# Men and Masculinities in Contemporary Japan

'There is already a rich and sophisticated literature discussing the complex and varied images and realities of the "Japanese Woman" and Japanese ideas of "femininity". It is good at last to have a complementary book that does the same for the "Japanese Man" and Japanese ideas of "masculinity". In short, this volume begins to fill a big gap in the literature on gender and sexuality in Japanese society.'
Dr Roger Goodman, *University of Oxford*

*Men and Masculinities in Contemporary Japan* provides the first comprehensive account of the changing role of men and the construction of masculinity in contemporary Japan. It moves beyond the stereotype of the white-collar salaryman to explore the diversity of identities and experiences found among Japanese men, including those versions of masculinity that are marginalized and subversive. By examining this diversity, the book also helps to bring the notion of 'masculinity' itself into question.

This edited collection includes discussions about transgendering men, working-class men, body aesthetics, transnational marriages, domestic violence, AIDS, representations of homosexuality, fatherhood and struggles for a masculine meaning in life beyond work within Japan.

This is a significant contribution to our understanding of contemporary Japanese society and identity. It will be of interest to students and researchers of anthropology, sociology and gender studies as well as Japanese studies.

**James E. Roberson** is Lecturer in the Department of Japanese and Korean Studies at the University of New South Wales. He is also the author of *Japanese Working Class Lives*.

**Nobue Suzuki** is a PhD candidate in the Department of Anthropology at the University of Hawaii.

D1598445

# Nissan Institute/Routledge Japanese Studies Series

# Men and Masculinities in Contemporary Japan

Dislocating the salaryman doxa

**Edited by**
**James E. Roberson and**
**Nobue Suzuki**

LONDON AND NEW YORK

First published 2003
by Routledge
2 Park Square, Milton Park, Abingdon, Oxon, OX14 4RN

Simultaneously published in the USA and Canada
by Routledge
711 Third Avenue, New York, NY 10017, USA

*Routledge is an imprint of the Taylor & Francis Group, an informa business*

Typeset in Baskerville by
BOOK NOW Ltd

*British Library Cataloguing in Publication Data*
A catalogue record for this book is available from the British Library

*Library of Congress Cataloging in Publication Data*
Men and masculinities in contemporary Japan : dislocating the salaryman doxa / edited
by James E. Roberson and Nobue Suzuki.
    p.  cm.
    Includes bibliographical references and index.
    1. Men–Japan–Social conditions. 2. Men–Japan–Identity. 3. Masculinity–Japan. 4.
Sex role–Japan. I. Roberson, James E., 1955– II. Suzuki, Nobue, 1957–

HQ1090.7.J3 M46 2002
305.32'0952–dc21                     2002068066

ISBN 0–415–24446–3 (hbk)
ISBN 0–415–27147–9 (pbk)

# Contents

# Contributors

**Tom Gill** received his doctorate in Social Anthropology from the London School of Economics and Political Science (LSE) in 1996. He is currently an Associate Professor at the Institute of Social Science, University of Tokyo, and managing editor of *Social Science Japan Journal*. His book on Japanese day labourers, *Men of Uncertainty*, was published by SUNY Press in 2001. His research interests centre on marginal groups such as homeless people, and on irregular modes of employment in Japan.

**Masako Ishii-Kuntz** is Associate Professor of Sociology at the University of California, Riverside. Her current research interests include the impact of economic hardship on fathers' work and family roles in Japan and the US. Her comparative research on men's participation in childcare and housework has appeared in *Journal of Marriage and the Family*, *Journal of Family Issues*, *International Journal of Family Sociology*, *Sociological Perspectives* and a number of book chapters. She is presently completing a book manuscript examining Japanese corporate fathers who are actively involved in childcare.

**Kazuya Kawaguchi** is Associate Professor of Community Studies and Gender/Sexuality Studies at Hiroshima Shūdō University and is a Director of Lesbian/Gay Studies at OCCUR (Japan Association for the Lesbian and Gay Movement). He has co-authored, with Keith Vincent and Takashi Kazama, *Gei Sutadīzu* (*Gay Studies*, 1997). His recent publications include '*Kenmei ni gei ni naru koto: shutai, teikō, sei no yōshiki*' (Becoming gay seriously: subjectivity, resistance and lifestyle), *Gendai Shisō* (March 1997) and '*Eizu jidai ni okeru "dōseiai ken'o": "Gei Sutorīto Yūsu" no jirei o tōshite*' (Homophobia in the age of AIDS: based on the case of 'Gay Street Youth'), *Kaihō Shakaigaku Kenkyū* 13 (1999).

**Takashi Kazama** is a doctoral candidate in the Department of International Sociology at the University of Tokyo. He has also been serving as Director of Research and Lesbian/Gay Studies at OCCUR. Recent publications include: *Gei Sutadīzu* (*Gay Studies*, co-authored with Keith Vincent and Kazuya Kawaguchi, 1997); *Jissen Suru Sekushuaritī* (*Practicing Sexuality*, part of the author collective of OCCUR, 1998); and '*Undō to chōsa no aida: dōseiai undō e no san'yokansatsu kara*' (Between activism and research: based on participant observation of homosexual movements), in Satō Kenji (ed.) *Toshi no Kaidokuryoku* (*Analytical Reading of the Urban*, 1996).

**Wim Lunsing** holds an MA in Japanese Studies from the University of Leiden and a PhD in Anthropology from Oxford Brookes University. He has been a Research Fellow in Anthropology at Tokyo University and Associate Research Professor of Japanese Studies at the University of Copenhagen. He is the author of *Beyond Common Sense: Sexuality and Gender in Contemporary Japan* (Kegan Paul, 2001).

**Gordon Mathews** is Associate Professor of Anthropology at the Chinese University of Hong Kong. He is the author of *What Makes Life Worth Living? How Japanese and Americans Make Sense of Their Worlds* (University of California Press, 1996) and *Global Culture/Individual Identity: Searching for Home in the Cultural Supermarket* (Routledge, 2000), and coeditor of *Consuming Hong Kong* (University of Hong Kong Press, 2001). He is currently doing research on 'the generation gap' in Japan today, and also on Hong Kong people's emerging senses of 'belonging to a nation'.

**Hisako Matsuo** is a freelance writer and researcher based in Hyōgo, Japan. She is the author of the first major book on transgender behaviour in Japan, *Transgenderism: The Twilight Between the Sexes* (Seori Shobō, 1996). She has written extensively about sex and gender issues including the Takarazuka Theatre, about which she has a book forthcoming. Her home page is located at: http://www.gpsy.com/matsuo/

**Laura Miller** is Associate Professor in the Department of Sociology and Anthropology at Loyola University of Chicago. Her research interests include language, gender and popular culture. Recently she served as guest editor for a special issue of *The US–Japan Women's Journal* focused on media models of women. She is currently working on a book manuscript tentatively entitled *Beauty Up: The Consumption of Body Aesthetics in Japan* investigating the *esute* ('body aesthetics') industry in Japan.

**Karen Nakamura** is Assistant Professor of Anthropology at Macalester College (Saint Paul, MN). She was born in Indonesia and grew up in Australia, Japan and the US. She has just completed her PhD dissertation research on deaf identity and minority social movements in modern Japan at Yale University. Her interest in the Takarazuka Theatre merges with her previous research on non-normative genders and sexualities as well as with girls' comic books and *anime* in Japan. Her home page is at: http://www.deaflibrary.org/nakamura/

**Tadashi Nakamura** is Professor of Sociology at Ritsumeikan University in Kyoto, Japan. He is active as both scholar and activist in the men's movement and in dealing with domestic violence in Japan. He is one of the founders of the Men's Center Japan and of the Men's Support Room, which provides rehabilitative support for men involved in domestic violence. His publications include *Kazoku no Yukue* (*Whereabouts of the Family*, Jinbun Shoin, 1997) and *Domesutikku Baiorensu: Kazoku no Byōri* (*Domestic Violence: Pathology of the Family*, Sakuhinsha, 2001).

**James E. Roberson** received his PhD in Anthropology from the University of Hawaii, Mānoa, in 1993. He has taught in the US and Japan and is currently Lecturer in the Department of Japanese and Korean Studies at the University of New South Wales. He is the author of *Japanese Working Class Lives: An Ethnographic Study of Factory Workers* (Routledge, 1998). His research interests include issues of class, ethnic and gender-related identities and marginality, presently focusing on the relations of music and cultural identity in Okinawa.

**Nobue Suzuki** is a PhD candidate in the Department of Anthropology at the University of Hawaii, Mānoa. She is completing her dissertation entitled, *Battlefields of Affection: Gender, Global Desires and the Politics of Intimacy in Filipina–Japanese Transnational Marriages*. Her research on the Filipina diaspora has been published in *Women's Studies International Forum* and *US–Japan Women's Journal* and her most recent work, 'Gendered surveillance and sexual violence in Filipina pre-migration experiences to Japan', will appear in *Gender Politics in the Asia Pacific Region*, edited by B. Yeoh, P. Teo and S. Huang (Routledge).

**Christine R. Yano** is Assistant Professor of Anthropology at the University of Hawaii, Mānoa. Her book, *Tears of Longing: Nostalgia and the Nation in Japanese Popular Song*, is forthcoming from Harvard University Press. Her current research interests include the global circulation of Japanese 'cute' products such as Hello Kitty, Korean singers of Japanese popular song and Japanese-American ethnic beauty pageants.

# Series editor's preface

If there is an unforgettable date that marks the beginning of the twenty-first century, it is that of 11th September 2001. Whether and how far the terrible events of that day will have changed the history of the new century and set it on a course other than that it would otherwise have taken will be for future historians to say. The terrorist attacks on the United States led to a war that largely eliminated the Taliban and Osama Bin Laden's organization from Afghanistan. Its rationale was proclaimed to be that of an international struggle against terrorism. In February 2002, President Bush publicly described Iraq, Iran and North Korea as an 'axis of evil', in that they were dictatorial states sponsoring terrorist activities. Subsequently, a hard-line Israeli government, faced with a spate of suicide bombings in Israeli cities, occupied many areas controlled by the Palestinian Authority, in an attempt to 'root out the terrorist infrastructure'. But Israel, in its turn, became the subject of widespread condemnation as the perpetrator of 'state terrorism'. The initial apparent simplicity of the 'crusade against terror' was becoming blurred, and European attitudes were coming to diverge from those of the United States administration.

One effect of 11th September has been a revival of interest in the concept of 'civilization' and of 'the civilized world'. An almost Manichean vision of the forces of civilization pitted against the forces of darkness infuses much of the commentary to which the events of that day have given rise. In practice, however, 'civilization' does not fit easily with those hundreds of millions of people that cannot escape from dire poverty, intolerance and exploitation. Unless these problems are tackled with determination and intelligence, it should surprise nobody that terror will be used to horrifying effect against the world deemed 'civilized'.

In all significant senses, Japan today is part of our 'civilized world'. The average standard of living of the Japanese people is high. The GNP of Japan is second only to that of the United States, and is larger than the combined GNP of all the other countries in Asia. Even the economy of China, though attracting much attention for the rapidity of its growth and for its success in Japanese markets, is many times smaller than that of Japan, though plainly it is catching up. The national interests of Japan, taking a hard-nosed view, lie with the interests of the advanced countries and their broad set of economic, political, social and moral values. Japan in most ways is an open democratic society. Since the early 1990s she has been suffering from severe problems of economic and political mismanagement. In the widest of terms the problem is that of a painful transition from a state-centred form of political economy to one that is more open, competitive and internationalized. The process of transition is far from over and mismanagement has cost the economy dear. Japan is also faced with deeper structural problems, including that of a rapidly aging population. Nevertheless, the key point is that this is a gigantic economy having enormous international weight.

The Japanese, being a proud people and heirs to an ancient civilization, have long been concerned to map out their own path in the world, and this creates a certain tension with the globalizing trends apparent in the world today. Even so, Japan is slowly forging her own set of compromises whereby assimilation to essential global norms of behaviour is tempered by the maintenance of structures and practices based on her own cultural experiences. But the next stage, in which Japanese expertise and commitment are desperately needed, is in the long and painful task of overcoming, not only the common terrorist enemy, but also the deepest causes of terrorism, namely global inequality, endemic poverty and squalor, exploitation and rejection.

The *Nissan Institute/RoutledgeCurzon Japanese Studies Series* was begun in 1986 and has now passed well beyond its fiftieth volume. It seeks to foster an informed and balanced, but not uncritical, understanding of Japan. One aim of the series is to show the depth and variety of Japanese institutions, practices and ideas. Another is, by using comparisons, to see what lessons, positive or negative, can be drawn for other countries. The tendency in commentary on Japan to resort to out-dated, ill-informed or sensational stereotypes still remains and needs to be combated.

Embedded in Western consciousness of Japanese society is the idea that Japan is highly male-dominated. In the popular (and even some academic) literature about post-war Japan, images abound of men generally – but particularly salaried employees of big conglomerated companies (the famed 'salaryman') – as the shock troops of the economic miracle. A metaphor in common use was that the 'salarymen' were latter-day *samurai*, selflessly dedicated to the national cause of economic expansion. If the *samurai* had been warriors, the 'salarymen' were warriors in economic rather than military battles. Two consequences followed from this paradigm. One was that the interests of the individual were subordinated to the interests of the broader whole (work group, company, nation). The other was that there was a sharp gender differentiation: women were not on a level with men, but were expected to play a supportive and subordinate role, aiding their husbands and caring for their families. If women worked, it was on a casual basis before marriage or after their families were mature and, of course, for much less remuneration than was earned by men.

In this fascinating book, Roberson and Suzuki, with their co-authors, examine what has happened to the concept of masculinity in modern and contemporary Japan. They show that, while the phenomenon of the dedicated 'salaryman' is far from dead, a striking range of diversity has emerged in male lifestyles and in relations between the sexes. They show that the nature of family life has changed markedly, especially in cities, with men's tensions between work and family gradually moving towards a concern with family. They examine gay lifestyles, and how these have tended to be more openly acknowledged, and they show how beautifying the human body is now pursued not only by women, but also by a substantial number of men. Popular culture is mined for clues about how masculinity has been changing, while less pleasant issues such as the spread of HIV/AIDS and domestic violence are explored. Day labourers on the margins of society, as well as farmers in remote regions who, being shunned by Japanese women, marry Filipina women instead, are presented as examples of divergence from a common norm.

The basic theme of the book is that, rather than a clear model of 'masculinity' in today's Japan, there is a diversity of 'masculinities'. This may be seen as an important aspect of a general diversification in Japanese society.

J. A. A. Stockwin

# Acknowledgements

This book has been a long time coming. Its origins begin with conversations between Suzuki and Roberson in the mid-1990s in which we discussed a three-way disjuncture which existed between many of the men we had encountered in our respective research projects, the common stereotypes and dominant representations of Japanese men, and the theoretical and ethnographic research in gender studies focusing on masculinities. These discussions led us first to organize a panel on 'Men and Masculinities in Contemporary Japan: Beyond the Urban Salaryman Model' for the 1998 Annual Meeting of the Association for Asian Studies in Washington, DC. The chapters in this book by Gordon Mathews, Laura Miller and Nobue Suzuki were originally presented there. Nakamura Tadashi also discussed his work in the men's movement in Japan, and Itō Kimio acted as discussant.

In the long processes of putting the book together, we have met many people, participated in various events, received encouragement and some criticism and incurred personal, professional and intellectual debts to more people than we can name here. Let us begin, though, by thanking all of the contributors for writing and for waiting; Laura Miller, for everything; Itō Kimio; Kawahashi Noriko; Anne Imamura; Roger Goodman; Bill Kelly; David Slater; Mary Brinton; Glenda Roberts; Wendy Smith; Tomoko Hamada; Fritz Gaenslen; Ted Fowler; Jeff Hester; Sabine Frühstück; and Cindi Sturtz. Thanks also to Vicky Smith, Craig Fowlie and Grace McInnes at Routledge for their interest and support.

Together with Laura Miller, we would also like to thank and acknowledge here the following for permission to use the images that appear in Laura Miller's chapter, 'Male Beauty Work in Japan': Ms Kawamata Sachiko, Manager of Tokyo Aesthetic Salon (for Figure 3.1); Mr Iimura Seiichirō of Yokohama Kanpō (for Figure 3.2); Mr Kase Hirotada of Bunkasha Publishing, publisher of *Ranking Daisuki* magazine (for Figure 3.3); the *Asahi Shinbun* and Mr Fukuda Toshiyuki, illustrator (for Figure 3.4); and Mr Hayashi Yasunari, editor of *Bidan* magazine (for Figures 3.5 and 3.6). Every effort has been made to contact copyright holders for their permission to reprint material in this book. The publishers would be grateful to hear from any copyright holder who is not here acknowledged and will undertake to rectify any errors or omissions in future editions of this book.

# Note on names

The names of all contributors to this book are listed in Western order, with given names followed by family names. However, unless noted otherwise, Japanese names mentioned in the text of each chapter are written in Japanese order, with family names followed by given names.

Names of Japanese government institutions given throughout the chapters are those used at the time of either the data's publication or collection and do not necessarily reflect the current consolidation of ministries and agencies. Thus, for example, Ministry of Labour and Ministry of Health and Welfare (pre-consolidation), and Ministry of Health, Labour and Welfare (post-consolidation) are all correct usages.

# 1 Introduction

*James E. Roberson and Nobue Suzuki*

In 1963, Ezra Vogel described the then newly (re)emerging lifestyle of Japan's 'new middle class', introducing Western readers to 'the salaryman', white-collar workers in large corporations and government bureaucracies (1971/1963: 5). Vogel portrayed the salaryman in terms of economic security, social status and sex role division. For Japanese people in the late 1950s and early 1960s, the salaryman represented a 'bright new life' (ibid.: 9). 'The young Japanese girl [*sic*] hopes to marry a salary man', Vogel (ibid.) wrote, while 'the new order of the salary man is not only a way of life for people in large organizations, but a model affecting the life of others' (ibid.: 268). Over thirty years later, Fujimura-Fanselow and Kameda describe the image of the typical Japanese man, held by people both inside and outside Japan, as that of

> a workaholic who toils long hours for Mitsubishi or Sony or some other large corporation, goes out drinking with his fellow workers or clients after work and plays golf with them on weekends, and rarely spends much time at home with his wife and children, much less does anything around the house, such as cleaning or changing diapers.
>
> (1995: 229)

Writing at different ends of Japan's postwar economic expansion, these two descriptions merge to encapsulate a set of images of Japanese men and masculinity which witnesses the transformation of the salaryman from emergent and desired to everyday and dominant. Descriptions such as these, while perhaps also recognizing diversity and critique, simultaneously participate in the reflexive manufacture of the salaryman as masculine stereotype in, of and for Japan. The salaryman as dominant (self-)image, model and representation of men and masculinity in Japan indexes overlapping discourses of gender, sexuality, class and nation: the middle-class, heterosexual, married salaryman considered as responsible for and representative of 'Japan'.

The essays collected here present research which critically engages with these intersecting discourses of masculinity in contemporary Japan. Discussing a variety of men and masculine practices, performances, performativity and politics, the chapters simultaneously demonstrate and deconstruct the power of the homologies of (salary)men–masculinity–heterosexuality. The goals of the book are thus twofold. First, the book offers gender-sensitive and critical views of the diversity of identities and experiences that may be found among men in contemporary Japan. Such complexity is seen within, and is sometimes the product of struggles against, contexts framed by ideological and institutional power and constraints. Second, by examining (the politics of) the multiplicity of Japanese masculinities, the book also helps problematize the notion of 'masculinity' in Japan, and beyond.

In this Introduction, we first mobilize some of the recent gender literature on men and masculinities to suggest the need for increased interchange between ethnographic (and other) research and the study of masculinities and men in Japan. In this, we warn against the complicity of scholarship with the reproduction of gender(ed) ideologies. We then discuss the ideological and representational hegemony of the salaryman model of Japanese manhood in more detail. Next, we describe the multiple and changing representations, relations and realities of men and masculinities in Japan and in Japan studies. Here we note the political and intellectual importance of critical recognition and interpretation of such diversity and dynamics. Finally, we provide a brief guide to the chapters to follow.

## Theorizing masculinities in contemporary Japan

Especially since the mid-1980s, an expanding body of academic literature has emerged in the West, and more recently in Japan, which critically analyses the constructions, performances and practices of men and masculinities.[1] The best of this work draws on the insights of feminist gender studies – most fundamentally that 'gender is a system of power and not just a set of stereotypes or observable differences between women and men' (Brod and Kaufman 1994b: 4). A major theme in critical studies of masculinities has been that 'of breaking down artificial unities of genders and sexualities' (Hearn and Morgan 1990b: 11). Indeed, some authors contend that masculinities and femininities may be viewed as objectified attributes that people 'do' and 'perform' (Butler 1990; Robertson 1998), while Sedgwick (1995) maintains that masculinity sometimes has nothing to do with men.

The significance of critically investigating the plurality of masculinities is at least twofold. Ethnographically, moving from the assumed and essentialized homogeneity and homology of men and masculinity to detailed descriptions of situated gender practice and performance permits us to view the 'multiple, contested, and at times contradictory' (Cornwall and Lindisfarne 1994c: 40) nature of gendered diversity in a given society. Researching multiplicity and difference involves recognizing and investigating the consequences of the fact that, as di Leonardo puts it: 'In any particular population, major social divisions – race/ethnicity, class, religion, age, sexual preference, nationality – will crosscut and influence the meanings of gender division' (1991: 30; see also Connell 1995: 75; Moore 1988: 80). Ong and Peletz similarly note the contribution of studies of masculinities to understandings of gender 'in relation to other forms of difference and inequality (class, race, etc.) which are in a very basic sense constituting, and constitutive of, masculinity and femininity alike' (1995: 10).

Thus, while recognizing that gender is interrelational, involving relations of power (including those of misogyny and homophobia) which have overwhelmingly benefited heterosexual men in most societies, it is also important, as di Leonardo notes of 'cultural feminist essentialism' (1991: 26), to avoid essentializing men or masculinities. It is crucial instead critically to interpret and understand the multiplicity of men and masculinities and to 'dislocate' (see Cornwall and Lindisfarne 1994a) notions which assume a homology of men with masculinity. Connell, moreover, argues that

> To recognize the diversity of masculinities is not enough. We must also recognize the *relations* between the different kinds of masculinity, relations of alliance, dominance and subordination. These relationships are constructed through practices that exclude and include, that intimidate, exploit and so on. There is a gender politics within masculinity.
>
> (1995: 37)

In addition to describing and deconstructing such ethnographic dimensions of the complexity of men and masculinities, there are other discursive reflexivities involved which implicate scholarship in a different fashion. Descriptions of the 'unities and differences between men and between masculinities' (Hearn and Collinson 1994: 97) bring these gendered relations into even closer view and under more detailed scrutiny. In a recent review of men's studies in Japan, Shibuya (2001: 454) argues against the tendency to pursue minute groupings of masculinities in a fashion which ignores if not avoids analysis of the structuring of gendered relations. This is an important reminder of the dangers of not seeing the forest for the trees, of 'recentering men at the center of the discourse' (Hearn and Collinson 1994: 98), and of self-servingly and reductionistically conceiving 'the study of men to [only] be about liberating men' (Hanmer 1990: 29).

However, studies of the diversities, differences and divisions among men and masculinities may also reflexively act to 'dislocate the hegemonic versions of masculinity which privilege some people over others' (Cornwall and Lindisfarne 1994b: 4). As Conway-Long puts it, 'The recognition of difference *within* this gendered category called masculinity and an identification of the plurality of masculinities are the beginnings of the deconstruction of dominant masculine "doxa" [taken-for-grantedness]' (1994: 63). Implicated here are both local and everyday as well as scholarly discourses of what Ortner calls the 'big man bias':

> We take the privileges of certain men – leaders, or elites, or . . . whatever – and assume them to apply to male actors in general. We thus obscure (and thereby unwittingly collude with cultural ideologies) what many men have in common with women in general, or with specific sectors of women.
>
> (1996: 133–4)

Sugimoto similarly indicts both Western and Japanese scholarship that has 'attempted to generalize about Japanese society on the basis of observations of its male elite sector' (1997: 2). Collusion with cultural ideologies in obscuring gender and sexual divisions within Japanese society risks complicity with interrelated *Nihonjinron* (theories about the Japanese) discourses of cultural nationalism which attempt to downplay or deny other dimensions of difference (see Lie 2001: 150–9). Such ideological 'hegemony of homogeneity', Befu notes, is produced by intellectuals, maintained and supported by the state and put into practice by the corporate establishment (2001: 81). Clammer, meanwhile, reminds us that '[d]ifference is a slippery concept. But far from this being a reason for abandoning it, it suggests that following its contours and transformations actually takes one into the heart of contemporary cultural debates in and about Japan' (2001: 26).

As Connell notes, 'The way we do our intellectual work of inquiry, analysis and reportage has consequences; epistemology and sexual politics are intertwined' (1993: 598). Critical scholarship which recognizes, investigates and writes about gendered diversity has the potential to contribute to discourses which deconstruct and dislocate the broader 'hegemony of homogeneity' and the 'dominant masculine "doxa"'. Such scholarship must involve critical analyses not just of the hegemonic but of the non-hegemonic, not assuming male homogeneity, the singularity of masculinity or the homology of men with (heterosexual) masculinity, but investigating divergences, differences, divisions. This further requires a simultaneous and reflexive interrogation of individual identities and experiences and of what di Leonardo refers to as the 'embedded nature of gender both as a material, social institution and as a set of ideologies' (1991: 30).

Connell (1995) usefully discusses three intersecting dimensions or sites of the 'gender configuring of practice' which basically correspond to individual, institutional and ideological levels of analysis (see also Kelly 1993). The individual site of gender configuration includes lifecourse and individual identity constructions (see Mathews, this volume, Chapter 7), personal psychology or character and the embodied nature of gender and sexuality (see Connell 1993: 602). This site may also be conceived of as the stage of gender performance and performativity (Butler 1990) and of what Sedgwick (1995) calls the 'n-dimensional space' of sex(uality) and gender in which men and femininity intersect (see Lunsing, this volume, Chapter 2). This is also the space of 'gender geometries' (Halberstam 1998: 21), where there is a field of female masculinities which are not simply the opposite of female femininity nor female versions of male masculinity (ibid.: 29; Nakamura and Matsuo, this volume, Chapter 4), the exploration of which 'affords us a glimpse of how masculinity is constructed as masculinity' (ibid.: 1).

The second site of the gender configuring of practice includes discourse, ideology and culture where 'gender is organized in symbolic practices' (Connell 1995: 72). This is obviously a very complex field and necessarily engages the notion of hegemony (see Connell 1987: 184; Ortner 1996: 145–6). As Donaldson notes:

> The ability to impose a definition of the situation, to set the terms in which events are understood and issues discussed, to formulate ideals and define morality is an essential part of this process. Hegemony involves persuasion of the greater part of the population, particularly through the media, and the

organization of social institutions in ways that appear 'natural', 'ordinary', 'normal' [or doxic].

(1993: 645; see also Allison 1994: 29, 100)[2]

However, no hegemony is historically static or complete: 'There are always sites . . . of alternative practices and perspectives available, and these may become the bases of resistance and transformation' (Ortner 1996: 18). Thus, as are described throughout many of the chapters collected here, if (representations of) the middle-class, white-collar, heterosexual salaryman powerfully invoke(s) ideologies of nation, class and sexuality in Japan, the practices and performances of other people must be seen as acts of challenge and change – potential, playful or purposeful.

The third set of sites of gender configuration includes 'institutions such as the state, the workplace and the school' (Connell 1995: 73); to which one must add the family. As Connell notes, '*masculinity is an aspect of institutions*, and is produced in institutional life, *as much as it is an aspect of personality* or produced in interpersonal transactions' (1993: 602; emphases in original). The state is especially important here since it is 'heavily masculinized', creates agencies and policies to deal with gender issues and acts to regulate gender relations (Connell 1996: 165–6). State interventions in the family in Japan have been discussed primarily in regard to women (see Garon 1997). However, together with other social and cultural factors influencing men's experiences of family, these have also affected men, both positively and negatively (see Mathews, Nakamura and Ishii-Kuntz, this volume, Chapters 7, 10 and 12, respectively).

Contestation and resistance against – as well as complicity with and support of – gendered ideological, institutional and interpersonally embodied hegemonies are practices which reflexively implicate the agency of both men and women. 'Gender identity', as Moore writes, 'is both constructed and lived' (1994: 49). Players in what Ortner (1996) terms the 'serious game' of making gender, while simultaneously 'defined and constructed (though never wholly contained)' by it, 'constantly stretch the game even as they enact it' (ibid.: 20). Recognizing the embedded nature of embodied gendered practice which 'stretches the game', we return to the significance of difference, now with a more grounded ethnographic focus on the lives, identities, practices and performances of men and women.

The chapters in this book, though written from a variety of positions and employing a range of perspectives, all work to provide ethnographically-based understandings which are sensitive to the reflexivities of the lived, constructed and embedded dimensions and diversity of masculinities in contemporary Japan. In this, they simultaneously mobilize and interrogate the individual, institutional and ideological manifestations and consequences of and resistances to hegemonic models of masculinity in Japan. While acknowledging the power of hegemonic masculine ideologies, policies and practices, by uncovering complexity and recovering agency, these essays simultaneously reveal and contribute to the deconstruction of the dominant masculine doxa embodied by the white-collar, middle-class, heterosexual salaryman in Japan and in Japan studies.

## Salaryman hegemony: representations and ideology

Reviewing the anthropology of masculinity, Gutmann notes that while important empirical and theoretical contributions have been made during the past several decades, gender studies are still largely equated with women's studies and that 'insufficient attention has been paid to men-as-men' (1997: 385–6). The same may be said of the ethnography of Japanese society. Writing by and about women in Japan has enriched, diversified and complicated our understandings of the range of cultural, social, economic and political contexts in which these women act, with which they struggle and through which they constitute their identities, inside and outside of the 'traditional' domestic sphere.

Images and understandings of Japanese men, however, remain limited and, as is often the case, must still largely 'be inferred from research on women and by extrapolation from studies on other topics' (ibid.: 387), including descriptions of various governmental, educational and corporate institutions, and discussions of particular role categories, especially that of company employee. As Miller notes, 'In popular media and books,[3] and even in scholarly work, *the general portrait of life and work* in Japan inevitably entails an *assumption* that the "typical" Japanese person is an urban, middle-class worker' (1995: 20; emphases added). Miller discusses representations of salarymen as part – together with a focus on elite firms – of a 'folk model' that 'functions as a tool for evaluating, explaining and predicting social behaviour and economic success' (ibid.: 19–20). There is thus an uneasy tension here between models of and models for (Geertz 1973) the Japanese that index the 'big man bias' noted above.

The salaryman has variously been viewed as social symbol (Takeuchi 1996); social–cultural construction (Kelly 1986, 1993); state/corporate ideology (Allison 1994), and social–historical reality (see below). Western ethnographic representations of the (new) middle-class salaryman, his family and his company began with the writings of Nakane (1970), Plath (1964), Rohlen (1974), Vogel (1971/ 1963) and others. The salaryman focus continues in work such as Allison's (1994) depiction of 'nightwork', which locates middle-class male leisure firmly within company and work-related contexts and views masculine sexuality as constructed by/within a pervasive corporate ideology.

The historical links between the salarymen of the modern Japanese capitalist system and the '*koshiben*' low-level samurai bureaucrats of the late Edo and white-collar employees of the Meiji eras have been discussed by a number of authors (Dasgupta 2000; Kinmonth 1981; Nakamaki 1997; Takeuchi 1996, 1997). However, one needs to be careful about collapsing historical difference into categorical and cultural–ideological sameness. The dangers of ahistorical reductionism are suggested by statements such as 'scratch a salaryman, find a samurai' (Plath 1964: 35) and Gilmore's remark that the samurai moral code of bushidō has 'lived on in modernized bureaucratic form . . . taken over by Japan's growing bourgeoisie . . . [and] gradually universalized to all other classes in Japan' (1990: 188–9).[4]

Okamoto and Sasano insightfully argue that representationally linking salarymen and samurai has in fact acted to legitimize the position and prestige of the former by using 'Japanese tradition' (2001: 25). Kelly (1986, 1993), meanwhile, has suggested that the salaryman/middle-class image, *as ideal*, is influential in the identities and lifestyles of many others (see also Plath 1964; Vogel 1971/1963). As long as one is critically aware of the tensions and distinctions among ideology, ideal and reality, extending the discourse on/of men as salarymen beyond the middle class can be an important exercise.

Tracing the rise (and, he claims, impending fall) of the salaryman as model of human formation, Takeuchi (1997) notes that as members of the new middle class their numbers increased from the end of the Meiji period (1868–1912). The term 'salaryman' itself dates back to the Taishō period (1912–26; see also Kinmonth 1981). However, during the prewar period, salarymen constituted less than 10 per cent of the employed population and so remained only a partial model of masculinity until after the war. According to Takeuchi (1997: 232), in 1955, half of all households were headed by salarymen, climbing to 75 per cent in 1970. While there are problems here with the definition of 'salaryman' (to include all full-time employees receiving monthly salaries), Takeuchi is surely correct to suggest that as a 'folk concept' (ibid.: 225) of masculinity the salaryman model has been dominant in the postwar period, linked to the processes and discourses of the re-emergence and successes of the state-capitalist system.

This does not mean, however, that representations of the salaryman have been unchanging or wholly laudatory and uncritical. Dasgupta, for example, notes that as depicted in *manga* (comics) and television, 'the flip-side of idealized salaryman masculinity has alternative readings which portray the salaryman not as figure of awe and respect, but rather as one for ridicule and caricature' (2000: 199; see also Schodt 1983; Skinner 1979).[5] Such comic criticism does not necessarily amount to a challenge, however, since 'modifications in various aspects of hegemonic masculinity [may] work to recuperate it' (Saco 1992: 34).[6] For example, while witnessing the difficulties of differentials in status and power between men, these (and other) comic representations often also reveal assumed or desired masculine power and privilege *vis-à-vis* women (see Allison 1996; Ito 1995).

Okamoto and Sasano (2001) describe changes in postwar representations of the salaryman, as revealed in *Asashi Shinbun* newspaper articles. They argue that with the rise of the '1955 System' (of Liberal Democrat Party stabilization and rule), and especially from the beginning of Japan's period of high economic growth in the early 1960s, men's roles became portrayed as those of taxpayers and workers, functioning – as 'correct' citizens – as part of a state-sponsored patriarchal industrial–capitalist system (see Dasgupta 2000: 192) that placed the family in subordinated support of the state. However, from around the time of the economic bubble of the late 1980s and its bursting in the early 1990s, salarymen have been portrayed as more independent of companies and with more diverse and individually relative roles (Okamoto and Sasano 2001: 27). Though changing, the representational focus remains on men as salarymen for whom working, paying taxes and supporting families remain basic.

As Okamoto and Sasano point out, the postwar system has relied on a sex-role-based division of labour in the family, simultaneously allowing and compelling men to fulfil roles as workers in capitalist corporations and taxpayers for the nation-state. This institutional system of roles, moreover, is interrelated with more general legitimating gender ideologies that both give meaning to and compel certain forms of gendered individual practices and identities. These emphasize and naturalize the public place, position, practice and power of men within the system of state-supported compulsory heterosexuality and transcend and subsume non-normative (non-salarymen) men and masculinities.

Especially important here are hegemonic notions of the male/masculine as head and provider of and for the family *vis-à-vis* the state. Although the male househead no longer has the same privileges and powers accorded him by the state prior to the Second World War, men are still commonly expected to want and to be able to become the official heads, primary providers and strong centres of heterosexual families. The term *daikokubashira* (literally, the large black pillar of traditional Japanese houses) expresses such gendered descriptions of and expectations for the ideal Japanese male. As Matsunaga notes, 'becoming the *daikokubashira* of one's own household is an index of mature manhood' (2000: 150; see Mathews, Gill and Ishii-Kuntz, this volume, Chapters 7, 9 and 12, respectively).

The family system in which men are *daikokubashira* househeads and providers has required the support of women as 'good wives, wise mothers' whose domestic labour is needed by corporations and the state to ensure the full-time physical commitment of men to 'productive' labour (see Garon 1997; Roberts 1994; Uno 1993). According to Japanese folk ideologies of gender, masculinity is constructed in complementary contrast to femininity in a discourse which naturalizes gender roles and attributes – men, it is said, are naturally good at some things (in the public social world – *shakai* – and work), women at others (in the domestic sphere – *katei* – of the household and family; see Edwards 1989: 122). Folk ideology here is rooted in and provides cultural support for the everyday enactments of the gender–state system. Such folk beliefs may also be seen as part of a set of cultural assumptions and institutional arrangements which effectively exclude homosexuality and homosexual relations in a cultural–political–economic system of compulsory (public) heterosexuality (see Lunsing 2001).

Such views of men and masculinity must also be seen in relation to dominant psycho-social discourses of idealized masculinity. Itō (1993, 1996), for example, suggests that there are three primarily socially constructed 'inclinations' – for interpersonal superiority, power and possession – said to characterize (hegemonic) masculinity in Japan. These ideologically dominant masculine 'inclinations' imply that unless a man is successful in terms of power, authority and possession (particularly *vis-à-vis* women), he cannot be considered to be a 'real man' (*ichininmae no otoko*) (1996: 105). Combined with discursive pedagogies of ideal masculinity embodied in the salaryman as capitalist employee, state taxpayer and family provider and with associated (family, school, workplace and state) institutional contexts, these more psychological dimensions of masculinity exist in reflexive interrelations of masculinist self-empowerment and legitimation. At the same time, however, these pervasive and multidimensional discourses of masculine power can engender fractures among men (between those who are successful and those who are not), in individual men's psyches, in interpersonal relations and in social institutions (most intimately, the family), as Nakamura (this volume, Chapter 10) discusses in terms of the domestic violence committed by male batterers and as Gill (this volume, Chapter 9) describes among day labourers who move away from family and company bonds.

## Changing realities, relations and representations

While men and masculinities in Japan must be understood in relation to historically hegemonic models, it is also important, as noted above, to be aware of the dangers of ahistorical reductionism and cultural essentialization. Here, we wish to describe briefly certain recent changes in the Japanese political economy, gender relations and gender representations which manifest, are contributing to or demand an awareness of the plurality of men and masculinities. The authors of the chapters in this volume have done ethnographic fieldwork and collected data within the historical context of such change, with its accompanying stresses, resistances and hopes.

The bursting of Japan's economic 'bubble' in mid-1991 has led into the now decade-long Hesei recession. Japanese men, including hegemonic and privileged salarymen, have come to experience various gendered and sexual constraints and crises, which may be described, in Jardine's terms, as 'loss of legitimation, loss of authority, loss of seduction, loss of genius – *loss*' (cited in Alarcón, Kaplan and Moallem 1999: 2; emphasis in original). On the one hand, as Kondo (1997) eloquently shows, elite men clad in 'the Japanese Suit' continue to 'fabricate' and embody a national masculine aesthetic sensibility which is part of the Japanese challenge to Western masculine world hegemony (see also Ling 1999). On the other hand, the example of Carlos Ghosn, the Brazilian-born CEO of Nissan Motors, lucidly demonstrates the vulnerability and inefficiency of 'Japan Inc.'. Ghosn, himself still in his forties, has mobilized the potentialities of younger rather than older senior managers and led an 'ultra V recovery' from near collapse back to profitability (Kanemitsu and Toyama 2000). This obviously non-Japanese leader has become a new symbol of masculine success in Japan. Upon his visit to Prime Minister Koizumi Jun'ichirō, the latter even barraged his guest with questions related to his own governmental reformation plans (*Asahi Shinbun* 2001a).

The recession has stripped many salarymen of their 'three treasures' of lifetime employment, the seniority system of promotion and company unionism, leaving them with the cold discourse and harsh realities of economic 'restructuring'. Unemployment rates as of August 2001 remain at a record high 5 per cent (*Asahi Shinbun* 2001b), while the impending reforms of the Koizumi administration promise further accompanying 'pain'. Suicides, especially among men in their prime, have become phenomenal and Kamata (1999: 1) suggests that suicides among salarymen holding managerial positions are particularly significant. In 1999, some 21,656 men committed suicide (Ministry of Health, Labour and Welfare 2001a; see also Gill and Nakamura, this volume, Chapters 9 and 10, respectively).[7]

Discussions of men's 'loss' in Japan have also focused on sexuality and men's power to reproduce new lives as well as the nation. Such sexual anxiety is expressed, for instance, in the discourse on environmental hormones, wherein the decreased number of sperm among young men supposedly endangers the nation (Kitahara 1999: 24–8). Kitahara maintains that the term 'environmental hormone' is crucial to this discourse since the 'environment' is located outside the self and 'hormones' inside. Together with the effects of 'femalization' (*mesuka*), this suggests the blurring of boundaries of heterosexual Yamato male power and privilege *vis-à-vis* women, 'unmanly' youth, gays and foreigners (see Miller, Suzuki, and Kazama and Kawaguchi, this volume, Chapters 3, 6 and 11, respectively). With Kitahara, we can also read the bill to legalize viagra, passed in the unprecedentedly short period of only six months (*Asahi Shinbun* 1999), as an attempt to reaffirm the virility that men once enjoyed as the (re)producers of national and economic miracles.[8]

These post-bubble economy losses, and more, threaten the hegemonic position and prestige of the middle-class, white-collar, heterosexual male (headed household and other institutions). At the same time, the legacies of the interrelated growth of a service economy and a 'culture of mass consumption' (Clammer 1997: 46) are firmly rooted in the Japanese social landscape. Consumers under conditions of late capitalism in Japan are knowledgeable and selective, and it is now common to talk of 'micro-markets' of consumption and style (see Ivy 1993; White 1993). Consumption, Clammer notes, is 'one of the chief ways through which identity is established and maintained and through which it is represented to others' (1997: 6), reflecting class, generational and gender differences. In this, 'men are increasingly expected to be discriminating consumers, and changing images of masculinity are closely tied to self-presentation and cultural performances' (ibid.: 13; see Miller, this volume, Chapter 3).

Contemporary identity construction increasingly also involves people as consumers in global markets (Mathews 2000). Globalization processes (re)structuring the parameters of gender and sexuality are at work as Japanese men and women draw from transnational flows of information, images and ideas (part of what Appadurai (1996) calls mediascapes and ideoscapes) in constructing identities for themselves and creating imaginations of and desires for others. Such information and ideas may also be used in local civil movements (see Nakamura, Kazama and Kawaguchi, and Ishii-Kuntz, this volume, Chapters 10, 11 and 12, respectively). Kondo (1997) illustrates how participation in transnational consumer culture can be woven into the fabric of nativistic and nostalgic national(ist) masculinities in Japan (see also Yano, this volume, Chapter 5). Transnational flows of people and extensions of human relations, including families, also increasingly mark Japanese modernity as men and women move into Japan to work and to wed (see Suzuki, this volume, Chapter 6). Conversely, fear of the threats to Japanese (cultural/national) identity believed to exist in or to come from/with outside 'others' may encourage conservative and nativist/nationalist reactions, attempting to define and preserve a 'pure or true' (and masculine) 'Japan(eseness)' (Lie 2001; see Yano, and Kazama and Kawaguchi, this volume, Chapters 5 and 11, respectively).

Men and masculinities in contemporary Japan have also been affected by changes in relations with women and femininity. For example, the birthrate has fallen yearly and in 1999 was at the historical low of 1.34 (Ministry of Health, Labour and

Welfare 2001b), shaking the foundations of Japan's biopolitics. Much of the blame here has been attributed to 'selfish' women and their resistance to marriage and reproduction. Young women, however, do not want to repeat the affectively deprived and/or economically constrained lives they have witnessed among their mothers (Jolivet 1997), instead choosing late marriage, non-marriage and low birth-rates. Many men suffer from the consequent 'bride famine' (see Suzuki, this volume, Chapter 6), even though marriage continues to be an important rite of passage especially for men dependent upon women's domestic labour. Single fathers, particularly those who are divorced, are conversely stigmatized as being 'good for nothing' (Kasuga 1989).

Other changes affecting men and masculinities in Japan come from men themselves in the form(ation) of a variety of activist groups. Two of the earliest of these groups were concerned with issues of childcare. Otoko no Kosodate o Kangaeru Kai (Men's Group for Rethinking Childcare) was founded in 1978, while Otoko mo Onna mo Ikuji Jikan o! Renraku Kai (Childcare Hours for Men and Women Network) was founded in 1980 (see Ishii-Kuntz, this volume, Chapter 12). Another group, Ajia no Baibaishun ni Hantai Suru Otoko-tachi no Kai (Group for Men Opposed to [Buying and Selling] Prostitution in Asia) was formed in 1988 (see Taniguchi 1997). Men's studies related groups began to appear in the 1990s, with the formation of Menzu Ribu Kenkyū Kai (Men's Lib Research Group; Itō 1996: 311), the Menzu Sentā (Men's Center) in 1995 (see Nakamura, this volume, Chapter 10) and Menzu Ribu Tokyo (Men's Lib Tokyo) in Tokyo also in 1995 (Toyoda 1997).

Lunsing describes gay and lesbian movements in some detail and notes that there are over thirty such groups (1998: 291–2). Among these are politically active groups such as JILGA (Japan International Lesbian and Gay Association) and OCCUR (Kazama and Kawaguchi, this volume, Chapter 11; see also Summerhawk, McMahill and McDonald 1998). Groups such as Project P in Kyoto, on the other hand, care 'less about parliamentary politics and law . . . and more about freedom of expression in a variety of contexts' (Lunsing 1999: 313). Lunsing also notes that many writers, though working more individually, are 'very much part of gay and lesbian activism in Japan' (1998: 295).

Finally, we want to point to recent changes in written representations of men and masculinities in Japan (studies).[9] There is, for example, a significant body of impor-tant new scholarship on male homosexuality. Among these are: historical analyses (Leupp 1995; Pflugfelder 1999); interpretations of modern media representations (Grossman 2000; McLelland 2000; Valentine 1997); and discussions of a variety of contemporary issues and experiences (see Ito and Yanase 2001; Lunsing 2001; Sunagawa 1999; Treat 1999; Vincent, Kazama and Kawaguchi 1997). Other work includes discussions of single-father families (Ikeda 1996; Kasuga 1989); domestic violence (Nakamura 2001, this volume, Chapter 10); Allison's (1994) description of the 'corporate masculinity' reconfirmed and refreshed in the 'nightwork' leisure of elite salarymen, and Standish's (2000) discussion of the cinematic construction of ideal masculine types in 'tragic hero' narratives/myths. Kondo's (1990) important description of male artisans has been complemented by other discussions of working-class men (Roberson 1998, this volume, Chapter 8) and day labourers

(Fowler 1996; Gill 2001, this volume, Chapter 9), contributing to the breaking of the representational dominance of the Japanese middle class.

## Guide to the chapters

The chapters that follow show both the power and the problematics of the ideological and representational dominance of hegemonic masculinity embodied in the middle-class, white-collar, heterosexual salaryman. They explore the experiences, identities, practices and performances of a diversity of men and masculinities in contemporary Japan whose existence has often been oppressed, obscured or otherwise representationally overlooked. Such complexity is examined in relation to a number of overlapping issues, including those of sexuality, lifecourse, changing gender and family relations, identity politics, class, nation(alism) and consumerism. While indexing the power of the salaryman ideal/ideology in embedding, constraining or acting as counterpoint to non-hegemonic practices and desires, the fact that such diverse, alternative practices (sometimes of resistance or inversion) actually exist, are struggled for or are dreamed and desired is significant at individual, institutional and ideological levels.

We begin in Chapter 2 with Wim Lunsing's discussion of various kinds of transgendering Japanese men whose gendered and sexual identities, practices and performance are mixed and multiplex. His query, 'What masculinity?' is in many ways the key question, differently posed and answered, in all the following chapters. The focus on the embodied nature of gender identities is maintained in Laura Miller's discussion in Chapter 3 of new body aesthetics among young heterosexual men. Miller combines a description of male consumer culture with an analysis of masculinity as sensual bodily presentation and practice constructed in relation to media-based discourses and in reflexive awareness of (imagined) female desire.

The performative dimensions of masculinity are again brought into focus and question in the chapters by Karen Nakamura and Hisako Matsuo and by Chris Yano. In Chapter 4, Nakamura and Matsuo argue that it is precisely the female masculinity of characters enacted on the Takarazuka Theatre stage and elsewhere in Japanese popular culture that allows fans, temporarily at least, to transcend the boundaries of gender and sexuality. In Chapter 5, Yano discusses the construction of masculinity in the production of performers, performances and song lyrics in the popular music form called *enka*, and shows how these are bound with constructions of nostalgic and nativized national identity.

The relations between national(ity/ism) and masculinity are also interrogated by Nobue Suzuki (Chapter 6), who describes the masculinity politics of (representations of) the Japanese men involved in transnational marriages with women from the Philippines. These become inflected with class-based ideologies which work to further representationally marginalize these transnationally married men. Chapters by Gordon Mathews, James Roberson and Tom Gill further discuss the interrelationships among masculine identities and lifecourse, (un)employment and class. In Chapter 7, Mathews employs the lens of *ikigai* ('that which most makes life worth living') to understand men's identity construction. In this central chapter, around which others must be read, he argues that given the gendered structuring of Japanese capitalism and men's own senses of masculine pride, it remains difficult for many men to live for their families or their dreams rather than their jobs, despite hopeful exceptions. Roberson (Chapter 8) examines how working-class Japanese men's masculinity construction is imbricated in the reproduction of their own class marginalization, at the same that it is implicated in a complicit, if changing, masculine privilege *vis-à-vis* women. Gill (Chapter 9) provides an ethnographically detailed description of the struggles of day labourers to maintain masculine identities based on physical machismo and personal independence in the face of waning strength in a job market crippled by a protracted recession and without support networks based on family or workplace.

The final three chapters present examples of groups of men engaged in activism which attempts to construct positive changes, alternatives and challenges to the current state-sponsored gender status quo. Tadashi Nakamura (Chapter 10) examines the problem of domestic violence, showing how this is related to family and state-contexted constructions of masculine identities. He also discusses the attempts of one group to 'regender' male batterers, guiding them away from violence. In Chapter 11, Takashi Kazama and Kazuya Kawaguchi critically analyse the nationalist and heterosexist constructions of HIV risk and representations of male homosexuality in Japan. They then describe acts and events organized by gay activists to counter such state heterosexism and the HIV threat. Masako Ishii-Kuntz (Chapter 12) closes the book with a description of the emergence of men who are trying to balance fatherhood and work, allowing a fuller and more creative participation by men in childcare and domestic responsibilities. As do Mathews, Nakamura and Suzuki, Ishii-Kuntz also disaggregates the hegemonic masculine group, not drawing sharp contrasts but showing the continuities and interconnectedness among masculinities.

Stuart Hall has argued that one of the culturally and politically most important events of recent times has been the 'coming into representation' of peoples on 'the margins' in Western countries such as Britain and the United States, compelling fuller recognition of the multicultural and multiethnic composition of those nations (1997: 36). The research about, writing by and activism among Japanese masculinities and men are similarly of significance in part because they signal the growing public representation, presence and recognition of a multiplicity of men, masculinities and sexualities, contributing to the dislocating of the current masculine doxa both in Japan and in Japan studies.

Other research remains to be done on issues including male sexuality, love and romance, pornography, the sex industry, sports, media representations and consumption, female masculinities, ethnic men and masculinities, nationalism, critical ethnographies of hegemonic men and masculinities and more. The current volume is an initial attempt to contribute to and encourage further critical analyses of men and masculinities in contemporary Japan.

## Notes

1 Useful English-language texts – which show both the diversity of topics and approaches and the relative paucity of English-language work on Asia – include: Berger, Wallis and Watson (1995), Brod and Kaufman (1994a), Cornwall and Lindisfarne (1994a), Gutmann (1997), Hearn and Morgan (1990a) and Stecopoulos and Uebel (1997). Japanese-language texts include those by Inoue, Ueno and Ehara (1995), Itō (1993, 1996), Nishikawa and Ogino (1999) and Tsutamori (1999).

2 Silverman's notion of the 'dominant fiction' is very similar, though her formulation emphasizes 'the images and stories through which a society figures consensus; images and stories which cinema, fiction, popular culture and other forms of mass representation presumably both draw upon and help to shape' (1992: 30). While acknowledging 'powerful constraints', she also recognizes the capacity of discursive practice, via representation and signification, 'to challenge and transform the dominant fiction' (ibid.: 48).

3 See Michael Crichton's (1992) *Rising Sun* and Meg Pei's (1992) (simultaneously representational and deconstructive) *Salaryman*. See also Johnson (1988).

4 The danger here is particularly clear in Crichton's (1992) *Rising Sun*, which depicts samurai salarymen with particular American patriotic paranoia. See Morris (2001) and especially Kondo (1997) for critiques.

   Gilmore compounds his problems by culturally essentializing Buruma's (1984: 143) dichotomization between 'hard school' (*kōha*) and 'soft school' (*nanpa*) types of cinematic masculinity. This static reductionism is reproduced by Henshall as well, though in part he uses this to claim that the postwar period a popular self-image among men has been not that of the *nanpa* salaryman but of the *kōha* 'corporate-warrior or latter-day samurai' (1999: 2). Pflugfelder (1999) provides a more sophisticated reading of the literary history and sexual politics of these terms and types of masculinity in Meiji period male student literature and culture.

5 The same was true during the prewar period as well, as reflected in the comic strips drawn by Kitazawa Rakuten describing the Taishō salaryman's 'heaven' and 'hell' (see Kinmonth 1981: 289; Takeuchi 1997: 228).

6 Another example of this may be found in television commercials for various kinds of vitamin drinks, which will supposedly supply the consumer with health and energy. These commercials may employ humorous, self-deprecating scenes of salarymen but in the end aid in recouping the salaryman hegemonic as the salaryman recovers his vitality (Roberson 1999).

7 In contrast, women's suicides in 2000 numbered 8,595. Suicides have generally been on the rise. The 2000 number for men was over 2.5 times that of 1970 (8,761). Suicides suddenly increased by 40 per cent between 1997 and 1999, from 15,901 (1997) to 22,349 (1998) and then to 22,402 (1999), declining somewhat in 2000. The sex ratio has also dramatically changed – from 55.6 per cent men and 44.3 per cent women in 1970, to 71.6 per cent men and 28.4 per cent women in 2000. Suicide is the sixth leading cause of death for men overall and the first for men aged 25–39; the second for men aged between 20–24 and 40–49; the third for men between 15–19 and 50–59; and the fourth for men aged between 10–14 and 60–64 (Ministry of Health, Labour and Welfare 2001a).

8 It required some nine years to legalize low-dosage contraceptive pills for women (*Asahi Shinbun* 1999).

9 See references in note 1, above.

## References

Alarcón, N., Kaplan, C. and Moallem, M. (1999) 'Introduction: between woman and nation', in C. Kaplan, N. Alarcón and M. Moallem (eds) *Between Woman and Nation: Nationalisms, Transnational Feminisms and the State*, Durham, NC and London: Duke University Press.

Allison, A. (1994) *Nightwork: Sexuality, Pleasure and Corporate Masculinity in a Tokyo Hostess Club*, Chicago: University of Chicago Press.

—— (1996) *Permitted and Prohibited Desires: Mothers, Comics and Censorship in Japan*, Boulder: Westview Press.

Appadurai, A. (1996) *Modernity at Large: Cultural Dimensions of Globalization*, Minneapolis: University of Minnesota Press.

*Asahi Shinbun* (1999) '*Teiyōryō piru no shōnin kettei*' (Low-dosage pill approved), June 3.

—— (2001a) '*Kaikaku no "senkusha" shushō ga shitumonzeme*' (Prime Minister barrages pioneer of reform with questions), June 27.

—— (2001b) '*Shitsugyōritsu hachigatsu mo 5%*' (Unemployment rate at 5 per cent in August too), September 28.

Befu, H. (2001) *Hegemony of Homogeneity: An Anthropological Analysis of Nihonjinron*, Melbourne: Trans Pacific Press.

Berger, M., Wallis, B. and Watson, S. (eds) (1995) *Constructing Masculinity*, London and New York: Routledge.

Brod, H. and Kaufman, M. (eds) (1994a) *Theorizing Masculinities*, Thousand Oaks: Sage Publications.

—— (1994b) 'Introduction', in H. Brod and M. Kaufman (eds) *Theorizing Masculinities*, Thousand Oaks: Sage Publications.

Buruma, I. (1984) *Behind the Mask*, New York: Pantheon Books.

Butler, J. (1990) *Gender Trouble: Feminism and the Subversion of Identity*, London and New York: Routledge.

Clammer, J. (1997) *Contemporary Urban Japan: A Sociology of Consumption*, Oxford: Blackwell.

—— (2001) *Japan and Its Others: Globalization, Difference and the Critique of Modernity*, Melbourne: Trans Pacific Press.

Connell, R. W. (1987) *Gender and Power: Society, the Person and Sexual Politics*, Stanford: Stanford University Press.

—— (1993) 'The big picture: masculinities in recent world history', *Theory and Society* 22: 597–623.

—— (1995) *Masculinities*, Berkeley: University of California Press.

—— (1996) 'New directions in gender theory, masculinity research and gender politics', *Ethnos* 61, 3–4: 157–76.

Conway-Long, D. (1994) 'Ethnographies and masculinities', in H. Brod and M. Kaufman (eds) *Theorizing Masculinities*, Thousand Oaks: Sage Publications.

Cornwall, A. and Lindisfarne, N. (1994a) *Dislocating Masculinity: Comparative Ethnographies*, London and New York: Routledge.

—— (1994b) 'Introduction', in A. Cornwall and N. Lindisfarne (eds) *Dislocating Masculinity: Comparative Ethnographies*, London and New York: Routledge.

—— (1994c) 'Dislocating masculinity: gender, power and anthropology', in A. Cornwall and N. Lindisfarne (eds) *Dislocating Masculinity: Comparative Ethnographies*, London and New York: Routledge.

Crichton, M. (1992) *Rising Sun*, New York: Alfred A. Knopf.

Dasgupta, R. (2000) 'Performing masculinities? The "salaryman" at work and play', *Japanese Studies* 20, 2: 189–200.

di Leonardo, M. (1991) 'Introduction: gender, culture and political economy: feminist anthropology in historical perspective', in M. di Leonardo (ed.) *Gender at the Crossroads of Knowledge: Feminist Anthropology in the Postmodern Era*, Berkeley: University of California Press.

Donaldson, M. (1993) 'What is hegemonic masculinity?', *Theory and Society* 22: 643–57.

Edwards, W. (1989) *Modern Japan Through Its Weddings: Gender, Person and Society in Ritual Portrayal*, Stanford: Stanford University Press.

Fowler, E. (1996) *San'ya Blues: Laboring Life in Contemporary Tokyo*, Ithaca and London: Cornell University Press.

Fujimura-Fanselow, K. and Kameda, A. (1995) 'The changing portrait of Japanese men', in K. Fujimura-Fanselow and A. Kameda (eds) *Japanese Women: New Feminist Perspectives on the Past, Present and Future*, New York: Feminist Press.

Garon, S. (1997) *Molding Japanese Minds: The State in Everyday Life*, Princeton: Princeton University Press.

Geertz, C. (1973) *The Interpretation of Cultures*, New York: Basic Books.

Gill, T. (2001) *Men of Uncertainty: The Social Organization of Day Laborers in Contemporary Japan*, Albany: SUNY Press.

Gilmore, D. (1990) *Manhood in the Making: Cultural Concepts of Masculinity*, New Haven and London: Yale University Press.

Grossman, A. (ed.) (2000) *Queer Asian Cinema: Shadows in the Shade*, special issue, *Journal of Homosexuality* 39, 3/4.

Gutmann, M. C. (1997) 'Trafficking in men: the anthropology of masculinity', *Annual Review of Anthropology* 26: 385–409.

Halberstam, J. (1998) *Female Masculinities*, Durham, NC and London: Duke University Press.

Hall, S. (1997) 'The local and the global: globalization and ethnicity', in A. D. King (ed.) *Culture, Globalization and the World System: Contemporary Conditions for the Representation of Identity*, Minneapolis: University of Minnesota Press.

Hanmer, J. (1990) 'Men, power and the exploitation of women', in J. Hearn and D. Morgan (eds) *Men, Masculinities and Social Theory*, London: Unwin Hyman.

Hearn, J. and Collinson, D. L. (1994) 'Theorizing unities and differences between men and between masculinities', in H. Brod and M. Kaufman (eds) *Theorizing Masculinities*, Thousand Oaks: Sage Publications.

Hearn, J. and Morgan, D. (eds) (1990a) *Men, Masculinities and Social Theory*, London: Unwin Hyman.

—— (1990b) 'Men, masculinities and social theory [Introduction]', in J. Hearn and D. Morgan (eds) *Men, Masculinities and Social Theory*, London: Unwin Hyman.

Henshall, K. (1999) *Dimensions of Japanese Society: Gender, Margins and Mainstream*, New York: St Martin's Press.

Ikeda, H. (1996) *Fushi Katei no Otōsan Funsenki* (*Single Father's Daily Battles*), Tokyo: Shinpūsha.

Inoue, T., Ueno, C. and Ehara, Y. (eds) (1995) *Danseigaku* (*Men's Studies*), Tokyo: Iwanami Shoten.

Itō, K. (1993) *'Otoko Rashisa' no Yukue: Dansei-Bunka no Bunkashakaigaku* (*The Direction of 'Manliness': The Cultural Sociology of Male Culture*), Tokyo: Shin'yōsha.

—— (1996) *Danseigaku Nyūmon* (Introduction to Men's Studies), Tokyo: Sakuhinsha.

Ito, K. (1995) 'Sexism in Japanese weekly comic magazines for men', in J. Lent (ed.) *Asian Popular Culture*, Boulder: Westview Press.

Ito, S. and Yanase, R. (2001) *Coming Out in Japan: The Story of Satoru and Ryuta*, trans. F. Conlan, Melbourne: Trans Pacific Press.

Ivy, M. (1993) 'Formations of mass culture', in A. Gordon (ed.) *Postwar Japan as History*, Berkeley: University of California Press.

Johnson, S. (1988) *The Japanese Through American Eyes*, Stanford: Stanford University Press.

Jolivet, M. (1997) *Japan: The Childless Society?*, London and New York: Routledge.

Kamata, S. (1999) *Kazoku ga Jisatsu ni Oikomareru Toki* (*When Family Members are Cornered into Committing Suicide*), Tokyo: Kōdansha.

Kanemitsu, T. and Toyama, T. (2000) '*Gōn majikku: Nissan masaka no kyūkaifuku shukudaizeme de shain sōjū*' (Ghosn magic: Nissan's unbelievable immediate recovery mobilizing employees with a barrage of homework), *Aera* (November 20): 10–13.

Kasuga, K. (1989) *Fushi Katei o Ikiru: Otoko to Oya no Aida* (*Living Single-Father Families: Between Man and Father*), Tokyo: Keisō Shobō.

Kelly, W. W. (1986) 'Rationalization and nostalgia: cultural dynamics of new middle-class Japan', *American Ethnologist* 13, 4: 603–18.

—— (1993) 'Finding a place in metropolitan Japan: ideologies, institutions, and everyday life', in A. Gordon (ed.) *Postwar Japan as History*, Berkeley: University of California Press.

Kinmonth, E. (1981) *The Self-Made Man in Meiji Japanese Thought: From Samurai to Salary Man*, Berkeley: University of California Press.

Kitahara, M. (1999) '*Kyōkai kakuran e no bakkurasshu to teikō*' (Backlash and resistance against the disturbed boundaries), *Gendai Shisō*, 27, 1: 238–53.

Kondo, D. (1990) *Crafting Selves: Power, Gender and Discourses of Identity in a Japanese Workplace*, Chicago: University of Chicago Press.

—— (1997) *About Face: Performing Race in Fashion and Theater*, London and New York: Routledge.

Leupp, G. (1995) *Male Colors: The Construction of Homosexuality in Tokugawa Japan*, Berkeley: University of California Press.

Lie, J. (2001) *Multiethnic Japan*, Cambridge, MA: Harvard University Press.

Ling, L. H. M. (1999) 'Sex machine: global hypermasculinity and images of the Asian woman in modernity', *positions* 7, 2: 277–306.

Lunsing, W. (1998) 'Lesbian and gay movements: between hard and soft', in A. Osiander and C. Weber (eds) *Soziale Bewegungen in Japan* (*Social Movements in Japan*), Hamburg: OAG Hamburg.

—— (1999) 'Japan: finding its way?', in B. Adam, J. W. Duyvendak and A. Krouwel (eds) *The Global Emergence of Gay and Lesbian Politics, National Imprints of a Worldwide Movement*, Philadelphia: Temple University Press.

—— (2001) *Beyond Common Sense: Negotiating Constructions of Sexuality and Gender in Contemporary Japan*, London and New York: Kegan Paul.

McLelland, M. (2000) *Male Homosexuality in Modern Japan: Cultural Myths and Social Realities*, Richmond, Surrey: Curzon.

Mathews, G. (2000) *Global Culture/Individual Identity: Searching for Home in the Cultural Supermarket*, London and New York: Routledge.

Matsunaga, L. (2000) *The Changing Face of Japanese Retail: Working in a Chain Store*, London and New York: Routledge.

Miller, L. (1995) 'Introduction: looking beyond the *sararīman* folk model', *The American Asian Review* 13, 2: 19–27.

Ministry of Health, Labour and Welfare (2001a) 'Vital statistics', <http://www.mhlw.go.jp/toukei/saikin/hw/jinkou/suii00/index.html> (October 17).

—— (2001b) 'Vital statistics', <http://www1.mhlw.go.jp/toukei/12nensui_8/index.html> (October 3).

Moore, H. L. (1988) *Feminism and Anthropology*, Minneapolis: University of Minnesota Press.

—— (1994) *A Passion for Difference: Essays in Anthropology and Gender*, Bloomington and Indianapolis: Indiana University Press.

Morris, N. (2001) 'Paradigm paranoia: images of Japan and the Japanese in American popular fiction of the early 1990s', *Japanese Studies* 21, 1: 45–59.

Nakamaki, H. (1997) '*Joshō: keiei jinruigaku ni mukete: kaisha no "minzokushi" to sararīman no "jōmin kenkyū"*' (Introduction: towards an anthropology of administration: company ethnography and the folk research of salarymen), in H. Nakamaki and K. Hioki (eds) *Keiei Jinruigaku Kotohajime* (*Toward an Anthropology of Administration*), Tokyo: Tōhō Shuppan.

Nakamura, T. (2001) *Domesutikku Baiorensu: Kazoku no Byōri* (*Domestic Violence: Pathology of the Family*), Tokyo: Sakuhinsha.

Nakane, C. (1970) *Japanese Society*, Berkeley: University of California Press.

Nishikawa, Y. and Ogino, M. (eds) (1999) *Kyōdō Kenkyū: Danseiron* (*Joint Research: Theories of Men*), Kyoto: Jinbun Shoin.

Okamoto, T. and Sasano, E. (2001) '*Sengo Nihon no "sararīman" hyōshō no henka: Asahi Shinbun o jirei ni*' (Changes in representations of 'salaried men' in postwar Japanese newspapers: a re-examination of Asahi Shinbun, 1945–1999), *Shakaigaku Hyōron* (*Japanese Sociological Review*) 52, 1: 16–32.

Ong, A. and Peletz, M. G. (1995) 'Introduction', in A. Ong and M. G. Peletz (eds) *Bewitching Women, Pious Men: Gender and Body Politics in Southeast Asia*, Berkeley: University of California Press.

Ortner, S. (1996) *Making Gender: The Politics and Erotics of Culture*, Boston: Beacon Press.

Pei, M. (1992) *Salaryman*, New York: Viking.

Pflugfelder, G. (1999) *Cartographies of Desire: Male–Male Sexuality in Japanese Discourse, 1600–1950*, Berkeley: University of California Press.

Plath, D. (1964) *The After Hours: Modern Japan and the Search for Enjoyment*, Berkeley: University of California Press.

Roberson, J. (1998) *Japanese Working Class Lives: An Ethnographic Study of Factory Workers*, London and New York: Routledge.

—— (1999) 'Fight! ippatsu!: "stamina" health drinks and the marketing of masculine ideology in Japan', paper presented at the Annual Meeting of the American Anthropological Association, Chicago, November 17–21.

Roberts, G. (1994) *Staying on the Line: Blue-Collar Women in Contemporary Japan*, Honolulu: University of Hawaii Press.

Robertson, J. (1998) *Takarazuka: Sexual Politics and Popular Culture in Modern Japan*, Berkeley: University of California Press.

Rohlen, T. P. (1974) *For Harmony and Strength: Japanese White-Collar Organization in Anthropological Perspective*, Berkeley: University of California Press.

Saco, D. (1992) 'Masculinity as signs: poststructuralist feminist approaches to the study of gender', in S. Craig (ed.) *Men, Masculinity and the Media*, Newbury Park: Sage Publications.

Schodt, F. (1983) *Manga! Manga! The World of Japanese Comics*, New York: Kodansha International.

Sedgwick, E. (1995) '"Gosh, Boy George, you must be awfully secure in your masculinity!"', in M. Berger, B. Wallis and S. Watson (eds) *Constructing Masculinity*, London and New York: Routledge.

Shibuya, T. (2001) '*"Feminisuto dansei kenkyū" no shiten to kōzō*' (A view and vision of feminist studies on men and masculinities, *Shakaigaku Hyōron* (*Japanese Sociological Review*) 51, 4: 447–63.

Silverman, K. (1992) *Male Subjectivity at the Margins*, London and New York: Routledge.

Skinner, K. (1979) 'Salaryman comics in Japan: images of self-perception', *Journal of Popular Culture* 13, 1: 141–51.

Standish, I. (2000) *Myth and Masculinity in the Japanese Cinema: Towards a Political Reading of the 'Tragic Hero'*, Richmond, Surrey: Curzon Press.

Stecopoulos, H. and Uebel, M. (eds) (1997) *Race and the Subject of Masculinities*, Durham, NC and London: Duke University Press.

Sugimoto, Y. (1997) *An Introduction to Japanese Society*, Cambridge: Cambridge University Press.

Summerhawk, B., McMahill, C. and McDonald, D. (eds) (1998) *Queer Japan: Personal Stories of Japanese Lesbians, Gays, Bisexuals and Transsexuals*, Norwich, VT: New Victoria Publishers.

Sunagawa, H. (1999) '*Nihon no gei/rezubian sutadīzu*' (Japanese gay/lesbian studies), *Queer Japan* 1: 135–52.

Takeuchi, Y. (1996) '*Sararīman to iu shakaiteki hyōchō*' (Salaryman as social symbol), in S. Inoue, et al. (eds) *Nihon Bunka no Shakaigaku* (*The Sociology of Japanese Culture*), Tokyo: Iwanami Shoten.

—— (1997) '*Sararīman-kei ningen zō no tanjō to shūen*' (The birth and end of the salaryman-style personal image), in H. Nakamaki and K. Hioki (eds) *Keiei Jinruigaku Kotohajime* (*Toward an Anthropology of Administration*), Tokyo: Tōhō Shuppan.

Taniguchi, K. (1997) *Sei o Kau Otoko* (*Men Who Buy Sex*), Tokyo: Pandora.

Toyoda, M. (1997) *Otoko ga 'Otoko Rashisa' o Suteru Toki* (*When Men Discard 'Manliness'*), Tokyo: Asuka Shinsha.

Treat, J. W. (1999) *Great Mirrors Shattered: Homosexuality, Orientalism and Japan*, Oxford and New York: Oxford University Press.

Tsutamori, T. (ed.) (1999) *Hajimete Kataru Menzu Ribu Hihyō* (*First Discussion of the Critique of Men's Lib*), Tokyo: Tokyo Shoseki.

Uno, K. (1993) 'The death of "good wife, wise mother"?', in A. Gordon (ed.) *Postwar Japan as History*, Berkeley: University of California Press.

Valentine, J. (1997) 'Skirting and suiting stereotypes: representations of marginalized sexualities in Japan', *Theory, Culture and Society* 14, 3: 57–85.

Vincent, K., Kazama, T. and Kawaguchi, K. (1997) *Gei Sutadīzu* (*Gay Studies*), Tokyo: Seidosha.

Vogel, E. F. (1971/1963) *Japan's New Middle Class: The Salary Man and His Family in a Tokyo Suburb* (2nd edn), Berkeley: University of California Press.

White, M. (1993) *The Material Child: Coming of Age in Japan and America*, New York: The Free Press.

# 2 What masculinity?

## Transgender practices among Japanese 'men'

*Wim Lunsing*

In this chapter, I investigate various phenomena concerning transgender practices among Japanese men. Taking as wide a view as possible, I examine the cultural tropes constructing transgender in relation to actual practice and the reasons people may have to engage in them. In conclusion, I discuss the questions of whether and how crossing gender boundaries may influence gender constructions and therefore the relation between the sexes. The stories I offer are partly based on in-depth interviews and participant observation I conducted in 1992–3, 1996 and 1999 and partly on published interviews and other publications. Names given are those under which those concerned are actually known, unless otherwise indicated.

## Transgender

I use the term 'transgender' in the broadest sense possible and refute the idea, as expounded for instance by Janice Raymond, that the 'majority of transgenderists are transvestite men' (Raymond 1995: 215). Transvestite men and men in drag – which, as I will discuss below, are different phenomena – may be the most visible phenomena of transgender activity. However, the majority of people have at least some attributes ascribed to the opposite gender and thereby can be seen to engage in transgender activity. Raymond's vilification of transgendering men as promoting sexist views of women by always performing hyperfeminine types is divisive and particularly damaging to transgendering men with feminist ideals, whose very existence is denied (Riddell 1995).

I regard gender as a set of constructions determined by culture, time and place. Therefore it varies from culture to culture and has the possibility to change (Lunsing 2001a, 2001b). One only has to look at historical developments in European dress codes to notice that, while nowadays wearing a dress is widely regarded as feminine, in earlier periods it was common for men to wear dresses or dress-like garments such as togas or kilts. I believe that, by appropriating attributes ascribed to the opposite gender, people have the possibility to change generally held perceptions of gender.

Various feminist scholars have maintained that gender exists because '[it] sustains patriarchy and the moral dominance of men' (MacInnes 1998: 72). In this view, gender is designed to keep women in a subordinate position and men are at liberty to use sexual violence against women as a tool to assert their dominance (e.g.

Brownmiller 1975; Pateman 1988; Rich 1980). According to John MacInnes (1998: 73), this view implies that men are naturally disposed towards violence. Patriarchy then is reproduced by the social construction of gender but the problem remains where patriarchy came from in the first place, if not from nature. Until recently, masculinity was discussed entirely as synonymous with men (Halberstam 1998: 13). In this view, men are simply seen as somehow inherently predisposed towards violence and dominance, which leaves them no space to question their masculinity on their own terms.

However, in Japan, as elsewhere, there have in fact always been men who have transgressed the socially constructed boundaries of 'masculinity'. The most obvious of these transgressions is that of female impersonation, the best known in historical Japan that of the *kabuki* theatre (Pflugfelder 1999). As will be discussed in detail below, in contemporary Japan a number of ways of impersonating females exist that must be clearly distinguished from each other. There are, for instance, drag queens (*doraggu kuīn*) – in most but by no means all cases gay men – who perform the feminine as an act and there are two distinctive types of transvestite, or *josōsha*.

In the general public conception, transgendering men are often conflated with gay men. Visible female gender attributes are typically seen as indicative of the presence of a sexual attraction to one's own sex. The strength of this conflation is shown by the fact that it is reproduced among Western scholars, even specialists in matters of sexuality. Jennifer Robertson, for instance, wrote that gay magazines carry hundreds of advertisements for transvestite clubs and that all patrons of such clubs identify as homosexual (Robertson 1998: 202). This is incorrect. There are not hundreds of such places, nor do gay magazines carry such advertisements. They do, occasionally, carry advertisements for new half clubs, which, as will be discussed below, are not the same as transvestite clubs (see Lunsing 1995). Judith Butler set the stage for such (American academic) confusion of matters of sexual preference and gender attributes in her book *Gender Trouble* (Butler 1990). Butler writes on the one hand that sexuality and gender can be uncoupled but on the other that sex is a construct, thus blurring the distinction between sex and gender all over again.

Drag performances are examples of performances of gender rather than of sex or sexuality. In *Bodies That Matter*, Butler (1993) discusses drag queens based on the film *Paris is Burning* and is sensitive to the various layers of performance and audience. In the end she finds that the film *sometimes* succeeds in remaking dominant gender norms, implying that most of the time it does not but instead ends up confirming what it supposedly intends to question.

Cross-dressing is not an alternative manifestation of oneself in order to show that one is sexually and/or romantically interested in one's own sex. This may be the case even more in Japan than in for instance the US. That sexual preference and trans-gender phenomena are not directly related is not a new finding,[1] albeit one that in recent years has been made more explicit (Butler 1990; Rubin 1993; Sedgwick 1990). The various transgender categories that can be discerned in contemporary Japan all have their own particular environments for practice and their own publications. However, the various categories of transgender that a cultural discourse provides are never adequate to fully describe actual transgender experience.

The Japanese word *sei* can be translated as sex as well as sexuality and gender. Perhaps because this can be terribly confusing, all three phenomena are often referred to by the Anglo-Japanese terms *sekkusu*, *sekushuariti* and *jendā*. It seems that Japanese specialists and those directly concerned have a comparatively good grasp of the differences of these terms. The gay writer Fushimi Noriaki (1991) shows exemplary lucidity. He developed a set of dichotomies through which people are positioned and/or position themselves. For sex, i.e. the sex one has, he uses the faunal terms *mesu* and *osu* (female and male), also represented by XX and XY symbols; for sexuality, i.e. sexual preference, he uses *hetero* and *homo* to refer to the object of sexual attraction; and for gender, which he regards as a product of people's imagination, he created the neologisms *josei* and *dansei* (female system and male system, whereby the character for system replaces that for sex, which is commonly used for *josei* [woman] and *dansei* [man]). Furthermore, he developed graphics that make it possible to represent hermaphrodites as well as bisexuality. Thus, he covers all thinkable forms of existence in relation to sex, sexuality and gender (1991: 192–243).[2]

## Japanese types of transgender males

While the typography below intends to clarify the fine lines of distinction and counter the common confusion of the various categories, when looking at people in real life matters are not always so clear. People may, for instance, not be aware of this typography and its various meanings and therefore not know how to categorize themselves. People may also change during their lifetime and, furthermore, the wordings themselves are subject to change, as in the case of the relatively new term 'new half'. Throughout, I introduce individual cases to illustrate how this may work for actual people.

### Josō *(male transvestism)*

The most famous and longest-lasting bimonthly male transvestite magazine is *Queen* (*Kuīn*), which since the early 1980s has consistently sold about 7,000 copies per issue (Lunsing 2001b: 267). In *Queen*, men show pictures of themselves in female attire, write about their cross-dressing experiences, and in some cases advertise for partners. *Queen* also contains articles on events staged by the magazine as well as occasional reports on, for instance, female impersonation contests held at university campus festivals in November. *Queen* is related to the Elisabeth club chain in Osaka and Tokyo, where men can go and receive assistance with and advice about applying make-up, selecting wigs and dressing in women's clothes. Readers of *Queen* and visitors to the Elisabeth chain typically dress up as women only within the confines of the Elisabeth clubs or other private quarters such as specially organized parties.

Different from these are men who like to dress as women and go out on the streets. Most famous is Candy Milky, who also runs his own magazine, *Himawari* (sunflower), with sales of about 3,000 to 4,000. *Himawari* is mostly filled with reports on outings, including for instance weddings. Candy and his likes make no attempt to pass as female. Candy himself dresses like a 12-year-old girl in Laura Ashley fashion, which makes him stand out in any context. This is different from the patrons of Elisabeth, who at least try to look like real women or girls and often succeed quite well.

Related yet different is another group of cross-dressers who wear women's clothes but do nothing else to make a feminine impression. They may for instance wear a dress while at the same time having a beard. According to Candy, this style is more specific to the Kansai area than to Tokyo (Fushimi 1996: 156–72). With Candy, they share a political agenda of rebelling against society's gender norms.

A famous example of someone engaging in *josō* is Tsutamori Tatsuru. Before he began his transgender activities, he looked like a rugged macho man, wrote about motorcycling, and was active on the motor scene. However, he came to feel dissatisfied with this performance and began adopting feminine attributes, in the end looking like a beautiful woman. He acquired a strong dislike for anything masculine, including his penis. For a period he worked for the transvestite magazine *Queen* and spoke with many of the men who frequented the Elisabeth club in Tokyo. Eventually, he felt unhappy with the weakness of the closeted character of this and left to write his own books, among them one on male beauty which focuses on the many methods of depilation (Tsutamori 1990). Another book describes the process of change he went through and the various occupations he held, including seam-stress, nude model and bar hostess. Apart from the nude model, he functioned entirely as a woman in these occupations (Tsutamori 1993).

Tsutamori's dislike of his genitals resulted from his embracing feminist thought in which all men are potential rapists. In his view, feminism taught that heterosexual sex was always and inherently oppressive to women and therefore he felt disinclined to engage in it any more. He experimented with sex with men but in the end he found that he was more attracted to the softness he found in the female body. Eventually he formed a relationship with a woman who worked during the daytime while he took care of the housekeeping and wrote. This woman enticed him to have sex with her, to which he reluctantly agreed:

> When finally my penis had entered her body, I became conscious of my body being male and I became petrified. My body, that until then had felt the same as hers, made me feel that I was a being with a penis, however much I disliked this. She had the same body as I, but was a being with a vagina. I felt awful about this and firmly closed my eyes. When she moved her thighs around I gritted my teeth to silence my voice. I didn't want to feel. When I heard her say: 'your clitoris feels very good to me' my head felt as if it was crushed into pieces. A penis is a variation of a clitoris. They are not different. When I thought this, I felt a relief emerge from the bottom of my heart, and suddenly my feelings of pleasure surged.
>
> (Tsutamori 1993: 199)[3]

He gained the insight that a penis is not essentially different from a clitoris and that the actual shape of a sexual organ is of little importance. This example undermines the view of men having a natural tendency towards dominance.

During the period I knew him, Tsutamori rarely wore make-up and dressed mainly in clothes not specifically women's, but his long hair and his delicate manner of speech and behaviour made him appear very androgynous. As the feminist Uemura Kuniko said (personal communication), he is extremely popular among young women. This may be related to his long hair and slender body shape and to his sensitive manner of conduct that make him appear like a character common in girls' comics (see McLelland 2000).

### Drag queens

Drag queens are a separate category of men who dress up in women's clothes solely for theatrical purposes. Unlike the two categories above, they have no magazine, but they do have contacts with the gay scene, in which many of their shows are performed. One of the more famous Japanese drag queens, Ogura Tō, whose drag name is Margaret, even functioned as chief editor of the bestselling gay magazine *Bádi* (*sic*; Buddy). Drag queens perform at parties in clubs throughout Japan or, like singer Shimōnu (Simone) Fukayuki, they may have one-person shows. While Fukayuki might appear to fit in a tradition set by the famous transvestite and gay singer Miwa Akihiro,[4] contemporary drag queens, including Fukayuki, divert from Miwa in that they do not try to look like beautiful women but make their performances more like grotesque parodies.

In the Kansai area, there are several overlapping troupes of drag performers, such as Diamond and the Shang Hai Love Theatre, which originally gathered in the mid-1980s around Fukayuki and the late Furuhashi Teiji. They have a distinct style and their programmes are constantly renewed. According to Fukayuki (personal communication), the majority of contemporary drag queens in Tokyo appear to have begun their activities in the mid-1990s after seeing the Australian film *The Adventures of Priscilla, Queen of the Desert* (released in 1994). Indeed, some of their drag costumes are copies of those in the film, as are many of their mannerisms. On the other hand, the Tokyo-based drag troupe Upper Camp has developed its own original style, in which being ugly and ridiculous play major roles. The troupes mostly include women as well as men. Fukayuki maintains that the Kansai performances are, in contrast to those in Tokyo, profoundly based in Japanese culture and refer to the underground culture (*angura bunka*) of the 1960s and 1970s, which greatly influenced his own view of Japanese society.

D. K. Uraji also referred to *angura bunka* as important for his position in society. He finds that young people nowadays lack a sense of what it is to be an outsider and believes that 'we have to create and show "outsiders" anew'. As a child, he regarded himself as female:

> I believe that love is performing a story . . . Unfortunately, I did not have a gay love story, but instead had imagined heterosexual stories like that of Walt Disney's Snow White . . . And I ended up thinking that I wanted to be that

heroine . . . I was late, at the age of 18 years, without even understanding that I had this wish to be a heroine, I decided upon a boy to play the opposite role and said that I liked him . . . But the story developed in a different direction. Even though the princess said that she liked him, the prince said that he disliked me . . . I was told that I was a man. Until then I had hardly ever realized that I was a man . . . It was terrible.

Denying his existence as he knew it, this event upset Uraji's view of what he was and led to a prolonged period of depression. He was jealous of women to the point that he was upset when a woman appeared on television. He wished he had been born a woman. Eventually he realized that it was impossible to become a woman and that, indeed, he did not really want to. He did not wish to menstruate or have children, and having breasts or not was not much of an issue. He joined Diamond in the early 1990s and the possibilities it provided to express himself were of major importance. He found that, if he could not become a heroine in reality, he could still perform (*enjiru*) like one. He did not need to be a woman to play the heroine. While Uraji's drag performances may at first sight be the most explicit example of his female impersonation, in fact on stage he finds it imperative to show that he is not a woman:

> I am masculine when I perform as a drag queen, [because] the impact is stronger if you bring to the foreground what is masculine about you, the bad part of masculinity. You have to find out your awkwardness and place that right in front of the people . . . Therefore, when I am a drag queen, I am more conscious of being a man than at any other time.

Uraji, a successful designer/artist, performs a variety of roles in everyday life. He believes that 'gender is something you have to use skilfully', but also feels that it is highly irrelevant how other people see him generally. As his delicate features prevent him from passing successfully as male, he adopted the strategy of wearing clothes that make him pass as female in public. In his present relationship he regards himself as a princess and his lover as a prince – though his boyfriend, to whom I spoke shortly after interviewing Uraji, was unaware of the fantasy in which Uraji casts their relationship.

    Fronsoir also participates in Diamond's events in Kyoto. He came in touch with this troupe through his girlfriend, who was already participating in the drag shows before they met. While some gay men in the group think that as a straight drag queen he is an outsider of sorts, he feels fully part of it. He enjoys drag as something that gives him the freedom to live out alternative roles and sees it mostly as a way of partying, though much time and effort go into preparation and rehearsals. When thinking about why he likes to make up and dress like a woman, he said: 'I was often told to behave like [a boy] and I hated that very much'. Like Uraji, drag provides a way of liberation from social norms. He regards himself as fully straight and so does his girlfriend. Thus, doing drag does not necessarily have anything to do with a person's sexuality. This is also underlined by the fact that many members of Diamond are women, the majority heterosexual. Female drag queens are of interest here since they 'impersonate' females, and audiences used to seeing men as female impersonators may believe that they are men, as happened to me when I saw a Diamond show for the first time.

The Kansai performers see the performances in *Paris is Burning*, which Butler (1993) used more or less as representative of drag performances, as different in nature from their own. Where the goal of the performances in *Paris is Burning* is to show actually existing examples of men and women as perfectly as possible, Diamond performances range from making the actually existing look grotesque to performances in which the sex of what is being performed is unclear. In Diamond shows, both women and men perform female as well as male roles, and the audience is made oblivious of what sex people actually have; a major point of the performances appears to be precisely to show that this is of no importance (see also Nakamura and Matsuo, this volume, Chapter 4). They engaged in these activities and gave them these meanings many years before Butler (1990) wrote on the performative nature of gender and before drag queens boomed in the US; so, indeed, it appears to be rooted in Japanese culture. Fukayuki said that they now use the term drag queen (*doraggu kuīn*) but only because that term has presently gained currency in Japan.

### Nyūhāfu *(new half)*

This is the most difficult category to pinpoint, as the term 'new half' is relatively new, having been coined in the early 1980s by the mass media (Matsuo 1997: 19). It is used very often to refer to men who work dressed as female hostesses in particular show pubs, where they give theatrical performances. Many people think that new half range from transvestites to transsexuals and anything in between and/or that they are gay (Robertson 1998: 202).[5] New half may be seen as an occupational category rather than a specifically gendered type of person. Establishments in which new half work are also widely known as *gei bā* (gay bars), and before the introduction of the term new half, those who worked there were called *gei bōi* (gay boys). This type of *gei bā* is in gay circles called *kankō bā* (tourist bars), and seen as places where straight people can go and watch what they perceive as gay people (see Lunsing 2001c). A term preceding new half is Mr Redī (Mr Lady). When I asked some gay men what the difference was between new half and Mr Lady, some thought the Mr Lady type had had his testicles removed and new half had not. Others maintained that there was no such difference and that there were new half as well as Mr Lady who had had full sex-change surgery as well as those who had not had any surgery.

The term new half has for most people a derogatory connotation. However, the few people who refer to themselves by the term new half regard themselves as halfway between men and women:

> Thinking about myself, I have developed a womanlike (*onnappoi*) body by using hormones and silicones in my breasts but my male sexual organs remain intact. It is an existence of neither male nor female. I think it cannot be expressed by any other word than new half.
>
> (Nekome 1998: 79)

New half can be equated to what in Western contexts may be called 'chicks with dicks' or 'she-males', i.e. men with breasts acquired by surgery and/or the use of oestrogen. They are similar to the *travesti* from Latin America (Cornwall 1994; Kulick 1998), with the difference that, unlike *travesti*, new half typically do not enhance their hips to appear more feminine and are less interested in having large breasts (Nekome 1998: 165).

The eight new half Nekome Yū introduces in the book *Nyūhāfu to Iu Ikikata* (*The Lifestyle Called 'New Half'*; ibid.) show great variety in motives, feelings, thoughts and future prospects. What they have in common is that they felt uneasy about living 'like a man' (*otoko rashii*). While one says that she became new half because as a man she was not desired by those she wanted to desire her (ibid.: 125), for the majority the reasons are independent of what is attributed to other people. They all have worked or are still working in the entertainment industry. While two cases actually concern transsexuals, one whose surgery was paid for by the club where she worked (ibid.: 54–5) and another who decided to appear in pornographic films to pay for the surgery (ibid.: 179–200), other cases concern new half in the sense outlined above, women with a penis or men with breasts. Again, the fluidity between the various categories must be stressed. Their preference for sexual partners is varied but new half are predominantly interested in men by whom they want to be seen and sexually related to as women (ibid.).

Shimada Toshiko is one of the people who were interviewed by Fushimi Noriaki for his book *Kuia Paradaisu* (*Queer Paradise*; Fushimi 1996: 37–52). From early childhood, Shimada felt attracted to and excited by dressing up in women's clothing. Like Tsutamori, he frequented Elisabeth for a period. He gradually began dressing as a woman to go to the company where he worked and this did not lead to any problems there. He used female hormones and grew breasts but never considered a sex change. The reason for using the hormones was not simply to grow breasts:

> I also didn't want to hurt my body too much and endured my whole life but in the end I didn't know whether I preferred to be male or female, so the idea was, if that is how things are, let me do this. I also had all the time some sexual obsession, a weird delusion of constantly being chased by sexual desire, which I hated. Thinking what to do about it, I decided to erase my masculinity (*danseisei*) ... The breasts are a premium. It was enough that by injecting female hormones my sexual desire dissipated.
>
> (ibid.: 42)

Different from Tsutamori, who stresses that he is neither male nor female, Shimada sees himself as both male and female. At times he wishes to engage in what he sees as rough masculine activities, such as riding a motorbike through rough areas, at others he feels like a delicate woman, travelling by train and eating lady-like box lunches.

At the time of this interview, he lived with a male partner, whom he regarded as straight. The partner had no negative feelings towards his penis, on the contrary. They met through an advertisement in *Queen*. While the partner also occasionally dresses as a woman, when they are together he prefers to act like a man while he prefers Shimada to look like a 'proper' woman. Their relationship mimics a typical heterosexual relationship. While Shimada's physique fits that of the new half discussed above, he does not use that term – which also reflects the fact that he does not have a stereotypical new half occupation – but rather calls himself 'transgender' or even 'overgender', referring to his overcoming the boundaries of gender (Fushimi 1996: 42).

### Male-to-female transsexuals (MTFTS)

As discussed, many of those who work as new half are male-to-female transsexuals. Once they have completed their sex-change surgery, male-to-female transsexuals can be seen as outside the category of the male. Nevertheless, I discuss them here as in some cases sex-change surgery can also be a final goal of men who work in typical new half contexts. They may choose to work in such contexts because the relatively high salary permits them to save enough money to pay for sex-change surgery or they may believe that their way of being precludes working in most other occupations. Kuroyanagi even devoted the bulk of a book to the danger of people obtaining full sex-change surgery under the peer pressure that may exist in such working conditions. The womanlier one is, the better. Indeed, he found some cases of people who regretted having acquired a female physique (Kuroyanagi 1992 [1987]).

Japanese law made it impossible to carry out sex-change surgery until very recently. The Eugenics Protection Law, passed in the 1940s, stipulated that it was not legal to carry out surgery that impeded the fertility of the people, which was taken by hospitals as a reason to stop performing such operations (Mako Sennyo 1996: 116). Consequently, much of the expertise that existed has disappeared. Only since 1998 has sex-change surgery been openly practised again, at the Saitama Prefecture Hospital near Tokyo. The specialist concerned learned to (re-)construct penises with male victims of traffic accidents and, consequently, actual sex-change surgery remains limited to FTM (female-to-male) surgery. MTF transsexuals undergo surgery abroad, varying from the US to Singapore and Thailand, or in obscure Japanese hospitals. It is not possible to change one's legal records upon the completion of sex-change surgery and therefore MTF transsexuals remain male in all official documents, leading to all sorts of problems (ibid.; Torii 1997).

Mako Sennyo – a nickname with a mythical quality, referring to Mako the fairy (*sennyo*) – was born with male genitalia but is now living as a lesbian woman after having had sex-change surgery inside Japan. What distinguishes her from most other transsexuals is not only that she is lesbian. More importantly, while her womanhood is of great importance to her and she places great value on being seen as a woman, she does not actually do much to adapt her behaviour to appear really feminine, i.e. to confirm to social constructions of femininity, as she is also an ardent feminist who believes that these constructions are oppressive. Therefore she does not mind having small breasts and short hair. She uses quite unfeminine ways of interacting with people and is generally seen as abrasive and even scary by people who do not know her well. Her uncompromising behaviour remains quite in tune with what is expected more of men than of women. At a party, a gay man even criticized her when she called herself lesbian because she did not speak like one (Lunsing 2001b: 277). She recognizes that because she was born as a man, she has remains of masculinity in herself and that therefore her position in lesbian and feminist groups is problematic.

Nevertheless, Mako has found acceptance as lesbian in lesbian circles in the Kansai area and she has an intimate relationship with a lesbian lover (Fushimi 1996: 111–12). Obviously falling outside the category of the transgendering male, as she has become a woman, Mako nevertheless often does not pass for female either, in constrast to Uraji, who often passes for female while being a male. She rather tends to raise people's eyebrows.

### Hermaphrodites/intersexual people

Hermaphrodites are born with both female and male sexual organs, which develop to varying extents. They are usually brought up to become either men or women and consequently may find at a later age that the sex assigned to them by their parents and/or physician does not agree with their feelings. At this point, they may decide to adopt the social behaviour of the opposite sex. Generally, hermaphrodism is seen as a natural phenomenon. The examples I found in Japan are generally seen more as men than as women, though there may actually be more who live as women. A third and new direction is that of activists who maintain that they are neither male nor female and should be accepted as such instead of being made to try to fit constructions of one gender or the other (Hashimoto 1998).

Hasshī, whose real name is Hashimoto Hideo, grew up as a boy and was educated to become a man. However, in his adolescence he felt some disagreement with his being male and found that he also had traits generally regarded as feminine. As it turned out, he was actually intersexual and also developed small breasts. An intimate relationship with a female friend ended after many years when she married. For a while he tried to be a gay man, as he felt attracted to men anyway, but eventually this was no solution, since his intersexual physique was not in agreement with what gay men sought. At age 32, he realized that he had spent ten years trying to be something he was not. This occurred when he had sex with a male colleague and friend, K:

> . . . we embraced on the bed. I could see flames of desire over his shoulder. But I have no penis or vagina. K finally reached his orgasm but my sexual organs were still reaching for his penis. The next morning I refused when K asked me to do it again. Because K could not detain the heart of his wife, he had made me into his object for the disposal of sexual desire. How vexatious! But my sexual organs did not reach an orgasm and kept reaching for K's penis. For the first time my passion was inflamed. I am neither male nor female, I am 'just a person'. I had just been performing a man for ten years.
>
> (ibid.: 90–1)

He also felt different from gay men, and a gay activist group he belonged to made it clear that they did not wish to deal with his problem, as they thought that it was a medical issue and they wished to deal only with social and political problems. The same group, however, does include FTM transgender people, whose concerns are not with their physique but with being socially accepted as men. Hasshī decided to form his own group of intersexual people, which he called Hijra Nihon (ibid.), after the Indian phenomenon of Hijras who cast themselves as neither male nor female (Serena 1990). The initial reaction to an advertisement for Hijra Nihon included all sorts of people, ranging from journalists to men who were sexually interested but none from other intersexual people (Hashimoto 1998: 105–6).

The advertisement did, however, lead to several magazine articles. The publication of an interview in the book *Queer Paradise* provided the chance for one intersexual to contact Hasshī (see Fushimi 1996: 137–49). This was Furukawa Miho, who lives mainly as a woman. After Hasshī contacted the American organization for intersexual people and met the American specialist Milton Diamond, he 'came out' as intersexual in an article in the opinion magazine *Views* in 1996. While, given the minimal response of intersexual people, Hasshī had become doubtful about whether Hijra Nihon was of any use to those it was meant for, he received a letter from the intersexual Tanaka Tomoko which gave him the courage to continue. Eventually the name of the group was changed to PESFIS (Peer Support for Intersexual People), which indicates the intentions of the group more clearly. The publication of an article in the women's magazine *Josei Sebun* led three other intersexual people to Hasshī and PESFIS, and only then was his goal of founding an organization for mutual support reached.

### Homosexuals

Homosexual men distinguish themselves from the categories above, since, despite popular imagination (see McLelland 2000), they do not necessarily have any visible attributes that are commonly constructed as belonging to the female gender. Among some gay groups, there exists great opposition to the general confusion of transgender phenomena and homosexuality (Lunsing 1998, 1999, 2001b). Indeed, several gay informants said that in their youth they had felt disgusted by the idea that they should live a life of cross-dressing and such because they felt attracted to men or boys – an idea they acquired from the mass media. Historically, '*okama*' has been an important construction of homosexuality in Japan. *Okama* are typically seen as effeminate and sexually passive. The term *okama* may also be used to refer to the anus (Lunsing 1997). The term is often regarded as derogatory and being called *okama* has, indeed, hurt many gay youths – though neither all gay youths nor only gay youths are confronted with this term. Having features seen as feminine is usually the determining factor (Lunsing 2001b: 271).

The Tokyo-based gay and lesbian organization OCCUR is at the forefront of those who deny that gay men are any different from straight men apart from their sexual preference. They appear to be quite influential in shaping the idea that *gei* (gay) is the politically correct word to refer to gay men (e.g. Lunsing 1998, 1999). Nevertheless, *gei* as it is used by mainstream Japanese also has a connotation of femininity and meanings that are similar to that of new half, as is also evidenced by the common understanding of the term *gei bā*, discussed above. While I agree with groups like OCCUR that not all gay men show feminine characteristics, I hold the view that their very sexuality makes it plausible to place all gay men among transgender males. After all, loving men is generally thought to be a female attribute.

However, there is more to the terminological difference of *okama* and *gei*. Shimōnu Fukayuki wrote that he finally felt that he had come to terms with his homosexuality when he felt at ease applying the term *okama* to himself (Fukayuki 1996). When I asked him to elaborate, he explained that he had felt very negatively about the word *okama* in his youth. At one point he met a woman who used the word all the time:

> When I asked why she used that word, she said that she didn't mean to hurt me but that she thought that *okama* was a splendid (*subarashii*) word and that she used it because she liked it . . . I was told that because it is Japanese – and the words that are today in fashion, like *homo*, *gei* and queer (*kuia*), don't convey the essential and direct style at all – people who have been educated in Japanese should place importance on the Japanese word *okama* . . . *Okama* may be a discriminatory term in mainstream society but inside myself, I don't have to treat it as discriminatory. I thought, if it sounds beautiful to me, then that's fine. When I accepted this idea I became very much at ease. In the end *gei*, *homo*, *kuia* or *okama* are all the same. If you say *gei* it may give a modern, new feeling but in essence it is the same. And the tradition of the meaning of the word *okama* that was created by people in the 1950s and 1960s has a very good essence and it is far better to follow them when you are Japanese.

Fukayuki may seem like a language purist but that is not the essence of his words. *Okama* has a tradition in Japan and one he feels attracted to. He wants to introduce younger generations to the world of the 1960s and 1950s *okama* culture, which he sees as part of the above-mentioned *angura bunka*. He finds the album *Baramon* (*Rose gate*), which like the term *okama* has connotations of effeminacy, representative of this culture.

Although gay men may not necessarily engage in transgender practices otherwise, there are some aspects that place them at the forefront of more general transgender practices. For instance, in the gay bar scene a distinct manner of speech has developed, called *onē kotoba*, literally meaning older sister's language. It is an effeminate manner of speech. Many gay men feel awkward in the company of those employing it (e.g. Ito and Yanase 2001: 309), which may be related at least partly to their internalized homophobia. Apart from that, it appears that gay men feel relatively more awkward using masculine terms of self-reference such as *boku* and *ore* and tend to make more use of the neutral, or even feminine, *watakushi*, *watashi* and the explicitly feminine *atashi* (Lunsing 2001b: 269–70).[6]

A large portion of gay men also tend to spend quite a lot of attention on their looks. In the 1990s the macho-man style came into vogue, particularly in Tokyo, where the gay bar area is awash with men with short hair or shaved heads, moustaches or goatees, and who wear jeans or leather, following models provided by gay styles popular in Western countries. However, the editor of the gay magazine *G-men*, which was first published in 1995 and can take much credit for popularizing this style, said that he thought that this itself was also a form of drag. Kamiya Toshihiro, a gay man from Kobe who has a shaved head and who dresses almost entirely in leather and rubber, said:

> If you didn't feel a yearning for men in leather inside yourself, if there wasn't a woman inside yourself that feels that yearning, I think it would be impossible. So you want to become that object you are yearning for, to wear the leather, and you like people who wear leather. So, I don't think it is possible to like people in leather without having such a female basis (*josei no hon'i*). But that is the first problem, Japanese gay men don't understand this connection, this situation. So if a leather man looks slightly feminine (*joseippoi*), they don't want to relate to him . . . So they say I hate feminine people but the ones that say it are often feminine themselves. Leather is a type of drag and it . . . is a very queer wear.

As in the case of drag, more than usual attention is given to appearance, albeit in this case a super-masculine one. Indeed, I found that a number of the more macho impersonators also engage in female impersonation as drag queens. On one occasion I witnessed Ogura Tō (above, best known in drag as Margaret) presenting a show in leather, saying that today he had come as a man.

## The boundaries of transgender

Other transgender phenomena can also be recognized in men, depending on the definition of the categories of masculine and feminine. One such area is that of speech. Men may choose to or feel unable not to use language that is generally regarded as feminine. This may include wording as well as tone and manner of speech. Curtness and quietness are supposed to be characteristics of masculinity in speech and being talkative a feminine feature. Hence men who talk 'too' much can be seen as practising transgender. Another example is that of food. Sweet food is associated with femininity and bitter food with masculinity. Thus, men eating sweet desserts can be seen as practicing transgender. In many job-related contexts, it is expected that men drink alcohol. Men failing to do so can equally be seen as practicing transgender. When taking into account such phenomena, it becomes clear that few men are wholly free of practising transgender and that some form or degree of femininity in men is commonplace.

In smaller ways, transgender activity seems to be gaining ground throughout Japanese society. Men have discovered the aesthetics business and are increasingly using make-up and seeking treatment in beauty parlours as well as plastic surgery (Frühstück 2000; Miller, this volume, Chapter 3). Tsutamori's introduction of depilation for men who want to be beautiful (Tsutamori 1990) also appears to have some following among young Japanese men. As Ishii-Kuntz (this volume, Chapter 12) shows, men have also become active in areas that during the 1950s and 1960s had come to be seen entirely as traditional female areas of activity such as home education and housekeeping. Men who do not wish to conform to the boundaries of the construction of the male gender act to undermine its rigidity.

In particular young men rebel against the norms for clothing that confront them. If they like to wear red and think they look good in it, they do so, regardless of the social construction of red as a colour belonging to female sex (Lunsing 2001b: 272–4). Dyeing hair and body piercing among men has taken an enormous flight from the late 1980s onwards. Young men, however, grow older, and most feel compelled to remove any visible piercings (which for instance do not include those in nipples, which I have seen even in the most modest *sararīman*) and to adapt more conservative looks. However, some persist in choosing their own style.

A famous example is Hirano Hiroaki, a gay high-school teacher who years before coming out as gay in the media had been widely reported for having a Mohican haircut (Izumi 1990: 329–30). In his forties, he still continues his own style, which, while he keeps changing his hair and so on, has become quite distinct for its colourfulness and often soft materials. Hirano has some following among straight men. A man who works as a day labourer said that he admired Hirano's individualistic looks and himself also took to wearing bright colors. The rebellion here is very much against the often heard phrase: *otoko rashiku shinasai*: behave like a man. Men who discover feelings, behaviour or, as for instance in the case of Uraji, physical features in themselves that do not fit the idea of *otoko rashisa* are obvious candidates for dissenting with what their surroundings expect of them.

## Discussion

What the examples above show is that the various categories of transgender people, while they can and must be clearly distinguished, are not necessarily always exclusive. In their search for what they are, people may pass through any number of settings. Since, for instance, the gay male setting is large compared to others, many people are likely to have (had) some contact with it. While the typical drag queen is thought to be a gay male, straight men can also do drag and in the case of Japan, this is not so uncommon. This is also true for the more withdrawn transvestites of Elisabeth, a majority of whom are straight men. Apart from that, the common occurrence of transvestism at company parties and university festivals suggests that in certain circumstances many men have no qualms about dressing up as women and wearing make-up and that this usually does not lead to stigmatization.

Do such activities, however, have any influence on prevailing social constructions of gender? In the case of companies, where I found that people may even feel obliged to perform in order to show themselves to be cooperative, this hardly seems to be likely. In other cases, however, it does seem to me that transgender activity serves to disseminate ideas concerning the constructed nature of gender. Like the drag troupe Diamond, which stresses that being male or female is of little importance in relation to one's performance, the demand of Hasshī that a third sex be recognized is also directed at a reappraisal of the existing gender order. The quest is for more space for people to express themselves as they are, regardless of their sex.

Feminism has made major efforts for women to be able to work in occupations that had been closed to them because of their sex, and thus effectively to transgress the limits set by the prevailing gender constructions. What the men discussed above do is similar, and not antithetical, as Raymond (1995) thinks of transgender males, who in her opinion reconfirm prejudice against women. In the sense that an effort is made to adjust the limits set by gender constructions, the political meaning is evident.

In some cases, this may be less evident, such as in the case of the MTF transsexual who ends up being a woman and often one who tries to fit neatly with conservative ideas of what women are. However, I believe that the important difference between them and women who were born and educated as women is that the former went through a major process of physical reconstruction. Typically, they have gone through many difficult times to be what they eventually have become, rather than conservative women who simply are as they were educated to become. Moreover, as the case of Mako shows, MTF transsexuals do not necessarily want to be utterly feminine.

Several book titles (Hashimoto 1998; Tsutamori 1993) make reference to the idea that transgender people are neither man nor woman. The problems Japanese law and society place before them are that they do not provide for more possibilities, as Hasshī and his group wish. What all the people discussed here do is to question and subvert gender as it is constructed in Japanese society. Together they form but one part of the many people who question the essentiality of femininity and masculinity as currently constructed. In a sense they can be seen as radicals, as their methods and ways of life are quite uncompromising. Thus, I feel that the explicit transgender people discussed here deserve the support of other groups like Ikujiren, men's lib, and gay and lesbian movements (see Nakamura, Kazama and Kawaguchi, and Ishii-Kuntz, this volume, Chapters 10, 11 and 12, respectively), as the front-runners of a great field of activity, the essence of which is that people should be freed from the constraints society and law place on them on the basis of their sex.

## Notes

1 See Whitehead (1981) for a standard work concerning the relation between transgender and homosexuality among Native American tribes and the mistakes that had been made by preceding researchers, most importantly the general confusion of cross-dressing with homosexuality.

2 Fushimi developed his ideas independent of American theorists like Rubin (1993), Sedgwick (1990) and Butler (1990), whose work was at the time neither available in Japanese nor part of academic or other discourse in Japan.

3 All translations are by the author.

4 Miwa Akihiro was born in 1935 and made his debut in 1952. One of his greatest hits was *Mekemeke* in 1957 (Miwa 1992).

5 Robertson compounds her confusion regarding the term 'new half' by relating it to *hāfu* (half), an older term denoting people of combined Japanese and non-Japanese parentage. In this context half refers to being half Japanese and half something else. For this reason, Robertson mistakenly believes that the term new half somehow suggests foreignness. The terms half and new half have nothing to do with each other.

6 See Ogawa and (Shibamoto) Smith (1997) for a discussion of the varieties of gay men's speech.

# References

Brownmiller, S. (1975) *Against Our Will: Men, Woman and Rape*, New York: Simon and Schuster.
Butler, J. (1990) *Gender Trouble: Feminism and the Subversion of Identity*, London and New York: Routledge.
—— (1993) *Bodies That Matter: On the Discursive Limits of 'Sex'*, London and New York: Routledge.
Cornwall, A. (1994) 'Gendered identities and gender ambiguity among *travestis* in Salvador, Brazil', in A. Cornwall and N. Lindisfarne (eds) *Dislocating Masculinities: Comparative Ethnographies*, London and New York: Routledge.
Frühstück, S. (2000) 'Treating the body as a commodity: "body projects" in contemporary Japan', in M. Ashkenazi and J. Clammer (eds) *Consumption and Material Culture in Contemporary Japan*, London and New York: Kegan Paul International.
Fukayuki, S. (1996) untitled, in Kuia Sutadīzu Henshū Iinkai (ed.) *Kuia Sutadīzu '96 (Queer Studies 1996)*, Tokyo: Nanatsu Mori Shokan.
Fushimi, N. (1991) *Puraibēto Gei Raifu: Posuto Ren'airon (Private Gay Life: Post-Love Theory)*, Tokyo: Gakuyō Shobō.
—— (1996) *Kuia Paradaisu: 'Sei' no Meikyū e Yōkoso (Queer Paradise: Welcome to the Labyrinth of 'Sex, Gender, Sexuality')*, Tokyo: Shōheisha.
Halberstam, J. (1998) *Female Masculinity*, Durham, NC and London: Duke University Press.
Hashimoto, H. (1998) *Otoko demo Onna demo Nai Sei: Intāsekkusu (Han-in'yō) o Ikiru (A Sex That is Neither Male nor Female: Living Intersex [Hermaphrodism])*, Tokyo: Seiyūsha.
Ito, S. and Yanase, R. (2001) *Coming Out in Japan*, Melbourne: Trans Pacific Press.
Izumi, A. (1990) *B-kyū Nyūsu Zukan (Illustrated B-Class News)*, Tokyo: Shinchō Bunko.
Kulick, D. (1998) *Travesti: Sex, Gender and Culture among Brazilian Transgendered Prostitutes*, Chicago: University of Chicago Press.
Kuroyanagi, T. (1992) [1987] *Samayoeru Jendā: Seibetsu Fukai Shōkōgun no Esunogurafi (Wandering Gender: An Ethnography of the Syndrome of Not Knowing One's Sex)*, Tokyo: Gendai Shokan.
Lunsing, W. (1995) 'Japanese gay magazines and marriage advertisements', *Journal of Gay and Lesbian Social Services* 3, 3: 71–87 (published simultaneously in G. Sullivan and L. Wai-Teng Leong (eds) *Gays and Lesbians in Asia and the Pacific: Social and Human Services*, Haworth: The Haworth Press, Inc.; also New York and London: Harrington Park Press, imprint of The Haworth Press).
—— (1997) '"Gay boom" in Japan: changing views of homosexuality?', *Thamyris: Mythmaking from Past to Present*, 4, 2: 267–93.
—— (1998) 'Lesbian and gay movements: between hard and soft', in A. Osiander and C. Weber (eds) *Soziale Bewegungen in Japan (Social Movements in Japan)*, Hamburg: OAG Hamburg.
—— (1999) 'Japan: finding its way?', in B. Adam, J. W. Duyvendak and A. Krouwel (eds) *The Global Emergence of Gay and Lesbian Politics: National Imprints of a Worldwide Movement*, Philadelphia: Temple University Press.
—— (2001a) 'Between margin and centre: researching "non-standard" Japanese', *Copenhagen Journal of Asian Studies*, 15: 81–113.
—— (2001b) *Beyond Common Sense: Sexuality and Gender in Contemporary Japan*, London, New York and Bahrain: Kegan Paul.
—— (2001c) '*Kono sekai* (the Japanese gay scene): communities or just playing around?', in M. Raveri and J. Hendry (eds) *Japan at Play*, London and New York: Routledge.
MacInnes, J. (1998) *The End of Masculinity: The Confusion of Sexual Genesis and Sexual Difference in Modern Society*, Buckingham: Open University Press.

McLelland, M. J. (2000) *Male Homosexuality in Modern Japan: Cultural Myths and Social Realities*, Richmond, Surrey: Curzon Press.

Mako, S. (1996) '*Genzai Nihon de TG ga chokumen suru mondaiten*' (Problems confronting transgender in contemporary Japan), in Kuia Sutadīzu Henshū Iinkai (ed.) *Kuia Sutadīzu '96 (Queer Studies 1996)*, Tokyo: Nanatsu Mori Shokan.

Matsuo, H. (1997) *Toransujendarizumu: Seibetsu no Higan, Sei o Ekkyō Suru Hitobito (Transgenderism: The Other Side of Sex Difference, People Overcoming Sex)*, Tokyo: Seori Shobō.

Miwa, A. (1992) *Murasaki no Rirekisho (A Purple Curriculum Vita)*, Tokyo: Sui Shobō.

Nekome, Y. (1998) *Nyūhāfu to Iu Ikikata (The Lifestyle Called 'New Half')*, Tokyo: Hiraku.

Ogawa, N. and (Shibamoto) Smith, J. (1997) 'The gendering of the gay male sex class in Japan: a case study based on *Rasen no Sobyō*', in A. Livia and K. Hall (eds) *Queerly Phrased: Language, Gender and Sexuality*, Oxford and New York: Oxford University Press.

Pateman, C. (1988) *The Sexual Contract*, Cambridge: Polity Press.

Pflugfelder, G. (1999) *Cartographies of Desire: Male–Male Sexuality in Japanese Discourse 1600–1950*, Berkeley: University of California Press.

Raymond, J. (1995) 'The politics of transgenderism', in R. Enkins and D. King (eds) *Blending Genders: Social Aspects of Cross-Dressing and Sex-Changing*, London and New York: Routledge.

Rich, A. (1980) 'Compulsory heterosexuality and lesbian existence', *Signs*, 5, 4: 631–60.

Riddell, C. (1995) 'Divided sisterhood: a critical review of Janice Raymond's transsexual empire', in R. Enkins and D. King (eds) *Blending Genders: Social Aspects of Cross-Dressing and Sex-Changing*, London and New York: Routledge.

Robertson, J. (1998) *Takarazuka: Sexual Politics and Popular Culture in Modern Japan*, Berkeley: University of California Press.

Rubin, G. S. (1993) 'Thinking sex: notes for a radical theory of the politics of sexuality', in H. Abelove, M. A. Barale and D. M. Halperin (eds) *The Lesbian and Gay Studies Reader*, New York and London: Routledge.

Sedgwick, E. K. (1990) *Epistemology of the Closet*, Berkeley: University of California Press.

Serena, N. (1990) *Neither Man nor Woman: The Hijras of India*, Belmont: Wadsworth Publishing Company.

Torii, M. (1997) '*Saitama Ika Daigaku no tōshin igo*' (After the report of Saitama Medical University), in Kuia Sutadīzu Henshū Iinkai (ed.) *Kuia Sutadīzu '97 (Queer Studies 1997)*, Tokyo: Nanatsu Mori Shokan.

Tsutamori, T. (1990) *Otoko datte Kirei ni Naritai (Men Too Want to Become Beautiful)*, Tokyo: Popeye Books.

—— (1993) *Otoko demo Naku Onna demo Nai: Shinjidai no Andorojinasutachi e (Neither Man nor Woman: To the Androgynes of the New Era)*, Tokyo: Keisō Shobō.

Whitehead, H. (1981) 'The bow and the burden strap: a new look at institutionalized homosexuality in native North America', in S. B. Ortner and H. Whitehead (eds) *Sexual Meanings: The Cultural Construction of Sexuality and Gender*, Cambridge: Cambridge University Press.

### Magazines

*Bādi, Himawari, Josei Sebun, Queen, Views*

# 3    Male beauty work in Japan

*Laura Miller*

In 1992 the young women's magazine *With* featured an interview with actor Akai Hidekazu, who had just starred as Miyazawa Rie's love interest in the hit TV series *Tokyo Elevator Girls* (*With* 1992). Akai, a former professional boxer from Osaka dubbed the 'Rocky of Naniwa', epitomized in physical form a version of standard male attractiveness. His large, blokeish, somewhat doughy ambience suggested desirable male traits such as strength, dependability, resolve and commitment.

More recently, Miyazawa's sultry co-star in another hit TV series *Concerto* was of an entirely different sort. Kimura Takuya exudes a frank sexuality that does not so easily endorse an uncomplicated portrayal of traditional masculinity. Yet Kimura, or Kimutaku as he is affectionately called, is invariably ranked as one of the most popular male stars by both men and women (*Mainichi Shinbun* 1995). For instance, the young men's magazine *Fine Boys* ranked him number one in a survey of 'Favourite male celebrities', or *tarento* (*Fine Boys* 1998). Similarly, since 1995, female readers of *An An* magazine have consistently voted Kimutaku the celebrity they like most, describing him as both 'sexy' and 'manly' (*An An* 1999, 2000). Each year Kimutaku heads their annual list of 'Guys we want to have sex with'.

The ascendance of male stars such as Kimutaku reflects a shift in Japanese canons of taste for young heterosexual men. While previous generations were evaluated primarily on the basis of character, social standing, earning capacity, lineage and other social criteria (Applbaum 1995; *PHP Intersect* 1987), young men these days are increasingly concerned with their status as objects of aesthetic and sexual appraisal. The recent emphasis on externalization of personal or social identity has given birth to new businesses which sell beauty products and services to those wanting to change or upgrade their appearance.

In this chapter I want to outline some of the new services and products now sold to men in their pursuit of beauty. These efforts at body and beauty transformation suggest that the ideological sphere of reference of masculinity has widened to include a greater diversity of physical styles, with beautification as another component of masculinity. This chapter is not intended as a critique of the capitalist industries engaged in promoting and selling gendered beauty norms.[1] Rather, the main questions I want to pursue are: What new practices have become part of men's beauty work? What parts of the body have become the objects of beautification? What is driving these efforts at surface change?

Historically, attention to male beauty in Japan is not unusual, so I am interested in understanding how current efforts at body improvement relate to aspects of contemporary social life. I believe that men's beauty consumption is linked to two intertwined forces: it is informed by female desire, while it concurrently symbolizes resistance to the 'salaryman' folk model (L. Miller 1995, 1998c). The model of masculinity being opposed is age-graded, and is associated with an older generation of *oyaji* ('old men') de-eroticized by a corporate culture that emphasized a 'productivity ideology of standardization, order, control, rationality and impersonality' (McVeigh 2000: 16). *Oyaji*-rejection also surfaces in women's popular media, where we find expressions of derision and dismissal for old-style salaryman types (L. Miller 1998b). An emphasis on male appearance counters the salaryman reification of men as workers, while women appreciate these new styles because they are aesthetically pleasing and erotically charged.

New forms of male beauty work go hand in hand with fashion trends and are integrated into a visually structured look. Morgan, noting a similar process in the US, states that the new focus on men's fashion and lifestyle magazines 'certainly points to the elaboration of consumption-led masculinities. The healthy body, the stylish body and the athletic body become part of a range of bodies that are available in commodified form' (1993: 87). Among Japan's current fashion styles for young men are Mode, School, Punk, American Casual, French Casual, Military and Outdoor. In each, some type of external alchemy is a necessary component of the selected style. Looks such as B-Boy, Surfer/Skateboarder or Dread may, for example, require skin darkening processes, tattooing or body piercing in addition to hair modification.

Magazines specializing in the new retro sensibilities and surface identities include *Bidan*, *Men's Non No* and *Fine Boys*, all of which offer a mix of fashion advice, facial care, hairstyling tips, interviews, music, horoscopes and surveys of trends. Also available are special publications, such as *Men's Body Manual*, which promises to provide 'face and body grade-up' for men (Gakken 2000). These publications provide an endless visual pedagogy (L. Miller 1998a) of the new male beauty work. Frequently, readers are taught about new beauty ideals through a format that provides meticulous visual representation of the beauty process, including before and after photographs of the aesthetically upgraded man.

## Beauty services for men: the men's *estute* salon

During the 1980s a new beauty industry developed separately from traditional beauty salons that mainly provide hair styling. These new businesses, called *esute* ('aesthetic') salons, provide body transformation services such as facials, body treatments and hair removal sessions. Although initially targeting women, some *esute* salons began offering beauty treatments for men as well. One of the earliest was Men's Joli Canaille Salon in Tokyo, which began doing so in April 1984. By 1989, *esute* salons solely for male customers were an established part of the urban landscape (*Nihon Keizai Shinbun* 1989a). Male-only salons now include establishments such as Prince, Ichirō, Dandy House and Tokyo Hands. Many of these became so successful that they were able to open franchises. Dandy House has more than eight salons in the Tokyo area and fifteen elsewhere in the country, and Men's Esute Raparare has more than forty shops throughout the country.

Men's *esute* salons typically offer services that address skin problems, body hair and body weight or shape. Some salons now also sell specialized packages such as 'men's bridal *esute*', a bundle of prenuptial treatments to prepare the groom for his big day (*Asahi Shinbun* 1999a), and in 1999 Men's TBC (an offshoot of the women's salon chain Tokyo Beauty Center) sold the 'Millennium party *esute*', a facial and massage to prepare men for the big New Year's event. Advertising for the men's *esute* salons frequently makes reference to the effects the beauty work, or a lack of it, might have on women. For example, in an advertisement for Tokyo Aesthetic Salon (see Figure 3.1), under a caption warning 'So that this doesn't happen to you', we see a drawing of a man crying as a woman walks off with a *binan* ('beautiful man'), saying 'Bye bye'.

In 1999, I visited several men's *esute* salons in the Tokyo area where I spoke to receptionists and managers, obtained informational brochures and observed what types of men were going there to get beauty work. It is clear that, similar to women's

*Figure 3.1* Get beautiful and get the girl.

*esute* salons, there are different micro-markets targetted by the salon proprietors. Some go after a young cohort of high-school or college-age men, while others are targeting older professional males. Some salons appeal to a largely gay clientele, while others are holding out the promise of complete transformation to decidedly frumpy men.

Since Kimutaku is the spokesman for Men's TBC, I went to the TBC branch in Shibuya. The salon reception area was furnished in ultra-modern chrome and glass. There was a poster of Kimutaku on the wall and speakers piped in music from Glay and other crucial J-Pop. This stripped-down practicality contrasts with the baroque ornateness customary in women's salons. Although the receptionists are always male, all the aestheticians are female. I was told that the typical customer is between twenty and thirty, although some younger men also go there. Some of the slogans Men's TBC was using were 'Men's new power' and 'Support for all the world's male beauty' (my translations). Men's salons operate very much like women's salons in their hard-sell procedures. When I accompanied my friend Masa to Dandy House for a pre-treatment counselling session, he underwent intense grilling and pressure to sign up for expensive treatments.

For those timid about exploring men's *esute* salons, or unable to afford the high costs, men's magazines regularly feature articles or advertisements that illustrate what one might expect when visiting. In an editorial advertisement found in *Bidan* (July 1997, p. 153), a certain 'Takahashi-kun'[2] leads us through each of the steps involved in getting a facial, including counselling, individual skin analysis, facial technology that uses a suction cup device to extract oils and blackheads, a peeling treatment, massage, application of a green seaweed pack followed by another white face pack and then a final massage.

As the salon business grew in popularity, so did related or spin-off services, such as *esute* tours or *esute* included as part of the travel experience. For example, men may now go on a one-day tour by sightseeing bus to various *esute* salons and beauty parlours. On one Tokyo-based tour, they get a hair cut, facial, make-up application, manicure and, at the end of the day, a formal portrait by a professional photographer (*Asahi Shinbun* 1999b). Overseas salons that have been providing beauty services to travelling Japanese women now offer facials and other treatments to men. *Esute* treatments have also been incorporated into travel entertainment packages to places such as Korea or Thailand, popular sex-tour destinations.

When I asked salon employees at several different locations about the leading treatments sought out by men, I was told that hair removal is certainly one of the most popular services. For example, at Men's TBC the number one service is body hair removal, followed by facials and tanning sessions, while at Men's Joli Canaille Salon body hair removal together with weight loss tops the list. For those who are too shy or too poor to go to an *esute* salon for a treatment, home-use products may be purchased to help achieve bodies that are hairless and smooth.

## Smooth, civilized bodies

For many centuries Japanese have held hairy bodies in some disfavour. In earlier times hairiness was exemplary of the uncivilized barbarian, as illustrated by the pejorative label for a white person, *ketō*, literally 'hairy Chinese'. In both China (Dikötter 1998) and Japan, excessive body hair came symbolically to represent ethnic or racial boundaries. The hairy body might represent the outside foreigner, or else the domestic 'other', such as Ainu or Okinawans.

Critics note that attitudes toward male body hair have undergone dramatic changes since the postwar period (Across 1989). From the 1950s until the 1970s, a new masculine ideal was promoted through bewhiskered or bushy Western movie stars such as Sean Connery and Charles Bronson. But a male desire to depilate began in the late 1980s, and chest hair ceased being a symbol of masculinity (*Nihon Keizai Shinbun* 1989b). Although recently beards have become fashionable among some young men, hairy chests are now decidedly *démodé*. Some men want to rid their bodies not only of chest hair, but of leg, armpit and arm hair as well.

Various reasons have been offered to explain this reversion to an old partiality, but preference for non-hairy men among women must be considered a primary force. A positive descriptor commonly used by women to catalogue the desirable man is *subesube* ('smooth'), and not surprisingly, this is a term that routinely appears in advertising for male beauty products. Male fear of negative female evaluation of their hairiness is frequently exploited by the *esute* salons. In an advertisement for a hair removal product named 10 Sex Functional Remover, there is a photograph of three young women expressing various forms of disgust at hairiness, such as crossing their arms in the 'no good' pose, or with speech bubbles saying things like 'It doesn't matter how cool he is, if he has a full-on hairy body, I'll pass'. In smaller, accompanying comic drawings, women looking at two hairy men say 'What's with that hair?' (see Figure 3.2) or, when they see two smooth guys, they unanimously say 'Cool'.

*Figure 3.2* 'What's with that hair?'

Young women queried about what they find obnoxious about the male body ranked chest and other forms of body hair the most offensive (*Rankingu Daisuki* 1999). The other detestable attributes, in descending order, were:

| | | | |
|---|---|---|---|
| 1 | chest hair | 6 | long hair (on the head) |
| 2 | body hair | 7 | skinny body |
| 3 | leg hair | 8 | body odours |
| 4 | beards | 9 | no muscles |
| 5 | fat body | 10 | small penises |

A drawing accompanying the poll shows a woman repulsed by the sight of a hairy man, saying 'Chest hair is gross!' (see Figure 3.3). It is noteworthy that the masculine traits so often focused on in the American (male) imagination, mainly muscles and penis size, do not receive the same attention on this list as does body hair. As a 20-year-old female aesthetician said, 'I hate men with thick leg hair. If I even see chest hair, I feel revolted' (*Akita Sakigawa Shinbun* 1996).

An article investigating the new trend interviewed men in Tokyo about why they rid their bodies of hair (Across 1989: 58). An 18-year-old man said he noticed that friends were using depilatories because 'Girls hate things like thick beards and body hair, and chest hair especially is loathsome. I myself haven't had chest hair for some time'. Another 22-year-old says he noticed he had thick body hair during his high-school days, and was so embarrassed he wouldn't wear shorts. He claims that since he hates thick beards himself, it is only natural that he likes women who also dislike body hair.

Electrolysis, the extraction of hair follicles with a needlenose electrode, is a staple offering of *esute* salons and medical clinics, but there are also less drastic and cheaper methods of hair removal that can be tried at home. Separate product lines of depilatory cremes and lotions, wax treatments, hair removal tapes, gels and various

*Figure 3.3* 'Chest hair is gross!'

shaving or extraction devices are actively targetted at men who desire smooth bodies. A variety of devices for use at home are widely sold as high technology that is almost as good as electrolysis. These usually have names that sound densely technological and masculine to distinguish them from identical female products. For instance, the Elimina 6X and the ProCare II are both dressed up shaver-tweezers which are connected to electric or battery-powered units.

Most of these products are careful to indicate that the target audience encompasses the heterosexual male by attaching admiring female commentary or endorsements. For example, a hair removal product named Valoir includes the words 'to get the skin girls love' in its advertisements. Another product named Verge also uses anxiety about female evaluation in its advertising. In one case, a photograph of a couple is shown with the woman gazing at her boyfriend, saying '*Tsurutsuru* ('smooth') feels good!' Occasionally banners with the text 'Women really do like *subesube*' ('smooth') run across the page.

The new focus on the slim and smooth male body means that entertainers take every opportunity to flash their bare, oiled torsos in concerts, TV dramas and advertising. Men in everyday contexts likewise display the smooth chest to onlookers. The popularity of male denuding has attracted its share of criticism, however, primarily from middle-aged men. One newspaper article that frets over the fact that some young baseball players are doing things like depilation, body piercing, nail manicures and hair removal is accompanied by a cartoon showing two men engaged in beauty work (see Figure 3.4). One is shaving his eyebrows while the other is trimming under his arm. A distressed observer watching them says 'Enough, leave the underarm!' (*Asahi Shinbun* 1998a).

There is also some resistance among young men to body hair removal. Interestingly, university students I interviewed who claimed not to like it used a sexist

*Figure 3.4* Making fun of male beauty work.

rather than homophobic logic to justify their position. They did not feel that it is wrong because it renders the male body more feminine and thereby suspect, but because it signals that the hairless man has no pride and has given in to the demands of women and their desires. Their denigrating term for men who remove body hair is *Tsurutsuru-kun*, 'Mr Smooth'.[3] *Tsurutsuru-kun*, they told me, are only interested in getting girls by whatever means necessary.

Despite the fact that an old Japanese proverb exists that says something like 'a hairy person is a sexy person' (*kebukai mono wa irobukai*), the majority of young Japanese women these days just do not like hairy men. Although *esute* marketing must have played some small role in establishing this preference, it is also the case that distaste for hairiness is another form of '*oyaji*-rejection'. Other scholars have noted that an aesthetic preference for hairlessness accompanies a penchant for youth and downy innocence (Dutton 1995). For many young Japanese women, patriarchal values, or at the very least a dowdy conservatism, go hand in hand with the cloned salaryman body style. A rejection of this aesthetic, therefore, and an appreciation of the ephebe style can be viewed as a rejection of male dominance and an assertion of an independent sexuality. The connection between sexual desire and men's beauty work will be returned to later.

## Cosmetic beauty work

Cosmetic products targeting men have long had great success in Japan. This may be related to the fact that from the beginning, the product category roughly equivalent to 'cosmetics' (*keshōhin*) was never strictly gendered as it is in the US (Fields 1985: 91). It is a category which has always included body products for both men and women, as can be seen in advertisements from the Meiji era (1868–1912) for products such as Bigan Sui (see Figure 3.5), a 'face water' for clearing up and beautifying the skin (Machida 1997).

*Figure 3.5* Meiji era unisex cosmetics.

These days the bulk of a young man's beauty work is devoted to his head hair. For this important task, according to one recent poll, the majority of young men (76 per cent) prefer to use the services of a specialized hair salon rather than an old-fashioned barber (*Fine Boys* 1998: 186). Hair dyes and various hair growth products have long been available for older men worried about grey hair and hair loss. Men have also long bought a variety of pomades, waxy hairdressings and liquids such as Vitalis Hair liquid.

Beginning in the mid-1990s, a fad for brown hair, or *chapatsu*, took hold of both men and women. The *chapatsu* look ranges from nutty brown to mahogany or chocolate tones and is popular in all parts of Japan, not just the urban centres. Hair may also be treated with streaks of various colours or dyed blond or orange. At the Salon de Kosson in Tokyo, men may have their hair dyed one or more of thirty-six different colours. For that fluffy, thatchy look there are numerous new product lines of hair dyes and bleaches for young men, and magazines routinely carry visual guidance on how to bleach and style one's own hair at home. In many cases instruction is given for how to style the hair after celebrities such as Kimutaku (see Figure 3.6).

Lines of men's cosmetics have been sold in Japan for almost two decades. In 1984 Isetan department store opened a make-up corner for men, and in 1986 Gear introduced a male line of face packs, eye liner and foundation products. Currently, the Mandom company produces twelve separate cosmetic products under the Mandom name, but most are hair tonics and after-shave lotions targetted at older men. Advertising for the *oyaji* crowd emphasizes masking of grey hair and conceal-ment of bald spots so that men look young as part of their work identity. For the younger market Mandom created the Gatsby line of more than twenty products, including facial scrubs, facial paper, nose pack, facial creme, facial astringent, deodorant, two types of hair bleach and various hairstyling foams, gels and sprays.

*Figure 3.6* How to get Kimutaku hair.

The Gerald line of male cosmetics, from Shiseido, sold more than one million dollars worth of products in one year (Ono 1999). The hottest items right now in young men's cosmetics are oil blotting papers and nose packs (*Asahi Shinbun* 1997b).

For men concerned about how to apply these new cosmetic products, classes and training programmes are available. For example, in September 1999 the Asahi Culture Center in Tokyo offered a two-hour 'Men's make-up' workshop. Flyers for the workshop included before and after photographs of a newly beautified man, and announced that men should 'Take advantage of the era when even men can be glamorous'. In a clear move to address the reason for the beauty work, the flyer specified that wives and girlfriends should accompany the men in order to observe their beauty transformation.

## The elegant crescent

Perhaps more than any other cosmetic procedure, the contemporary manipulation of the eyebrow challenges the 'naturalness' of gender stereotypes. Male cosmetic treatment of the eyebrows has a long history in Japan, dating to at least the Heian era (AD 794–1185; see Tsuda 1985). Eyebrow plucking and shaping is just one of numerous beauty activities many contemporary women do in order to create female-gendered looks (L. Miller 2000). When men engage in such craftsmanship, the degree to which women's faces are the product of beauty work and cosmetics is exposed, or at least it is brought to another level of conscious awareness.

The current preference among young men is for thin rather than thick eyebrows. In a poll of male readers, 70.9 per cent of the respondents said they think men look better with thin eyebrows (*Bidan* 1997a). Men emulate celebrities who sport plucked eyebrows, including Funaki Kazuyoshi, the Japanese gold-medal winner in the ski jump, who engendered a widespread desire for the *Funaki-mayu* ('Funaki eyebrow') look. The press has often linked this fad to the beauty of idols like Kimutaku and pop music star Ishida Issei, whom the *Yomiuri Shinbun* (1997) cites as good eyebrow men. Of course, really bushy eyebrows were always frowned upon, as indicated by the insult *gejigeji mayuge* ('centipede eyebrows') used towards both men and women.

Advice on how to create and manage a nice eyebrow shape is found in many men's magazines (see Figure 3.7). One such article claims that it 'seems like 100 per cent of the cool guys on the street are shaping their eyebrows' (*Bidan* 1997a). Before and after photographs instruct readers in the improvements to one's looks this beauty work brings about, and advice is tailored to various eyebrow types. To ensure that eyebrow work is seen as an acceptable heterosexual activity, articles and advice pieces insert quotes from admiring girlfriends or testimonies from the guy on the street who reports that his girlfriend approves or that, in fact, it was a girlfriend who first taught him how to do it. One fellow even positions this beauty work as a form of courtship when he says 'Doing eyebrows together with a girlfriend is my dream'.

Special tools for eyebrow construction are also available. The Gerald For Men Eyebrow Design Kit, launched in November 1996, includes eyebrow brush, tweezers, scissors and eyebrow pencil. One may also buy eyebrow templates, clear

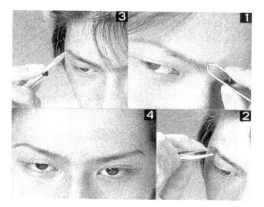

*Figure 3.7* Eyebrow beauty work.

plastic guides with exact measurements imprinted on them. Men may do their eyebrows at home or go to a hair salon for eyebrow shaping.

Just as male body hair removal has its detractors, so too eyebrow plucking is viewed by some critics as unmanly, debauched behaviour. In the controversial yet bestselling comic castigating postwar moral decadence, Kobayashi (1998: 8) depicts young men plucking their eyebrows as an example of the vile self-indulgence that accompanies democracy. The macho, war-glorifying principles espoused by older men like Kobayashi, however, are some of the values most despised by younger generations.

## Dabbling in beauty

Young men are actively experimenting with many types of cosmetic and beauty products, but often feel a bit inept or inexperienced. One way to reassure consumers that it's normal, everyday practice to use cosmetics is through features that highlight what some men carry around with them to maintain their appearance. In one piece, readers get to examine the contents of the small cosmetic bags carried around by a group of young men (*Bidan* 1997b). One 18-year-old student's pouch, for example, contains a mirror, hair brush, a vial of perfume he got from his current girlfriend, an eyebrow comb and pencil left over from an ex-girlfriend, nose-hair scissors, lip creme and a hair band for when his teacher makes him pull back his long hair.

Ear piercing, body piercing and tattoos have become more common among straight men after decades of being seen as having strictly underworld or gay connotations. But, style advice for the heterosexual man warns that if one does get piercing, cute or sweet earrings ought to be worn to soften the potentially 'hard' look. Ear and body piercing is available at some beauty salons and at cosmetic surgery clinics. Both procedures are relatively inexpensive. The Shibuya Sarah Beauty and Health Salon offers piercing services to men for as little as US$4.00 for the ears, and starting around US$40.00 for piercing any other place on the body.

Of course, it is difficult to determine the actual percentage of men who buy or use cosmetic products, since not everyone is confident about their excursions into this domain or the degree to which their beauty secrets should become public knowledge. Surveys suggest that men are relatively open about hair colouring and bleach, which is hard to play down, but less so about other procedures. A poll of men between the ages of 20 and 24 by the magazine *Nikkei Trendy* (see Figure 3.8) found that 65 per cent of the respondents had used hair colouring products, 38.2 per cent admitted to shaping their eyebrows and 17.2 per cent had received some type of hair removal treatment (*Nikkei Trendy* 1997).

A different survey of a younger cohort in *Fine Boys* (see Figure 3.9) gave similar results, but included other body treatments such as tattoos, make-up use and body piercing (*Fine Boys* 1998: 187).

Both surveys make it clear that many young men are experimenting with a spectrum of new types of beauty work. In an interview, a 20-year-old university student says he uses a woman's electric eyebrow shaver and uses a facial pack once a week. He says 'Even when I turn 50, I'll continue to do it'. A 15-year-old uses oil-blotting paper and foundation, and when he gets enough money, wants to try a salon (*Asahi Shinbun* 1999c).

While older men may be reluctant to try out make-up and eyebrow plucking, many are still interested in improving their appearance with the assistance of salon facial treatments or tanning sessions. Among the *oyaji* set, a good tan is considered a masculine attribute, denoting youth and robustness and suggesting dedication to work-related activities such as corporate-sponsored golf (*Asahi Shinbun* 1998b; *Nihon Keizai Shinbun* 1999). A father and son getting their tanning treatments together may

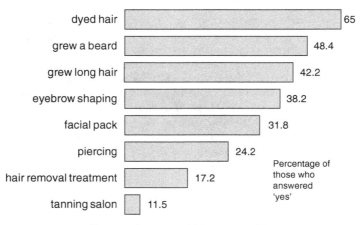

**Which of these have you done?**

*Nikkei Trendy* survey, February 1997

Survey of men aged 20–4 years old

*Figure 3.8 Nikkei Trendy* magazine poll of male beauty work.

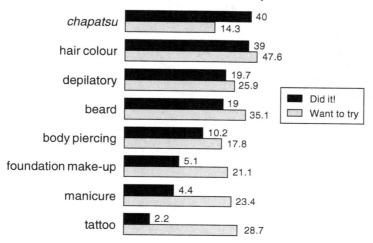

**Esute** I did, *esute* I want to try
*Fine Boys* survey, February 1998
Percentage who answered 'yes'

chapatsu — 40 / 14.3
hair colour — 39 / 47.6
depilatory — 19.7 / 25.9
beard — 19 / 35.1
body piercing — 10.2 / 17.8
foundation make-up — 5.1 / 21.1
manicure — 4.4 / 23.4
tattoo — 2.2 / 28.7

Did it! / Want to try

*Figure 3.9 Fine Boys* magazine poll of male beauty work.

therefore be doing so for very different reasons – the young man to look good for women, the *oyaji* to look good for his clients and company.

Male engagement with many of these forms of beauty work not only challenges conventional gender constructions, it also contends with traditional notions about the malleability of the self. Earnest efforts to accommodate to the new aesthetic are also seen in the development of other services, both surgical and less permanent, for modifying the body.

## Surgical and non-medical body modification

It is often said that Japanese women hate three things: the short, the bald and the chubby. Advertisements for weight loss and hair growth products rely on this anxiety by including reference to women's opinions or by including surveys of female tastes. For example, an advertisement for a product named Men's Super Speed Diet HCA 780 includes a survey asking two hundred women 'What type of man do you hate?' The majority, 89 per cent, gave 'chubby' as their pet peeve.

The average height for a man of 20 in 1995 was 171.1 centimetres, or around 5 feet 6 inches (*Asahi Shinbun* 1997a: 226). But these days young men do not want to look average, they want to look like the models and stars they see on TV and in magazines. According to Hashimoto (1994: 320), the typical Japanese male celebrity or model is around 6 feet tall, as is Sorimachi Takashi, who is often featured on lists of favourite *tarento*. For those who view tall celebrities as their aspirational yardsticks, a quest for methods to increase height has led to a variety of dubious products being huckstered through every media form. The Kyōrin Medical Company sells something called the Gulliver #3, which employs pulleys and a traction extension machine they claim will straighten the legs and lengthen the body. Models exclaim that sports ability will improve and that 'with this I'll be a regular guy and get a girlfriend'.

Increasingly, surgery is also called on to beautify the body. According to the director of a hospital in Tokyo, 'Especially for young Tokyoites, it is merely an extension of having your nails done or your ears pierced. It is a more active form of an *esute* salon' (Itoh 1996). Another cosmetic surgery clinic in Tokyo has noticed a gradual rise in the number of its male clients, so that now they comprise around 30 per cent of the total (Stuhlman 1999). For men, the face is the most frequent site for 'fashion surgery' (Balsamo 1996: 62), particularly operations that build up a flat nose, sculpt the nasal tip, enhance the chin line or change the eyelid. Eyelid surgery, which in the US is primarily intended to counteract the process of ageing, is enlisted foremost to address eye shape in Japan. Temporary folds to the eyelids may also be obtained with the help of over-the-counter eye glues and tapes. These are often sold in gender-neutral packaging and are advertized in both women's and men's magazines.

There are numerous cosmetic surgery clinics devoted exclusively to men which provide specialized procedures in addition to facial surgery. One can get aroma-therapy for male 'power up' or impotence, as well as various types of genital surgery, such as penile implants, silicone injections, bead insertions or cosmetic circumcision, also offered as techniques to upgrade a man's appearance and performance.[5] While most Japanese men are not usually circumcised at birth (Williams and Kapila 1993), many young men are now having the foreskin surgically removed at male-only clinics ('Circumcision in Japan becoming popular' 2000). A desire to be more appealing to women, who say that the circumcised penis is 'cleaner' and 'looks better', is often concealed in rhetoric about health concerns. In advertising for the Shinjuku Clinic, for instance, the claim is made that an uncircumcised penis is 'not popular' with women, who feel it is *fuketsu* ('impure'). New worries may stem from the role of international pornography, in which the circumcised American penis is available for emulation, as well as mass media commentary from young women who openly discuss penile qualities (*Seventeen* 2001; *Egg* 2000). For instance, an uncircumcised penis is often derogatively referred to as *menashibō* ('eyeless stick') or *suppon* ('mud turtle').

## Interpreting change

Why has there been a change from decades in which men who wore anything but dark blue suits were suspect, to an era in which eyebrow plucking and hair colouring is *de rigueur*? In trying to understand the male quest for surface beauty, one researcher suggests that use of cosmetics by men is the outcome of 'copying every-one' (Ono 1999: B1). Although there may be a degree of peer pressure involved, this does not explain why such fads began in the first place, nor why it is the body itself which is the object of change. Other explanations are that a change to a new model of masculinity, in which mass media images of hairless men are prevalent, is linked to the sports craze, especially cycling and skateboarding (Across 1989: 47).

Various political, economic and social perspectives have also been used to interpret changes in the modern representation of gender and masculinity. According to some, it is the advancement of consumer capitalism which promotes changes in the beauty and fashion industries (McCracken 1988; Simmel 1973; Turner 1980). So, for upward-hustling Japanese men, having the right look – the right hair, face, skin and clothes – means that one has both the sensibilities to recognize this new aesthetic and also the time and resources to achieve the socially desired body for compulsory heterosexual marriage. Their bodies are now 'projects' (Featherstone 1991; Frühstück 2000; Shilling 1993) that fuel an economy of beauty goods and services.

Edwards (1997) sees the expansion of interest in men's fashion as linked to developments in marketing and advertising, and to the nature of modern consumption. He says:

> It has become more socially acceptable for men to be consumers *per se* and, more importantly, to be consumers of their own masculinity, or in short, to look at themselves and other men as objects of desire to be bought and sold or imitated and copied.
>
> (ibid.: 73)

Masculine identity, once defined through work, now hinges on consumption, a sort of 'commodified selfhood' (Langman 1992: 734). Androgynous writer Tsutamori (1990) suggests that rather than accommodating the female or male 'gaze', male beauty work enables one to 'redeem the body for oneself' while social critic Seki claims that the new beauty work is an outcome of 'aesthetic communication' in which men have acquired female sensibilities and bodily sensuality as an aspect of self-expression (*Mainichi Shinbun* 1996; Seki 1996).

Japan is a major co-participant in a global consumer-oriented ethos diffused through transnational corporations, advertizing agencies and media. Many critics and scholars interpret the rise of new body aesthetics as emanating from an imported racist beauty ideology that denigrates Asian physical appearance. For example, Kaw (1993) vehemently disparages cosmetic surgery among Asian American women as the result of a colonialist and racist discourse. Deceased film director Itami Jūzō also insisted that young Japanese who change their bodies are earnestly trying to 'become American'.[4] However, if looking Euro-American includes having a hairy body, I doubt that very many young Japanese men would be interested. This is an aesthetic that pulls in ideas from outside Japan for inspiration but also draws on local concepts and proclivities, and is not merely 'failed Western' or 'faux-American'. Japanese use of body styles that include things like preference for large eye shape and new and diverse hair colours should not automatically lead us to claim that they are simply emulating non-Japanese. Wouldn't that be confounding the rejection of older Japanese models of male identity, particularly the salaryman, with a rejection of ethnicity?

This new male concern with beauty work may also be linked to socio-political issues. Hebdige (1979: 28) saw the significance of 1970s British youth styles as political phenomena that disrupted the dominant culture. This way of thinking accounts, somewhat, for the new body aesthetics for men in Japan. It is a style that 'offends the majority, challenges the principle of unity and cohesion and contradicts the myth of consensus' (ibid.: 18). The rejection of imposed and proscribed norms, of the world of schools and corporations, and especially of images of short, stocky, dark-suited *oyaji* with pomade-plastered hair, is notable in the new fashions and beauty culture among younger Japanese men.

This is perhaps most clearly seen in the appeal of 'hip hop' subculture (Condry 2000) and the fashion rebellions of early groups such as *bōsōzoku* ('hot rodders'; Sato 1991). The wearing of uniforms in schools, and suits in the business world, diverts attention away from individual, particular bodies. Young men who give detailed attention to their surface ornamentation are refusing the bland imprint of corporate sameness and rejecting this suppression of individuality. Their visible grooming activity creatively opposes the rigid male salaryman icon, or at the least provides a 'refuge' from the suffocation of the salaryman ideal. Ironically, though, their fashion insurgency ultimately supports the status quo by accommodating female desire, leading to participation in a state-endorsed ideology of heterosexual bonding and reproduction.

According to some observers, the new focus on androgynously erotic men reflects what Seki (1996: 36) and Lunsing (1997) term Japan's 'gay boom', in which gay sensibilities and tastes have informed wider social trends and aesthetics. Although a gay boom may well be under way, and a female receptiveness to gay men as characterized in popular culture reflects changes in attitudes and feelings towards traditional masculinity, gay culture is probably not the inspiration for female preferences in male appearance. As pointed out by McLelland (1999), the over-the-top masculinity of the male body as presented in gay media is not at all the same as the beautiful young men espoused in girls' comics, but is instead a hypermasculine embodiment of the very traits women are rejecting (particularly aggressiveness). The taut men pictured in gay magazines such as *Barazoku* are quite different from Kimutaku and other stars who make it onto *An An*'s annual lists of 'men I want to have sex with'. The idea of 'gay' best friends for women, and the new beauty norms for straight men, both stem from a similar rejection of a narrow and traditional capitalist-dictated masculinity.

New male beauty work indicates a deconstruction or breakdown in rigid 1970s gender categories and images, and in doing so it disturbs many critics (Imamura 2000). Rather than see the new emphasis on male beauty as contributing to a reconstruction of masculinity, critics often view it as straightforward 'feminization' of men. This is based on the assumption that 'beauty' is *de facto* 'feminine', and supports an extremely polarized view of gender.[5] When based on a blunt contrast with grey salarymen drabness, men like Hyde, lead vocalist for the group L'Arc-en-Ciel, and Kimutaku might indeed seem 'feminine'. But viewed from the perspective of women's desires, these men retain their masculinity which is concurrently presented with a surface beauty. When a woman says of an androgynous J-Pop icon that 'He's not vulgar, and seems like he'd be calm and steady in bed', she is hardly describing someone overly effeminate (*An An* 1997).

Numerous feminist scholars have claimed that when women do beauty work, they are making themselves the 'object and prey' (de Beauvoir 1968: 642) of men or of an imagined male connoisseur. Does this in turn mean that when the male body is the candidate for assessment, it legitimizes women as the observers of male bodies? A few intellectuals would say no. Gay and lesbian scholars, for example, have pointed out that homoerotic imagery can exist in a homophobic culture since representations of male bonding and the reification of the male body are necessary components of patriarchy (Fuss 1995; Sedgwick 1991). Consequently, an increase in the so-called 'feminizing' of male behaviour or appearance could be viewed as a means of reinforcing patriarchal masculinities (Horrocks 1995: 11). According to Chapman (1988), male narcissism and fashion interest amounts to a confiscating of femininity, in which men adopt only the behaviours without suffering the consequences. Social critic Ueno (1997: 21) created the term 'transvestite patriarchy' to describe just this process in the 'feminization' of Japanese men.

From this perspective, it appears that women have become doubly marginalized and that the rise of male beauty aesthetics has done little to change existing power relations between men and women. One wonders, then, if the creation of beautiful men is truly for appreciation by a female audience, or if it is simply providing a safe space where men, both gay and straight, may view and admire each other. Fuss (1995) noted that for female fashion photography to 'work', the female consumer, be she heterosexual or lesbian, must look at and appreciate eroticized images of the female body. Is it possible that the new body aesthetics for men is merely a similar principle in operation and is completely unrelated to women's desires or social roles?

Even acknowledging this last point, it is still the case that Japan's heterosexual marketplace is suffering some serious problems these days. During the first decades of the postwar era, the man of 'pure action and sincerity' (Plath 1980) was attractive to women because of his dedication to family, community and emperor. Whereas previously men were not expected to be beautiful as long as they offered economic stability and social capital (also see Yano, this volume, Chapter 5), women now employ a more critical eye, one which includes aesthetic criteria, when they evaluate potential lovers and spouses.

Among the many theories which have been proposed to explain the new beauty fads for Japanese men, few of them acknowledge the role which female desire might be playing in male anxiety about appearance. One of the most overlooked aspects of the *esute* fad among Japanese men is its erotic meaning. The beauty work of heterosexual men is, after all, intended at least partly to stimulate interest in women.[6] Perhaps this point is overlooked due to widespread acceptance of the idea that all visual codes serve to position women as the objects of a viewing 'male gaze' (Mulvey 1975; Pollock 1988). Yet, according to M. Miller (1998: 432), in Japanese visual media the position of the viewing subject is not exclusively male, and 'the female gaze is recognized and incorporated'. In pre-Meiji prints, for example, men are often depicted as objects for the female viewer, particularly in erotic prints or *shunga*. Increasingly, other scholars are questioning the complete dominance of the so-called 'male gaze' (Chow 1995).

Female expressions of desire for the beautiful male body are commonly found in a variety of popular Japanese media. For example, a women's magazine asked readers to talk about the latest crop of beautiful male idols and what they find most appealing about them (*An An* 1997). A few women used the term 'boyishness' as one of the qualities they find attractive. But these lads also inspire more carnal impulses. The following assessments from the *An An* poll, which I have also heard echoed in conversations, suggest something other than a maternal urge to 'indulge' (*amayakasu/ amaeru*) the 'boys'. A 30-year-old housewife, commenting on one of the young idols, said 'He's manly yet there's still some boyishness remaining. If you have sex with him, he'd have good energy'. Speaking about Takenouchi Yutaka, who has a slightly dangerous image, one 19-year-old says 'Although he's slim, he's got muscles, so he has a body you want to have sex with'. About Kimutaku, with his air of impudent carnality, women say things like 'I want to spend a passionate week with him at some villa in the mountains'; 'He seems like a guy who would use various techniques to give you pleasure', and 'I want to press my face into his chest!' In addition to the social resistance to the *oyaji* salaryman model of masculinity noted above, then, sexual selection should be seen as an important reason for the new male beauty work industry.

In a recent book, Jolivet (1997) discusses the contemporary problems related to women's refusal to enter marriage and motherhood. The number of unmarried women and men doubled in two decades (Shōgakkan 1999: 277). In a 1999 Prime Minister's Office survey, conducted to explain the decline in marriage and birth-rates, 40 per cent of the women polled said that marriage is a 'burden' (*Japan Now* 2000). During the bubble era the media claimed that Japanese women specified three things before they were willing to tie the knot. Dubbed the 'three highs', these were 'high salary, high educational credentials, high physical stature'. The three Hs were actually the product of an in-house customer survey conducted by a marriage service, and therefore only reflected the 'requirements' demanded by women who wanted to get married (Jolivet 1997).

One wonders what women only interested in dating or sleeping with men were after. These days there is said to be a new list, the three 'Cs', which stand for 'comfortable, communicative and cooperative' (Shōgakkan 1999: 283). Perhaps we may look forward to a time when Japanese men and women use and enjoy a new set of terms created by another media spin doctor, such as the three Es, 'elegant, egalitarian and erotic'.

## Notes

Special thanks go to James Roberson and Nobue Suzuki, who see research and writing as an ongoing scholarly dialogue, and from whom I've learned much. I would like to extend my thanks to others who have been helpful in providing ideas, feedback or assistance, including Jan Bardsley, Rebecca Copeland, Joseph Hawkins, Laura Hein, Kevin Henson, Yukihiro Nagaoka, Yoko Hoshino, Masakazu Iino, Hiroko Kawazoe, Hiroko Hirakawa, Yuka Nonami, Shigeko Okamoto, Carolyn Stevens and Wei Wei. I am also grateful to the Northeast Asian Council of the Association for Asian Studies for funding, and to a Loyola University of Chicago Paid Leave of Absence which supported research. An early version of this chapter was presented at the 1998 Association for Asian Studies Annual Meeting,

Washington, DC. A draft was also presented at the Triangle East Asia Consortium at Duke University, in 2000. I greatly appreciated the critical written comments I received from the discussant for my paper, Kazuko Watanabe of Kyoto University.

1   A criticism I have received from colleagues is that this chapter does not present a sufficiently 'critical' approach to the beauty industries and the commodification of the body that is driven by capitalism. My analysis of men's beauty work is part of a larger book manuscript in progress, tentatively entitled *Beauty Up: The Consumption of Body Aesthetics in Japan*. One chapter of this project is devoted to the *esute* salon business, where I more critically examine the fraudulent nature of the services sold.
2   The use of the address term *kun*, an intimate form that replaces *san* ('Mr'), is intended to establish the reader as a peer of the just-one-of-the-guys undergoing the *esute* treatment.
3   Decades ago the label *tsurutsuru* was used to mean someone who is bald.
4   The Itami assessment is from a conversation I had with him on October 17, 1997.
5   In Robertson's (1998) investigation of historically situated constructions of androgyny in Japan, she finds that, despite the workings of a normalizing principle, neither femininity nor masculinity has been deemed the exclusive province of either male or female.
6   Some readers have rejected my linking of men's beauty work to female desire, noting that the majority of consumers are too young for the 'marriage' market. Nevertheless, they are not too young to be socialized into gender expectations and the beauty politics linked to sexual desire.

# References

Across (1989) '*Otoko no taimō to sengo nihonjin*' (Men's body hair and the postwar Japanese), August 8: 47–61.

Akita Sakigawa Shinbun (1996) '*Otoko datte kirei ni*' (Even men go after beauty), July 26.

*An An* (1997) '*An An ga erabu dakitai otoko, dakaretai otoko*' (Selected by *An An* subscribers, men they want to embrace, men they want to be embraced by), June 20: 10–25.

—— (1999) '*Suki na otoko, kirai na otoko*' (Men we like, men we hate), No. 1172: 54.

—— (2000) '*Dokusha ga eranda suki na otoko, kirai na otoko*' (Readers' choice for men we like, men we hate), No. 1223, August 7: 53–67.

Applbaum, K. (1995) 'Marriage with the proper stranger: arranged marriage in metropolitan Japan', *Ethnology* 34: 37–51.

*Asahi Shinbun* (1997a) *Japan Almanac 1998*, Tokyo: *Asahi Shinbun*.

—— (1997b) '*Dansei mo aiyō abura torigami*' (Men also habitually use oil-blotting paper), September 4.

—— (1998a) '*'98 Tokyo kyūji dēta fairu*' ('98 Tokyo [high school] ballplayers' data file), July 14.

—— (1998b) '*Chūkōnen ni ninki*' (Popular with the middle-aged), April 16.

—— (1999a) '*Boku, hanayome yori kirei desu*' (Me, I'm more beautiful than my bride), June 10.

—— (1999b) '*Kirei na otoko ni naru*' (In order to become a beautiful man), July 10.

—— (1999c) '*Otoko o kirei ni hirogaru biyō shijō*' (The expanding beauty market for male beauty work), June 5.

Balsamo, A. (1996) *Technologies of the Gendered Body*, Durham, NC: Duke University Press.

*Bidan* (1997a) '*Mayu mēku no tatsujin daishūgō*' (Gathering of experts on eyebrow shaping), No. 7, August: 35–8.

—— (1997b) '*Pōchi no naka no byūtei guzzu o misete kure!*' (Show me what beauty goods you have inside the pouch!), No. 7, August: 30–1.

Chapman, R. (1988) 'The great pretender: variations on the New Man theme', in R. Chapman and J. Rutherford (eds) *Male Order: Unwrapping Masculinity*, London: Lawrence and Wishart.

Chow, R. (1995) *Primitive Passions: Visuality, Sexuality, Ethnography and Contemporary Chinese Cinema*, New York: Columbia University Press.

'Circumcision in Japan becoming popular', <http://www.circlist.org/critesjapan.html> (December 2000).

Condry, I. (2000) 'The social production of difference: imitation and authenticity in Japanese rap music', in U. Poiger and H. Fehrenbach (eds) *Transactions, Transgressions, Transformations: American Culture in Western Europe and Japan*, New York: Berghan Books.

de Beauvoir, S. (1968) *The Second Sex*, New York: Bantam Books.

Dikötter, F. (1998) 'Hairy barbarians, furry primates and wild men: medical science and cultural representations of hair in China', in A. Hiltebeitel and B. D. Miller (eds) *Hair: Its Power and Meaning in Asian Cultures*, New York: SUNY Press.

Dutton, K. (1995) *The Perfectible Body: The Western Ideal of Male Physical Development*, New York: Continuum.

Edwards, T. (1997) *Men in the Mirror: Men's Fashion, Masculinity and Consumer Society*, London: Cassell.

*Egg* (2000) '*Eroero dai kenkyū*' (Major research on the erotic), No. 46, August: 50–4.

Featherstone, M. (1991) 'The body in consumer culture', in M. Hepworth, B. Turner and M. Featherstone (eds) *The Body: Social Process and Cultural Theory*, London: Sage.

Fields, G. (1985) *From Bonsai to Levis*, New York: Mentor Books.

*Fine Boys* (1998) '*Bokura no raifusutairu hakusho*' (White paper on our lifestyles), No. 142, February: 183–90.

Frühstück, S. (2000) 'Treating the body as a commodity: "body projects" in contemporary Japan', in M. Ashkenazi and J. Clammer (eds) *Consumption and Material Culture in Contemporary Japan*, London: Kegan Paul.

Fuss, D. (1995) 'Fashion and the homospectatorial look', in K. A. Appiah and H. L. Gates, Jr (eds) *Identities*, Chicago: University of Chicago Press.

Gakken (2000) *Men's Body Manual*, January 20, Tokyo: Gakken.

Hashimoto, O. (1994) *Bidan e no Ressun* (*Lessons for Beautiful Men*), Tokyo: Chūō Kōronsha.

Hebdige, D. (1979) *Subculture: The Meaning of Style*, London and New York: Routledge.

Horrocks, R. (1995) *Male Myths and Icons: Masculinity in Popular Culture*, New York: St Martin's Press.

Imamura, I. (2000) '*Kakkoii koto wa, nante kakko warui n darō*' (Coolness can somehow be unhip), *J-Pop Hikyō* 479, January: 48.

Itoh, K. (1996) 'Seizing control of your facial destiny', *The Japan Times*, <http://www/japantimes.co.jp> (July 15, 1997).

*Japan Now* (2000) 'Birth rate still declining', February: 4.

Jolivet, M. (1997) *Japan: The Childless Society?* trans. A. Glasheen, London and New York: Routledge.

Kaw, E. (1993) 'Medicalization of racial features: Asian American women and cosmetic surgery', *Medical Anthropology Quarterly* 7, 1: 74–89.

Kobayashi, Y. (1998) *Sensōron* (*An Essay on War*), Tokyo: Gentōsha.

Langman, L. (1992) 'Neon cages: shopping for subjectivity', in R. Shields (ed.) *Lifestyle Shopping: The Subject of Consumption*, London and New York: Routledge.

Lunsing, W. (1997) 'Gay boom in Japan: changing views of homosexuality?', *Thamyris* 4, 2: 267–93.

McCracken, G. (1988) *Culture and Consumption: New Approaches to the Symbolic Character of Consumer Goods and Activities*, Bloomington: Indiana University Press.

McLelland, M. (1999) 'Gay men as women's ideal partners in Japanese popular culture: are gay men really a girl's best friend?', *US–Japan Women's Journal* 17: 77–110.

McVeigh, B. (2000) *Wearing Ideology: State, Schooling and Self-Presentation in Japan*, Oxford: Berg.

Machida, S. (1997) *Jintan wa, Naze Nigai? (Why is Jintan Bitter?)*, Tokyo: Boranteia Jōhō Nettowāku.

*Mainichi Shinbun* (1995) '*Kimutaku genshō o saguru: kawaii otoko ga suki?*' (Probing into the Kimutaku phenomenon: do you like cool guys?), November 7.

—— (1996 ) '*Binanron josetsu: shakai ga dansei ni mo "bi" o motomeru jidai*' (Commentary on male beauty: the era in which society demands 'beauty' even from men), August 19.

Miller, L. (1995) 'Introduction: beyond the *sarariiman* folk model', *The American Asian Review* 13, 2: 19–27.

—— (1998a) 'Visual pedagogy of male beauty work in Japan', *Newsletter of the American Anthropological Association* 39, 9: 51–2.

—— (1998b) 'People types: personality classification in Japanese women's magazines', *Journal of Popular Culture*, 31, 2: 133–50.

—— (1998c) 'Hidden assets: Japan's social transformations for the 21st Century', *The American Asian Review* 1, 3: 43–63.

—— (2000) 'Media typifications and hip *bijin*', *US–Japan Women's Journal* 19: 176–205.

Miller, M. (1998) 'Art and the construction of self and subject in Japan', in E. Ames, T. Kasulis and W. Dissanayke (eds) *Self as Image in Asian Theory and Practice*, Albany: SUNY Press.

Morgan, D. (1993) 'You too can have a body like mine: reflections on the male body and masculinities', in S. Scott and D. Morgan (eds) *Body Matters: Essays on the Sociology of the Body*, London: Falmer Press.

Mulvey, L. (1975) 'Visual pleasure and narrative cinema', *Screen* 16: 3.

*Nihon Keizai Shinbun* (1989a) '*Otokogokoro o sasou biyō saron*' (Beauty salons tempt the inner man), November 12.

—— (1989b) '*Otoko rashisa yori subesube ohada wakamono ni takamaru eikyū datsumō*' (Smooth skin before manliness: the increase in electrolysis among young men), August 16.

—— (1999) '*Chūnen dansei esutegayoi*' (Middle-aged men frequent *esute* salons), May 3.

Nikkei Trendy (1997) '*Chapatsu, piasu no tsugi wa mayu no teire*' (After *chapatsu* and piercing, eyebrow care), No. 117: 164–5.

Ono, Y. (1999) 'Beautifying the Japanese male', *The Wall Street Journal*, March 11, pp. B1–2.

*PHP Intersect* (1987) 'You handsome hunk of man, you', January: 4.

Plath, D. (1980) *Long Engagements: Maturity in Modern Japan*, Stanford: Stanford University Press.

Pollock, G. (1988) *Vision and Difference: Femininity, Feminism and Histories of Art*, London and New York: Routledge.

*Rankingu Daisuki* (1999) '*Otoko no ko no karada ni tsuite, kore wa yurusen! to omou koto*' (Women think that, as for the male body, this is not allowed!), March: 91.

Robertson, J. (1998) *Takarazuka: Sexual Politics and Popular Culture in Modern Japan*, Berkeley: University of California Press.

Sato, I. (1991) *Kamikaze Biker: Parody and Anomy in Affluent Japan*, Chicago: University of Chicago Press.

Sedgwick, E. (1991) *Epistemology in the Closet*, London: Harvester Wheatsheaf.

Seki, O. (1996) *Bidanron Josetsu (Introduction to Theories of Male Beauty)*, Tokyo: Natsume Shobō.

*Seventeen* (2001) '*Otoko no ko no kahanshin Q & A*' (Q & A about a boy's lower body region), No. 6, February: 126–7.

Shilling, C. (1993) *The Body and Social Theory*, London: Sage.

Shōgakkan (1999) *Dētaparu: Saishin Jōhō, Yōgo Jiten* (DataPal: Up-To Date Information and Encyclopaedia of Terms), Tokyo: Shōgakkan.

Simmel, G. (1973) 'Fashion', in G. Wills and D. Midgley (eds) *On Individuality and Social Forms*, Chicago: University of Chicago Press.

Stuhlman, A. (1999) 'See the world through different eyes', *Tokyo Journal* 18, 212: 15.

Tsuda, N. (1985) *Mayu no bunkashi (A Cultural History of Eyebrows)*, Tokyo: Pōra Bunka Kenkyūkai.

Tsutamori, T. (1990) *Otoko datte Kirei ni Naritai (Even Men Want to Become Beautiful)*, Tokyo: Keisō Shobō.

Turner, T. (1980) 'The social skin', in J. Cherfas and R. Lewin (eds) *Not Work Alone: A Cross-Cultural View of Activities Superfluous to Survival*, Beverly Hills: Sage.

Ueno, C. (1997) 'In the feminine guise: a trap of reverse Orientalism', *US-Japan Women's Journal* 13: 3–25.

Williams, N. and Kapila, L. (1993) 'Complications of circumcision', *British Journal of Surgery* 80: 1231–6.

*With* (1992) 'People: Akai Hidekazu', No. 132, September: 28–9.

*Yomiuri Shinbun* (1997) '*Mayuge binan: "Kimutaku mitai ni" biyōshitsu ni kayou dankai*' (Beautifully eyebrowed men: the crowd who visit beauty salons in order to 'look like Kimutaku'), April 17.

# 4 Female masculinity and fantasy spaces

## Transcending genders in the Takarazuka Theatre and Japanese popular culture

*Karen Nakamura and Hisako Matsuo*

A young man stands in front of the ocean dreaming of the adventures he will have. A young woman in a café opens the lid of the feminine waste receptacle and sees the end of her life.

(*Shōjo Kamen* [The Young Girl's Mask]; Kara 1970)

## Introduction

In a volume that concerns itself primarily with alternative images of male masculinity in Japan, this chapter looks at female masculinity as found in the Takarazuka Theatre and related genres of popular culture featuring heroines and heroes who transcend gender categories. We argue that the particular forms of female masculinity found in the contemporary Takarazuka Theatre, *shōjo* (young girl) culture, *manga* (comic books) and *anime* (animation) create spaces where both female and male fans, regardless of their sexual orientations, can temporarily transcend their everyday gender expectations and roles. These, and Takarazuka in particular, are in essence special types of asexual, agendered spaces created through the actor–fan relationship. In order to understand how this happens, we need to analyse the nature of this relationship on the stage as well as the particular details of the performance of female masculinity in the creation of these fantasy spaces.

In this chapter, we first discuss how female masculinity has been theorized in the West by feminist scholars. Differentiating ourselves from those studies by our interest in non-lesbian female masculinity, we introduce the Takarazuka Theatre and its highly organized fan clubs. We then explore the dynamic that exists between the top stars and the fans, explaining how this is a form of suturing or *bunshin* process by which the stars become the temporary embodiment of fan desire. Broadening our scope, we give examples of men within the Takarazuka space – as fans, directors and playwrights – and argue that their reading of the Theatre is similarly about the creation of an agendered, asexual fantasy space. We conclude by connecting Takarazuka Theatre with popular girls' and boys' *manga* comic book and *anime* traditions in Japan, illustrating how these too serve as vehicles for escaping gender roles in modern Japan.

## Theories of female masculinity in the West

What is special about the figure of the masculine woman? There has been growing academic interest in the field of female masculinity in the United States. Most of this has evolved from gay and lesbian studies out of a desire to understand the image of the butch lesbian (and her femme counterpart) and to re-approach the issue of alternative genders within alternative sexualities. Early feminists focused on what they saw as a conservative heterosexism implicit in butch–femme relationships, i.e. that it was some sort of 'mimicry' of male–female heterosexuality.

Queer feminist scholar Judith Butler has challenged such simple readings of sex and gender. In her seminal work *Gender Trouble*, she notes that 'gender is a kind of imitation for which there is no original' (1990: 21), for there is the 'fact that "being" a sex or gender is fundamentally impossible' (ibid.: 19) because these are ideal constructs which we can approach but never become. Building on anthropologist Esther Newton's work on drag queens (1972) and Foucault's (1980b) notion of systems of resistance and power, Butler further argues that mainstream genders are co-dependent on alternative genders for their very existence. Side A of a sheet of paper only exists because there is a Side B.

Butler and Foucault have been at the forefront of a larger movement systematic-ally deconstructing the 'objective' premises on which scientific knowledge of sex, gender and sexuality are based. Far from being limited to the humanities and social sciences, the work of disassembling the notion of binary sex classifications has also been undertaken by biological scientists such as Anne Fausto-Sterling (1993, 2000). In her 1993 article, Fausto-Sterling famously asserted that 'five sexes aren't enough' (ibid.: 20) to classify all of the possible human sexual phenotypes available. Our division of the world into only two (male and female) sexes does not reflect the reality of human variation. Far from *gender* being a 'cultural construct' imposed on the 'reality' of *sex*, both sex *and* gender are cultural constructs.

Thus back to Judith Butler's assertion. If there is no essential biological reality to maleness,[1] then masculine women are not necessarily imitations of masculine men. In that vein, Judith Halberstam's (1998) *Female Masculinity* suggests that the study of female masculinity can be approached quite separately from male masculinity and men. As Halberstam argues in her introduction:

> Female masculinity is a particularly fruitful site of investigation because it has been vilified by heterosexist and feminist/womanist programs alike . . . Within a lesbian context, female masculinity has been situated as a site where patriarchy goes to work on the female psyche and reproduces misogyny within femaleness . . .
>
> I want to carefully produce a model of female masculinity that remarks on its multiple forms but also calls for new and self-conscious affirmations of different gender taxonomies. Such affirmations begin not by subverting masculine power or taking up a position against masculine power but by turning a blind eye to conventional masculinities and refusing to engage.
>
> (1998: 9)

Unfortunately, most of the scholarship on female masculinity in the United States has tied it intimately to lesbianism, with a strong emphasis on the physical body and physical sex acts of those involved. This may be traced to the fact that the original work on sex/gender in the West came from the psychopathologization of sex/sexual 'inversions' (cf. Krafft-Ebing 1903; Foucault 1980a).

Foucault and Butler both use the life history of the nineteenth-century hermaphrodite Herculine Barbin as the point from which the 'happy limbo of non-identity' (Butler 1990: 100) no longer exists. This, coupled with the popularity of Freudian psychoanalytical theories in the early twentieth century, means that individuals in the United States can no longer be considered and analysed separately from the gendered and sexualized bodies they occupy.

As a result, perhaps, there has been scant attention paid to non-lesbian female masculinities that do not involve forms of sexuality. Halberstam notes that she elides this subject but then makes the error of assuming that non-lesbian implies hetero-sexual:

> Finally, there are likely to be many examples of masculine women in history who had no interest in same-sex sexuality. While it is not within the scope of this book to do so, there is probably a lively history of the masculine *heterosexual* woman to be told . . .
>
> (1998: 57; emphasis added)

What we see as one of the greatest tragedies of post-Freudian society in the United States is the sexualization of all human relationships from mother–infant onwards (cf. Bem 1993). This has affected critical scholarship in disallowing the possibility of asexualized relations or the transcendence of gender in non-Freudian societies.[2]

This is, however, what we suggest occurs within the space provided by female masculinity in the Takarazuka Theatre, some aspects of *shōjo* culture, *manga* and *anime* in Japan. The particular gender of the space centred around the masculine female heroes/heroines in each allows for the creation of a space where sex, gender and sexuality are suspended for a carefully delineated amount of time. We turn now to a more detailed consideration of these spaces, with a particular focus on the Takarazuka Theatre.

## The Takarazuka Theatre: actors and fans

Founded in 1913 by a railroad baron, the 340-member Takarazuka Revue Company is one of the larger theatre groups in Japan and features an all-female cast playing both male and female roles in musicals, stage dramas and dance revues. All the performers are graduates of the Takarazuka Music School where they study theatre, dance and singing for two years. During their two years at the school, the women decide whether to play female roles (*musume-yaku*, literally 'the role of a young woman/daughter'; or *onna-yaku*, literally 'the role of a woman') or male roles (*otoko-yaku*, literally 'the role of a man'). With very few exceptions, they will continue as either *musume-yaku* or *otoko-yaku* through their tenure at the Theatre.

Takarazuka has its own special language. The performers are called 'students' (*seito*) even after they graduate from the Music School and enter the Revue Theatre. The fans talk about the performers as if they were grade-school children, using special in-group nicknames and the *-chan* nominative suffix (*Zunko-chan* for the former top star Shizuki Asato, for example). Most of these 'students' will 'graduate' (*sotsugyō suru*) by their mid-thirties. In the past, most stars used to marry and become housewives, but these days many enter the movie or television show businesses. There are also Takarazuka 'students' who are in their late forties, and even one who is in her eighties, making their nominal childhood status even more difficult to sustain. However, as we will discuss, this very childhood status is critical in maintaining the fundamental asexuality of the performance space.

The large majority of ardent Takarazuka fans are married, middle-aged women who are members of 'fan clubs' centred around particular top stars. The fan clubs arrange group tickets for their members, who usually see each show around ten or twenty times. This is part of the reason why regular tickets are so hard to come by for people who do not belong to a fan club and serves to heighten the exclusivity of the Takarazuka world. The fan clubs also arrange tea parties (*ochakai* or *ochanomikai*) with the objects of their adoration, make lunch boxes, give flowers and presents and so forth. The fan clubs are unique in that while they are organized under the rubric of the Takarazuka Theatre, they follow the careers of particular stars. When a star 'graduates' from the Theatre, the fan club attached to that actor disbands. It is through the mechanism of the fan clubs that audience members are encouraged to identify with one and only one top star in Takarazuka.

Our fieldwork has focused on those fans who belong to these types of organized fan clubs and who regularly attend Takarazuka showings, 'professional' fans to use Goffman's term (1963: 108). There are certainly many other people who appreciate Takarazuka and who occasionally attend a showing, but we have not included them in the scope of this project. When we refer to 'fans', we are referring to this professionalized group.

For many of these fans, the camaraderie of the Theatre experience is important and is what differentiates the Theatre from television or movies. One fan responded in an interview that the Theatre provided a way for her temporarily to escape loneliness in her family life:

> At the time, my mother was hospitalized so that I was living alone with my father. It was like a single-father situation. I was an only child, so when I watched television I was all by myself. But when I went to Takarazuka, I was surrounded by a huge crowd. We were all watching the same thing. If something was funny, we'd all laugh together. That's why I enjoyed going to the Theatre. After that, I'd always go once a month. At the time, the S-seats only cost ¥800 and ¥300 for standing room tickets. Back then, even high school students could afford to go.
>
> (Matsuo 1998b)

The fan clubs remind many of their members of their happy-go-lucky high-school days or college clubs and circles. They provide a space for empty-nesters to congregate during the day and share their experiences as middle-class, middle-aged women. At a very basic level, the fan clubs are fun and it is their frivolous nature that should not be forgotten in any analysis.

## Women seeking masculine women: fans and top stars

Why do these women come to watch the Takarazuka Theatre? Most fans would reply that it is to see their favourite top star actors and to be taken away by the 'Takarazuka Dream' (*Takarazuka no yume*). The *otoko-yaku* or male impersonators in particular attract legions of female fans and have often been portrayed in the context of an 'ideal male' image. They are outstandingly handsome, pure, kind, emotional, charming, funny, romantic and intelligent – that is, the complete antithesis of the salaryman/*oyaji* stereotype of Japanese men. With hordes of female fans adoring the masculine female actors, it would be tempting to interpret their adoration of their top stars as some form of latent lesbian sexual desire. Takarazuka playwright Ogita Kōichi responded to our question on this topic:

> There are those who, looking at Takarazuka from the outside, try to understand it in terms of sexuality. That is not enough. Analysing only the raw bodies (*namami* [the physicality]) of Takarazuka will lead you to ignore a completely different dimension of the Theatre – that Takarazuka is ultimately a fantasy, a fictional creation.
>
> That is why the Theatre has been able to continue for over eighty years without experiencing any limitations in regards to the *otoko-yaku* as the main role. Furthermore, I have never written a play with the intention of portraying [real] men. That is because the *otoko-yaku* are *otoko-yaku* and are not men. The same goes for the *onna-yaku* (female roles) – both the *otoko-yaku* and the *onna-yaku* are constructs that exist within a particular fantasy [or fictional space]. I do not equate them at all with the raw bodies (*namami*) of [actual] women.
>
> (Matsuo 2000b: 120)

If it is not out of a latent lesbian desire to see masculine women, what draws women to the Takarazuka Theatre in such numbers? We interviewed one Takarazuka fan about her first experience:

> Since I was born and grew up in Hyōgo Prefecture [where the Theatre is based], I had seen the posters in the trains and knew about the Theatre but I had never gone to a performance. Until I actually went, my general feeling about the Theatre was, 'What??? Takarazuka??? [Give me a break!]'. I guess that's pretty much a typical reaction.
>
> So I first went to see [top star] Natsume-san's *The Rose of Versailles* as an adult. When I entered the theatre lobby, my first reaction was one of surprise, 'What is this?!' All around me were women and only women. The room was packed and the atmosphere was hot with excitement. There were life-size posters of the

stars pasted onto the walls. It seemed to me like it was a different world (*ijigen*) altogether.

Finally the curtain went up. The actor playing the role of [Axel] Fersen rose up from the centre of the stage through a hidden trapdoor carrying the doll Stephan. For the next three hours I was transfixed. Every time an actor walked on the apron stage, I could only sigh, '*hā*', that's all, '*hā*'. I was surprised by what was a totally new experience for me. Then, by accident, my eyes drifted towards the André character played by Ruko-san. 'Ah! She's so cool (*kakkoii*)!' Oh no, I thought to myself, 'she's so cool!' The most vivid memory was when the actor playing the role of Oscar [Jarjayes] revealed herself as a woman and danced in a duet. Wow! I felt like I overcame something [inside of myself]. So this is what Takarazuka is like.

(Matsuo 1998a)

Her story shares many common themes with other women we have talked with. The first is the feeling that Takarazuka represents a place outside of normal time and space. As the interviewee notes, most 'normal' (that is, non-Takarazuka) people have a somewhat prejudiced image of the Takarazuka Theatre and its fans as being rather over the top. She overcomes her own internal resistance during the theatre performance when she allows herself to realize the 'coolness' of the actor Ruko-san who is playing the male role of André. It is at this point that she is able to enter into the Takarazuka world, allowing Ruko-san to be her *bunshin* or alter-ego on the stage (see below).

It happened that this fan was also a lesbian in her personal life. We asked her if there was any connection between her lesbian sexuality and her adoration of the Takarazuka Theatre:

Even if there was a lesbian among one of the students [i.e. stars], I have the feeling that they would only be [lesbian] during their time in that world. After leaving the Revue, I don't know what would happen to them [i.e. they might get married and have children]. About the fans . . . well, I don't participate in the [festivities] surrounding the stars coming into and out of the Theatre, I just come to the Theatre to watch the show and go home. So how am I supposed to meet [any other lesbians]? . . . There are other places for that, for example the group *Tokyo Shōnen* [with vocalist Sasano Michiru, who came out as a lesbian]. It's much easier to go to other groups to look for that kind of thing.

(ibid.)

When the same fan was asked what she saw in one of her favourite *otoko-yaku* stars (i.e. to see if she experiences sexual desire for them), she responded:

When Non-chan [*otoko-yaku* top star Kuze Seika] performs . . . even before you get into whether being an *otoko-yaku* is natural or unnatural . . . she fits perfectly into the character itself. I feel a lot of warmth from her character. Perhaps that's what I seek in the Takarazuka *otoko-yaku*, that feeling of warmth.

(ibid.)

When asked further about whether she experiences any sexual desire for the Takarazuka stars, the fan again rejected that interpretation of her feelings for the stars. We have encountered this with other fans who are lesbian as well, who do not connect their sexuality with the appeal they feel for Takarazuka. They are lesbians who are fans of Takarazuka, not Takarazuka lesbian fans.

## Becoming a fan: suture and *bunshin*

If not through sexual desire, then what is the process by which audience members enter and engage in fictional works like Takarazuka and identify with *otoko-yaku* actors? In *The Subject of Semiotics*, film theoretician Kaja Silverman develops the concept of 'suture . . . the procedures by means of which cinematic texts confer subjectivity upon their viewers' (1983: 195), or the process by which the viewers identify (and interpellate themselves into) the position of the subjects on the screen. That is, Silverman argues that we cannot analyse the process of viewing film as merely reactive; rather it is inherently an active process, a discourse that can itself be subject to discourse analysis. Although the film experience differs from being in a stage audience, we can borrow some of Silverman's ideas relating to gender relations on the stage. The process of identification with one of the protagonists is of course an essential part of the suturing process. The character we identify with becomes our alter-ego, or, to use the Japanese term, *bunshin*.[3]

The problem, especially for women audience members, is finding the appropriate protagonist on screen or stage to suture into. In an opaque style driven by Lacanian psychoanalytic theory, Silverman explains why women cannot participate equally as audience members with men. She argues that the traditional film structure denies female viewers full subjectivity because of their inability to fully suture with the male actors because of female viewers' lack of a penis. Furthermore, they have a wary relationship to women who represent symbolic insecurity. Male viewers, however, can fully suture with the male leads who act both as mirrors of their idealized self-image and of fathers and role models. They can further suture with the female actors who represent 'warmth and nourishment' (i.e. the mother) (ibid.: 234).

Removing the psychoanalytic penile baggage from Silverman's argument, female audience members cannot fully invest in the film or stage experience because they cannot identify with either the male heroes because they are male or the female leads who are not portrayed as empowered. We have heard this in our own interviews with fans when asking them why they are not attracted towards traditional (male) Japanese theatre on one hand, or towards the female *musume-yaku* in Takarazuka on the other. For example, Natori Chisato, a married female critic of Takarazuka, put it this way:

> The presence of men no longer creates any desire (*akogare*)[4] in me. Through the male body of my husband, the image of 'man' (*otoko*) has changed from what used to be a distant yearning to becoming that of a friend, an enemy and that of a kindred spirit in the loneliness of our human existence . . . When I see female actors trying to approach an ideal image of femininity on the stage, I sometimes

feel painfully like I am looking at myself. But when I see the *otoko-yaku* actors in their endless struggle to distance themselves from [their] femaleness, I enjoy the refreshing thrill of seeing the delicate balancing act between possibility and impossibility.

(1990: 113)

Takarazuka is often portrayed as a fantastic space. For fantasy to work, it must provide something outside of the normal. The fans remark that they find it difficult to 'enter' (*hairikomu*) or suture to the bodies and roles of male stage actors because of their male sex, as well as into the bodies of feminine female actors because of their female gender.[5] Nimiya Kazuko, another married female Takarazuka critic, remarks:

If I wanted to see real men, I'd go to another theatre . . . Among female fans of Takarazuka, there are much fewer fans of the *musume-yaku* female performers when compared to the *otoko-yaku* male impersonators . . . Women know the female condition very well, thus it is hard to cherish the dreams [that the female characters have on stage]. That's why women can't become fans of the female leads.

The main reason I cannot accept the explanation that 'women are attracted to the *otoko-yaku* male impersonators because they perform the role of being ideal men' (*risō no otoko*) is because I have no ideals (*risō*) that I hold men up to. I have no expectations (*kitai*) towards men either. Or perhaps I should say that I do not want to have any expectations towards men. This might serve only as an explanation for myself, but I arrive at the conclusion that when women look at the *otoko-yaku* male impersonators, what draws their attention is not the 'ideals we hold to men' but rather the 'despair we attach to men'.

(1995: 132)

When interviewing Takarazuka playwright Kimura Shinji about the male roles in the Theatre, he responded in very similar fashion to Ogita Kōichi, above. Fantasy is a key element that allows people (the stars, playwrights and fans) to transcend the physicality, the moment, and to immerse themselves into the Theatre where they can experience pure emotion.

I think the existence of the *otoko-yaku* is wonderful. To give an example, the story of *Romeo and Juliet* is about a young daughter and son caught in the fate caused by the war between their two families. It is difficult to represent this [on the stage] in a contemporary and realistic way. However, I can directly engage the themes of love and fantasy into the storyline by borrowing the fictional construct (*kyokō*) of the *otoko-yaku*. As an artistic creator, a storyline that exists within a fictional construct gives me extremely flexible material to work with. Through the Theatre, our own human souls experience yearning (*akogare*), despair, depression and other emotions.

The 'Dream Story' [that Takarazuka provides through the *otoko-yaku*] becomes a way for us to find the real Truth [about the human condition]. It is only through the fictional construct of the *otoko-yaku* that we are able to directly engage and get pulled into the Theatre experience.

(Matsuo 2000b: 117)

Building on the theories of experimental theatre director Jerzy Growtoski, Japanese theatre critic Suzuki Tadashi wrote in *Engeki to wa Nani ka* (*What is Theatre?*) that the theatre is 'an area where the audience and the actors co-exist simultaneously' (1988: 53). Audience members use the body of the *otoko-yaku* to directly enter and engage in the world presented on the stage. This is the process of building an alter-ego or *bunshin* alluded to in the first interview.

By acting through the *otoko-yaku* as alter-ego, the audience experiences emotional catharsis and can play with roles outside of their own. It is precisely because the *otoko-yaku* is a female masculine/masculine female fictional construct that the audience can do this – they cannot immerse themselves quite as easily with male-actors-playing-male-roles or female-actors-playing-female-roles. For the fans, this is what fundamentally differentiates Takarazuka from other theatre and revue acts in Japan in which men play lead roles. The introduction of physical sexuality either between the male and female roles on stage or between the fans and stars would only serve to block the process of this emotional catharsis. The Western settings of most of the musical dramas, the garish costumes and make-up, and outlandish stage names of the Takarazuka further combine with the female masculinity of the *otoko-yaku* to create the unreality that allows for an escape into the fantasy realm and identification with the *otoko-yaku*.

The unrealness of the stage experience itself aids in the direct suturing process. As suggested by Suzuki Tadashi, there is a special quality to the live stage experience that brings actors and audience into close relationship. Unlike film, where each perfect shot and cut creates an illusion of seamless perfection, the stage has a 'sticky' human quality. Each actor tries their best and their fans hang on their every word, sharing their emotions as well as their failures. One of the fans relates her experience of a star missing her lines:

> Out of the eighty actors on the stage, one really caught my eye. That was [*otoko-yaku*] Mami Rei. Her individuality really stuck out. First, she's really tall, right? She has a really high-pitched voice, right? Her eyes are bright and clear, like a Westerner, right? And then she's really tall . . . perhaps it's because they made the sleeves and hem of her kimono too short and she had on a [male] wig with a bald spot . . . there was something about the Western-ness of her body along with the Japanese-ness of the role that didn't fit together. It was that disparity and her extraordinary beauty that caught my eye. I just couldn't keep my eyes off her.
>
> Mami-san then sang, 'From Atago-yama I saw the horses pulling the carts, the dogs pissed and made a hole!'
>
> The whole crowd burst into laughter after she finished that line. Next to her were Nao Sumire and Uraji Natsuko. After the song finished, Mami-san turned over to Sumire-san and whispered her, 'What was the next line?' That was picked up by the wireless mike and the crowd burst into laughter again.
>
> The real line wasn't 'the dogs pissed and made a hole' but 'the horses pissed and made a hole'. I didn't understand that at the time. But the whole crowd was laughing and I was taken along with their merriment.

(Matsuo 1998b)

As the majority of the fans in the audience have already seen the same play at least several times, these small slips are immediately recognized. But the audiences come back each time because the drama unfolds in new ways with small variations. Each time, the fans can re-immerse themselves in the fantasy space and the illusion of reality is maintained by the humanness of the performance, something that cannot be said about film, in which each screening is exactly the same.

### Men and the Takarazuka space

As this volume is about masculinity in Japan, in this chapter we should additionally mention of the presence of actual men in Takarazuka, who also enjoy female masculinity. Most of the directors and playwrights are male, as are many of the backstage crew.[6] There is a small but growing percentage of men who attend Takarazuka – usually first on the insistence of their wives and girlfriends, but who then find their own space within the theatre experience. Although we would expect heterosexual men to be primarily attracted to the *musume-yaku* stars, on the contrary most of the male fans seem to be attracted to the *otoko-yaku* top stars, perhaps finding in them a way to transcend their own physical maleness and enter the fantasy world of Takarazuka. The artifice of female masculinity allows men to suture themselves just as efficiently as women.

We interviewed one of the male orchestra staff about sexuality within the Takarazuka space:

> When rehearsing, there are the *otoko-yaku* as well as the *onna-yaku* and *musume-yaku*. The *musume-yaku* usually wear a long skirt over their dance leotards. They are dressed, at the very least, in a feminine way. But I don't think a single male staff members feels any 'female sexual attraction' (*onna no iroke*) from them. Similarly, the *otoko-yaku* have sharper movements and are more dashing than normal women. They also have shorter hairstyles. But I think it would be very difficult to see them as 'lesbian–butches' (*rezubian no tachi yaku*). The reason for that would be that [at their core] they exist as actors – they must kill any remnants of their own gender within themselves. Another way to say this would be that they must eradicate any notion of 'male' or 'female' – as actors they exist as only as [empty] figures. They do this to the utmost limit so that they can become the frame for the roles of the *otoko-yaku* or *onna-yaku*.
>
> For example, [top *onna-yaku* star] Hanafusa Mari recently played the role of Elizabeth [in the musical of the same name]. One of the male staff members said to me, 'Even when she wears a leotard, I can't detect any "woman" [femaleness] in that child'. I don't think that is limited to just Hanafusa Mari, it's impossible to detect [sexual] pheromones from any of the Takarazuka students.
>
> (Matsuo 1999)

In the types of letters and commentary that fans write to Takarazuka magazines as well as in our interviews, we have not seen an appreciative difference between male and female fans in their attraction to the stage and the actors. Their attraction to the

Theatre is not a sexual one, although it is driven by a mutual desire to escape the gendered normal world of Japanese society for even a few hours.

## Female masculinity, *shōjo* and freedom from sexuality

In his 1996 article, John Treat highlights the importance of *shōjo* (young girl's) commodity culture in modern Japan. Acting like *shōjo* (a small girl) provides a space for Japanese women outside of the bounds of adult Japanese female responsibility:

> The word most often associated with this *shōjo* culture is *kawaii*, or 'cute'. This aesthetic value is directly linked to the consumer role that *shōjo* exist to play. A *kawaii* girl is attractive, and thus valorized, but lacks libidinal agency of her own. While others may sexually desire the *shōjo* – and indeed, another phenomenon in the Japan of the 1980s was the talk of the *rorikon* 'Lolita complex' of adult heterosexual males – the *shōjo*'s own sexual energy, directed as it is towards stuffed animals, pink notebooks, strawberry crepes and Hello Kitty novelties is an energy not yet deployable in the heterosexual economy of adult life in Japan.
>
> (1996: 363)

> In English, gender is binary – at every stage one is either 'male' or 'female'. But in Japan, one might well argue that *shōjo* constitute their own gender, neither male nor female but rather something importantly detached from the productive economy of heterosexual reproduction.
>
> (ibid.: 364)

Performing *shōjo* is one active and dynamic way that Japanese women can control their sexuality. As the opening quote from writer Kara Jūrō depicts, men have been portrayed as being able to dream of transcending their current state, going off to faraway lands. In contrast, women are constantly reminded of the responsibilities that their bodies and gender roles restrict them to within Japanese society.

In her historical analysis of early twentieth-century Takarazuka, Jennifer Robertson (1998) argues that the performance of what she calls the 'androgyny' in Takarazuka is an amalgamation of both male and female, a zone of deep eroticism. Robertson bases her argument in part on prewar Japanese newspapers and conservative social critics who fret about the increasing sexual deviance that they saw in Takarazuka and popular culture, as part of a larger concern about aberrant sexuality in that period. In the postwar period, however, we find that most of that discourse has disappeared and our own ethnography of modern Takarazuka does not reveal the 'lesbian subtexts' (ibid.: 61) that her earlier study did. Most of our informants, both lesbian and straight, as revealed in the interview data we present here, explicitly reject a sexualized reading of modern Takarazuka.

Although most *shōjo* forms focus on reversion to a prepubescent girlhood with ribbons and frilly skirts, Takarazuka is a *shōjo* fantasy space that allows grown Japanese women – for the space of a few hours – to revert to a prepubescent stage of tomboyism, thus escaping the immanence of their bodies and their sexuality. The female masculinity on the Takarazuka stage is fundamentally a prepubescent asexual one – a reversion to the tomboy years of freedom before adult female responsibility symbolized by the blood of menarche. As Judith Halberstam writes:

> We could say that tomboyism is tolerated [in the West] as long as the child remains prepubescent; as soon as puberty begins, however, the full force of gender conformity descends on the girl . . . Female adolescence represents the crisis of coming of age as a girl in male-dominated society. If adolescence represents a rite of passage . . . and an ascension to some version (however attenuated) of social power, for girls, adolescence is a lesson in restraint, punishment and repression. It is in the context of female adolescence that the tomboy instincts of millions of girls are remodelled into compliant forms of femininity.
>
> (1998: 6)

In Japan, escape for women is possible through reversion to a prepubescent state. We believe that for most Takarazuka fans, sexuality in the interactions between the fans and stars is inconceivable.[7] The stars – who are symbolically presented as 'students' and 'young girls' – are not the objects of sexual desire. They serve instead as the empty vessel for fan dreams, the *bunshin* or alter-ego. Everything about Takarazuka, from organization of the 'fan clubs' as childlike spaces to the 'graduation ceremonies' when stars step down from the stage, re-emphasizes the essential childishness and childhood purity (i.e. freedom from sullying sexuality and sexual responsibility) of Takarazuka.

Top Takarazuka *otoko-yaku* star Makoto Tsubasa comments on how the *otoko-yaku* role is just that, a role: 'Acting [as an *otoko-yaku* for me] is essentially about deceiving (*damasu*) the audience' (Matsuo 2000a: 8). Many top stars also use the metaphor of 'killing themselves' in order to get into character. Top *otoko-yaku* male impersonator Shizuki Asato was famous for sewing teddy bears together during show intermissions, in great contrast to her strong, masculine stage performance. Many are aware, from the stars to the fans, that the Theatre is just theatre and the actors are just actors.

We must emphasize that the 'escape' from adult responsibility and reversion to childhoodness in Takarazuka and *shōjo* culture is both temporally and spatially bounded in order for the viewers to be unbounded from normative expectations. Takarazuka serves as a vacation from adult responsibility; but it operates in similar ways to real vacations, which are appreciated because of the presence of the work that centrally provides one with a core *ikigai* or meaning to life (Mathews 1996). Takarazuka is a bracketed experience that fans go to and return from. They do not live within that space permanently.

In many ways this mirrors the consumptive freedom of male erotic comics that Anne Allison analyses in her *Permitted and Prohibited Desires*:

> I [argue] that play and desire are always interconnected with the paths people assume to make a living, reproduce a community and move from childhood into adulthood. In this sense, desire is not reduced or repressed as much as it is

actively produced in forms that coordinate with the habits demanded of productive subjects. The 'dullness' and 'arduousness' of the tasks Japanese must execute over a lifetime, starting in childhood, are made acceptable not by the mere threat or force of an external structure (fear of failure on exams, for example). More powerful is the internalization of a different sort of process, one based on desires that make the habitual desirable as well as making escape from the habits of labour seem possible through everyday practices of consumptive pleasure.

(2000: xv)

In his critique of Japanese comics, Frederik Schodt (1986) notes that Japanese readers are able to make distinctions between fantasy and reality in ways that most American cultural critics are not. The extreme violence and sexuality in *manga* and *anime* for men and boys are not representations of deep repressed desires. Similarly, the gender transcendence in Takarazuka Theatre and homosexuality in women and girls' comic books do not necessarily speak to a larger yearning for homosexuality and gender transgression in the housewives who make up the majority of the fan audience. The fantasy spaces in both instances have utility only because they have no connection with reality.

## The origins of 'beautiful warrior girls': Takarazuka, *shōjo manga* and the Tezuka connection

Starting in the mid-1980s, there has been a growing theme of beautiful aggressive girl warriors in Japanese *anime* and *manga* such as *Nausicaä of the Valley of the Winds* (1984), *Bubble Gum Crisis* (1985), *Ghost in the Shell* (1995), *Battle Angel Alita* (1994)[8] and so forth. With lithe bodies often strengthened by exoskeletal armour, these young women replace the earlier generation of young male heroes fighting evil. In his book titled *Sentō Bishōjo no Seishin Bunseki* (The Psychology of Beautiful Girl Warriors), Japanese author Saitō Tamaki (2000) argues that the increase in female heroines displacing male heroes in boys' comics is a response to the growing feeling of inadequacy among young Japanese men. In order to escape into the world of *anime*, they can no longer immerse themselves in fantasies involving male figures, whose responsibilities (to fight; to improve themselves; to protect their families) and flaws all too closely mirror their own. The *sentō bishōjo* warrior–princesses provide them with a vehicle of purity, strength and purposefulness that they find lacking in their own lives.[9]

In her groundbreaking literary analysis of Japanese *anime*, Susan Napier quotes Tamae Prindle on the centrality of *shōjo* images even in male culture:

Surely the nation's gaze is more and more focused on girls. Girls occupy a distinctive place in Japan's mass media, including films and literature. What fascinates the Japanese is that the *shōjo* nestle in a shallow lacuna between adulthood and childhood, power and powerlessness, awareness and innocence as well as masculinity and femininity.

(Prindle, cited in Napier 2000: 119)

We argue that the female masculinity of Takarazuka occupies the same 'shallow lacuna . . . between masculinity and femininity'. Napier goes on to link *shōjo* with *anime* directed towards men and boys:

> In contemporary Japanese society, girls, with their seemingly still-amorphous identities, seem to embody the potential for unfettered change and excitement that is far less available to Japanese males, who are caught in the network of demanding workforce responsibilities. It is not surprising, therefore, that it is the female Kusanagi [playing the central role] in *Ghost in the Shell* who melds with the [androgynous/masculine] Puppet Master, or that it is [male character's] Ranma's transformation into a girl that gives the series its narrative pleasure.
>
> (ibid.)

The original gender-bending warrior girl was of course the *Princess Knight* (1978; *Ribon no Kishi*) by Japanese *manga* and *anime* demi-god Tezuka Osamu. The story involves a young girl, Saphire, born as a princess to a royal family. For various reasons Saphire is raised as a son and heir to the throne. The story line revolves around plots by evil courtiers to reveal Saphire's true gender, all of the time while s/he struggles with balancing both sides of his/her gender presentation. At moments a dashing prince and later reappearing as a gorgeous princess, Saphire seems to have it all. *Princess Knight* is important because it is seen as the first real *shōjo manga* as well. In the postscript to the bound-book edition of the *manga*, Tezuka responds to why he started drawing it:

> I can say with absolute certainty that the *Princess Knight* which appeared [in the magazine] *Shōjo Club* is the first appearance of a Japanese story *shōjo manga*.
> Up to then, *shōjo manga* consisted of funny and humorous comics about everyday life (*seikatsu manga*), *Anmitsu Hime* (Princess Anmitsu) is a good example of this.
> In the Fall of 1952, I was visited by the then-Editor of *Shōjo Club*, Mr Makino. He asked me whether I could draw a story *manga* like [my previous works] *Tetsuwan Atomu* [Atom Boy] or *Janguru Taitei* [Kimba] but for girls (*shōjo*). I immediately thought of transposing the Takarazuka Theatre, which was immensely popular with girls, into *manga* form. I told him I would give it a try.
>
> (cited in Murakami 1998: 104)

It should be mentioned that the young Tezuka grew up in Takarazuka City and was a common visitor to the Takarazuka Theatre with his mother, who was a huge fan of the stage. From the original *Princess Knight*, the genre of *shōjo manga* grew, developing such classics as the *Rose of Versailles* (1972–4) by Ikeda Riyoko, which also features a cross-dressing prince who is really a princess. By that time *shōjo manga* in general was playing heavily with themes of gender role transgression and subversion.[10] The immense popularity of the 1974 stage production of the *Rose of Versailles* by Takarazuka caught the attention of all of Japan. As *manga* commentator Schodt notes, 'As a result boys as well as men – including academics and literary types – finally took note of what was happening in girls' comics' (1986: 100).

It took about a decade for the developments in *shōjo manga* to filter into the main-stream. In 1984, bestselling *manga* artist and animator Miyazaki Hayao created his enormously popular *Nausicaä of the Valley of the Winds* (*Kaze no Tani no Nausicaä*) with a strong young female lead drawn strongly from the *shōjo* tradition. The foil or antagonist is provided by a powerful princess who, while motivated by her own goals, cannot be classified as wholly evil as in the Western comics tradition. Miyazaki commented on his need to have female heroines and anti-heroines rather than male heroes and anti-heroes: 'If we try to make an adventure story with a male lead, we have no choice but to do *Indiana Jones*, with a Nazi or someone else who is a villain in everyone's eyes' (Miyazaki 1988, cited in McCarthy 1999: 80).

In order to transcend gender, to emphasize his themes of purity and strength, he had to make his heroes female: 'Nausicaä is not a protagonist who defeats an opponent, but a protagonist who understands, or accepts. She is someone who lives on a different dimension. That kind of character should be female rather than male' (Miyazaki 1984, cited in McCarthy 1999: 79).

Takarazuka playwright Ogita in one of our interviews relates this to his own need for having female heroines on his stage: 'Superficially, the heroines in Miyazaki Hayao's *anime* are female, but more important than their gender is their purity and asexuality (*musei*) . . . That is perhaps the similarity between his work and Takarazuka' (Matsuo 2000b: 120).

## Female masculinity and the future of gender relations in Japan

At the end of the day, the Japanese housewives who are enchanted by the dashing figures of the *otoko-yaku* stars still have to return to their families, cook and clean for their husbands and children. The Theatre provides an escape but it is temporally bounded. Is this kind of gender escapism merely a type of 'weapons of the weak' (Scott 1985) with no real long-term impact?

Perhaps we are expecting too much from the Takarazuka Theatre. It is, after all, commercial entertainment – neither an evil standard-bearer of gender conservatism and commodity fetishism nor the saviour of all womankind and lesbian – feminist transcendence. But our own observations suggest that the collapse of the Japanese economy and the ensuing dissipation of the Japanese dream ('My car, my home, my wife', etc.) have created more space for alternative gender configurations to erupt. Furthermore, by reading more deeply into the reasons why both men and women go to the Takarazuka Theatre, we can better understand gender relations in Japan today.

The growing popularity of the Takarazuka Revue among men in Japan can be seen as part of a larger movement away from stereotyped forms of male masculinity. Gender is being recreated in new, active and dynamic ways, whether it is a new generation of Japanese men seeking refuge and solace from the pressures of their gender in the warrior–princess *anime* adventures of young women, or Japanese housewives finding transcendence and purity in the *otoko-yaku* male impersonators of the Takarazuka Theatre. Both are in some ways reactions to what the critic and housewife Nimiya Kazuko describes as the 'despair we attach to men' in contemporary Japanese society, the absence of purity, innocence and hope.

# Notes

1  Although we like to imagine the penis as symbolizing the difference between men and women, it is truly only that: symbolic. In our everyday interactions with people who we imagine to be male or female, we usually have no way of accessing the 'truth' (i.e. checking for the presence of the symbol). Instead, we treat their sex as if it is congruous with their gender performance.
2  We posit that Japan is such a nation. That is, the popular discourse on the self in Japan has not been structured through the lens of gendered Western biomedicine and Freudian psychoanalysis as it has in the United States. For one discussion of Japanese psychotherapies, see Reynolds (1980).
3  Related to the Buddhist concept of *henshin*, *bunshin* originally referred to appearances of the Buddha and Bodhisattvas in various guises (cf. Gill [1998] for a discussion of *henshin* in Japanese popular *anime*). Especially on the stage, *bunshin* has taken on a meaning close to that of alter-ego – the other self or projection of self.
4  Although *akogare* is most often translated as 'desire' or 'yearning', it should be remarked that it is a purely platonic desire or yearning, distanced from sexual attraction.
5  One exception, however, has been the enormously popular *Elizabeth* role played by top *musume-yaku* star Hanafusa Mari in the musical of the same name. The strength of this character (based on an Austrian opera), who struggles against the limitations set by her female gender, allowed for fans to suture themselves into her.
6  We should mention that there are two female Takarazuka playwrights who have debuted their work at the Theatre. There are also female conductors and the main composer of the Takarazuka Theatre is a woman.
7  That is not to say that there are absolutely no fans (either male or female) who sexually fantasize about Takarazuka. They can easily be found (as with anything else imaginable) on the Internet in their own chat rooms. However, the quotes provided here suggest that many if not most fans do not engage Takarazuka in a sexual fashion.
8  Titles are from the US releases (only *Battle Angel Alita* differs significantly, it was originally released as *Gunm* in Japan). Release dates are from the original Japanese releases. All are available in translation in DVD or graphic novel form now in the US.
9  It should be noted here that similar motifs of the warrior–princess have emerged in the US, also attracting legions of heterosexual male fans: Lara Croft (*Tomb Raider*); Buffy the Vampire Slayer; and Zena Warrior Princess. Saitō's entire thesis is rather complex and very difficult to summarize in one paragraph as it also involves the phallic sexualization of the beautiful warrior girls. By attaching a penis to the warrior girls, Saitō argues that the image is complete for the '*otaku*' dispossessed men who find them so appealing. The girls have all of the purity of femininity and, because they have a penis, they become the vessel (*bunshin*) for the men to suture themselves to. This analysis of feminine masculinity requires, of course, an entire separate chapter.
10  For example, a common theme in contemporary adult *shōjo manga* is male homosexuality. One interpretation is that because the women who are reading this feel constrained by the limits of female heterosexual roles, the body of the male homosexual and homosexual relationships allow them to explore the full domain of emotions and pleasures. Because *manga* characters are fictional and, due to censorship laws, do not have penises, they do not have the same penile suture problem that women encounter with real human actors on the stage or in films. Lesbian relationships are rare in mainstream *shōjo manga*.

# References

Allison, A. (2000) *Permitted and Prohibited Desires in Japan: Mothers, Comics and Censorship in Japan*, Berkeley: University of California Press.
Bem, S. L. (1993) *The Lenses of Gender: Transforming the Debate on Sexual Inequality*, New Haven: Yale University Press.

Butler, J. (1990) *Gender Trouble: Feminism and the Subversion of Identity*, London and New York: Routledge.

Fausto-Sterling, A. (1993) 'The five sexes: why male and female are not enough', *The Sciences* (March/April): 20–5.

— (2000) *Sexing the Body: Gender Politics and the Construction of Sexuality*, New York: Basic Books.

Foucault, M. (1980a) *Herculine Barbin: Being the Recently Discovered Memoirs of a Nineteenth-Century French Hermaphrodite*, trans. R. McDougall, New York: Pantheon.

— (1980b) *Power/Knowledge*, C. Gordon (ed.), New York: Pantheon.

Gill, T. (1998) 'Transformational magic: some Japanese super-heroes and monsters', in D. P. Martinez (ed.) *The Worlds of Japanese Popular Culture: Gender, Shifting Boundaries and Global Cultures*, Cambridge: Cambridge University Press.

Goffman, E. (1963) *Stigma: Notes on the Management of Spoiled Identity*, Englewood Cliffs: Prentice-Hall.

Halberstam, J. (1998) *Female Masculinity*, Durham, NC and London: Duke University Press.

Kara, J. (1970) *Shōjo Kamen* (*The Young Girl's Mask*), Tokyo: Gakugei Shorin.

Krafft-Ebing, R. von (1933 [1903]) *Psychopathia Sexualis: With Especial Reference to the Antipathic Sexual Instinct: a Medico–Forensic Study*. Translated and adapted from the 12th German edn by F. J. Rebman, New York: Physicians and Surgeons Book Company.

McCarthy, H. (1999) *Hayao Miyazaki: Master of Japanese Animation: Films, Themes, Artistry*, Berkeley: Stone Bridge Press.

Mathews, G. (1996) *What Makes Life Worth Living?: How Japanese and Americans Make Sense of Their Worlds*, Berkeley: University of California Press.

Matsuo, H. (1998a) Fan Interview 1, October 24, unpublished.

— (1998b) Fan Interview 2, October 26, unpublished.

— (1999) Fan Interview 3, January 7, unpublished.

— (2000a) 'Watashitachi wa Takarazuka, hoka to dōka wa shinai. Tsukigumi toppu Makoto Tsubasa' (We are Takarazuka, we will not assimilate with others; an interview with Makoto Tsubasa: the top star of the Tsukigumi), *Takarazuka 1999–2000 Memories to Millennium*, Tokyo: Mainichi Shinbunsha.

— (2000b) 'Takarazuka wakate enshutsuka ni kiku Takarazuka mireniamu: 21 seiki no Takarazuka kageki wa?' (Takarazuka Millenium: interviews with young playwrights about Takarazuka Theatre in the 21st Century), *Takarazuka 1999–2000 Memories to Millennium*, Tokyo: Mainichi Shinbunsha.

Murakami, T. (1998) '*Tatakau shōjo no genshō: "Ribon no Kishi" ron*' (The phenomenon of the fighting young girl: my theory on 'The Princess Knight'), in T. Saitō *et al.* (eds) *Shōjotachi no Senreki: 'Ribon no Kishi' kara 'Shōjo no Kakumei Utena' made* (*The Battle History of Young Girls: From 'The Princess Knight' to 'Revolutionary Girl Utena'*), Tokyo: Seikyūsha.

Napier, S. J. (2000) *Anime: From Akira to Princess Mononoke*, New York: Palgrave.

Natori, C. (1990) *Dorīmu Shiatā: Ai, Yume, Takarazuka* (*Dream Theatre: Love, Dreams, Takarazuka*), Osaka: Kansai Shoin.

Newton, E. (1972) *Mother Camp: Female Impersonators in America*, Chicago: University of Chicago Press.

Nimiya, K. (1995) *Takarazuka no Kōki* (*The Fragrance of Takarazuka*), Tokyo: Kōsaidō Shuppan.

Reynolds, D. (1980) *The Quiet Therapies: Japanese Pathways to Personal Growth*, Honolulu: University of Hawaii Press.

Robertson, J. (1998) *Takarazuka: Sexual Politics and Popular Culture in Modern Japan*, Berkeley: University of California Press.

Saitō, T. (2000) *Sentō Bishōjo no Seishin Bunseki* (*The Psychology of Beautiful Girl Warriors*), Tokyo: Ōta Shuppan.

Schodt, F. L. (1986) *Manga! Manga!: The World of Japanese Comics*, Tokyo: Kodansha International.

Scott, J. (1985) *Weapons of the Weak: Everyday Forms of Peasant Resistance*, New Haven: Yale University Press.

Silverman, K. (1983) *The Subject of Semiotics*, New York: Oxford University Press.

Suzuki, T. (1988) *Engeki to wa Nani ka (What is Theatre?)*, Tokyo: Iwanami Shinsho.

Treat, J. (1996) 'Yoshimoto Banana writes home: *shōjo* culture and the nostalgic subject', *Journal of Japanese Studies* 19, 2: 353–88.

# 5   The burning of men

## Masculinities and the nation in Japanese popular song

*Christine R. Yano*

## Introduction

The highly gendered expressions of Japanese popular song and its staged performances give ready access to constructions of what it means to be a man or a woman, masculine or feminine. In *enka*, a popular ballad genre considered the most 'traditional' in its forms and cultural values, men and women take the stage not only as gendered beings, but as particularly Japanese ones. This chapter examines one half of the constructions, that of masculinity, through texts, music, movement and images of its stars. At the same time, I acknowledge that masculinity and femininity are relational concepts, which cannot be understood without reference to each other (Kimmel 1987: 12; see also Gutmann 1996) as well as to articulations of multiple masculinities within one socio-cultural setting (Connell 1987; Ortner 1996).

At the outset, I should make the limitations of this chapter clear. Although consumption is a part of my research, my focus here is on the texts and images of *enka*, including their production and promotion in Japan in the 1990s. Therefore, I examine constructions of masculinities rather than men. This chapter is based on fieldwork conducted during 1991–3 in Tokyo, during which I interviewed producers, performers and fans of *enka*, recorded and analysed television broadcasts, attended numerous concerts, participated in two fan clubs and analysed fan magazines.

Another aspect I want to make clear is the context for these images. Japan in the 1990s and 2000s has been in the midst of its greatest economic challenge since dramatic postwar success and intensification of globalization. The economic crisis commingles with social crises questioning the values, ethos and morals of Japanese people today. Some of these crises involve questions of identity, asking, 'Who are we Japanese?' It is a question which spans pre-modern as well as modern times (see Nosco 1990), with answers most recently devolving into *nihonjinron* (theories of being Japanese)[1] which gained prominence in the introspective, nationalistic 1970s. The fact that gender frames some of the answers to the question of Japaneseness makes national–cultural identity central to this chapter.

*Enka* is a product of the 1970s. Although music and texts are drawn from prewar Japanese sentimental ballads, *enka* became reconfigured as a genre ('genrified') in the 1970s as a particularly Japanese form of popular music, to be pitted against popular music influenced more strongly from Euro-America. What was previously all considered *ryūkōka* ('popular song') became divided into two major divisions: (1) *enka* ('Japanese' songs) and (2) *poppusu* (Euro-American-derived songs). It does not matter that the instruments accompanying *enka* are by and large Western, although there may be an occasional *shakuhachi* (Japanese bamboo end-blown flute) or *shamisen* (Japanese plucked lute) added for 'flavour'; nor does it matter that the harmonic form is basically a Western import. What matters far more is the belief, fuelled and reinforced by the music industry, that the genre is quintessentially Japanese. One critical aspect of this Japaneseness is emotion – in particular longing – as well as the highly gendered situations in which emotion is invoked. Through emotion and gender, *enka* becomes known as 'song of Japan', expressive of the 'heart/soul of Japanese'.

Consumption of this 'song of Japan' is limited, but continuing. At the end of the 1990s, *enka* accounts for less than 1 per cent of the market share of recordings sold in Japan annually. Characteristically, this is not youth culture, but the culture of older consumers. Moreover, *enka* carries with it the reputation of being particularly popular in the more conservative segments of the population: rural (outside of Tokyo) dwellers and blue-collar workers. This stereotype ignores the many white-collar salarymen who fill the karaoke establishments of Tokyo in the after-hours with the heartfelt sounds of *enka*. It also ignores the many urban housewives who patronize karaoke booths during the day, singing the songs of their favourite *enka* singers.

One of *enka*'s largest boosters is NHK (Nihon Hōsō Kyōkai – Japan Broadcasting Corporation), Japan's state-sponsored media magnate, which devotes a significant portion of its regular and special programming to *enka*. This includes live radio shows, televised weekly musical shows, and the annual year-end all-star televised music extravaganza, the *Kōhaku Uta Gassen* (Red and White Song Contest). The *Kōhaku*, a benchmark of the music industry and a yearly ritual for viewers,[2] never fails to include *enka* songs and singers, especially in the latter, more prestigious half of the programme.

*Enka* is the 'song of Japan' not by accident, but by design, produced by culture industries, and supported by state institutions such as NHK. This form of national culture, however, more than other forms, is met with contention and dissent. Part of that dissent comes from the ways in which *enka* becomes linked with class culture: what are considered working-class excesses of emotion, melodrama, formula-driven expressions and gender constructions are critiqued in particular by intellectuals who uphold, by contrast, disciplined control and rationality. Other sources of dissent come from *enka*'s linkages with generational culture: older adult culture's reification of past values, expressions and gender roles are critiqued in particular by youth (see Miller, this volume, Chapter 3). Yet other sources of dissent come from *enka*'s linkages with regional culture: a constructed sense of rural culture as harbinger of old-fashioned, conservative ways and ideas is critiqued in particular by many urbanites (see Creed and Ching 1997). Yet *enka*'s production centres lie in the cities of Japan, especially Tokyo, and many of its urban fans avidly consume *enka* as a nostalgized form of rurality, as an aural, emotional, national–cultural rootedness.

Fraught with ironies, contradictions and contentions, amidst the threat of youth culture, globalization and a continually shrinking share of the market in Japan, *enka* retains its place not mystically, but through the direct interventions of a music industry committed to keeping the genre afloat. *Enka* remains viable through special record industry awards for the genre, karaoke activities specifically targetting the genre, and commercial and NHK broadcasts on radio and television. The industry is controlled primarily by older men, which is not surprising in a country known for its public male dominance. It is also an industry which has historically developed links with both the national government and international corporations.

## Constructing gender in performance

*Enka*'s highly gendered, heterosexual and homosocial world for men (but not women) rests upon stereotypical formulae of masculinity and femininity. The formulae create a code of gender, whose very patternedness makes gender separable from the biology of its players. The unmooring of masculinities from men's bodies suggests that anyone may perform them. Indeed, one of the hallmarks of *enka* is the acceptability of crossed performances, even as the integrity of the singly-sexed body is retained. That is, more often than not, men's songs are performed by biological males, and women's songs by biological females. However, men's songs performed by biological females, and women's songs performed by biological males, are not uncommon or necessarily associated with same-sex practices.

In the following, I discuss masculinities at three interactive levels of song, performance and performer. Following de Lauretis (1987), I consider the apparatuses by which pluralized masculinities (and singular femininity) in *enka* are constructed and performed as technologies of gender (see Butler 1990; Robertson 1998).

At the level of song, technologies include text and music. Song texts themselves are gendered, typically sung in the first person. The maleness and femaleness of a song text may be determined by the language of the speaker and the situation of the song. Because of the heteronormativity of the *enka mise en scène*, gendered expressions (e.g. pronouns, sentence endings, 'soft, indirect'/female versus 'abrupt, direct'/male speech patterns) and overt information (e.g. lamenting over one's lover being 'someone else's wife') typically make the gender coding of a song fairly unambiguous. Of the 115 songs I analysed from the 1950s to the 1990s, 33 are men's songs and 76 are women's songs.[3]

Musically, men's and women's songs show great overlap and are often stylistically indistinguishable. However, when they diverge, men's songs more than women's have the following traits: (1) major keys; (2) faster, harder-driving rhythms (some borrowed from rock music), and (3) use of non-semantic vocalizations, such as grunts and shouts.

Technologies of gender at the level of performance include lighting, stage effects, costuming and bodily movement. Men in *enka* stand in contrast to mainstream salarymen, but not nearly so much as the contrast between women in *enka* and the urban housewife. That is, although both men and women in *enka* are imaged as distant from contemporary peers, women are drawn as especially remote from life at the beginning of the twenty-first century. In general, performances by male singers tend to be less theatrical and dramatic than those by female singers. Stages for female performers often feature out-of-the-ordinary lighting and effects, especially that of manufactured fog, which conveys a sense of a dream world. The female singer, more than the male singer, wears kimono, an out-of-the-ordinary costume in contemporary Japan. She appears in glittery gowns and dresses as well, but these typically evoke a kind of fantasy female, even in Western dress. The female performer may strike dramatic poses while singing or punctuate her performance with small dance-like movements.[4]

By contrast, stages, lighting and costuming for male performers tend to be more subdued and less theatrical. Male performers typically sing wearing Western suits or tuxedoes, mimicking the gender divide of the late nineteenth and early twentieth century when men, but not women, were exhorted to adopt Western clothes in a public exhibition of modernity. In those fewer instances where male singers wear kimono or *hakama* (formal traditional male costume), the performance itself becomes a signifier for 'Japanese tradition', often accompanied by other icons such as *matsuri* (festival), cherry blossoms and sword fights. In other words, whereas wearing kimono is the performing norm for females, traditional costuming marks a man's performance with special significance. Costuming, lighting, staging and movement place *enka* women in a dream world far more distant from her contemporaries than *enka* men from theirs.

Male singers tend to restrict their movements to few gestures, even while vocally expressive, suggesting great bodily control. Clad in suits, standing with little motion upon a relatively simple stage, male *enka* singers are striking by their very unspectacularity. This is not necessarily to say that they are less performative, but that masculinities on the *enka* stage are noticeably unremarkable, even ordinary.

At the level of performers, record company producers have no prescriptive physical order for males, as they do for females. Whereas prospective female singers may be selected in part for their approximation to facial and bodily standards made popular by *enka bijin* (female *enka* singers known for their beauty; also known as *kimono bijin*/kimono beauty),[5] no such comparable normative category exists for male singers. Men on the *enka* stage include a wide range of faces and bodies, many of them remarkably unremarkable. One might consider this an oblique comment on Ortner's well-known, much-debated formulation linking women with nature and men with culture (1996; see also Gilmore 1990). Whereas Ortner's equation refers to the power men often yield in creating and controlling culture, this Japanese example shows another domain, that of performance, in which precisely because women may be equated with nature, they must be culturalized in order to be controlled. Women, more than men, are constantly made and re-made as art or artifice. Conversely, men, more than women, need far less making.

At the levels of performer and performance, the unremarkable male *enka* singer doing unremarkable things with his body on stage makes just this point. His facial expression (or lack thereof), clothing and presentational style are the unmarked elements in performance (see Phelan 1993), making a mundane performance not only acceptable, but, according to several fans I spoke with, even virtuous. One middle-aged female fan spoke glowingly of the stoicism and seriousness (*majime*) of her favourite male singer. He performed that seriousness by presenting songs in a straightforward manner – that is, not embellished with overt physical expression or stage patter. She contrasted his rather stoic, even solemn performance style with the facile, talkative showiness of another male *enka* singer considered to be his rival. In her interpretation, within these competing masculinities, the solemn performer is the one who is more honest and therefore praiseworthy. What she does not say, however, is whether that praise is particularly gendered: in other words, does seriousness become a man but not a woman? Do Japanese *enka* audiences expect not only more, but also different kinds of theatricality from performances by a female singer than a male one?

A comparison of publicity photos of male and female singers suggests that this may be the case.[6] Whereas women are photographed at acute angles, from the side, from above, their bodies turning, their eyes downcast or gazing into the distance, men are photographed more often straight on or from slightly below to enhance their stature. They look directly into the camera more often than women, or sometimes gaze at a point above the lens (placing the camera below the eye level of the man). Men's bodies are positioned in straight lines: arms down at the sides, weight evenly distributed between both legs. Women's bodies, on the other hand, turn and twist gracefully: head cocked, limbs curving inward upon themselves, one hand touching an *obi* (sash) or collar of a kimono, knees slightly bent, feet pigeon-toed with one foot on scant tiptoe. I speak here dichotomously to overemphasize the binariness which the visual language makes clear. The code is binary (masculine versus feminine), even if the recombinations of the elements of the codes are multiple. These recombinations include the frank, freely acceptable cross-gendered performances mentioned previously.

The contrast lies not only in men to women, but in multiple masculinities to a narrower, even singular version of femininity in *enka* songs and their performances.[7] Because *enka* derives from a male-centred frame with predominantly male pro-ducers, directors, composers and lyricists, its female characters, songs and singers become products and projections of male desire. As a result, the range of acceptable femaleness is far narrower than the plurality with which maleness is approached. At the level of song, women may include mothers, lovers, bar hostesses and prostitutes, but all share in common their suffering. They, in effect, become one in the conditions of their suffering: lovers who leave them, impossible affairs, one-night stands, sons long gone. These women suffer incessantly, without recourse, not necessarily through any fault of their own, but because suffering is structural to patterned situations, characters and expectations. Suffering for women becomes a one-note song.

*Enka* constructs its men at the levels of song, performance and performer with greater range and complexity. Whereas women are physicalized into a single ideal (whether or not that ideal is always met), and culturalized as patterned emotion, men are drawn within a range of types. There are not only the masculine stereotypes of *kōha* (tough guy) and *nanpa* (romantic) of which Buruma writes (1984: 143; Gilmore 1990: 187–8; Henshall 1999: 2–5), but also combinations and internal contradictions of these two. The same Kyūshū man of the sea who beats the drums wildly, 'weeps as a man weeps' (*'otoko naki suru'*, from *'Abare-daiko'*/Wild Drums; lyrics by Taka Takashi, music by Inomata Kōshō, 1987). The sailor who prefers 'warm *sake* (alcohol), grilled squid and women who do not say too much' sheds tears which spill over (*'namida ga porori to koboretara'*, from *'Funa-Uta'*/Sailor's Song; lyrics by Aku Yū, music by Hama Keisuke, 1979).[8] Several *enka* songs genderize the particularities of emotion, singing of the 'tears of a man' (*'otoko no namida'*), the 'crying of a man' (*'otoko naki suru'*), lubricated with 'men's *sake*' (*'otoko-zake'*).

Other men's *enka* songs sing of celebration. In the song *'Shiawase-zake'* (Celebratory *Sake*; lyrics by Takada Naokazu, music by Tomita Katsuji, 1991), a father celebrates the marriage of his son. *'Otoko-bore'* (Admiration between Men; lyrics by Hoshino Tetsurō, music by Inomata Kōshō, 1992) glorifies the long-lasting power of men's homosocial bonds, drawn over many cups of *sake*, more noble than fleeting heterosexual ties with women. Patriarchal desires express themselves most strongly in familial attachments of brother to brother, son to father, father to sons. The song *'Kyōdai-bune'* (Ship of Brothers; lyrics by Hoshino Tetsurō, music by Funamura Tōru, 1982)[9] sings of fishermen-brothers working together, the pride of their father, bound to one another by blood which runs 'hot' (*'atsui kono chi wa'*) across generations. Daughters come and go in this extended patriarchy; sons are those who stay.[10]

Some men characterize themselves ruefully as 'selfish men' (*'wagamama bakari no otoko'* from *'Nukumori'*/Warmth, lyrics by Miura Yasuteru, music by Kanō Gendai, 1992); others sing of their devotion to friends, lovers and mothers. Rarely do men sing of devotion to their wives. Some men's songs sing close to the moral fibre of the community. For example, the song *'Senshū Harukikō'* (Osaka Harbour; lyrics by Mozu Shōhei, music by Funamura Tōru, 1992) sings from the point of view of an aged fisherman, one of five sons, who exhorts his fellow fishermen to live life with dignity (*'Dosshiri ikiro!'*).

This multiplicity of masculinities in *enka* suggest that there is no singular 'he'. Rather, there are many 'hes', some within the same person, each particularized as part of a complex of masculinities, public and private, at work and at play, pulled by conflicting ties. At the level of performer, the *enka* man may be short and squat, as easily as tall and thin, and neither physical form adds or detracts from his maleness. Unlike a woman, who, by *enka* standards, may become more 'womanly' by her approximation to a physical 'kimono-ideal', a man does not necessarily become more manly by inhabiting a particular kind of body or dress. Rather, manliness inheres within a range of bodies and attire, relying instead on non-physical, spiritual qualities.

*Enka* songs sing of *otoko-michi* (the path of a man) as a man's passionate devotion to a cause. The song entitled *'Otoko-Michi'* (lyrics by Fukuda Yoshio, music by Tomita Katsuji, 1991) sings of a man's commitment to a dream etched in his heart. He is one who lives by fighting spirit (*konjō*) alone, pursuing his 'path' without tears or regrets. Although some songs place male heroes in the seat of power, more typically in *enka* a man becomes publicly virtuous in basing his actions upon loyalty not to a master or group, but to his individual convictions (see Morris 1975). In this way, he refutes Buruma's and Gilmore's characterization of both *kōha* and *nanpa* Japanese masculinity, both of which are bound by their strong sense of duty to the group, whether family, nation or business (Buruma 1984: 162; Gilmore 1990: 199). The convictions of the *enka* man's path/*michi* tend to go against, not with, the grain of society. He is the rebel rather than the citizen, torn between the duties and obligations of society, as opposed to his internal feelings and beliefs. Following pre-modern plots of kabuki, *bunraku* (puppet plays) and narrative ballads, *enka* men struggle between *giri* (duty, obligation to the group) and *ninjō* (individual, personal feelings). The masculine figure thus becomes a meta-narrative for acts against the public grain, a disruption to the smooth and harmonious ordering of society, purposely distanced from the community, the public and the nation. One may harp on Ortner's male–female/culture–nature dichotomy again and find contrast here. *Enka* man-as-rebel represents untamed nature, rather than orderly culture which Ortner would have us expect.

Not all *enka* constructions of masculinity are of this form of noble, rebellious virility. As several song lyrics attest, 'to be strong is not all there is to being a man'. In one instance, an *enka* man celebrates public ideals of loyalty (often to his own 'path'), perseverance, endurance and strength. In another instance, he bares his weaknesses in heartbreak, admitting his indiscretions. He sings of both the hometown and the mother for which he yearns and the lover from whom he is parted. He may be publicly virile, forceful and potent, while privately vulnerable. If *amae* (dependency system) requires a dyad of activities and persons (*amaeru*/to depend; *amayakasu*/to be depended upon), then he places himself in the position of one who does *amaeru*, who relies upon the benevolent support of dependable others (Doi 1973; Lebra 1976: 54–5). The public rebel in this way becomes the private child, locked into a dependent relationship with the women who surround him, who do *amayakasu* in indulging him by their actions: lover, mother, bar hostess (or owner, often referred to by customers as 'mama'), prostitute. This form of masculinity rests in the ability to depend, even as others look to depend upon him. He shifts and slides from role to role: in private and for particular individual needs, he may *amaeru*; in public and serving the group's needs or his own principles, he may *amayakasu*. This alternating show of heart within a relationship of dependency gives greater complexity to the construction of maleness.

This is not to say that all masculinities carry the same kinds of cultural value. As Connell points out, different masculinities within a single cultural frame constitute their own internal gender politics of inclusion, exclusion, intimidation and exploitation (1995: 37). The contrast this chapter explores, then, lies not only in male versus female, or multiple masculinities versus singular femininity, but also in competing masculinities within one cultural frame. The internal gender politics of masculinities in *enka* lies within issues of class, region and history, even as they embed themselves within the umbrella concept of the nation.

## Masculinities and the nation

This complex of masculinities occurs within the larger framework of Japan itself. *Enka*, the 'song of Japan', sings to no less than the 'man (or men) of Japan'. Each song, each performance, each performer provides a public lesson on not only what it means to be a man (or men), but in particular what it means to be a Japanese man. This comes within an ongoing public discourse of Japaneseness, constructed in large part through contrast with Euro-America.[11] This is manhood created not only by negation of femalehood, but also by negation of Western-hood.

One of the most pervasive ties of masculinities in *enka* to the nation is through the figure of mother, the *amayakasu* half of the *amae* dyad. If, as Ortner and Whitehead suggest (1981: 21), one or another different relational role tends to dominate gender categories, then in the case of *enka*, that relational role is of a son. Being a son permanently and emotionally ties an *enka* man not only to his mother, but also to the hometown he has long left, and thereby to the nation of hometowns called Japan (Yano 1999).

In a hit song such as '*Miso Shiru no Uta*' (Song of Miso Soup; lyrics and music by Nakayama Daizaburō, 1980), a man is defined as one who is always and forever a son yearning, even crying, for his mother's breast. He wears traditional Japanese clothes (especially *fundoshi*, loincloth), drinks Japanese soup (miso soup), sleeps on a Japanese futon and upholds what are defined as Japanese values and traditions. He chooses to live amidst physical hardship in the rural heartland, the northeast of Japan, rather than in the upscale neighbourhoods of Tokyo.[12] This song is sung by Sen Masao, a man indeed originally from the rural north, dressed in tuxedo, his hair at times in his career drawn back in a very untraditional ponytail.

Sen's biggest hit, '*Kitaguni no Haru*' (Spring in the North Country; lyrics by Idehaku, music by Endō Minoru, 1977), has been one of *enka*'s most successful exports throughout Asia. The earnings from that song and others enabled the singer to live a highly publicized cosmopolitan life, with a blonde wife (now divorced), home in Hong Kong and series of dramatic financial successes and failures. This 'son of Japan' profitably sings of traditional Japan even as he leads a life markedly distant from it. While a song such as '*Miso Shiru no Uta*' sings like a textbook on masculinity and the nation, its performance and performer may be seen within an ironic, multilayered frame. Here is Sen, the cosmopolitan country bumpkin, performing this song on the NHK stage, as well as Sen, the rural 'exotic', still sporting the wart in the middle of his forehead which marks him as a man of the countryside,[13] even while dressed in a tuxedo.

Another *enka* hit, '*Matsuri*' (Festival; lyrics by Nakanishi Rei, music by Hara Jōji, 1984), glorifies men in their production of crops, their spirit and Japan itself. The song celebrates young men who till the soil, as well as men of the sea, both of whom work in cooperation with the gods to produce the means by which a community may survive. These men work hard and play hard, living life as the spiritual and economic mainstays of this nation of villages. '*Matsuri*' celebrates this version of masculinity in what it calls a 'festival of Japan'. In its nostalgic glorification of men and gods, the song ignores the considerable work of women in the rice paddies of Japan, as well as the increasing mechanization of crop production and harvest. Musically, this song invokes a masculinist spirit with its electric guitar and driving rock beat. The performer of this song is Kitajima Saburō, once banned from the NHK stage for his connections to *yakuza* (gangsters), but here placed at the pinnacle of that same stage. His long, successful career in the *enka* world (debuting in 1962) authorizes his role as the representative man of Japan, singing, 'The life of a man is one of sweat and tears. I am living to the fullest. This is a festival of Japan!'[14] He performed this song not only in NHK's famous end-of-year 'Red and White Song Contest' of 1993, but within that show in its most prestigious *tori* (finale) position amidst familiar national icons of cherry blossoms, female festival dancers and the rising sun printed on fans. Again, one finds ironies, not within the song, but in its performer and performative frames.

Where do these representations of masculinities come from? *Enka*'s reputation as blue-collar (see Roberson, this volume, Chapter 8), peasant and rural expression draws upon gendered constructions from these very segments of the population. The masculinities upheld in *enka* perform underclass representations. It is worth noting who is not generally present in these songs: the salaryman, managers, landowners, politicians – in other words, those who control the large companies and upper political echelons of Japan today.[15] Instead, the songs present a range of male 'others', normally excluded from the international Japan Inc. picture. These include farmers, sailors, fishermen, day labourers (see Gill, this volume, Chapter 9), itinerant workers (*dekasegi*) and *yakuza*. At the level of song, these men within the *mise en scène* of *enka* occupy 'other Japans', even as the singers at the level of performance sing clad in the attire of those within official power structures. The ironies of the stage render the invisible ('other Japans') visible, while simultaneously dressing them in acceptable forms.

These 'other men' become representations expressing the 'heart/soul of Japanese' both by their difference as well as by their commonality. The discourse of *enka* asserts that these men may be different on the outside, but just like men of mainstream Japan (i.e. salaryman) on the inside. The men of *enka* can be representatives because they are just like the 'us' of mainstream Japan. More importantly, men of mainstream Japan are just like them. Here is the 'warrior' aspect of the corporate warrior idiom, retrieved from blue-collar, peasant, rural gender expressions. *Enka* presents the warrior/farmer/itinerant worker who is supposed to lurk just beneath the suit and tie of the salaryman, even as presented on stage in suit and tie. The salaryman by day, in effect, borrows and even recuperates masculinities from these underclass representations through his night-time singing of *enka* at karaoke. The corporate warrior in this interpretation remains an emasculated shell of pencil-pushing activity by day, waiting to be re-masculinized through song or sex by night (see Allison 1994). In this way, privileging masculinities borrowed from 'other Japans' is but the flip side of asserting nativized masculinities of the salaryman mainstream.

Class-embedded and regional practices such as *dekasegi* and working at sea help define practical representations of masculinity which subvert deeply held cultural values and norms of rootedness by its very itinerancy (see Gill, this volume, Chapter 9). Wandering gains cultural legitimacy through *dekasegi*[16] and working at sea. In contradiction to the relationship of men and women to the kinship structure discussed earlier, men here are those who physically come and go, while women stay. Through *dekasegi* they come and go not by individual whim but for the economic benefit of the group, even while their itinerancy produces emotional hardship.

These are not only class and regional issues, but temporal ones as well. Nativized masculinities of the underclass locate the past in the present. The authority of these recuperated masculinities lies in their power to invoke the distant past: this is who we were and still are. The critical message these male characters perform is that Japan, a nation which has undergone tremendous political, social and economic upheavals since the nineteenth century, has not fundamentally changed.

*Enka* singers have been reconstructed and sometimes construct themselves as repositories of 'traditional Japan'. Both male and female singers perform in serial *jidai-geki* (period dramas) on television (typically NHK), building upon their image as men and women from and of the past. Top-ranked singers also perform in month-long engagements at theatres in Tokyo, Osaka and other cities. These feature both a *jidai-geki* and a concert. During the period drama, the *enka* singer appears as a character in pre-modern Japan, often complete with sword fighting. These period pieces link *enka* closely with *taishū engeki* (mass theatre), an itinerant populist theatre form which uses this same combination of period drama and song show. As analysed by Ivy (1995), *taishū engeki* is an example of a cultural form from the margins of twentieth-century Japan, which gets co-opted by the mainstream as a means of recuperating and consuming the past and distant. I suggest here that *enka* participates in this process as well, but with greater accessibility because of its mass media exposure and state institution support.

Some men's actions in *enka* do not support the stability of social structures, but undermine them. Like the practical representations of Malay men in Michael Peletz's study (1995), some men in *enka* are less reasonable, less responsible than women and elite, failing to honour basic social obligations associated with marriage, parents and kinship generally. They are not the glue that holds society together; instead they pose constant threats. Other men in *enka*, however, represent the stable social structure. They till the soil, fish the seas and form the centrepiece of household productivity. These competing masculinities provide both the structure (as creators, as on-stage dominance) and the anti-structure (as individuals challenging the structure).

Dorinne Kondo's recent work on the fashion world of Japanese designers presents another kind of Japanese masculinity which asserts itself as a progressive challenge to Western hegemonies (1997: 168–9). In contrast to Japanese fashion's affluent, young, urban Japanese masculinity chic (see also Miller, this volume, Chapter 3), the masculinities of the *enka* world present a different set of nativized genderings, retrogressively looking back rather than forward. Here are masculinities situated within nostalgic retreat on a number of axes: pitted against Euro-American hegemony, against salaryman lifestyles, against Japanese femininity, against globalizing cultures, including Japan's own youth. The complex of masculinities asserted by *enka*'s technologies of gender forms a preserve of the past in the present. The boundary that *enka* inscribes is as much about defining what is within as keeping at bay what is without.

# Conclusion

In closing, let me reiterate some of the contentions with which I initially embedded *enka* as a genre. *Enka*'s many critics heatedly disentangle the music from the nation. For them, *enka* is anachronistically old-fashioned, even feudal, ignoring present-day realities. How can this be 'Japan' when so little of it connects to many people's lives? These lessons of masculinities and the nation, therefore, often fall upon unheeding ears.

For its older fans, as well as state institutions such as NHK, however, the distance between the Japan of *enka* and that of everyday surroundings creates exactly the gap to be filled in by nostalgia (see Robertson 1997). The Japan of *enka* is one which still makes sense to them, and therefore which makes sense of them. *Enka* gives these particular lives validity, not necessarily as farmers, fishermen or itinerant workers (although some may be), but as men and women of Japan who feel passionately, cry easily and understand the vagaries of hardship and suffering. It matters far less what people specifically do, than what people feel. Feeling gives meaning to these gendered lives.

The rebels of the anti-structure work within this frame. Driven by how they feel, their actions challenge the stability of the social order. Elevating these men glorifies not the bureaucrat who follows commands, but the individual with initiative and drive. As the film critic Richard Dyer suggests, the image of the rebel on screen and stage points to the 'legitimacy of rebellion or its inadequacy' (1998: 53). In the case of *enka*, rebellion becomes ennobled, not through the failure that Ivan Morris asserts (1975), but through the passion which fuels it. Passion shades masculinities into heroisms of the national heart, even those – perhaps especially those – whose actions challenge the legitimacy of society. The social and political order take a back seat to what many songs sing of as the 'flame' which burns as individual passion, as masculine desire in a public forum.

The 'burning' of men galvanizes their positions, as well as threatens the very order of the nation-state. These are not mainstream salaryman masculinities, but masculinities drawn from the margins of space, time and society (see Ivy 1995). Instead, they are rebels who recuperate that desire as national expression. The margins become the very source from which men of the mainstream are said to recover their own nativized masculinites. This is a 'song of Japan' which simultaneously upholds and challenges the stability of the community by laying laurels at its margins.

This complex of masculinities suggests that, rather than the form that order takes, it is the processes which create and maintain individual involvement that are important for the nation. Those processes carry their own double-edged sword: loyalty to one's ideals may stand in direct conflict with loyalty to one's family, community or nation. The long-standing battle between *giri* (duty, obligation) and *ninjō* (human feelings, individual passion) played out in centuries-old dramas in Japan remains at a stand-off. *Otoko-michi* raises the possibility of both public acclaim and censure, depending on the path one chooses.

Passion, however, disregards the specificities of paths and choices, pointing instead directly to *kokoro* (heart, mind, soul), the cultural dead end of questionings. If one acts with *kokoro*, with seriousness of intent and sincerity of purpose, then that justifies, even aestheticizes, any action.[17] The lessons of *enka* boil down to this: *kokoro* is the heroic seat of individual actions, masculinities and the nation. It is here that the contradictions of rebels and nations, of loyalties divided, of *giri* and *ninjō*, of songs and performances, are laid to rest. Invoking *kokoro* spreads a cultural blanket of ambiguity, 'wrapping' tensions, struggles and ironies within layers which go beyond presentation and politeness (see Hendry 1993). The blanket answers all questions, even while maintaining the contradictions.

Passion-filled masculinities shaped around *kokoro* perform this 'song of Japan' with its contradictions unchallenged. The challenging goes on elsewhere, outside the frame of *enka*, as part of life in Japan in the late twentieth and early twenty-first centuries. *Enka*'s nostalgized expressions sound familiar, and this in itself draws listeners, some in retreat from a world which has become increasingly unfamiliar and bewildering. This is music which deliberately invokes the past and the distant, even when accompanied by electric guitars, even when sung by singers in tuxedo. *Enka* – its masculinities, its emotions, its nationhood – shows one refraction of Japan intact, hard at work in the practices of its own imagining.

## Notes

1  Part of the question of identity revolves around the shifting, ambivalent attitudes in Japan toward 'the West', characterized variously as admiration and disdain, envy and contempt, infatuation and fear. In many spheres of consumption, Japan and Euro-America still coexist not as elements to be mixed in a soup of hybridity, but as oil-and-water fundamental differences. One makes a consumer choice to lodge in a Japanese inn or Western hotel, to squat above a Japanese toilet or sit on a Western one, even as these two are placed in adjacent stalls at a train station, to eat rice for breakfast or bread. (When people in Japan meet me, a Japanese-American, they often ask me what I have for breakfast, rice or bread, making the food I choose a way of understanding who I am *vis-à-vis* the hyphenated identity. Likewise, a middle-aged Japanese housewife in Aomori characterized her husband for me as one who will only eat rice for breakfast, and will not touch bread.)

It does not matter that what may be considered Japanese by many (for example, tempura) may have European (Portuguese) roots; or that what may be considered Western (for example, spaghetti) may have Asian connections. What matters is the kinds of meanings and categories in place, the continuing concern with markers of distinctiveness. The presence of these choices suggests multilinear paths to coexisting modernities.

2  Begun as a radio show in 1951 and moving successfully to television in late 1953, the *Kōhaku*, as it is commonly known, reached its peak of popularity in the 1960s and 1970s, with ratings as high as 70 to 80 per cent. Since that period, its popularity has declined to approximately 50 per cent, which still warrants its status as a New Year's viewing ritual in Japan (Schilling 1997: 94–8).

3  I derived the corpus from a compilation of the following: (1) songs performed from July 1992 to July 1993 on the television show '*Enka no Hanamichi*', the only programme dedicated solely to *enka*; (2) most frequently requested songs in karaoke from August 1992 to August 1993 as compiled by *Karaoke Fan*; (3) top-selling *enka* songs from August 1992 to August 1993 compiled by Oricon (the Japanese equivalent of America's *Billboard*); (4) 1992 and 1993 editions of yearly song compilations by *enka* composer and singing teacher Mr Noda Hisashi; (5) songs taught by composer/teacher Mr Ichikawa Shōsuke in the NHK series '*Karaoke Enka Kahō-hō*' from 1991 to 1993; and (6) 1992 listing of 100 most

popular karaoke songs compiled by Nihon Amachua Kayō Renmei (Japanese Amateur Singing Federation).

    I left the determination of which are men's and which women's songs to older Japanese informants. In the corpus, I found agreement on all but two songs, which I subsequently labelled 'gender ambiguous'. The other songs in the corpus not discussed here are duets.

4  The sense of posing, but not the poses themselves, recalls the *mie* (patterned poses which highlight particular dramatic moments) of *kabuki*.

5  Record producers make clear that *enka* singers, both male and female, must at minimum be musically proficient. *Enka* is, by both producers' and consumers' accounts, a music genre first, and an image-driven visual genre second. This is not to say that image is unimportant, but that musical talent and expressivity lie foremost in the selection of new singers.

    It is also important to point out that not all female *enka* singers meet these standards.

6  The following generalizations are based upon publicity photos published in *Enka Jānaru*, the leading *enka* fan magazine, from May 1989 to November 1994.

7  These axes intersect as well with other discursively constructed, embedded binaries of difference: Japanese versus non-Japanese (within that, Asian versus 'Western' [within that, 'white' versus 'black']).

8  '*Funa-Uta*' is an example of a man's song made famous by a female singer, Yashiro Aki, who performs the song typically clad in pink gown and tiara.

9  The song '*Kyōdai-bune*' is sung by Toba Ichirō, a male singer whose image is built on coming from a fisherman's family and having a brother who is also an *enka* singer. The two brothers sometimes perform together, not as a duo, but as a two-man concert.

10  The permanency of sons varies by position in the family. Because the system honours primogeniture, the eldest son is the most permanent member who theoretically inherits all the assets and responsibilities of the household. Junior sons may set up related households. By contrast, daughters leave their natal household to join their husband's household.

11  See note 1, above. See Tobin (1992) for further discussions of Japan and its shifting relationship with things from the West.

12  Northeastern Honshū is constructed as a distant homeland subject to severe winters and famine. It is also a repository of 'traditional culture' including shamanism (Ivy 1995) and *shamisen* (lute) virtuoso playing.

13  Unlike most entertainers in Euro-America, *enka* singers generally do not remove moles or warts from their faces or straighten their teeth. Instead, these become signifiers of their rural origins. The degree to which these elements do signify the rural in Japan is no better seen than in celebrated animator Miyazaki Hayao's 1988 feature film, *Tonari no Totoro* (*My Neighbour Totoro*). In the film, the old peasant woman of the countryside who befriends the city children is drawn as short, squat, brown-skinned and with a wart dead centre on her forehead. Sen's wart is positioned exactly as hers.

14  Translation by author.

15  This holds true in general not only for *enka*, but also for other popular music genres.

16  See Yoshida's (1981) analysis on themes of the wanderer in Japanese folk mythology and its relationship to deities, strangers and the general concept of outsider.

17  In my conversation with a sushi chef in Tokyo, he explained that the key ingredient in good sushi was the *kokoro* of the maker. See Moeran (1986: 72–4) for an analysis of *kokoro* as a keyword in various settings within Japanese life, including advertising, pottery and baseball.

# References

Allison, A. (1994) *Nightwork: Sexuality, Pleasure and Corporate Masculinity in a Tokyo Hostess Club*, Chicago: University of Chicago Press.

90   *Christine R. Yano*

Buruma, I. (1984) *Behind the Mask: On Sexual Demons, Sacred Mothers, Transvestites, Gangsters, Drifters and Other Japanese Cultural Heroes*, New York: Pantheon Books.

Butler, J. (1990) *Gender Trouble: Feminism and the Subversion of Identity*, London and New York: Routledge.

Connell, R.W. (1987) *Gender and Power*, Stanford: Stanford University Press.

—— (1995) *Masculinities*, Berkeley: University of California Press.

Creed, G. W. and Ching, B. (eds) (1997) *Knowing Your Place: Rural Identity and Cultural Hierarchy*, London and New York: Routledge.

de Lauretis, T. (1987) *Technologies of Gender*, Bloomington: Indiana University Press.

Doi, T. (1973) *The Anatomy of Dependence*, Tokyo: Kodansha International.

Dyer, R. (1998) *Stars*, London: British Film Institute Publishing.

Gilmore, D. D. (1990) *Manhood in the Making*, New Haven: Yale University Press.

Gutmann, M. (1996) *The Meanings of Macho: Being a Man in Mexico City*, Berkeley: University of California Press.

Hendry, J. (1993) *Wrapping Culture: Politeness, Presentation and Power in Japan and Other Societies*, Oxford: Clarendon Press.

Henshall, K. G. (1999) *Dimensions of Japanese Society: Gender, Margins and Mainstream*, New York: St Martin's Press.

Ivy, M. (1995) *Discourses of the Vanishing: Modernity, Phantasm, Japan*, Chicago: University of Chicago Press.

Kimmel, M. (1987) *Changing Men: New Directions in Research on Men and Masculinity*, Thousand Oaks: Sage.

Kondo, D. (1997) *About Face: Performing Race in Fashion and Theater*, London and New York: Routledge.

Lebra, T. S. (1976) *Japanese Patterns of Behavior*, Honolulu: University Press of Hawaii.

Moeran, B. (1986) 'Individual, group and *seishin*: Japan's internal cultural debate', in T. S. Lebra and W. P. Lebra (eds) *Japanese Culture and Behavior: Selected Readings* (2nd edn), Honolulu: University of Hawaii Press.

Morris, I. (1975) *The Nobility of Failure: Tragic Heroes in the History of Japan*, New York: Holt, Rinehart and Winston.

Nosco, P. (1990) *Remembering Paradise: Nativism and Nostalgia in Eighteenth-Century Japan*, Cambridge, MA: Harvard University Press.

Ortner, S. (1996) *Making Gender: The Politics and Erotics of Culture*, Boston: Beacon Press.

Ortner, S. and Whitehead, H. (1981) 'Introduction: accounting for sexual meanings', in S. Ortner and H. Whitehead (eds) *Sexual Meanings: The Cultural Construction of Gender and Sexuality*, Cambridge: Cambridge University Press.

Peletz, M. (1995) 'Neither reasonable nor responsible: contrasting representations of masculinity in a Malay society', in A. Ong and M. G. Peletz (eds) *Bewitching Women, Pious Men: Gender and Body Politics in Southeast Asia*, Berkeley: University of California Press.

Phelan, P. (1993) *Unmarked: The Politics of Performance*, London and New York: Routledge.

Robertson, J. (1997) 'Empire of nostalgia: rethinking "internationalization" in Japan today', *Theory, Culture and Society* 14, 4: 97–122.

—— (1998) *Takarazuka: Sexual Politics and Popular Culture in Modern Japan*, Berkeley: University of California Press.

Schilling, M. (1997) *The Encyclopedia of Japanese Pop Culture*, New York: Weatherhill, Inc.

Tobin, J. J. (1992) *Re-made in Japan*, New Haven: Yale University Press.

Yano, C. (1999) 'Distant homelands: nation as place in Japanese popular song', in K. Yoshino (ed.) *Consuming Ethnicity and Nationalism: Asian Experiences*, Richmond, Surrey: Curzon Press.

Yoshida, T. (1981) 'The stranger as god: the place of the outsider in Japanese folk religion', *Ethnology* 20, 2: 87–99.

# 6 Of love and the marriage market

## Masculinity politics and Filipina–Japanese marriages in Japan

*Nobue Suzuki*

Transnational romances have always attracted the public gaze. In Japan, the increase of intermarriages since the mid-1980s has incited the curiosity of people at local, national and international levels. From 1992, when the Ministry of Health and Welfare began providing more detailed breakdowns by nationality, the formerly dominant place of intermarriages between ethnic Koreans in Japan and Japanese nationals was superseded by marriages between Filipino women (Filipinas) and Japanese men. These latter intermarriages continued to occupy first place until 1996 (Ministry of Health and Welfare 1993–2000).

When such relationships are discussed, it is usually the women who become the topics of popular and academic discourses, while the men have tended to remain stereotyped as over-aged, unattractive men who are rejected by local women and who 'take advantage' of their foreign wives. Contrary to such popular views, this chapter aims to provide more nuanced and complicated pictures of men who are married to Filipinas. The men's experiences demonstrate various forms of struggles over their masculine identities. In discussing these men, I suggest that banal compartmentalizations and the men's struggles are situated in the politics of masculine identity in changing Japanese society in the 1990s.

Intermarriage everywhere has long been considered taboo (Johnson and Warren 1994). However, not all intermarriages are equally problematic. In Japan, while Caucasian–Japanese marriages have often been viewed with admiration, envy and spite (e.g. Kamisaka 1999; Setouchi 1989), liaisons between Japanese and non-Japanese Asians (hereafter Asians) have often been representationally mocked. Metaphorically and physically, relations where the first world 'possesses' and 'penetrates' the third world have been 'a male power-fantasy', and the policing of such associations along racial–national lines evokes power struggles between states and between men (Said 1978). Incongruent views of Caucasian–Japanese and Asian–Japanese relations, which are historically contingent, articulate patterns of relative strength (see Ching 1998), and these intermarriages have thus come under differential social surveillance.

The choice of spouse reflects one's 'taste' and accordingly the spouse's class, race and nationality become important markers of difference in one's own social position (Bourdieu 1984: 108–9). In the case of Filipina–Japanese associations, images of the men are relatively unambiguous. On one hand, they are hypermasculinized as violent, and as predatory consumers of the sex and gender-based services of 'trafficked' women from the 'poor Third World' (Suzuki 2000b). On the other hand, resembling Japan's feudal *shi–nō–kō–shō* (samurai–farmers–artisans–merchants) hierarchy, they are demasculinized *nō–kō–shō* because they hold less economic and symbolic capital than urban 'corporate warriors' (*shi*), who are seldom found in representations of Filipina–Japanese marriages. In this scenario, the possibility of love and care being nurtured between the intermarried spouses tends to be denied, oppressing not only the husbands but also wives, who claim 'My husband is a good man!'

By reducing the whole range of their marital experiences to phallic desires satisfied by money and aggression and to disparaged manhood, Filipina–Japanese spouses have been cast into a category of 'international marriages' (*kokusai kekkon*), which is juxtaposed with the 'standard family' (*hyōjun kazoku*), consisting of a formally married Japanese couple living together with two children.[1] Although gradually declining in number, ethnic endogamies are presumed to be part of this 'standard' as they have been the vast majority. The discourse of sexual unions thus blurs other political aspects of the affective relationships and contested masculine identities involved in Filipina–Japanese intermarriages.

In this chapter, I explore masculinity politics in Japan's marriage market, defined as men's mobilization and struggles over the meanings of masculine gender and men's positions in gender relations (Connell 1995: 205). Gender consists of negotiated practices in complex hierarchical relations, which are most intense at the borders of cultures and nationalities (Ortner 1996). In this light, by seeking to locate what it negates, subordinates or valorizes by way of difference, I first inquire into the discursive marginalization of intermarried husbands' positions in the Japanese masculine hierarchy. The masculine experiences among Japanese men associated with Filipinas are imbricated within pervasive cultural ideologies, social institutions and capitalist discipline. These obscure and justify social practices and serve as conduits between oppressive macro-structural inequalities and micro-level power relations (Bourdieu 1984; Foucault 1980).

Next, I analyse the experiences of husbands of Filipinas residing in the Tokyo area, focusing on the meanings of masculine gender that these men have been seeking in their everyday lives. Thus far, the Japanese husbands' narratives have seldom appeared publicly, except by way of backgrounded contrast. The men's stories, however, demonstrate their individual differences. They also show that in the process of negotiating and performing male gender, the men transform their identities, thereby further complicating the category of men married to Filipinas. They also, however, ironically reproduce the dominant social schemes in which they enjoy privileges as men. I begin with an overview of the institutionalization of marriage along the axes of gender, sexuality, class and nationality and of the representations of men's positions in the masculine hierarchy in Japan.

## Men and marriage in capitalist Japan

The productivity of capitalist modernity requires that sex be regulated, and state technologies have thus demanded 'compulsory heterosexuality' and marriage

(Foucault 1980; Rich 1980). These not only require that women make themselves sexually available to men but are also forced upon men (Connell 1995). In Japan, marriage helps the state sustain its global economic domination and its welfare scheme, which the state has primarily relegated to individual households (Ida 1995). Although the continuing recession and changing gender relations in Japan in the 1990s have altered the meanings of marriage and family among younger people, social mechanisms have not yet substantially accommodated divergent values and lifestyles.

Social welfare and reproduction are still accomplished largely through the culturally endorsed gender roles. As in many other societies, a man's role is primarily financial, making him the household head. Wives are expected to keep their breadwinner husbands fit for work by performing housework. Gender division and hierarchy are reinforced through economic, social and psychological mechanisms and have shaped the 'structure of cathexis', or relationships around one's emotional attachment to another (Connell 1987: 111–12). This regime has spawned bifurcated spousal relationships, especially among the upper strata (Iwao 1993).

The labour market has intensified this gender division of labour within the household. Japan's seniority and lifetime employment systems secure workers' economic life;[2] however, behind these are supervisors' differentiating assessments of subordinates' performance (Ida 1998). Internationally criticized long hours of work are a consequence of workers' efforts to secure their supervisor's favourable assessments, which turn the workers into 'company-domesticated animals' (*shachiku*). In order to respond to the demands made by Japan's capitalist discipline, men are compelled to marry so that they can relegate reproductive work at home to their (presumably Japanese) wives. To facilitate marriage for men, many leading companies maintain contacts with marriage bureaux (Yoshida 1990). Once married, men are rewarded with various forms of compensation for the support of their families. In 1990, for example, 88.2 per cent of all corporations and 91.4 per cent of those employing more than 500 workers gave family allowances (Ida 1995: 220). When both spouses are full-time workers, usually the husband receives this benefit. Other social welfare schemes continue to privilege the 'standard' family (*Asahi Shinbun* 2000). Conversely, unwed men are categorized as 'youths' (*seinen*), and are often placed together with women at workplaces and excluded from important decision-making.

Men who do not form 'standard families' may receive negative sanction. For example, Hamamatsu, a manager at a large corporation, said that upon learning about his marriage to a Filipina, a client told him, 'You must be a fool!' Terami's supervisor lamented, 'You'll undergo hardships'. These men clarified to me that the client and supervisor thought that the husbands would be distracted from their work because their foreign wives were assumed to be 'unable to manage their households by themselves'.

Aside from the capitalization of gendered labour, state techniques have constituted marriage and subsequent procreation as inevitable and as granting 'full-fledged adulthood' (Ida 1995). Conversely, unmarried and non-procreating Japanese continue to be considered socially 'incompetent', 'incomplete' and 'irresponsible'.

Accordingly, as shown below, some of the intermarried husbands I interviewed gave primarily social reasons as their motivation for marrying Filipinas. Although the numbers of voluntarily single people and childless couples are increasing, the vast majority of Japanese marry and procreate by their forties in order to become 'real' adults (Itamoto 1992).

Through such social mechanisms, marriage in Japan becomes hegemonic. This gendered process yields economic and social 'dividends' especially to men (see Connell 1995).[3] However, such dividends are not equally distributed among all married men.

## Geopolitics and farmers

In the literature on Filipina–Japanese relationships, one of the most 'typical' groups of men are farmers in their mid-thirties to early forties who live in rural 'depopulated hamlets' and are facing the 'bride shortage' (NHK 1988). These men are often the heirs of *ie* (households) which demand the succession of gender-based roles within their residential premises. Within the *ie* institution, even newly married couples are expected to prioritize gendered household functions over affective spousal relations. Knowing these structural constraints, young Japanese women often leave rural villages for employment and marriage in cities and avoid marrying such heirs (Shukuya 1988). Consequently, since the succession of households is essential for the survival of their communities, local administrators in various areas have sought Asian women.

On the other hand, many rural heirs feel discouraged about proposing marriage to Japanese women because they are unsure whether as household 'heads' they can support their families. This uncertainty has essentially been caused by governmental neglect of rural development, simultaneously negative demands for primary industry – e.g. reduced rice production – and the freer market for agricultural products (NHK 1988). Moreover, the overpowering parental wish for *ie* succession by their own heirs has made such men feel discouraged about even searching for mates. Paying little attention to such economic and psychological consequences of Japan's modernization and institutional constraints, village administrators have blamed individual men for being 'unable to marry', 'unqualified' or 'lacking special abilities to find a spouse' (Imagawa 1990: 11, 219). One male marriage agent also lamented, 'There's no "man" in them!' (Sakuma 1997: 48).

Moreover, according to the prevailing popular rhetoric, Asian 'brides' have been 'imported to Japan to overcome the shortage of women' and there are substantial age gaps between the spouses (Matsui 1997: 136). Filipina–Japanese marriages therefore violate the sexual normativity of capitalist society based on monogamous, reproductive, same generation and non-commercial relationships (see Rubin 1984).[4] The opposites of these are considered 'bad' and 'unnatural'. Indeed, like many of his fellows, a rural man aged 36 who married an 18-year-old Filipina became intimidated, saying: 'At the end of a symposium [where I was a panellist], a man [came to] the stage and said to me, "at least I don't want to commit human trafficking"' (Shukuya 1988: 301). The capitalist logic of the 'market' deployed here has demonized these individuals and negated the possibility of affective relationships developing between spouses.

The assumption of rural farmers' 'commodification' of 'Filipina brides', moreover, masks the fact that many urban men who meet *Japanese* marriage candidates at matchmaking parties also leave the impression of 'shopping' for women, insisting on 'low cost', 'efficiency' and 'investment loss protection' (Itamoto 1992; Wakui 1990).[5] The mocking of de- or hypermasculinized farmers then takes on political implications and conceals broader issues in Japan's capitalist modernity and social institutions.

## Sex, race and 'bad' marriage

Urban centres may be more disdainful of Filipina–Japanese liaisons on moral grounds than are rural villages. Since the 1970s, numerous Filipinas have been working as '*Japayuki*' (Japan-bound) entertainers or sex workers in night businesses throughout Japan. Like their Japanese counterparts (Allison 1994), Filipina entertainers largely facilitate social intercourse in bars, spiced with sexual talk and demeanours (Ballescas 1992; Suzuki 2000a, 2000b). Others are prostitutes, forced or voluntary, though the number of the former seems to have shrunk since the mid-1980s as information about '*Japayuki*' has circulated widely in the Philippines (Ishiyama 1989). In either case, Filipina workers in these establishments have hardly won social respect. Representationally contained within 'bad' sexual relationships between 'prostitutes' and 'patrons', Filipina–Japanese unions have rarely been considered emotionally significant while husbands have been viewed as those at the margins.

Aside from rural farmers, marriage agencies specializing in nuptials with Filipinas commonly target men who run small businesses, are artisans, factory workers and drivers, and are (junior) high school graduates (Shukuya 1988: 105–6). These are exactly the opposite of the 'three high' qualifications – high income, high education and high physical stature – that Japanese women are thought to want in their husbands. Other Japanese 'candidates' for marriage with Asian women include those who own no assets; have two or more children and are marrying for the third time; have physical disabilities; wish to marry a woman younger by ten years and are physically short, fat and/or bald (ibid.; Sakuma 1997).

Other marriage agents contend that these 'undesirable' attributes do not always prevent marriage (Wakui 1990).[6] Yet all of these characteristics nevertheless resonate with other *images* of Filipinas' suitors: salarymen at dead ends in the career race; men who abandon their wives and children and commit bigamy; *hisabetsumin* (*burakumin*) 'outcasts'; members of the Korean minority in Japan; and *yakuza* gangsters (David 1991; Matsui 1998; Sai 1993). Filipina–Japanese liaisons have also been aligned with other 'heretics' under heterosexism: gay couples, partners of fake marriages, swapping couples and pimps and their women (Sasabe 1996).

In the much debated television drama, *Firippīna o Aishita Otokotachi*, which was shown in December 1992, the protagonist Toshio embodies the images of such 'unpopular' men. 'Backward' Tōhoku-born divorcee Toshio works as a denigrated office employee in Tokyo. While entertaining his sexual desires at night, he comes to love a Filipina prostitute and upon her return to the Philippines, he also moves there. He tries to establish business enterprises, but instead loses everything. Feeling sorry for him, the Filipina marries him and the couple begin their life in a slum built on a huge garbage dump. Toshio is enabled to start a marital life by speaking Tagalog and living in pauperism in the Third World. His 'First World' identity is sustained only by extravagantly throwing their matrimonial gifts to his neighbours from a truck.[7]

However, as among my subjects, Japanese men registering their marriages with Filipinas at the Japanese Embassy in Manila also include salarymen (Imagawa 1990: 10). Such salarymen, too, appear in the book, *Firippīna o Aishita Otokotachi* (Hisada 1989), on which the television drama was based. Yet in the process of representation, they were absorbed into the powerful visual image of Toshio. Reflecting on the strong public doubt about the possibilities of developing affective relationships, Maruyama, a trailer truck driver, related his experience to me, saying: 'Even young kids [in Tokyo] stare at us at restaurants and places like that. What's wrong with us? Their eyes look so nasty!' (see also Terada 1994: 26).[8]

The public gaze also encodes concerns for Japanese race and nation. In the wake of the massive inflow of '*Japayuki*', assumed sexual contacts and subsequent procreation between Japanese and Filipinas began to destabilize the national phantasm of a 'homogeneous' Japan (Suzuki 2000b). Relationships with these 'prostitutes' involve access both to the life of the body and to the life of the Japanese 'species' (see Foucault 1980: 146). Children born to *Japanese* fathers and Fili*pino* mothers are derogatorily called '*Japino*'. This neologism indexes the children's disparaged status since the majority are thought to have been abandoned by their fathers and to be leading impoverished lives in the Philippines (Matsui 1998).[9] Their stories have been circulated in the media, inciting both worry and guilt feelings among Japanese.

One of the early reports on these children was a television documentary broadcast nationwide during prime time one Sunday in 1988 (Gunji 1991). The programme focused chiefly on two toddler boys given their fathers' surnames, 'Kawamata' and 'Ishida'.[10] Living in extreme poverty, the grubby, hungry and sickly toddlers wear only worn out shorts and eat watery porridge with salt and maggots. After the documentary, female observers responded to the programme, saying: 'As a Japanese, I think the idea of 100 million pan-middle-class people has been well established. What was shocking to me was that children with the same faces as ours live like the homeless' (ibid.: 49). Another woman said, 'My father went to the Philippines fifteen years ago. I don't know if that was a sex tour. If so, I may have younger siblings' (ibid.: 50). One journalist commented on these children, saying men who joined sex tours to the Philippines in the 1970s 'may meet their "*Hinomaru* (Japan's national flag) babies" at Philippine bars in Tokyo. The days when such grotesque scenes become no surprise are approaching' (Imaeda 1990: 98). The children straddle and blur the divisions of First World and Third World. Although children who are indeed suffering do exist, their spectral presences especially conjure up feelings of anxiety, guilt and fear, spawning antagonism among some Japanese for being offspring of a 'sexual affront' to the Japanese nation (Kosuge 1998; Stoler 1992).

These pervasive views of Filipina–Japanese relationships have worked to rationalize critiques of 'bad' sexual associations and simultaneously valorize 'good' marriages, with all their institutional baggage, between Japanese corporate 'warriors' and Japanese women. In this process of differentiation, scant attention has thus far been paid to individual men's choices, emotions and lifestyles. As in all marriages, Japanese husbands of Filipinas have their own desires and motivations for love and sharing. As their stories demonstrate, the husbands' subjectivities as men, and their expressions of love for and partnership with their wives and families, show no monolithic pattern. I now turn to the masculinity politics in which Japanese husbands try to give personal meanings to their gender in their everyday struggles.

## Japanese husbands: of love and dilemma

Starting in 1993 and continuing to 1996, I met several dozen Japanese husbands and contenders for marriage with Filipinas. Of 76 husbands whose jobs are known to me, many fit the occupational stereotypes mentioned above, including blue-collar workers (n = 14), transportation operators (n = 8), small business owners (n = 15), cooks (n = 2), carpenters (n = 1) and *yakuza* gangsters (n = 1). However, others are, with various ranks and affiliations, professionals (n = 4), managers in large corporations (n = 10), other white-collar employees (n = 3), engineers (n = 7), journalists (n = 4) and public employees (n = 7). A significant minority (n = 22) met their wives while working or travelling in the Philippines. Over one half (n = 25) of formally interviewed subjects (n = 43), from all occupational backgrounds, met their wives at bars in Japan where the women were hostessing. Other men were introduced to their wives through acquaintances or marriage agents.

Wherever they first met each other, the men's gendered and erotic imaginations were ignited by the women's attributes, including: 'unrivalled cheerfulness'; 'exotic beauty'; being like a 'Marilyn Monroe of the tropics'; 'girlish but coquettish'; 'joyous conversations in incomplete Japanese'; 'musical sense in singing and dancing', and 'affective mannerisms'. Filipinas' ability to speak English is also appealing, especially to the baby-boomer men, who grew up admiring American popular culture. The women's 'feminine' attentiveness to people around them, including their dedication in supporting their families in the Philippines even at a young age, also tickled men's patronizing desires. Some men felt, 'I've got to help her!'

As they wed, however, this initial excitement began to wrestle with the Japanese husbands' and their Filipino wives' notions of gender and family relationships. Although I also met problematic husbands, who were violent or womanizing and whose lives need to be analysed in a critical gender light,[11] in the following I introduce less extreme men. I do this because pursuing already dominant images tends to constitute and censor 'undesirable' hyper- and de-masculinized 'differences' while subsuming other expressions of masculine identity and politics. Conversely, putting competing voices into alternative discursive circuits exerts power, helping to intervene in the stereotypes of Japanese husbands and Filipina wives. Such acts complicate the images and create new imaginations about masculinity, gender and transnational marriages.

Among the Japanese husbands who spoke to me are Terami Yukihiro, Nishida Eiji and Kurama Kiyoshi (pseudonyms), who at the time of our interviews in 1996 had been married for three, six and one year(s), respectively. The marital contexts in which the three men introduced here related their experiences to me were more balanced, and their higher tolerance of my presence allowed me to have multiple interviews and to make observations of their lives at their homes. During the prolonged recession in the late 1990s, and for other familial reasons, the men's lives have changed for better and for worse since our first meetings. Although there are characteristics shared by these men and other husbands, rather than being typifications of husbands of Filipinas in Japan, what follows should be better understood as illustrating how individual men sustained and transformed their masculine identities and lifestyles through their marriages to Filipinas in the mid-1990s.

### Terami Yukihiro

Terami was born in the mid-1950s. After graduating from technical college, he joined a large transnational corporation as a salaryman. He is a section chief, making an annual income of nearly ten million yen (US$90,000 @ $1 = ¥110). He also owned a condominium, which enabled him to enjoy greater financial freedom. He appeared to be close to the 'ideal man' in the marriage market except, as the eldest son, for being responsible for his mother, who lives with him.

Terami met his wife Rita when she was a hostess at a 'Philippine club'. He once took me to the club, saying, 'It's not the kind of place you may be imagining'. It was, though, similar to the four other Philippine clubs I had visited where hostesses provide their usual services of talking, pouring drinks and singing karaoke. Terami described his initial feelings as follows:

> The trigger? Her cheerful character makes me feel relaxed. Unlike going out with Japanese women, [with her] I don't have to make the 'I'm somebody' front (*erasō*). She wasn't even moved to hear that I'm a manager at [my company]! You know, normally people say, 'Wow!' or something. She didn't even know [my company]. If I had a Japanese wife, she'd worry what title her husband holds and how far he's advanced in the corporate hierarchy. With Rita, I can forget about it and just be myself. It's all right if I drop out of the company [competition].

Terami began to develop this attitude after the oil crisis during the 1970s, a few years after he joined the company. The vulnerability of company life led him to think that being professional means fulfilling his assignment but not totally subjecting himself to corporate discipline. Coming to know Rita seemed to have confirmed his desires because she, as a Filipina with a strong family orientation, would enable him to pursue the kind of life he had begun to search for. For him, 'it's not work, but my family [that comes] first! Japanese men's identity is now primarily work. If one values his work, he won't understand his Filipina wife'.

Unlike some other family-oriented Japanese men (see Ishii-Kuntz, this volume, Chapter 12), Terami's insistence on the importance of the family does not, however, make him a man who shares housework with his wife. Rather, especially as one of a(n involuntarily) childless couple, he has been trying to become a partner who shares other activities with his wife. He described his everyday life with Rita, saying:

> Before, when I was only with my mother, I returned home at one or two [in the morning]. I'd never phoned her. Now, if I don't tell Rita that I'm coming back, she scolds me. I have [Rita's] curfew [at 7:00 pm]. My mother said, 'you *can* call home!' . . . If Rita feels that I'm not nice to her, she gets really mad! She kicks empty cans on the roadside and bangs the wall! Then, she goes to sleep and the next day, she completely forgets why she was so upset! Japanese couples don't talk much once they establish a household. But really, if I don't pay attention to her, she gets angry. 'Oh, in the Philippines, you do it in that way, huh?' If I don't think things interesting, our relationship won't last too long. Sometimes, it's good to be alone, but I'm no longer young. So, I don't feel like going out just by myself. It's better to be together.

The time he makes available after work and on weekends has also allowed him to learn about the Philippines through books and symposia. Terami thus understands Rita's strong commitment to the welfare of her natal family. In order to materialize her wishes, Terami has extended financial support in various ways. One is to give Rita a generous monthly personal allowance of 50,000 yen, and a 'food and daily goods' allowance of 110,000 yen just for the two of them. Terami said, 'Once I give her our budget, it is up to her to allocate it and she can spend it as she wishes'. Rita then remits her allowance to her bank account in the Philippines. In the spring of 1996, Rita was also pursuing another big dream: building a new house for her parents. Terami is happy to see that due to their contributions, Rita, the youngest among ten siblings, has gained the 'No. 2' voice after her oldest brother and is treated well in her natal family.

It is noteworthy that Terami's assertion of the priority of family over work sometimes fluctuated. He occasionally negated his 'family orientation', saying 'I too really am a "corporate being!"' His longtime friend attested that Terami has been 'extremely patient with Rita. He's been making so many adjustments to make their marriage work'. Terami's resistance to housework, being a claim to masculine power, may then be a result of the ongoing negotiation of his masculine self – whether to be an accommodating partner or a 'man', especially a 'Japanese' salaryman.

### Nishida Eiji

While Terami's narratives reflect an elite salaryman's struggle to turn away from the work discipline of a large corporation, Nishida's story is that of a man who had wanted to marry but who had previously been unsuccessful. I met the Nishidas when they contacted me after a Filipinas' event in which I had served as an interpreter. Nishida's elder stepdaughter, May, wants to become an English–Filipino–Japanese interpreter and they found me reassuring. I later learned that Nishida's masculine identities and struggles were also implicated in this particular encounter.

Nishida, in his late forties, graduated from a junior college night school and had remained single until his early forties. He said he had attended some twenty weddings of friends, who in turn asked when he was going to have his. An opportunity never seemed to come, and he related his feelings to me saying, 'After all, I felt lonely and I thought I could not marry. What the hell! I was desperate'. Knowing his feelings, friends introduced him to Pinky, then in her late twenties. She was visiting her sister, who was married to a Japanese and living in Nishida's hometown. Pinky was a single mother and needed a means to raise her two daughters. At the time of the introduction, she had already arranged to return to the Philippines in three weeks. For Nishida, their meeting evolved as follows:

> I thought this would be my last chance. Everybody was worried about me. So, I met her. From the beginning, I was determined to marry her. 'You know why we were introduced to each other, right?' I asked her. 'Well, if that's the case, let's get married.' Then, I took her to the airport. When she came back, I was worried if she'd remember me. But at the airport, she found me and called out, 'Mr. Nishida!' Boy, was I happy!

After one year of marriage, Nishida adopted Pinky's two daughters, who had been left in the Philippines. After overcoming their initial awkwardness, the daughters started to fight over their stepfather's attention. He reflected on those days, saying, 'Anyone would notice [our relationship] by looking at our faces. But I thought it would be clear to everyone that we were the happiest family in the world! We were together wherever we went'. The children brought him happiness and a sense of responsibility as a father and as the head of the family. This sense of responsibility, however, has ironically also spawned ambivalence in him.

Although they enjoyed life in the countryside, after a while the family moved to northern Tokyo. This was because Nishida wanted to grant May's request to live in Tokyo. He also thought that the city might offer better educational opportunities for his stepchildren. He contacted a relative in the city and arranged to get a job there. The family moved to Tokyo only to realize that the work arrangement had to be cancelled. After this broken promise, Nishida landed a low-paying factory job, and due to this financial constraint he had to agree to his wife's request to work in a nightclub. Nishida, however, remains the chief provider for his family since Pinky's income, which is larger than Nishida's, has mostly been used for her own investments and support for her Filipino family. After having satisfied his desire to marry and raise a family, Nishida soon began to face financial difficulties because of this very desire. The following reveals his dilemma as the head of a household:

> For us, Mom earns more and Dad is no good. When I think about the rent, if I can't work for a month, we'll be knocked out. The children tell me that after we came to Tokyo, I get upset easily. I know. I'm driven by necessity here in Tokyo. When your spouse's family needs support, it doesn't matter if they are Japanese or foreigners, it's natural to help. But I don't have the earning power. And the children. Especially the younger one, Flora came here innocently. We changed their destiny. So, I want them to become happy.

Resembling some working-class husbands in Australia (Connell 1995), Nishida began to do chores he had never done before marriage in order to compensate for his inability to bring home a large paycheque. When I commented on entering their home and seeing Nishida folding the laundry, he responded to me, saying:

> It's my job. At work I occasionally wonder if I hung the laundry this morning [laugh]. Sometimes I come back at two or three in the morning, but Pinky returns even later. So, I feel I have to do the chores. I'm hungry and I sip some beer. After drinking beer, I feel, 'it's too much trouble. All right, I'm gonna sleep!' Then, she comes back and gets upset. She washes the dishes and the noise wakes me. Ridiculous! Hey, I'm also working! I clean the bathroom and take care of the children. What else am I supposed to do? Well . . . , she's different from Japanese. I sometimes wonder what she'd think if she were Japanese. Conversely, the reverse is also true for her. So, I'm trying, trying to fill the gap. Then, the girls. May lived in the Philippines until ten, so she must remember the meals there. But now, they say, 'Oh, I can't eat this stuff!' I feel like telling them, 'Hey, sometimes you had nothing to eat over there!' But in Japan kids have been exposed to a certain diet. What we eat is nothing special here. Their complaints are only natural. Things like that, there is this gap.

In his struggles to maintain his family in the high-cost city, these 'gaps' have been troubling Nishida's masculine identities. The 'gaps' emerge not only between different cultural backgrounds but also between his desire to offer a good, secure life for his family according to the Japanese standard and his limited (earning) capacity to realize it.

The difficult time that Nishida has been experiencing has often been lightened by his relationships with his stepchildren. When they arrived in Japan, they had no one to ask for help for homework that they had to do in Japanese. As soon as Nishida came back from work, May, then a third grader, rushed to him to ask questions 'even when I was using the toilet or taking a bath!' He was reminded that he 'was the only person in the family for her to rely on for Japanese'. Five years later, Nishida was paying high tutorial fees to help prepare May for high school entrance examinations and in order to help her realize her aspiration of becoming an interpreter. His daughters also keep Nishida busy at weekends, driving them to their softball practices.

Marriage to Pinky has enlivened Nishida's life and masculine identities, especially as father, since through his stepdaughters he has been depended on and included in these everyday familial exchanges. His desire to realize May's wish to live in Tokyo has, however, dramatically changed their financial situation. Nishida reflected on his life saying, 'If I was only with Pinky, [things would be different]. In any case, she relies on me saying, "Daddy (*otōchan*), Daddy". But, because of the daughters, I can go on'.

### Kurama Kiyoshi

Like Nishida, Kurama Kiyoshi also struggled to find a wife. In Kurama's case, his difficulties derived from the tension between his past and present identities:

formerly an 'elite salaryman' and subsequently a middle-aged single father. Kurama was born in southwestern Tokyo in the early 1950s, the last of three brothers. As he repeatedly claimed, he 'was an elite salaryman' at a large electronics corporation which he joined in the early 1970s immediately after graduating from one of the major universities in Tokyo. He soon married his longtime Japanese girlfriend and had three children.

Blown by the fair winds of the booming consumer economy of the time, he quickly moved up the career ladder. He said, 'thinking only about providing a good life for my family', he became a 'complete "company being"'. In less than ten years, as the 'head runner among my contemporaries', he was promoted to branch manager. He continued working long hours, from morning to midnight, and took numerous business trips even when his wife asked him 'not to go'. At one point, he learned after the fact that his wife had suffered from an extra-uterine pregnancy. Eventually, she left for another man, leaving the children with Kurama. Only a few months before this incident, he had been honoured with the presidential award as the best branch manager of the year. Looking back, Kurama regretted that 'because I was truly workaholic, I neglected my family'. His present identities and paths to marriage with Ligaya are deeply rooted in this past.

Soon after his wife left him, Kurama resigned from his company in order to attend to his children's needs. Although there was really no room for Kurama, he requested that his father take him into the family business. He volunteered to serve tea to everyone in the office, work commonly done by female workers. He described the situation saying, 'Well, it was the consequence of my own deed. I turned from an elite salaryman to a physical worker and my salary, too, was slashed in half'.

With little time to deal with his sense of defeat regarding the loss of his 'former elite' identity, Kurama was driven to care for his children. He described his feelings, saying:

> My work had been my raison d'être. Then, partly I felt comfortless, and partly playing the two roles simply became taxing. For a while, I wanted to marry anyone. Anyone would be fine, but I wished someone would come rescue me! So, when the children went to sleep, I stepped out to drink. Now, when we are to meet [single] women – and for me, a dispirited, middle-aged man (*ojisan*) – there is no other place but drinking establishments.

The lack of opportunities to develop romantic relationships is a common reason why people in Japan have difficulty finding marital partners (Itamoto 1992). Although for four years after his wife left Kurama had stopped drinking in order to make his children's lunches, which are publicly scrutinized (Kasuga 1989), he later spent time at drinking establishments in hopes of meeting someone. Kurama was 'enchanted' (*hamaru*) by Filipina hostesses at 'Philippine pubs' who tickled his masculine ego and 'even *ojisan* like me feel that we are popular' (see also AFK 1996). He developed a sexual relationship with one of these Filipinas. Unfortunately, he later learned that she was married in the Philippines and that he had been cherished primarily for his material contributions to her. Realizing that the women were doing business in Japan, Kurama was then determined to pursue the 'image of a typical Filipina–Japanese couple – an *ojisan* pursuing "fresh and lively" (*pitchipichi*) Filipinas in their teens or early twenties'.

One day, he visited a pub and met Ligaya, who was known at the club as a 28-year-old single woman with no children. As soon as Ligaya and Kurama began a private conversation, she told him that she was actually in her late thirties and had five grown children in the Philippines. Impressed by her honesty, he soon stopped pursuing younger Filipinas. He frequented the club for one year to meet her. Since by this time his children had also grown up, Kurama and Ligaya eventually decided to live together in order to see if their relationship would develop for good. They married after confirming their mutual love and trust during two years of cohabitation.

Kurama was attracted to Ligaya because she was an 'honest and wonderful woman!' Unlike the women – Japanese and Filipina – who rejected him, Ligaya has shown thoughtfulness towards him as well as to her natal family. Ligaya works hard at her sister's pub in order to support them all. Ligaya also carefully allocates their financial and material resources. Like Terami, Kurama gives Ligaya a monthly household allowance of 100,000 yen with the thought that she will budget the money in order to save some for her natal family. Contrary to his assumption, she saves the money in their (joint) bank account, not in her personal account.

As he had hoped, Ligaya does all the chores and Kurama has resumed the breadwinner role for their household. Unlike his relationship with his first wife, however, Kurama and Ligaya have denser exchanges of spousal affection and sexual communication. Ligaya gives Kurama many signs of love and care, including, he said, 'calling me "love", taking a bath together, and even scolding me for drinking too much'. Sex with Ligaya is also important and he once boasted at a gathering of Filipina–Japanese couples that he 'would have sex with her every day'. While this '*ojisan*' kind of sex talk (see Mathews, this volume, Chapter 7) was also meant to valorize his male prowess, he immediately added the unusual public statement that 'because I love her, so it's only natural'. Kurama stated to me that marriage for him 'is to be with the one I love'.

Having largely graduated from parental responsibilities, Kurama and Ligaya are currently together pursuing dreams for retirement some ten years hence. The gap in economic conditions between the Philippines and Japan will most probably enable Kurama to materialize his dreams to own a jazz club and a soccer field and to live comfortably in a large house with their own land. Monetary and material contributions that Kurama and especially Ligaya – who through her marriage to Kurama has been able to work legally – have provided to her family in the Philippines have paved the way. Kurama observes that Ligaya's influence in her natal home is 'of course, absolute' and will enable them to enjoy a comfortable old age in the large house that Ligaya has built in her home town.

## Marriage and masculinity politics

The meanings of these three men's masculine experiences are multifariously inflected within various social and capitalist disciplines and with the Japanese version of compulsory heterosexuality. The increase in intermarriages between Japanese and Asian women and their subsequent procreation has concurrently refracted these national projects. Whereas marriage is a way to accumulate power and privilege, especially for (heterosexual) men, masculine identities are embedded and ranked within state technologies and public discourses. In this final section, I try to re-weave the men's narratives, showing how they are imbricated in these broader contexts.

Due to various social mechanisms, many Japanese men have come to be concerned about marriage primarily as a means to gain social credentials, fulfil social obligations and enjoy male privileges, including being cared for (Wakui 1990). Many men have no concrete ideas about marriage beyond just getting a wife (Itamoto 1992). Nishida's initial notion of marriage indeed seems to have been one of 'acquiring a wife' for social reasons. Pressured by his friends' queries, for Nishida marriage was compulsory and he was ready to marry even a foreign stranger. Kurama, who is now self-critical of his first choice, as an 'elite' salaryman needed a wife so that he could climb up the corporate ladder. He consequently wanted 'anyone' to 'rescue' him from both a disparaged masculine identity and housework.

Divorced by their wives, men like Kurama are ranked below married men and widowers in an 'adult' male hierarchy because they are considered 'good-for-nothing' (*kaishōnashi*) (Kasuga 1989). Structurally, while single-mother families can claim various welfare subsidies because of the lack of breadwinners, single-father families do not benefit from such state provisions because of the logical impossibility of compensating for women's *unpaid* work (Ida 1998: 57). Socially, as men, they are expected to remain strong and autonomous and, if they need help, they should seek it privately (Kasuga 1989). The economic difficulties of single-mother homes are irrefutable.[12] However, Japan's welfare scheme, built around the 'standard family', not only ignores single fathers like Kurama, but denigrates them for raising a 'family of loss' (*kesson kazoku*) (ibid.). Knowing of no support groups and with his female kin unwilling to help, Kurama's sense of disparagement compelled him to want to remarry *anyone*. Having lived as a socially slandered '*ojisan*', he found Ligaya not only 'feminine and thoughtful' but also sincere. Upon cohabiting, however, Kurama quickly resumed the normative gender division of labour at home.

Exposed to the economic vulnerability of the oil crisis (and of the current recession), Terami, in contrast, is sceptical of Japan's capitalist discipline and structure of cathexis in marriage that distance men from their families. He married Rita to avoid these constraints. With her, he does not have to perform a masculine façade of being 'somebody'. He felt that he could drop out of the promotion race, although this is itself based on the privileges of his financial power and stable employment. These have simultaneously enabled him to provide both a better life for his wife in Japan and substantial economic support for her natal family. This, in turn, satisfies his masculine wish 'to realize my wife's dream' in the Philippines.

These husbands, Kurama and Terami in particular, have to varying degrees gained masculine dividends by attaining the statuses of household 'heads' and 'full-fledged' – married and providing – men. With these statuses and financial power, men symbolically place themselves above their wives and excuse themselves from doing 'women's jobs'. Nishida, too, enjoys some masculine confidence by being relied on by Pinky and his stepdaughters, although he must also share some chores since Pinky also works. His comments reflect his ambivalence and self-criticism.[13] Yet Nishida's identities have also been impressed with Flora's child-like expressions such as, 'Because you're short, I'm short, too!' (meaning 'Yes, you are my (real) Dad and you are responsible for what we are!')

The gender division and hierarchy are also the consequences of the labour market, which does not offer many options for Asian immigrant women, most of whom cannot read Japanese well and who remain outside Japan's andro- and ethnocentric employment system. Also, given the tarnished images of their being 'commodified' women, Filipinas' alternatives are largely limited to bar hostessing, ethnic businesses and low-wage jobs. The gender division of labour, which encodes both the assertion of masculine identities and correlated social configurations in Japan, then tends to intensify for Filipina–Japanese couples, except for cases like Nishida's.

Role segregation in Japan has bifurcated spousal affective–sexual relationships and, as seen in Kurama's first marriage, is related to the rise in divorces between Japanese. Terami married Rita because of his ideas about men's roles *vis-à-vis* Japanese housewives who worry mostly about their husbands' promotions. The men's efforts to enjoy more emotionally reciprocal spousal relationships are partly motivated by their realization that their marriages with Filipinas are commonly not considered 'real' but those between 'prostitutes' and their 'customers'. This is perhaps also the motivation behind Terami's decision to show me the club where he had met Rita.

By marrying Filipinas, these Japanese men are trying to affectively unleash themselves from Japan's gender yoking and enjoy denser spousal relationships, even if this involves new forms of domestic discipline such as accepting their wives' 'curfews', 'anger' and 'scolding'. Verbally and behaviourally expressing their love for their wives in public and at home seems to be more common among the husbands I have dealt with. Kurama, for example, does not hesitate to express his love and care for his wife, creating scenes rare in Japan, especially when enacted by men of his age. Although many Filipina wives continue to complain about their husbands being 'cold', many husbands of Filipinas, at least ideally, share Terami's wish to prioritize family over work. While these husbands also wittingly and unwittingly reproduce gender inequality, they have in many ways more significantly challenged Japan's gendered structures of cathexis and practice.

The offspring of these liaisons have often been conceptualized as leading impoverished lives that are 'affronts' to Japan's 'pan-middle-class' ideology. While there are abandoned Japanese–Filipino children, there are also fathers like Nishida, who has willingly adopted Pinky's daughters and attempts to give them the best he can.[14] Nishida has taken his stepdaughter May's wishes seriously, especially that to become an interpreter, with the hope that she will bridge, rather than divide, the multiple languages and national affiliations between Japan and the Philippines. Although these adopted children, as well as racially 'double' children, continue to be disruptive of Japan's 'homogeneous' nation, they also enable men like Nishida to find meanings as fathers in their difficult lives.

Filipina–Japanese marriages have further worked to parody nationalists' spins on the 'pan-middle-class' phantasm. Critics have argued that Japanese men's sexual associations with Filipinas are based on the uneven power between an 'affluent' Japan and a 'poor' Philippines. This inequality, however, has taken an ironic colonial twist. Men from the 'wealthy' country of Japan are able to enjoy the 'men's dream' of masculinist middle-class life – being the 'lord of his own castle' – only at the time of retirement and with the compassion of their 'Third World' Filipina wives and affinal families in the Philippines.

What is doubly ironic here is that this poignant 'Japanese dream' has also been promoted by the Philippine Retirement Authority, an office of the Philippine President, which has provided various incentives to Japanese retirees to move to the Philippines and enjoy, as the office's brochure puts it, 'low living cost, medical fees and services' and a 'natural national character respectful of the elderly'. As in Rita's case, many Filipina wives, furthermore, put up with racial, sexual and gender slurs in both Japan and the Philippines with the hopes of building '*Japayuki* palaces' and leading princess-like 'señorita lives' back home.

Seen in these individual struggles, masculinity politics and the marriage market in Japan at the turn of the century are multifariously embedded both within the reproduction of the existing systems and within numerous concurrent redefinitions of desirable and possible gender, sexual and familial relationships. It is still easy to criticize the men discussed here for being colonialist, chauvinist and racist. Yet the men's behaviours have also created various cracks, however small as yet, in conventional social relations and institutions, calling into question pernicious state ideologies and regimes within Japanese society and its geopolitical borders. Filipina–Japanese marriages thus articulate individual battles and, simultaneously, masculine divisions, gender troubles, capitalist discipline, class demarcations and Japanese state body politic and national identity in the globalizing world, all in different measures and not all at the same time.

## Acknowledgements

I thank Roger Goodman, Engseng Ho, Anne Imamura, Kawahashi Noriko and Nagafuchi Yasuyuki for their comments. The Japan Foundation and the Matsushita International Foundation provided generous funds that enabled me to carry out this research.

## Notes

1 This 'standard family' actually occupied only 8.75 per cent of all households in Japan in 1997 (*Asahi Shinbun* 1999). The most common form of households consists of single adults (25.0 per cent), followed by two persons (24.5 per cent), four persons (18.9 per cent) and three persons (18.3 per cent).
2 Although the prolonged recession has partially breached these practices, *structural* change has not been forthcoming.
3 For this reason, numerous homosexual men feel compelled to marry, even visiting marriage bureaux (see Yoshida 1996). For more examples and critiques of the criss-

crossed hetero/sexist practices based on capitalist development, pedagogy, legal decision-making and homophobia in Japan, see Ida (1995, 1998), Fukushima (1997) and Lunsing (2001).

4  Although Rubin's 'cross-generational' chiefly means paedophilia, the age difference among Filipina 'brides' has rendered a similar interpretation.
5  This is not to say that only men are 'shopping'.
6  While the 'three highs' continue to be ideal, many young women today prefer '3C' men, who are communicative, comfortable and cooperative.
7  For more details, see Go and Jung (1999).
8  Even if they started out with 'bad' associations, sex(ual) workers and their clients do not always develop 'foul' relationships, as many entertainers and their husbands demonstrated to me.
9  The circumstances surrounding these children are more complex (Suzuki 2000b).
10  I am not certain how common giving children their fathers' surnames is among single Filipina mothers. These children's names may be a result of the practice by which married Filipinas in Japan who have worked at bars sometimes call their Japanese husbands by the latter's surnames just as they had when they initially met.
11  For the issues of domestic violence and divorce, see Suzuki (forthcoming).
12  In 1992, single-mother, single-father and 'standard' households on average made 2.2, 4.2 and 6.5 million yen, respectively (Yoshizumi 1999: 21).
13  Unfortunately, among some other husbands, lack of financial power seems to have been translated into violence against wives and children in order to compensate for their lowered masculine sense of identity.
14  Many Filipinas I met were single mothers before their marriages to Japanese.

# References

AFK (Asia Fūzoku Kenkyūkai) (1996) *Firipīna Aizō Dokuhon* (*The Love–Hate Filipina Reader*), Tokyo: Dētahausu.
Allison, A. (1994) *Nightwork*, Chicago: University of Chicago Press.
*Asahi Shinbun* (1999) '*Kazoku no "hyōjun" kuzure kiro ni*' (Collapsed 'standard' of the family standing at the cross-roads), January 1.
—— (2000) '*Soboku na gimon (ge)*' (Simple question 2), December 15.
Ballescas, M. R. (1992) *Filipino Entertainers in Japan*, Quezon City: The Foundation for Nationalist Studies.
Bourdieu, P. (1984) *Distinction*, Cambridge, MA: Harvard University Press.
Ching, L. (1998) 'Yellow skin, white masks', in K. H. Chen (ed.) *Trajectories*, London and New York: Routledge.
Connell, R. W. (1987) *Gender and Power*, Stanford: Stanford University Press.
—— (1995) *Masculinities*, Berkeley: University of California Press.
David, R. (1991) 'Filipino workers in Japan', *Kasarinlan* 6, 3: 8–23.
Foucault, M. (1980) *The History of Sexuality I*, New York: Vintage.
Fukushima, M. (1997) *Saiban no Joseigaku* (*Women's Studies in Justice*), Tokyo: Yūhikaku.
Go, L. and Jung, Y. (1999) *Watashi to Iu Tabi* (*The Journey Called Me*), Tokyo: Seidosha.
Gunji, S. (1991) *Nihonjin no Wasuremono* (*The Left-Behind of the Japanese*), Tokyo: Bungei Shunjū.
Hisada, M. (1989) *Firippīna o Aishita Otokotachi* (*The Men Who Fell in Love with Filipinas*), Tokyo: Bungei Shunjū.
Ida, H. (1995) *Seisabetsu to Shihonsei* (*Sexual Discrimination and Capitalism*), Kyoto: Keibunsha.
—— (1998) *Shinguru Tan'i no Shakairon* (*Sociology of Single Units*), Kyoto: Sekai Hyōronsha.
Imaeda, K. (1990) '*Kokkyō o koeta yokubō*' (Desires crossing national borders), *Bessatsu Takarajima* No. 106, Tokyo: JICC.

Imagawa, I. (1990) *Gendai Kekkon Kō* (*On Modern Marriages*), Tokyo: Tabata Shoten.

Ishiyama, E. (1989) *Firipinjin Dekasegi Rōdōsha* (*Filipino Migrant Workers*), Tokyo: Tsuge Shobō.

Itamoto, Y. (1992) '*Otoko wa naze kekkon dekinai ka*' (Why men cannot marry), in K. Ichikawa (ed.) *Dansei Junan Jidai* (*Age of Crucified Men*), Tokyo: Shibundō.

Iwao, S. (1993) *The Japanese Woman*, New York: The Free Press.

Johnson, W. and Warren, M. (1994) *Inside the Mixed Marriage*, Lanham, MD: University Press of America.

Kamisaka, F. (1999) *Haru Raishawā* (*Haru Reischauer*), Tokyo: Kōdansha.

Kasuga, K. (1989) *Fushikatei o Ikiru* (*Single Fathers' Lives*), Tokyo: Keisō Shobō.

Kosuge, K. (1998) *Furyō Gaikokujin Danjo ni Damasarenai Hon* (*Book for Not Being Deceived by Delinquent Foreign Men and Women*), Tokyo: Dētahouse.

Lunsing, W. (2001) *Beyond Common Sense*, London and New York: Kegan Paul.

Matsui, Y. (1997) 'Matsui Yayori', in S. Buckley (ed.) *Broken Silence*, Berkeley: University of California Press.

—— (1998) *Nihon no Otōsan ni Aitai* (*We Want to Meet Our Fathers in Japan*), Tokyo: Iwanami Booklet.

Ministry of Health and Welfare (1993–2000) *Vital Statistics*, Tokyo: Ōkurashō.

NHK (Nihon Hōsō Kyōkai) (1988) *Ohayō Jānaru* (*Good Morning Journal*) I & II, television documentary, June 13–14.

Ortner, S. (1996) *Making Gender*, Boston: Beacon Press.

Rich, A. (1980) 'Compulsory heterosexuality and lesbian existence', *Signs* 5, 4: 631–60.

Rubin, G. (1984) 'Thinking sex', in C. Vance (ed.) *Pleasure and Danger*, Boston: Routledge and Kegan Paul.

Sai, Y. (1993) *All Under the Moon*, Cine Qua Non Film.

Said, E. (1978) *Orientalism*, New York: Vintage.

Sakuma, T. (1997) *Chikyū no Hanayome o Moraō* (*Let's Get Global Brides*), Tokyo: Ken'yūkan.

Sasabe, T. (1996) '*Imadoki no kekkon no imi*' (Meanings of marriage today), *Spa!* 2491: 122–7.

Setouchi, H. (1989) *Kokusai Kekkon no Reimei* (*Dawn of International Marriage*), Tokyo: Kōdansha.

Shukuya, K. (1988) *Ajia kara Kita Hanayome* (*The Brides Who Came from Asia*), Tokyo: Akashi Shoten.

Stoler, A. (1992) 'Sexual affronts and racial frontiers', *Comparative Study of Society and History* 34, 2: 514–51.

Suzuki, N. (2000a) 'Between two shores', *Women's Studies International Forum* 23, 4: 431–44.

—— (2000b) 'Women imagined, women imaging', *US–Japan Women's Journal English Supplement* 19: 142–75.

—— (forthcoming) 'Battlefields of affection: gender, global desires and the politics of intimacy in Filipina–Japanese transnational marriages', PhD dissertation, University of Hawaii.

Terada, Y. (ed.) (1994) *Tsuma wa Firipīna* (*My Wife is a Filipina*), Tokyo: Hanashi no Tokushū.

Wakui, Y. (1990) '*Komatta yatsura*' (Troublesome guys), in M. Fukushima (ed.) *Otokotachi no Gosan* (*Men's Miscalculations*), Tokyo: Komichi Shobō.

Yoshida, K. (1996) *Kekkon Sōdanjo Koko dake no Hanashi* (*Marriage Bureau's Secret Stories*), Tokyo: Waseda Shuppan.

Yoshida, R. (1990) 'Getting married the corporate way', *Japan Quarterly* XXXVII, 2: 171–5.

Yoshizumi, K. (1999) '*Fueru rikon ni yoru tanshin setai*' (Single households caused by increasing divorces), in T. Inoue and Y. Ehara (eds) *Josei no Dētabukku* (*Data Book on Women*), Tokyo: Yūhikaku.

# 7   Can 'a real man' live for his family?

## *Ikigai* and masculinity in today's Japan

*Gordon Mathews*

Masculinity is not an easy subject to broach in Japan; if you ask Japanese men 'what does it mean to be a man?' you are liable to receive only embarrassed shrugs, or perhaps a joking comment about sex. But there are other, more indirect routes into the meanings of Japanese masculinity. One such route is through *ikigai*, a Japanese term meaning 'that which most makes life worth living' (see Mathews 1996). *Ikigai* may sound philosophical and abstract to Western readers, but it is an everyday term in Japan, a subject of occasional discussion and dispute in mass media and in daily life. 'A real man lives for his work!' some men told me during my research into *ikigai*. 'A man should live for his family; that's what's most important!' other men said. 'A man should find *ikigai* in following his dream!' still other men said. These different responses indicate, I argue, different ideas of masculinity in Japan today. In approaching Japanese masculinity through *ikigai*, I am approaching only one aspect of masculinity; areas such as sexuality are mostly neglected in this chapter. None the less, because so many men I interviewed brought up what it means to be a man during our discussions about *ikigai*, it seems clear that *ikigai* may serve as a window into Japanese senses of masculinity.

Japanese society has in recent decades held to a clear gender-role division of *ikigai*. Men have been expected to devote themselves to their work to support their families, while women have been expected to devote themselves to nurturing their families and raising their children, working only part-time at most. The gender division of *ikigai* has been deeply disadvantageous to women. Women make only 50 per cent of the wages that men make in Japan as opposed to 74 per cent in the United States (by 1992 statistics); in 1996, only 9.2 per cent of corporate managers in Japan were women, as opposed to 43.8 per cent in the United States (*Asahi Shinbun* 1999b). But this gender division of *ikigai* has also been deeply disadvantageous to men: 'Men's lives in Japan . . . are confined and regimented by their jobs to an extreme' (Iwao 1993: 15).

In recent years, this gender-role division of *ikigai* has been to some extent crumbling, linked to such diverse factors as the decline in the Japanese birthrate, the increasing prominence of foreign companies allowing female employees opportunities for advancement and the erosion of the white-collar ideal of lifetime employment. But while the gender division of *ikigai* is increasingly challenged today, this division remains the reality of many Japanese lives. As we will see in this chapter, Japanese men may seek to live for their families or for their dreams rather than for their work; but the weight of work in their lives makes an *ikigai* beyond work difficult to pursue.

Surveys of *ikigai*, as occasionally found in Japanese mass media and government publications, do not tend to reveal the massive presence of work in men's lives. One such survey (cited by Minami 1989: 129) showed that men of ages 30 to 60 hold their *ikigai* to be work or family, with men over 45 seeing *ikigai* as work more than family, and men under 45 seeing *ikigai* as family more than work. But what does this designation of *ikigai* as family actually mean? Ueno states that 'even today, some men mistake money and success at work for love for their family' (1995: 216). These men, she is implying, may believe that their *ikigai* is family since they are their families' main breadwinners, but really their *ikigai* is work, since that is what they are truly devoted to in their lives. Other men, however, may suffer from no such misunderstanding. These men may truly seek to make their families the centre of their lives, but they are constrained in this because they are forced to devote so much of themselves to their work.

In this chapter, rather than relying on the data of surveys, I explore masculine *ikigai* through interviews conducted with twenty-seven Japanese men of various ages and from various walks of life in 1989–90 in Sapporo, Japan, and follow-up interviews in the decade since. I also make use of interviews and mass media reports obtained in Tokyo in 1999–2000. Many of these men are, broadly speaking, urban salarymen – white-collar workers, from high-school teacher to bank employee to insurance salesman – but their words transcend the 'urban salaryman model', I believe, in showing the complexities of their experiences as men in a world of multiple cultural discourses and conflicting social pressures. In the pages that follow, I will discuss what I have found, in terms of three commitments often in conflict: *ikigai* as work, *ikigai* as family and *ikigai* as self.

## *Ikigai* as work

The survey discussed above depicts a generational shift that I have found in my interviews. Men in their fifties and sixties in 1989–90 tended to hold work as their *ikigai*, but men in their thirties and forties in 1989–90 were often unwilling to make that commitment to work. This may reflect a historical shift: those who were in their fifties and sixties grew up in a less affluent Japan, and spent their lives in pursuit of affluence, whereas those in their thirties and forties had always known affluence, and were thus less single-mindedly devoted to work and company.

For many of the older men I spoke with, living for work was a source of unambiguous pride: a man is supposed to live for his work. A corporate executive in his fifties said:

> For the past thirty years, my *ikigai* has been the companies I've worked for; they've been more important to me than my family. I don't expect much from my family; they don't expect me to be at home on weekends anymore. Yes, I can't say that I'm a family man. I have more human communication with the young girls (*onna no ko*) in my office than I do with my own daughters . . .

A high-school teacher in his fifties said:

> Maybe Americans can separate business and private life, but I can't, and most Japanese can't. If you don't have business, you can't have any private life . . . In my house, my wife was like a widow; I was busy, even on Sundays, with my school clubs. So now, if I'm not home, everyone feels more relaxed!

There is an undercurrent of regret in these men's statements: they are emotionally cut off from their wives and children, in that their lives have for so long been lived in the workplace. Now that these men are close to retirement, they realize that they must surrender their *ikigai* of work; and this makes them feel considerable unease. None the less, these men expressed no doubt as to the wisdom and propriety of the gender division of *ikigai*, and neither did their wives: it was these men's pride that they had lived utterly for work. This pride is reflected in their harsh criticism of younger Japanese men for not sharing the single-minded devotion to work that they themselves have had. As the high-school teacher said:

> Young people today overwhelmingly value being with their families. They calmly say, 'My child's sick. I'll take the day off'. Nobody ever did that when I was young! Today's young people don't have any fighting spirit! They relax with their families before they think about work!

As the company executive said,

> There are fewer and fewer company men like me these days; there are many more 'my home' types – these kind of people aren't at all happy if I tell them to come to the office on Sunday! I've never said no to any of my job assignments – I was always there when they needed me. I like men who do that: manly man (*otoko rashii otoko*), like Western cowboys! Men living for their companies are better than those who live for their families; that's why Japan's developed! I get upset when I see a young man with dyed hair driving around in a fancy car with a pretty girl. Fifty years ago, people his age all died in the war; they didn't have the chance to enjoy their youth! I want to drag that young man out of his car and put a judo hold on him, teach him a lesson!

These men view living for work as the essence of masculinity: a man who sacrifices himself for his company is like a cowboy, we are told, truly a manly man. Such statements may indicate 'false consciousness'. As Lukes has written, 'Is it not the supreme exercise of power to get . . . others to have the desires you want them to have – that is, to secure their compliance by controlling their thoughts and desires?' (quoted in Pyke 1996: 529). This is the power of the Japanese state and economic order, moulding workers such as these to believe that their sacrifice of themselves to the organizations they work for represents not their exploitation but rather their apotheosis as men – just as their wives have been moulded to believe that their place at home represents their apotheosis as women (see Allison 2000: 81–122). Some I interviewed expressed exactly such views about men's *ikigai* of work. A man of 30 who had fled conventional middle-class expectations (see Mathews 1996: 118–23) said, 'Companies take priority over everything else in Japan, and people working in such places are just cogs (*haguruma*). They don't have selves. They don't know what freedom is; they don't know their own identities'.

However, the older men I interviewed, as might be expected, totally rejected this view: they felt not that they had been exploited by a Japanese system that had rendered them slaves to work, but rather that they themselves had willingly and eagerly given their lives rebuilding Japan from ruin to affluence. In one bank worker's words (see Mathews 1996: 57–62): 'It's my generation that built Japan . . . . I still remember those day of hardship after the war, when I was a child. My generation wanted to escape that low level of existence – that was the driving force of Japan's development'. These men believed that the gender division of *ikigai*, whereby men devote themselves single-mindedly to work and women raise the sons and daughters who become the workers and mothers of the future, is what has enabled Japan to develop into a prosperous and moral society.

These men's pride has, however, been shaken by Japan's economic downturn over the past decade. This downturn has clearly been due not to the lack of devotion to work of the young, but rather to the problems of the Japanese economic system built by their elders, men such as those quoted above. As a salaryman in his fifties told me in 1999,

> The problem was that we worked too hard, generated too much money, that had to be ploughed back into the system, into stocks and land, creating 'the bubble economy' . . . If only Japanese hadn't worked so hard, maybe the economic downturn would never have happened.

Whatever the validity of this man's economic theorizing, the social implications of his words are important: if only Japanese men hadn't lived for work, but had lived in a broader way – such as for their families or for their dreams – Japan's economy would not have stalled, he is saying.

Indeed, because of the economic downturn, the image of the Japanese white-collar worker has been tarnished of late. Older salarymen have been compared in one magazine column, aimed at young Japanese 'office ladies', to cockroaches: '*Ojisan* [company men in their forties and fifties][1] and cockroaches: if you had to choose between them as to which was worse, which would win out?' Cockroaches win by a small margin, its readers decided (reprinted in Shimizu 1998: 75–82). More tellingly, a new deodorant has been produced aimed at masking '*ojisan no nioi*', the smell of older men. 'The fear of bothering other people with one's odour has led to a kind of [pathology] . . . among many middle-aged and older men in the past one to two years . . . This may be related to their loss of confidence' in an age of economic downturn and possible layoffs, one newspaper article states (Satō 1999). Some of the proud creators of Japan's economic miracle have, in Japan's new straitened age, become terrified about offending the people around them by their stench, the stench, they sense, of failed older men. This is a small but pungent symbol of what one earlier sense of Japanese masculinity has come to in Japan today.

The younger men I interviewed did not have the beliefs of their elders about work. It was rare to find a man under 45 who would claim that his *ikigai* was 'living for the company'. A salaryman in his thirties working for a famous Japanese company said:

> If you ask my coworkers whether they find *ikigai* in work for this company, they might say they do. But they'd be lying . . . But, then, maybe they really do find *ikigai* here. If you don't have time to do anything but work, then isn't that your *ikigai*?

This statement indicates that although work for the company is no longer one's taken-for-granted *ikigai*, the natural basis for one's masculine purpose in life, none the less work remains all-powerful. When most men have to spend most of their waking lives at work, work necessarily remains what might be termed their '*de facto ikigai*', and *de facto* definition of who they are as men.

Today in Japan, it is difficult to find any voices in mass media proclaiming that one should 'live for one's company'. Walk into any bookshop and one will find dozens of titles saying the opposite: 'Live as you yourself want! Don't be chained to working for your company!' as the cover blurb for one recent bestseller proclaims (Ōhashi 2000). 'We have no loyal army of company men in Japan any more', the business consultant Ohmae Kenichi recently stated (*Economist* 1999); popular Japanese magazines today offer counsel on what to do 'when love for one's company vanishes' (Ōshima 1999). The ideal for many aspiring young people today is to be not a salaryman but an entrepreneur. This may be linked to a new conception of work as *ikigai* in Japan, formulated not as 'commitment to company' but as 'individual self-fulfilment'. Only a very few of the people I interviewed conceived of their work this way; a television producer in his thirties said, 'This programme I'm working on demands all my energy. This is what I devote myself to . . . I want this programme to be really good!' But perhaps this more self-oriented conception of work as *ikigai* will increase in Japan in the future.[2]

In a cultural sense, working for one's company has lost its sheen as a masculine *ikigai* in Japan today; but in an institutional sense, the matter is more ambiguous. On the one hand, 'Japanese companies, which once demanded the undivided loyalty of their employees, have executed an about-face and are frantically trying to reduce staff' (*Asahi Shinbun* 1999a). On the other hand, however, the demands of work seem more onerous than ever:

> In spite of the recession, I haven't heard of any salarymen who go home early because they don't have work to do. Rather, there are a great number of salarymen who work so hard that they die from overwork or are driven to suicide.

> (Morinaga 1999: 434)

Even though younger men no longer take for granted that a man should live for his company as his *ikigai*, it seems that many find themselves still having to live as if that were the case. In spite of their own interests and intentions, it seems that the *de facto ikigai* of many younger men in Japan today remains work.

### *Ikigai* as family

If *ikigai* is not found in work, then perhaps it may be found in family; but for most Japanese men I interviewed, this seemed problematic. This is partly because of the continuing adherence to rigid gender roles, and the lack of emphasis on communication between husband on the one hand and wife and children on the other. This is also because of the continuing pressure for men to spend the bulk of their lives at work.

Some of the older Japanese men I interviewed claimed family as their *ikigai* because they were breadwinners, but almost no one claimed a deep emotional commitment to family – given their senses of themselves as men, such an assertion seemed impossible. Indeed, for some older men, family seemed to function as an outlet for their frustrations at work. A recently retired railroad worker in his sixties said:

> You know how work is. The husband has to be subservient to his boss, and so when he comes home, he wants to boss around his wife and children: 'Turn off the TV! Put the kids to bed!' And communication between husband and wife, father and children, goes bad . . .

This attitude, of 'husband as boss of the family', was most strongly held by those who were not white-collar but working-class. A self-employed repairman, a man whose working hours were set by himself rather than by any company, and who thus could not securely speak of a home at work as opposed to his actual home, said:

> I believe that the husband's the boss of the family. A wife should know what her husband is thinking by looking at his face. She should properly send him off to work in the morning; and when he comes home at night, there should be a drink and some good food waiting for him. A husband should educate his wife to do that . . . When I got married, my wife fell in love with me; I didn't care whether I married her or not. She works part-time at the supermarket as a cashier – she's a little overbearing now, since she's got her own money.[3]

This man seemed totally dependent on his wife from all I was able to observe over many hours at his house; but by his rhetoric he sought to preserve his ideal that the man is to be head of the family, while the woman is to be subservient. Pyke has written that in the United States, 'working-class husbands' subordinated class status . . . in the labour force seems to exacerbate their need to use their marriage as a place where they can be superior' (1996: 539); perhaps this is what we see in this Japanese example as well.

However, the younger men I interviewed had wives much less willing to accept the role of their husband as head of the family, and not nearly as willing as their mothers had been to accept 'a husband who is healthy and absent' (*teishu wa jōbu de rusu ga ii*), as the popular old saying goes. One company worker in his late thirties described his marriage to a wife who sought more from him than his salary:

> Early in our marriage, my wife was always angry because I came home late from work, and because I wasn't *yasashii* (affectionate); I didn't take her anywhere on weekends, I didn't convey to her that I loved her. We came very close to divorce several times. Once my wife left with the kids and didn't come home for three days; I still don't know where they went. I wasn't thinking much about my family then; that's why my wife got so upset. I realized that I'd have to change. My wife made me promise that, unless I was out of town on business, I'd have breakfast with the family no matter how late I came home the previous night. I also spend every Sunday – at least half the day – with my family. Saturdays I use for myself: I go fishing....I feel exhausted because of stress on my job – that's why I need Saturdays for myself. When I'm with my family, I just can't get rid of stress.

This is a key statement, in that it shows the negotiation of the gender-role division of *ikigai* between husband and wife, a negotiation that becomes necessary once the nature of that division is no longer taken for granted by husband and wife in common. Although this man has agreed to devote himself more to family, his family is not his *ikigai*, he told me. His devotion to family seems to be a matter of *kazoku sābisu* ('family service': men's activities with their families at weekends): not something that men enjoy doing, but rather feel that they have to do (Ōsawa 1993: 122–3). One reason why his family is not his *ikigai* is personal: he and his wife do not, apparently, have the most fulfilling of relationships. But another reason is structural: he is under great pressure at work, but now feels pressure in his family as well, in that his wife, who does not work, wants him to be not only the breadwinner but an emotional presence in the family as well. He thus feels that family is not a solace from work's stress, but rather one more source of stress.

Japanese media in recent decades have often discussed 'the absent father': 'Where is the father? He is a corporate warrior . . . More than being a member of his family, he is a member of his company' (Myōki 1997: 220–1). There has been a growing movement urging men to become more than just 'corporate drones', and live not simply for their companies but for their families as well (Kashima 1993); and this has increasingly been framed as an argument over what it means to be a man. One recent guide to 'how to be a real man' tells its readers, 'A man who sticks out his chest and says, "I leave family matters to my wife" should feel ashamed of himself' (Hirokane 1997: 208). Recently, the government has added its voice to this debate: in early 1999, the Ministry of Health and Welfare distributed a poster showing Sam (the husband of pop idol Amuro Namie) holding a baby and saying, 'A man who doesn't raise his children can't be called a father' (see Yamada 1999b: 143). This has aroused controversy: one young man I spoke with said, 'I guess I agree with the poster, but really it's none of the government's business how a man raises his family. The government should stay out!'

But of course the government can't possibly stay out, for a wide range of government policies, plans and exhortations have implications for the gender division of *ikigai*, and for the meanings of masculinity in Japan. Allison (2000) and Garon (1997), among other scholars, have written about how the Japanese state shapes women to be devoted to family in the service of the nation: the state has clearly helped to shape the rigid separation of Japanese gender roles. Today, however, this shaping is no longer so clear in its emphasis.

On the one hand, there is the 'Sam' poster discussed above, encouraging men to find their masculinity in raising their children; and there is the revised 1999 Equal Employment Opportunity law making illegal any discrimination against women in employment (*Nihon no Ronten 2000* 1999a: 662). On the other hand, however, there are Japanese tax statutes: 'When a mother works and her income exceeds a certain amount [¥1,030,000 per year: somewhat under $10,000 at today's exchange rates], she will be worse off because of taxes . . . than a full-time housewife. It is as if the state is encouraging women to be full-time housewives' (Suzuki 1999: 686), and encouraging their husbands to devote themselves wholly to work. (In fact, the law doesn't penalize women *per se*, but rather the second of two working spouses, but in Japan today this almost always means women.) Does the Japanese state seek to preserve the gender division of *ikigai*, and thus men's senses of masculinity as found through devotion to work rather than commitment to family? Or does the Japanese state seek to end the gender division of *ikigai*, and enable men to find their *ikigai* in family and women to find their *ikigai* in work? There are huge consequences at stake in this issue, in terms of the future of the Japanese economy and of Japan itself (see Jolivet 1997 for a discussion of Japan's potential 'childless society'); but the state's position seems ambiguous.

The government's ambivalence about how men should live reflects and is reflected in the views of women today. Some social critics have discussed a 'gender gap' between young men and women in Japan,

> a gender gap regarding expectations of the future spouse . . . Women seek companionship based on affection and understanding . . . Men seem more interested in the traditional division of domestic roles. It is women who are changing the dynamics of the marriage market, while men . . . are being urged to comprehend and catch up.
>
> (Kawanishi 1999)

This may be true, but many women also seek to be financially supported by their husbands. A term bandied about by young Japanese women today is '*san-shī*', the '3 Cs' that they seek in a prospective mate: he must bring home a 'comfortable' income, be 'communicative' and be 'cooperative' with housework and childcare. One recent government survey showed that some half of women in their twenties believe that the husband should support his family through work, while the wife should stay at home; another shows that 70 per cent of *sengyō shufu* (full-time homemakers) believe that their husbands should share equally in housekeeping and childrearing (Sugihara 2000).

In fact, Japanese men at present do remarkably little housework and childcare. Another survey shows that in families with children under six years old, wives do an average of 2 hours 39 minutes of childcare each day, while their husbands do only 17 minutes (*Nihon no Ronten 2000* 1999b: 688). But if in fact men in Japan continue to do very little housework and childrearing, the cultural ideal and expectation has shifted: many men today can no longer simply be their family's absent breadwinner, as was the case in the past, but also must participate physically and emotionally in the home. Indeed, mass media of late feature many stories (for example Yamauchi 2000) in which husbands say, 'I'm cooperating with childcare so much!' but their wives say, 'no, it's not enough!' Japanese men today may face double pressure from work and home, pressure that their fathers did not face; and this may make being a man in Japan today more difficult than it was in the recent past.

The younger Japanese men I interviewed faced these conflicting cultural concepts and opposing social pressures in different ways. A bank worker in his twenties spoke of how work rather than family should be a man's *ikigai*, but expressed doubt as to the validity of such a formulation, even admitting, reluctantly, that he might wish he were a woman:

> I don't like my work – I really hate it – but I wouldn't want to stay at home either, taking care of my children. Maybe that's my pride – maybe I don't want to deviate from the ideal image of a man. A man is supposed to work outside the home. In Japan, if a man says his child rather than his work is his *ikigai*, he'll be considered a sissy (*memeshii*); I could never say that . . . In Japan women are discriminated against in the workplace, but at the same time they have less obligation; they have more time to follow their own pursuits. Do I wish I could be a woman instead of a man? Well . . . I could never say that; but it's possible that it's true . . .

For this man, the image of what a man should be may override his own natural inclinations. Given the work culture in which he lives, and the cultural image of masculinity that he adheres to, it seems that he must profess his deepest commitment to a job he hates over a family that he might come to love. In this thinking, from what he told me, he is following the footsteps of his father a generation earlier.

A few men I interviewed, however, *were* able to find a sense of masculine *ikigai* within their families. A junior-high-school teacher in his late twenties said:

> I want to be with my wife when she gives birth; I'll need to take three days off from school for that. When I told that to the mothers in the PTA, they said, 'That's great – go ahead!' I thought they were going to say, 'What? Why so long a vacation!' But they didn't. They really appreciate me! . . . I usually get home by 7:30 or 8:00; sometimes not until 9:00 or 10:00. All I can do after I come home so late is bathe, eat and sleep; that's tough on my wife. I'm really tired. Sometimes it's just too much trouble to listen to her, to be honest. I'd really like more free time . . . My family – my wife and child to be – is more important than

my work. I'd quit my work, if I had to, for my family. My family is my *ikigai*. I just wish I had more time to be with my family.

This man in some ways seems to embody the new concept of Japanese masculinity offered in some of the books and articles discussed above, a concept affirmed by the mothers of his students, who applaud rather than criticize his desire to be with his wife during childbirth. He was one of the few men I interviewed who maintained unambiguously that he lived for his family, an assertion seconded by his wife, a school nurse. But his work, by its demands on his time, seems designed to insinuate itself into his life as his *ikigai*. Yes, he can take three days off from teaching to be with his wife; but the demands of work force him to stay until late every day, after which he is too tired to pay much attention to his wife and soon-to-come child. Even though this man has overcome the cultural barriers to living for family, the structural barriers remain: work claims by far the greatest share of his time and his energy. This man seeks to preserve what he feels to be his humanity as against the relentless pressures of work (see Ishii-Kuntz, this volume, Chapter 12 for more on Japanese men's struggles to act as fathers).

What we have seen in this section is that while culturally the ideal of men living for their families has become increasingly advocated in Japan, structurally this remains problematic, since work continues to require so much of men. Perhaps when a new generation of managers takes the reins of Japanese companies and organizations, the structures of Japanese working life will catch up with this new cultural ideal, giving men more leeway in their lives. At present, however, the situation is ironic: the progressive Japanese cultural ideal of men living for their families seems to have become not a source of fulfillment for men but a source of pressure.

## *Ikigai* as self

Thus far, we have considered the words of men who express masculinity in terms of living for work; and we have seen how an alternative ideal, in print and in the words of at least a few men I interviewed, may be emerging: a man should live for his family. But aside from these, there is another *ikigai* ideal that has become widespread in Japan. One should not find one's *ikigai* in one's commitment to work or family; rather, *ikigai* should involve one's own 'self-realization' (Kobayashi 1989), one's deepest expression of one's self.

We saw earlier how Japanese formulations of work as *ikigai* may be changing in their emphasis from 'commitment to company' to 'self-fulfillment'; but the same trend may be happening to *ikigai* in general (Mathews 1996: 12–26). One reason for this is that as Japan has become more affluent, life choices have increased: one can more easily pursue self-fulfillment today than in the past. A bigger reason may be that many people continue to feel that they have little choice in their lives, given the social pressures they must conform to: their dreams of self-fulfillment function as a sort of escape hatch, making bearable their lack of choice in reality. This was true for a number of men I interviewed. Consider this salaryman's words, a man in his forties (see Mathews 1996: 82–7):

I hate this work – it could never be my *ikigai* . . . If I could, I'd quit the company and do something I want to do. But I can't, because I have to support my kids . . . One night I looked at my wife, and at our kids sleeping beside us. She looked so tired from taking care of them – I felt I couldn't quit the company, however much I hated it . . . I guess I don't have any *ikigai*. I love my kids – I want to teach them to be fine human beings. But my kids shouldn't be my *ikigai* – they'll have their own lives to live. My wife can't be my *ikigai* either . . . I want to live a life with meaning; I want to have an individual purpose to my existence! That's the ideal; my own life is far from that ideal . . .

This man embodies Itō's call (1995: 85) for men to cast aside their outmoded senses of masculinity, to find their own selves. But he also embodies the difficulties inherent in that call: where, for a man long living a standard salaryman's life, is any such self to be found? He seems deeply committed to his family, but also sees his family as a barrier to his own fulfillment: he stays chained to a job he hates, he tells us, for the sake of his family – this is the role he must play as breadwinner. He dreams of a purpose in life that transcends work and family, but he will probably never find such a purpose.

This man had never in his life deviated from the standard salaryman's path; and the source of much of his life's frustration was that he had never felt able to deviate, and did not know who he really was. My impression is that there are many men like him in Japan today: men who can find real personal fulfillment in neither work nor family, but who feel they cannot deviate from the social roles they are obliged to play. The economic stall over the past decade has exacerbated this sense of frustration for many men, since work can no longer provide the obvious markers of fulfillment – the salary increases and promotions – that it once did. One disillusioned salaryman is quoted in a recent article as saying, 'I cannot imagine what makes me happy. At least I can say it may not be my company, my job, or my family' (Iitake and Saito 2000).

But other men today, particularly those who have avoided the cultural and structural constraints of the standard white-collar path, have not been confined to unimaginable dreams as their *ikigai*. The salarymen I interviewed generally entered the white-collar workforce immediately after leaving school; they thus never had a chance in their adult lives to follow their dreams, if, indeed, they ever had any. Other men, however – blue-collar workers, the self-employed, artists – had often had more chequered work histories that precluded them from enjoying the high occupational status that salarymen until recently have enjoyed, but that also gave them the leeway, at least for part of their lives, to pursue their dreams. Consider the words of a former rock musician in his late thirties, now turned construction worker:

I like myself now because I'm working hard for my family, but I hate myself because I gave up music. I'm not a bad father – I'm supporting my family – but maybe it'd be better for my two kids if I showed them a father who's pursuing his dream. Life isn't only a matter of making money; that's why I half regret my life now. I want to quit my job and play music again. But it'd be hard. The older you get, the less courage you've got. Compared to five years ago, I'm much more of a coward than I used to be. Maybe I've become a better husband and father to the extent that I've grown chicken-hearted! . . . I live for my dream of music, but I also live for my wife: she too is my *ikigai*. But yeah, I guess that my real *ikigai* is music. I don't play the guitar much these days, but I have that desire – I'll have that for the rest of my life . . .

This man, unlike his more stifled white-collar counterparts, attempted for seven years to live out his dream of being a professional rock musician. It was the birth of his children that led him to give up that dream, to lead a stable life as a regular wage-earner. He does not feel embittered that his children led him to give up his dream – indeed, his love for his family almost outweighs his dream as his *ikigai* – but the dream wins out, in his sense of who he is, if not in the day-to-day practical conduct of his life.

This man has tempered his pursuit of self-realization for the sake of his family; but I interviewed one man who claimed to live only for his enjoyment of self. This man, in his early forties, had held some twenty jobs in his life, from night watchman, to factory worker, to real estate executive, to, at present, owner of his own tiny import company: 'My company now? It's fifth-rate: the absolute bottom . . . But I'm free! Nobody orders me to work!' When a job didn't suit him, he would leave, 'go to the restroom and never return', something he might yet do today, he joked. As for his family, he said:

Yeah, it's true that I've slept with lots of women outside of my marriage. Why do I need so many women? Well, why should I have to be with only one woman? My wife wouldn't understand; I want to talk about it with her, but she's too busy taking care of our kids. In the context of marriage, what I do is bad, but the context is bad! It all depends on whether you consider me as a husband or as a fuller person . . . I'm not so interested in sex; it's just the simple human encounter. I don't want to be bound by family: maybe I'm selfish, but . . . I can't teach my kids that you have to work, work, work. I'd rather give them myself than my money! . . . My *ikigai* is myself. My wife says that I'm the kind of person who thinks about nothing but himself. She's amazed: she wonders how she could spend her life with someone like me. I tell her, 'It's because I think of myself that I'm so interesting!'

For this man, work means nothing as a source of value – although he still must somehow earn a living to support his family – and family seems to mean little, although he did say that he loved his wife and children. His source of value seems to lie primarily in himself. In some ways, he is a caricature of the pursuit of self-realization in Japan today, in his unembarrassed self-centredness. In other ways, he epitomizes that pursuit – at least as described in Japanese mass media – in his ability to ignore the conventional cultural dictates of work and family, to follow his own path in life.

The ideal of self-realization is generally written about in Japan as being free of gender specificity: men and women can equally pursue such an ideal, by most accounts. Yet this man is clearly in a privileged position to pursue self-realization; Japanese women – married women anyway – are culturally forbidden from living as he has lived. Although he has, by his freewheeling attitude towards work, cut himself off from conventional Japanese notions of masculine success, he is celebrated among some of his male friends for being the epitome of masculine freedom, bound in his life by neither work nor family. Many of the Japanese men portrayed in this chapter have seemed beleaguered, pressed by the conflicting demands of work and family; but as this man reveals, the pursuit of freedom remains for at least some men a privileged masculine prerogative.

As we have seen in this section, the pursuit of self-realization may have different meanings for different men. For some, it may represent no more than a distant dream, of a self not swallowed by the demands of work and family; for others, it may represent an alternative path in life to that of labouring at a mundane job to support one's family; and for still others, it may represent a justification for self deified over all else. Despite these differences, however, this new *ikigai* may serve for a spectrum of Japanese men as a jump from work to self as *ikigai*, bypassing family. (This leap from living for work to living for self has also taken place among men in the United States, as Baumeister [1991: 365–7] and Ehrenreich [1983] discuss.) Most of the Japanese men I interviewed who spoke of living for their dream of self-realization also deeply valued their families. Yet, in at least an abstract sense, work and self have in common the fact that they are not family – as if preserving a non-family realm as the prerogative of masculine *ikigai* in Japan.

## Conclusion: can 'a real man' live for his family?

We have looked at three varieties of masculine *ikigai* in this chapter: *ikigai* as work, *ikigai* as family and *ikigai* as self and self-fulfillment. *Ikigai* as work for one's company or organization has been the taken-for-granted masculine *ikigai* for older Japanese men, but younger Japanese men no longer profess such an *ikigai*. Yet, because work continues to demand so much of men's time and energy, it continues to be, in effect, the *de facto ikigai* for many men today. *Ikigai* as family meant, for some older Japanese men, that they economically supported their families while being emotionally devoted to work; but many younger Japanese women have sought more – that their husbands be emotionally committed to their families. Some men have obliged, but others have found an emotional home in neither work nor family, but only stress from both. *Ikigai* as self has been a prominent theme in Japanese mass media in recent years, but has been more a dream than a reality in Japanese life. Some men use this dream as a sort of escape hatch, to make tolerable a constraining reality, but a few others actually pursue this dream, a cultural prerogative of husbands more than wives in Japan today.

Underlying these different *ikigai* is the gender-role division and its contestation, over whether or not 'men should live for work and women for family'. In a number of post-industrial societies today, the division of 'men at work, women at home' has become less salient than it was fifty years ago, with women playing increasingly prominent roles in the workplace. However, if women in these societies can thus live more for work than in the recent past, this has not necessarily meant that men have come to live more for family. Connell (1987: 100) cites studies from England and Australia showing how men regard housework and childcare as 'unmanly'. Hochschild (1989) explores how American working women must engage in 'the second shift' of housework and childcare because their husbands, although often expressing belief in gender equality, leave these tasks to their wives. This is an expression of men's ongoing domination of women, a domination that cannot easily be expressed in the workplace today, but that can be and is expressed at home.

In Japan, more than in the societies mentioned above, women continue to be discriminated against at work, earning far less, as compared to men, than their counterparts in other post-industrial societies. One consequence of this is that many Japanese women don't seek careers. However, these women may contest the gender division of *ikigai* not through themselves seeking to live for work but rather through seeking their husbands' devotion to family. As we have seen, this has placed men under considerable pressure in Japan today. None the less, it seems likely that most Japanese men will continue to resist living for family, as have their counterparts in other societies; a few men will live for family, but more will live for work or for self.

Why should this be the case? One reason is the particularities of Japan that I have discussed in this chapter. The gender division of *ikigai*, for all the cultural changes taking place, remains stronger in Japan than in many other societies; and the commitment to work and long working hours required of many Japanese men makes any deep commitment to family difficult to put into practice in day-to-day life.

A second reason relates to the broader patterning of cultural masculinity not just in Japan but in the world at large. Ortner (1996 [1972]) has argued that the ideology of women as belonging to nature/the domestic sphere and men as belonging to culture/the public sphere has been a universal cultural construct oppressing women. The resistance of men to living for family that we have seen in this chapter may embody a particular cultural reflection of this ideology.

A third reason is contemporary capitalism. Yamada (1999b: 145–6) argues that only when women can play as full a role in Japanese work life as men do, including higher salaries for women, will men be able to play a full role in their families. However, if Japanese women could live for work as easily as men, then might not both men and women live for work, leaving no one to find *ikigai* in family?[4] Hochschild (1997) describes how for some men and women in the United States, 'work becomes home and home becomes work': work offers both men and women the feeling of self-fulfilment that home does not. In one American woman's words (see Mathews 1996: 76),

> If you've been active in the professional world, you get a lot of strokes; when you're at home and have these little kids . . . that's not enough. Society doesn't affirm you in that role of mother because you're not making any money.

Family is devalued, as work is not, she is saying, because in the capitalist world one does not get paid for raising one's children. Although Japan has tried to resist this logic by preserving the gender division of *ikigai*, this capitalist logic may be inexorable. One apparent illustration of this logic is that more and more Japanese women and men are remaining single (Yamada 1999a), and the Japanese birthrate continues to plummet (Jolivet 1997). Increasingly it seems that many young Japanese don't believe that it is worthwhile to have families.

Can 'a real man' in Japan live for his family? Of course, and some men do, as we've seen, abetted by current progressive cultural ideals. But this is hard in Japan today, and will only get harder in the future, I suspect. In an ideal future Japan, as in an ideal future United States, both men and women would live for their families. In the real future Japan, as the gender division of *ikigai* continues to crumble, perhaps neither men nor women will live for their families.

## Notes

1  *Ojisan* is a generic term for middle-aged men, but the term carries disparaging overtones, especially when used by young women. When I ask my Japanese students about what the term *ojisan* implies for them, I am told that it refers to 'older salarymen who always get drunk and talk about sex'.

2  Japanese and Americans, I've found, tend to formulate the *ikigai* of work in different ways, with Americans tending to think of work in self-oriented terms ('If I didn't have this job, I'd lose a lot of self-esteem') and Japanese often thinking of work in more group-oriented terms. It will be interesting to investigate whether, as the ideal of lifetime employment fades in Japan, Japanese formulations of *ikigai* as work will begin to resemble those of many Americans. This relates to the larger issue of whether living for self, rather than for family or work or religion, is becoming the general value base of contemporary modernity, as Baumeister (1991) implies.

3  Although close to half the wives of the men I interviewed worked, in only two cases was that work of a sort that could rival that of their husbands. Mostly they worked at part-time jobs, and told me that the priority of their lives was not work but family.

4  This is particularly likely to happen if work in Japan becomes reformulated not as a commitment to company that is seen as inferior to commitment to family, but as a pursuit of self-fulfillment that is seen as superior to commitment to family. This may already be happening (see Mathews 2001).

## References

Allison, A. (2000) *Permitted and Prohibited Desires: Mothers, Comics and Censorship in Japan*, Berkeley: University of California Press. Previously published in 1996, Westview.

*Asahi Shinbun* (1999a) 'Managers protest their sacrifice on "restructuring" altar', *Asahi Evening News*, November 3.

—— (1999b) 'Women find unexpected turns on road to work equality', *Asahi Evening News*, December 11–12.

Baumeister, R. (1991) *Meanings of Life*, New York: Guilford Press.

Connell, R. W. (1987) *Gender and Power*, Stanford: Stanford University Press.

*Economist, The* (1999) 'Who wants to be a sarariman?', Business in Japan Survey, November 27.

Ehrenreich, B. (1983) *The Hearts of Men: American Dreams and the Flight from Commitment*, New York: Doubleday Anchor Books.

Garon, S. (1997) *Molding Japanese Minds: The State in Everyday Life*, Princeton: Princeton University Press.

Hirokane, K. (1997) *Tahu na 'Otoko' ni Naru 80 Kajō (Eighty Ways to be a 'Real Man')*, Tokyo: Kōdansha.

Hochschild, A. (1997) *The Time Bind: When Work Becomes Home and Home Becomes Work*, New York: Henry Holt.

Hochschild, A., with Machung, A. (1989) *The Second Shift*, New York: Avon.

Iitake, K. and Saito, J. (2000) 'Workers searching for new meaning in life as values change', *Asahi Evening News*, January 1–2.

Itō, K. (1995) '*Otoko no sei mo mata hitotsu de wa nai*' (There's more than one way to be a man), in T. Inoue, C. Ueno and Y. Ehara (eds) *Danseigaku (Men's Studies)*, Tokyo: Iwanami Shoten.

Iwao, S. (1993) *The Japanese Woman: Traditional Image and Changing Reality*, New York: Free Press.

Jolivet, M. (1997) *Japan, the Childless Society?: The Crisis of Motherhood*, trans. A. M. Glasheen, London: Routledge.

Kashima, T. (1993) *Otoko no Zahyōjiku: Kigyō kara Kazoku, Shakai e (Men's Position Today: From Company to Family and Society)*, Tokyo: Iwanami Shoten.

Kawanishi, Y. (1999) 'Japan's declining birthrate: a good thing?', *Japan Times*, December 18.

Kobayashi, T. (1989) *'Ikigai' to wa Nani ka: Jikojitsugen e no Michi (What is Ikigai? The Path Toward Self-realization)*, Tokyo: Nihon Hōsō Shuppan Kyōkai.

Mathews, G. (1996) *What Makes Life Worth Living? How Japanese and Americans Make Sense of Their Worlds*, Berkeley: University of California Press.

—— (2001) '*Ikigai no bunkateki bunmyaku–Nihon to Amerika*' (The cultural context of *ikigai*: Japan and the United States), in Y. Takahashi and S. Wada (eds) *Ikigai no Shakaigaku (The Sociology of Ikigai)*, Tokyo: Kōbundō.

Minami, I. (1989) '*Chūnen dansei no seikatsu to ikikata*' (The ways of life of middle-aged men), in K. Misawa *et al.* (eds) *Gendaijin no Raifukōsu (Contemporary Lifecourse)*, Kyoto: Mineruva Shobō.

Morinaga, T. (1999) '*Mazu keieijin mizukara chinsage o fukumu risutora o dankōshi genba no koyō o mamorubeshi*' (Protect employment by carrying out restructuring, including reduced salaries for managers), in *Nihon no Ronten 2000 (Issues for Japan 2000)*, Tokyo: Bungei Shunjū.

Myōki, H. (1997) *Chichioya Hōkai (The Collapse of Fatherhood)*, Tokyo: Shinshokan.

*Nihon no Ronten 2000* (1999a) '*Sekuhara no Teigi to Koyō no Byōdō o Kangaeru' Tame no Kiso Chishiki (Basic Knowledge for Thinking about the Definition of Sexual Harassment and Equal Employment Opportunities)*, Tokyo: Bungei Shunjū.

—— (1999b) '*Seibetsu Yakuwari Bungyō to Chichioya no Ikuji Sanka o Kangaeru' Tame no Kiso Chishiki (Basic Knowledge for Thinking About Sex Roles and the Father's Participation in Childrearing)*, Tokyo: Bungei Shunjū.

Ōhashi, K. (2000) *Kyosen: Jinsei no Sentaku (Kyosen: Choices in Life)*, Tokyo: Kōdansha.

Ortner, S. (1996) [1972] 'Is female to male as nature is to culture?', in *Making Gender: The Politics and Erotics of Culture*, Boston: Beacon Press.

Ōsawa, M. (1993) *Kigyō Chūshin Shakai o Koete: Gendai Nihon o Jendā de Yomu (Overcoming the Corporate-centred Society: A Gendered Reading of Contemporary Japan)*, Tokyo: Jijitsūsinsha.

Ōshima, T. (1999) '*Aisha seishin kieru toki*' (When love for one's company vanishes), *Aera*, November 22.

Pyke, K. (1996) 'Class-based masculinities: the interdependence of gender, class and interpersonal power', *Gender and Society* 10, 5: 527–49.

Satō, Y. (1999) '*Ojisan no nioi: sonna ni ki ni naru?*' (The smell of middle-aged men: is it really that bad?), *Asahi Shinbun*, December 8.

Shimizu, C. (1998) *Ojisan Kaizō Kōza 9: Yūki o Motte Tobidasō! (Lectures for Remodelling Middle-aged Men, no. 9: Be Brave and Leap!)*, Tokyo: Bungei Shunjū.

Sugihara, S. (2000) ' *"Kekkon de seikatsu teika iya"* ('I'd hate to have my standard of living lowered because of marriage'), *Asahi Shinbun*, April 4.

Suzuki, K. (1999) '*Haki o ushinatta Nihonjin – ima hodo ikuji ni "fusei" ga hitsuyō to sareru jidai wa nai*' (The lost vigour of Japanese: now is the time when 'the father' is needed in childrearing), in *Nihon no Ronten 2000 (Issues for Japan 2000)*, Tokyo: Bungei Shunjū.

Ueno, C. (1995) Introduction to Chapter 5, '*Kigyō senshitachi*' (Corporate warriors), in T. Inoue, C. Ueno and Y. Ehara (eds) *Danseigaku (Men's Studies)*, Tokyo: Iwanami Shoten.

Yamada, M. (1999a) *Parasaito Shinguru no Jidai (The Age of Parasite Singles)*, Tokyo: Chikuma Shobō.

—— (1999b) *Kazoku no Risutorakucharingu (Restructuring the Family)*, Tokyo: Shin'yōsha.

Yamauchi, K. (2000) '*Ikuji sanka papa no yūutsu*' (Papa's feeling depressed participating in childrearing), *Asahi Shinbun*, April 7.

# 8 Japanese working-class masculinities
## Marginalized complicity

*James E. Roberson*

Making use of the recent literature on men and masculinities, in this chapter[1] I bring a gender-informed perspective to bear in refocusing my attention on the men working at the small metals factory where I have conducted research (see Roberson 1995a, 1995b, 1998a, 1998b). The goal of the chapter is to contribute to the discussion of the multiplicity of masculinities manifest in Japan by considering the inter-articulation of class and gender among the working-class men I studied. I hope to show how, through practice, these men simultaneously reproduce a class-based masculinity that in many ways is different and marginalized from hegemonic middle-class masculinity and yet is complicit with the hegemony of the white-collar, middle-class salaryman model of masculinity and the patriarchal system of gendered relations in Japan.

I first briefly suggest a practice-theory-based view of the diversity, dynamics, connections and contradictions among class, gender, identity/agency and context/ structure. I then describe aspects of the construction of gendered practices and experiences among the men working at the Shintani Metals Company, where I conducted ethnographic fieldwork in 1989–90. This firm employed around 50 to 55 people during this time (more at the beginning, less at the end), including some 35 to 40 men. In particular, I will discuss such masculine practices in interrelation with educational, employment and work, and non-work family and leisure contexts.

## Perspective: a gendered theory of practice

Practice-theory approaches to the study of gender have been advocated and employed most notably by Sherry Ortner (1996), whose research deals primarily with women, and R. W. Connell (1987, 1995), whose research and writing focus on men. Both Ortner and Connell emphasize the 'making of gender' in individual agency and practice and as simultaneously contexted within and interrelated with various broader social, economic, historical and cultural structures. Connell suggests that 'Gender is a way in which social practice is ordered' (1995: 71), and notes: 'Taking a dynamic view of the organization of practice, we arrive at an understanding of masculinity and femininity as *gender projects*. These are processes of configuring practice through time, which transform their starting-points in gender structures' (ibid.: 72).

Henrietta Moore, meanwhile, notes that recent work in feminist anthropology has emphasized the need to recognize that class and gender are 'mutually determining systems . . . [and] that gender differences find very different expression within different class levels' (1988: 80; see also di Leonardo 1991: 31). In an earlier statement, Ortner and Whitehead noted that 'Gender conceptions . . . are seen as *emergent* from varying forms of *action, or practice*, within varying forms of organization of social, economic, and political life' (1981: 5; emphasis added). Recent writing in masculinities studies (Connell 1987, 1995; Hearn and Morgan 1990; Morgan 1992) has similarly emphasized the importance of class context in understanding the multiplicity of masculinities. From a practice perspective, class and gender, themselves always also interrelated, become significant structural contexts reflexively implicated with(in) individual identity and action. Connell more generally writes: 'To understand gender, then, we must constantly go beyond gender. The same applies in reverse. We cannot understand class, race or global inequality without constantly moving towards gender' (1995: 76).

Connell distinguishes among hegemonic, subordinate, complicit and marginalized masculinities in discussing the interrelations of 'gender and power' (1987) and the multiplicity of 'masculinities' (1995). Hegemonic masculinity is 'the configuration of gender practice which embodies the currently accepted answer to the problem of the legitimacy of patriarchy, which guarantees (or is taken to guarantee) the dominant position of men and the subordination of women' (ibid.: 77) and, furthermore, the dominant position of certain men over other men. As Morgan notes, 'patriarchy is also about the dominance of men by men as well as the dominance of women by men' (1992: 196), and 'any society has a range of masculinities, historically shaped, which are hierarchically, if not always in an absolutely fixed fashion, arranged' (ibid.: 203).

Connell uses the term 'marginalization' to refer to 'the relations between the masculinities in dominant and subordinated classes or ethnic groups' (1995: 80–1). Such subordination may engender a 'protest masculinity' among some working-class men (ibid.: 109ff.). However, marginalized men may also be 'complicit in the collective project of patriarchy' (ibid.: 114–15). Connell explains such 'complicity' with the hegemonic masculine project as based on the fact that non-hegemonic men also 'benefit from the *patriarchal dividend*, the advantage men in general gain from the overall subordination of women' (ibid.: 79; emphasis added). Though socially and economically marginalized, they remain complicit with the dominant cultural (and political–economic) ideology of masculinity.

It is this dynamic, among hegemonic, marginalized and complicit masculinities that I want to explore in describing the lives and gendered practices among the men working at Shintani Metals. In Japan, hegemonic masculinity has most commonly been associated with or ascribed to middle-class, white-collar salarymen and the ideologies – masculinist, capitalist, statist – they embody and employ. Salarymen are in a privileged class position, accorded social prestige, assumed to have or perform corporate and work-centred identities and practices, and benefit fully from the 'patriarchal dividend' of male superiority and separation from the domestic sphere.

The salaryman becomes the embodiment, real and ideal, of the ideological model of masculine superiority and success, which other men are assumed to aspire to through educational and employment achievements, which parents presumably desire for their sons and which corporations and other state institutions powerfully instil and support. The actual social, economic and political power of salarymen and their representatives over other (subordinated and marginalized) men and (all) women is in part a manifestation of differences in masculinities as embedded (di Leonardo 1991) in class differences.

If variations in class result in/from variations in (self-)gendering practice (and, as Connell suggests, gender as practice), then working-class men in Japan should manifest relative, though not absolute, differences from salaryman members of the middle class. Writing with reference to Japanese women, but in a statement that may also be applied to men, Kondo has noted that 'when one is delineating the various cleavages among women, class differences are replayed in a powerful, distilled form' (1990: 284). Despite such theoretical and, when applied to women (see also Roberts 1994), ethnographic recognition of the diversity engendered by the interconnections between class and gender, the dominant representations of Japanese men have portrayed them as (like) middle-class, white-collar salarymen. Little has yet been written about other men and different masculinities in Japan as these relate to class (see Mathews and Gill, this volume, Chapters 7 and 9 respectively).

## Japanese working-class men: gendered class practice

According to Bourdieu (1984), a class (or 'fraction' thereof) is composed of agents whose lives are characterized by similar sets of economic and cultural conditions and capital. These in turn produce 'systems of dispositions capable of generating similar practices' (ibid.: 101). Individual agency and practice are in ongoing and reflexive interrelationships with class context and with class reproduction and change. Like other structuring contexts, class must be understood to be both constraining *and* enabling.

Various discussions of the class structure of contemporary Japan recognize some occupational, blue-collar versus white-collar, basis for distinguishing among classes (see Roberson 1998a; Sugimoto 1997). While not consistently so in all dimensions, Japanese blue-collar working-class men and women are generally recognized as having lower educations, incomes, home ownership, investment, luxury possessions and so forth. Ishida's (1993) work is of particular importance here. He notes that 'Firm size appears to be a powerful factor differentiating employees within classes' (ibid.: 224). The class structure of Japan, he concludes, 'is characterized by a combination of polarization and inconsistency of status characteristics with a further differentiation among employees by firm size' (ibid.: 259).

The importance of firm size in the constitution of class distinctions in Japan is suggested by a number of economic indicators. Contrary to dominant domestic ideals and foreign representations, most Japanese people (white- and blue-collar) are in fact not employed by larger corporations but by medium–small enterprises. Some 70 per cent of all Japanese employees are employed by firms with fewer than 100 workers, 50 per cent by firms with 30 or fewer employees (see Roberson 1998a). Firm size is generally correlated with wages, bonuses and benefits: the smaller the company, the less received. Firm size is also correlated with rates of unionization (see Chalmers 1989; Sugimoto 1997). The lower wages, etc. in smaller companies must also be understood in relation to the fact that these firms also provide less corporate sponsorship than do larger enterprises of housing, recreational and leisure facilities and activities, loans and so forth (see Roberson 1998a).

Rates of intra- and interfirm mobility also differ among employees of large and small enterprises. Seiyama notes that employees of smaller companies have higher levels of intercompany mobility and lower levels intracompany mobility, and that blue-collar workers are less internally mobile than are white-collar workers (1994). Such mobility is in part related to historically higher rates of failure found among smaller enterprises (see Roberson 1998a).

John Lie further points out that 'The gulf between white-collar employees in large corporations and blue-collar workers in small firms remains striking not just in terms of income [and other material conditions] but in terms of class culture' (1996: 37–8). Though of a different order than the mobility of the day labourers described by Gill (2001, this volume, Chapter 9), I have argued elsewhere (Roberson 1998a) that the relatively higher rates of inter-firm mobility among blue-collar workers in smaller firms must be seen in terms of class economic conditions such as company closures, as well as in interrelation with working-class perceptions and practices regarding work, employment and company affiliation. Kondo has similarly noted that 'the distinction between small and large firms is a culturally meaningful one . . . [and] these distinctions among firms are laden with symbolic, cultural and moral value' (1990: 53).

The class context outlined above, in both economic and cultural dimensions, is one of the principal structuring contexts of the social–economic marginalization of – and is reproduced by the agency and practice, including the 'gender projects' of – Japanese working-class men and women. One implication of such class-based marginalization is that becoming and remaining the '*daikokubashira*' (main pillar) provider and head of the family and household – one of the main tenets of idealized/ideologized masculinity in Japan – is more contingent and shaky for working-class men than for middle-class men. Greater employment insecurity, thinner pay packages and weaker commitment combine to suggest that, even if the great pillar does not 'evaporate' (see Gill, this volume, Chapter 9), this dimension of masculinity, among others, is realized in class-relative styles and practice.

### Education: tracks and paths

A number of authors in and outside Japan have discussed the class nature of education, in particular the interrelation of education and class reproduction. The works of MacLeod (1995), Okano (1993) and Willis (1977) are of particular interest because of their articulation of class culture and students' agency as individuals in constructing educational careers that, intentionally or otherwise, lead them to employment positions within the working class (of America, Japan and England, respectively). The interrelation of working-class notions of masculinity and class reproduction is most directly and fully explored by Willis. The 'lads' he describes develop 'an oppositional masculinity which led them towards the factory floor' (Connell 1995: 37). The tough machismo of Willis's lads and MacLeod's 'hangers' is perhaps similar to the 'ultramasculinity, bravado, defiance and . . . emphasis on violence' (including sexual violence) described by Sato (1991: 69) among 'Yankee' and '*bōsōzoku*' (motor gang) youth in Japan. While not necessarily of working-class backgrounds, these young men 'may be categorized as working-class or blue-collar in terms of their occupations and tastes' (ibid.: 138).

Such 'ultramasculine' machismo was, however, not apparent among the working-class men I describe below. I will argue that there are class-based masculinities involved in their educational (and other) trajectories, but unlike the 'lads' and '*bōsōzoku*' youth these do not appear to have involved a 'protest masculinity' (Connell 1995), defiance or rebellion against middle-class norms of educational achievement, career paths or masculinity. This suggests that further distinctions of 'class fraction' (Bourdieu 1984) within the working class need to be kept in mind when investigating the articulations of class and gender.

Popular and academic representations of educational careers in Japan have come to portray Japan as a country with a highly structured educational system producing a uniformly highly educated populace, whose members are singularly motivated for their children's, especially sons', educational advancement through college graduation (White 1987; Brinton 1993). While it is also recognized that not all (or, less commonly admitted, even the majority of) students continue to (junior) college, it is commonly suggested that not continuing on to higher education is the result of the failure on the part of the individual student (and perhaps his parents, primarily his mother). No doubt such failures of individual intelligence or preparation do occur. However, educational careers in Japan, as elsewhere, are also class- and gender-related phenomena.

The class backgrounds of the families of the men at Shintani Metals (here based on fathers' educations and occupations) may generally, though not uniformly, be considered to have been working class in nature (see Roberson 1995a, 1998a), and a set of class and gender reflexivities may be seen in the educations of these boys becoming working-class men. While talking about their educational backgrounds and school experiences, it was fairly common to hear the men say that they did not get into higher-ranked institutions or go on to higher levels of education was because their 'heads were no good' (*atama ga warui*) or similar such things. This, of course, reproduces the middle-class discourse of the meritocratic nature of the educational system, (self-)legitimizing their marginalization.

However, talking in more detail, most of the men provided other, more contextual or circumstantial, and more positive and proactive, explanations for their educational paths that simultaneously implicate historically contexted class and gender positionalities. For example, Mr Ikeda, a Tokyoite who began working after finishing junior high school in the 1950s, explained that he had wanted to continue on to high school but, he said:

I'm the first son, right? There were other children below me. At the time, life wasn't easy for my father and for my mother. So, if possible we want you to work, they said. I gave up on going to high school and so 'went out into society'.

Mr Ikeda's gendered position within the family as first son, who as successor to family headship is ideologically and commonly in practice responsible for maintaining the family, combined with the class-based conditions of poverty, lead him out of school and into society to work.

In other cases, families as the mediators of class position acted in more culturally constituted/ing ways. For many men, parents seem not to have placed great importance on educational achievement as such or entry into a university in particular. Several of the older men (and women), themselves now parents, held similar views. Mr Honda, for example, said 'I leave it up to the kid's desires (*kodomo no ishi ni makaseru*) . . . I was a junior high graduate myself, so that way of thinking is strong in me'.

Other men talked of the influences of older male family members in pursuing the acquisition of manual skills. Horiuchi,[2] whose father worked as a machinist, explained that it was his father's idea for him to go to an industrial high school in order to learn practical skills. Miyata likewise said:

> I had already decided to enter an industrial high school from my first year of junior high school. That was because my uncle had gone to an industrial high school and I'd heard various stories from him. And then there was also the fact that I really liked electronics construction and that sort of thing, and so I went to an industrial high school.

In addition to reflecting the importance of influential male role models in deciding on educational trajectories, reflected in Miyata's comment, and in those of others, are more personal preferences to acquire industrial and craft skills or to work with machines. Some of the (especially middle-aged or older) women at Shintani Metals had also gone to vocational schools, but they had studied nursing, dressmaking and early childhood education. While it is also true that educational content, work and machinery are not inherently or ahistorically gendered either male or female, within the historical context of postwar Japan in which they were constructing life paths, the vocational educations pursued or preferred by the Shintani Metals workers reflect gender differences in the class-contexted construction of both education and employment.

A number of the men at the factory told me that they were not really interested in school or studying while they were still in (junior or senior high) school. Takayama, the youngest man not to go to high school, explained that he had thought that doing so would not make much difference and that he had wanted to begin learning a skilled craft and make money. For men such as these, as with Willis's 'lads', starting to work, earn money and acquire a skill were more important, interesting and satisfying (at least at first), but their actions also work to reproduce working-class masculine gender trajectories.

## Employment: gendered careers and practice

Having graduated from one level or rank of educational institution or another, the men at Shintani Metals all began and continue to work. Work, of course, is one of the central contexts of everyday experience and practice in the construction of masculine identities in Japan (Mathews 1996, this volume, Chapter 7) as in many other modern societies (Gilmore 1990). One must be wary of directly associating different masculinities with different occupations (Morgan 1992: 80), and I will argue below that one must also be cautious about assuming the singular centrality of work in the construction of male identities. Nevertheless, the perceptions and experiences of work and the interrelationships among personal identity, lifecourse and work as seen among the men at Shintani Metals suggest that there *are* (also) work-related class distinctions among men and masculine identities in Japan. As Morgan notes: 'It is in the interplay between agency and structure, between employee and workplace that themes of gender, and in this case masculine, identity are elaborated' (ibid.).

### Work careers and life paths

The typical description of male work careers in Japan has long represented these, like education, as rather linear, structured, secure and predictable, bound after graduation from school to and within one institution of employment and progressing through a standard set of lifecourse-correlated stages (see Nakane 1970; Plath 1983; Rohlen 1974; Vogel 1971). For some working-class men a similarly constructed life trajectory is achieved, for other men such is at least desired, reflecting the normative nature of the idealized middle-class life trajectory. For many other working-class men, even if not marked by the uncertainty of more fully marginalized men (Gill 2001, this volume, Chapter 9), the construction of work histories and lifecourse paths is more diverse and complicated, to some extent resembling the 'fragmentary' and 'contingent' work histories Kondo (1990: 260) has noted of the women working part-time in the small factory where she conducted research. However, while there are similar class-related factors involved, there are also differently gendered reasons for such movement. Women move in and out of paid employment while giving priority to domestic work and responsibilities. Men, on the other hand, may move from one job to another, but try to stay gainfully employed in order to (or because they must) remain the primary providers for their families.

Several men at Shintani Metals explained that, while working in a larger company might provide better wages and greater prestige and security, they preferred the opportunities available in smaller firms to make use of a variety of skills; to receive more personalized recognition for their work, and to avoid getting stuck doing the same thing. The reasons for working at Shintani Metals given by many of the men were related to personal preferences, including the enjoyment of making things, of working with one's hands and/or of working with machines. In a typical statement, Shinoyama, who had previously worked at various other manufacturing enterprises, explained entering Shintani Metals thus:

I felt that if it's this, it's in the range of my experience so it looks like I can do it. And then, afterwards, there's also the sense that it's because I like this kind of work. Because I like to make things.

Like others of the men, Shinoyama also said that he felt more suited to working with machines and doing blue-collar work than to doing sales and working with people. His statement is one of identity that in its valorization of manufacturing work must be read as simultaneously gendered and class reflexive, indexing a particular working-class context in which 'the familiar connection between masculinity and machinery' (Connell 1995: 55) was, if even then changing, still intact.

There were several men working at Shintani Metals who had remained at the company for (nearly) the entirety of their work careers, after having graduated from junior high or (industrial) high schools, or after having worked elsewhere while younger. Mr Ikeda, at the time 50 years old, once explained the appeal to his generation of finding employment in a stable company, using the phrase '*nagai mono ni makarero*' (meaning, more or less, to attach oneself to someone powerful). Others of the older men spoke of their sense of personal indebtedness to the Company President as part of what has kept them at the firm for the length of their careers. However, the working-class and small-company contexts of the lives and work of these men must not be forgotten. Robert Cole noted some time ago that smaller firms may (attempt to) offer 'employment security *as long as the company lasts*' (1979: 21, emphasis added).[3]

In the second part of the above sentence, Cole further notes that even if a particular company remains more or less stable, 'workers may still choose to move on in search of better wages and working conditions' (ibid.), breaching the culturally sanctioned ideal of lifetime employment constructed in reference to white-collar salarymen and the working-class aristocracy employed in large companies. Gordon (1985), Koike (1983) and others have pointed out that working-class men have historically been peripatetic in their pursuits (as workers, or, eventually, as entrepreneurs) of employment, skills and independence. Such movement is simultaneously classed and gendered in the sense of being a manifestation of a masculinized pursuit of skills and in terms of being enabled and constrained by gender relations in which women prioritize management of the home (see Kondo 1990) while men do what they will or what they can within the Japanese capitalist economy to earn a living in support of their families. I will return to this point later.

I believe that especially among working-class Japanese men we must make a distinction between 'work(ing)' and 'job' similar to Pyke's suggestion that American working-class men 'do not have male "careers" but "jobs"' (1996: 533). While I would agree that work and working are important for the men at Shintani Metals, I argue that for many men having a job at a particular company is of much less significance. The 'commitment' which salarymen and employees of larger firms are supposed to have, and even the desire to 'join a firm' and have a company-centred identity reported by Kondo (1990: 255), seem to me to overly privilege the (ideology and/or the discourse of the) company as site or centre of masculine identity, especially among working-class men in smaller firms.

Kondo has, however, also noted the significance placed on having embodied skills among the male artisans she studied. In the case of working-class men at Shintani Metals as well, having their own skills, earning their living and being able to support their families by making things is, I believe, part of their construction of masculine identities and courses of work and life. Among these men, personally desired or embodied skills, personal obligations or the more straightforward need to make a living were of more importance than 'company affiliation' or 'company identity' described and prescribed among white-collar, middle-class salarymen.

*Work (and) experience*

Connell notes that 'There is an irreducible bodily dimension in experience and practice' (1995: 51), such that the body is implicated in what he terms 'body-reflexive practice' (ibid.: 61) which also involves broader social–historical relations and symbolism (ibid.: 64). Thus he writes that 'Particular versions of masculinity are constituted in their circuits as meaningful bodies and embodied meanings. Through body-reflexive practices, more than individual lives are formed: a social world is formed' (ibid.). 'The making of working-class masculinity on the factory floor', he notes, 'has different dynamics from the making of middle-class masculinity in the air-conditioned office' (ibid.: 36).

Among the confectioneries craftsmen at the factory where she did her research, Kondo has similarly noted the prevalence of 'physical idioms of technical capability' and the sense of interconnectedness between men, their tools and machines (1990: 238, 244). While the discourse of the men at Shintani Metals did not necessarily index the importance of a sense of interconnectedness, the embodied, material- and machine-dependent nature of the manufacturing work they did may more generally be seen to be part of the everyday practice which structures and gives expression to certain working-class masculine identities. These are men for many of whom being able to work with machines and tools, being able to work with one's hands, getting dirty and tired, having the physical marks (of rough hands and calluses) of such work, were simultaneously marks of their manliness.

Part of the manufacturing of masculine identities among working-class men may thus be intimated in bodily practice, helping to differentiate these men from 'pen-pushing' white-collar members of the middle class. This reflexivity of bodily practice may also create distinctions among 'working-class men'. Such differentiation was apparent to me one day at the Shintani Metals factory when I and others of the men watched and commented on the physical strength and prowess of workers from a moving company who were transporting heavy lathes and other equipment into the factory. Fowler (1996) similarly describes power- and prowess-based distinctions among day labourers.

Such differentiation of embodied skills, as Kondo (1990) notes, separates the boys from the men. It is also one example of the factory-floor manufacture of masculinity dividing the men from the women. Men were assumed to be most knowledgeable of and skilled at the work to be done. Based on and reasserting broader assumptions of male authority and privilege, this did not always sit well with all of the women. For example, one of the reasons Ms Shimada, a young woman employed full-time, left the company was that although she had wanted to learn the skills involved in making jewellery she was instead made to do the paperwork for the section into which she was placed.

Gender relations at the Shintani Metals factory were fundamentally patriarchal and because of that sometimes conflictual, but they were also contradictory and to some extent changing. Men assumed most positions of formal authority – with only one exception at the time of my fieldwork, all of the fourteen sections in the company were headed by men. Men's exercise of their authority could become a source of criticism from the women. Mrs Naitō told me that she and others of the part-time women workers disliked being told, often in rough language, to stop an unfinished task and begin working on something else. She also said that when a foreman's way of doing things is bad, 'I just want to oppose it' (*hanpatsu shitaku natchau*). Although (no doubt in part because of restricted access to more private conversations among women) I did not hear or witness the kinds of 'everyday resistance' by women that Ogasawara (1998) describes, disagreements with male foremen were one reason for women to leave the company (see Roberson 1998a).

Men were also assumed to have the greatest responsibility towards the work. At one meeting of the section in which I worked, the section head Mr Shintani (the owner's nephew) explained the need for the two young men (and myself) working under him to do increased overtime in order to meet an upcoming deadline. He attempted to justify the amount of work, in part, by saying that '*otoko wa hatarakanakya naranai*', that men must work, that it is the role of men to work. When Mrs Sugimoto, the part-timer assigned to the section asked if she too needed to work late, Mr Shintani again answered in a gender-stereotypical manner. He excused her, saying that although part-timers left at four or five (earlier than the full-time employees, male or female), he understood that they then had to go shopping and/or prepare dinner for their families. Otherwise, their husbands would complain at the women; after all, he said, it's really '*iya na koto*' (disagreeable) (for a man) to return home and not find dinner prepared.

Partly in response to the labour shortage making it difficult to recruit young male factory workers, the strictness of this gendered division of labour at the factory had, however, already begun to change while I was there. While part-timers have, of course, always done less skilled manual jobs, one full-time woman was primarily involved in jewellery production and another woman, whose main responsibilities were in design and office work, was occasionally brought into the shop area to do various manual jobs. On a return visit to the factory some years later, there were several new women employees apparently working full-time on the shop floor. Whether these women represent an 'invasion' or are 'tokens' (Morgan 1992) of female entry into a previously masculine occupation and zone of authority remains to be seen, but their presence surely represents a class-contexted necessity for at least some measure of change in the confluence of work and gender in the Shintani Metals factory.

## *After and outside of work: leisure and family*

Discussing the male working-class culture in a Canadian town, Dunk notes that 'the activities pursued during leisure time are useful places to begin a description and anaylsis of the cultural themes important to the working-class' (1991: 65) and that 'it is impossible to separate [working-class men's] ideas about masculinity and femininity from their ideas about work and play' (ibid.: 100). Morgan similarly writes that

> it is clear that in matters of gender as well as in other matters we cannot confine our analysis to the workplace . . . we are often dealing with the points of intersection between work and other relationships, particularly domestic and familial ones but also to do with class and community.
>
> (1992: 98)

In the following, I describe some of the reflexive interrelationships that may be seen among my Japanese working-class informants in terms of class, non-work leisure and family-based action and the construction of masculine identities as gendered practice.

### *Ideology at work in play?*

'The leisure behaviour of white- and blue-collar workers is rather different,' Sepp Linhart notes, 'despite the notion that Japan is a big middle-class society without clearly visible class differences' (1998: 9). Discussions of (male) leisure in Japan still manifest and reproduce class-biased views of play. Particularly problematic are continuing tendencies to focus on homosocial (see Bird 1996) after-hours leisure activities and relationships among white-collar middle-class Japanese men and, related to this, to view men's leisure (and sexuality) as singularly structured and given meaning by company, work and co-worker contexts (see Allison 1993, 1994).

Views of male leisure as company-contexted, corporate-ideologically structured or otherwise work-related (if only as bodily rest and recuperation interstitial to and necessary for work), while describing undeniable aspects of what many men do in their leisure hours, are overly reductionistic and essentializing. I argue that leisure among the working-class men at the Shintani Metals differs in significant ways from masculine leisure as typically portrayed among white-collar salarymen. At the same time, similarities in male family roles and domestic practice reproduce the overall structure of gender relations, or what Connell (1996) calls the 'gender order', of Japanese society and so are complicit in hegemonic patriarchal masculinity.

As I have discussed in more detail elsewhere (Roberson 1995b; 1998a), neither the company, particular workgroups or other (semi-)formal groups such as the workers' association organize frequent leisure events or outings. The company owns no recreational facilities, as is more common of smaller than of larger enterprises. Furthermore, presence at 'sponsored' events is not as obligatory as has been suggested by some writers discussing white-collar employees (Atsumi 1979, 1989).

All of these are consequences of the marginalized working-class context of Shintani Metals and of the men and women working there. Sponsored leisure events in smaller companies are not very effective means of creating corporate and/or masculine bonds of solidarity (Rohlen 1974) or of embodying a corporate masculine ideology (Allison 1993, 1994).

In addition to sponsored leisure events, the men (and women) at Shintani Metals also participate in leisure events organized by informal groups of *nakama* co-worker friends. These *nakama* groups are characterized by their flexible, non-workgroup-based and frequently heterosocial (Bird 1996) memberships, relatively infrequent outings and the non-obligatory nature of presence of members (though there are certain social limits to frequent absence). The infrequency, small scale, local venues, self-made and cost-sensitive nature of many of the activities (see Roberson 1995b, 1998a) are reflections of the economically marginalized class positions of the participants.

Work-related leisure practices were manifest among a number of men who claimed to enjoy using skills employed at work in hobbies making things – for one man, jewellery, for another man, hunting-knives.[4] For others, the connection to work is not as direct. For example, Mr Okakura, who specialized in jewellery-making and repair at the factory, painted, practised calligraphy and more recently has begun making violins. As he himself once pointed out, these are all like the work that he has done at Shintani Metals and elsewhere (as a shoe craftsman), making things with his own hands. Conversely, private hobbies and interests in making things led a number of men (and a few women) to work at the factory (see Roberson 1998a).

Not all leisure among men that has interconnections with work necessarily does so in ways that a corporate-hegemonic representation would suggest. And not all male leisure is company or co-worker contexted or related – in practice or ideology. Although I believe that more work on leisure among middle-class men remains to be done to investigate the extent of their co-optation by company contexts and corporate ideologies, there do appear to be distinctions in how blue- and white-collar workers (are able to) spend their leisure time.

While such leisure activities may be seen as reflecting the marginalized class position of the men (and women) at Shintani Metals, relations between men and women at play, while complex, suggest the complicity of the men (at least) in maintaining a hierarchical gender order. The self-regulatory assumption of masculine privilege is suggested in, for example, claims by Mr Shintani and Mr Honda that when going out after hours they never call their wives to say that they will be late, since if they were to always do so they would be given a hard time by other men. I was also teased about calling my wife on those occasions when an impromptu invitation kept me out.

Sexualized discourse privileging the male gaze similar to those described by Allison (1993, 1994) could occasionally also be heard in the conversations at heterosocial leisure events. At one party, the factory manager and one of the older men, both well into their cups, seemed to be questioning Ms Imai, one of the young full-time women workers, about and commenting on her breast size. On another occasion, at a '*niji-kai*' (the second party after a main event), a very drunk Mr Abe expressed his desire to have sex with one or two of the part-time women present (like him, well into middle age). Such explicitly male/phallocentric comments were rarely made directly to women, and then only when drinking (often heavily), but may none the less be heard as expressions of hierarchical patriarchal privilege.

However, leisure-contexted gender and sexualized relations and discourse were also more complex, suggesting that extreme expressions of male discursive privilege must also be qualified and put into a broader context of gender relations. As has been noted by others, older women who are either married or in their thirties or forties have greater license to playfully express their sexuality during leisure events. Conversations among the younger men and women, meanwhile, often focused on who liked or might (not) be dating whom and on whether or not certain of the men approaching 30 had any prospects of getting married, simultaneously indexing general heterosexual concerns and the difficulties in finding mates among men in smaller companies who make less money and have fewer opportunities to meet women than employees of larger firms – especially given the popular discourse on attractive men as having a high education and a high salary, in addition to being tall in stature (see Miller, this volume, Chapter 3).

Overall, the fact that the men working at Shintani Metals are members of the Japanese working class is revealed and reproduced in these, and other, leisure practices. Some forms of play reflect economic constraints, some reflect class-cultural preferences or tastes and some leisure practices make use of work-based skills. These events and practices of play simultaneously index, reflect and reproduce a broader set of masculine privileges *vis-à-vis* women – which, however, does/can not deny women subjectivity, sexual or other. In seeing leisure and class as interconnected, we must understand that the interrelationships are class and gender inflected and multiplex.

## Marginalized complicity at home

In discussions of workers in Japan, the intersections between work and domestic and family relationships have been commonly commented on only in regard to women. The failure to extend research about men beyond factory or office walls – real or discursive – is gender based and biased, often *presuming* that Japanese men's identities are essentially and essentialistically company (or, at least, co-worker) contexted.

However, a number of authors have commented on the more active involvement in home and family life of working-class men (see Mathews and Ishii-Kuntz, this volume, Chapters 7 and 12, respectively). Sugimoto has recently noted that Japanese blue-collar workers

> find more satisfaction at home and in community life than do white-collar employees. Generally, they value family life and take an active part in community affairs. In community baseball teams, after-hours children's soccer teams and other sports clubs, blue-collar workers are prominent.
>
> (1997: 87; see also Linhart 1988)

Imamura has similarly observed that 'The family-oriented man is either the young husband . . . *or the blue-collar worker who is freed from some of the obligatory after-hours socializing*' (1987: 68; emphasis added). Roberts, meanwhile, notes that while some of the husbands of her blue-collar women informants fit the stereotypical pattern of rarely helping their wives at home, 'there were also not a few [men] who actively contributed to household activities, especially childcare, cooking and dish washing' (1994: 167).

For some men at Shintani Metals, being at home seemed to be a consequence of not having the monetary freedom to spend time and money outside. For young men in their late twenties to early thirties, the combination of a new (and, sometimes, newly independent) family life and relatively low wages could necessitate their presence at home, even during the hey-day of the late 1980s bubble economy. Men whose wives worked outside seemed pragmatically to accept (the necessity of) their wives' employment, candidly reporting that their wives' wages in some cases amounted to one-third or more of their own. Mr Murakami's wife, for example, was employed at a pharmaceuticals firm, made more money than he did, and due to her work was often away from home. He said that because of these things, it was he who did much of the shopping, cooking and cleaning – perhaps an extreme case, but one which points to the flexibility of practice I find more generally characteristic of the Japanese working class (but see Ishii-Kuntz, this volume, Chapter 12).

Men appear to spend more time at home with their families when children are young, more or less up to junior high-school age. Mr Tozawa, for example, claimed to have acted as a baseball coach for a group of neighbourhood children for five or six years while his own two sons were in elementary school. During this time he would spend many Sundays coaching and, when possible, he would play catch with his sons on weekday evenings after work as well. Mr Ikeda spoke of the past enjoyment he had found in making plastic models together when his son was still young.

While I did not ask enough about what the men did at home or with families, these men appear to have enjoyed/exercised the male privilege of being able to only play with children (but see Ishii-Kuntz, this volume, Chapter 12). The complicit reproduction of masculine privilege may also be seen in the fact that, as is common for men in all class positions, most of the men from Shintani Metals also seem to spend time at home in essentially passive fashion napping, lounging around or watching television (see Linhart 1988).

## Conclusion

The masculine gender projects being constructed by the men working at Shintani Metals were both recognizably 'Japanese' and in a diversity of ways very much of working-class character and manufacture. It is the multiplicity of identities suggested in this chapter – born of the ongoing intercourse of class and gender – that I want to reflect on a bit further here.

As noted at the beginning of this chapter, the notions of 'hegemonic', 'marginalized' or other kinds of masculinities are useful when discussing the diversity of 'masculinities' in Japan. Such diversity and difference may be found and analysed at various levels. Though not followed closely here, Connell (1995) suggests three levels of analysis: that of the individual lifecourse; that of discourse, ideology and culture, and that of institutions such as schools, companies and the state (see also Roberson and Suzuki, this volume, Chapter 1).

Thus, on the one hand, we may talk of the 'marginalized masculinity' of working-class Japanese men such as those at Shintani Metals, whose lives and identities, whose models of perception and of practice are, in fact, doubly marginalized. On the ideological or representational level, these men's identities and experiences, as men, are not given the same cultural legitimacy as is accorded to middle-class salarymen. On the social-institutional level, these men are excluded from core positions of control and power – starting at the factory level where, for example, the company president was described as making decisions in a unilateral, 'one-man' fashion and where positions of authority are limited in number.

The marginalization of the Shintani Metals men is also a matter of class culture and practice which reject, resist or manifest preferences for the construction – at the individual level – of lifecourses and identities other than those of the 'hegemonic masculinity' of the salaryman. The educational, employment, leisure and, to some extent, family-related or contexted practices and experiences of the men working at Shintani Metals show that these men are faced with pragmatic class-related conditions that require or enable different gender(ed) practices and suggest that these men hold different, class-relative notions of what men should do, who men should be. Thus many of the men preferred to pursue the possession of practical skills rather than further education; many men desired or had to accept changes in companies and work content when called for by opportunity or necessity; and, for many, leisure is a site of ludic individuation rather than corporate ideological reaffirmation.

On the other hand, such exclusion or marginalization must be seen in inter-relationship with the hegemonically complicit practices of these working-class men. The men at Shintani Metals, as Kelly (1986, 1993) more generally suggests, are certainly aware of and to one degree or another influenced by images of the middle-class salaryman (and his family). Some of the men, for instance, occasionally used the word 'salaryman' as a normative term for company employees, and a few men commuted to the factory in tie and jacket (though not business suits). In other ways, especially when our focus shifts to male–female interactions, the working-class men here also act in a manner which reproduces the patriarchal gender order and which is based on or (attempts to) assure them of what Connell (1995) calls the patriarchal dividend.

Marginalized from the centres of ideological and political-economic power, the working-class men at Shintani Metals, in their dealings with women, remain complicit with the very system of masculine ideology and power within which they themselves are marginalized. Yet such complicity is itself mediated by the working-class context – and the broader postwar capitalist and nation-state systems – in which it is embedded. And it is in part in interrelation with such embedding contexts that we may see not just relative difference from the middle-class standards but the possibility of change, still class-inflected, as men increasingly share full-time employment with women. The examples of the gender practices and projects of these working-class men suggest that discussions of masculinity, as well as of class, in contemporary Japan need more fully to consider how 'gender relations themselves are bisected by class relations and vice-versa' (Donaldson 1993: 643).

## Notes

1  This is a revised version of a paper first presented at the Chicago–Hitotsubashi Conference on Class Society in Contemporary Japan, Hitotsubashi University, Tokyo, Japan, October 10, 1997. A shorter version was published in the *Hitotsubashi University Journal of Social Sciences* (Roberson 1998c). I would like to thank Mary Brinton, Laura Miller, Gordon Mathews, Bill Kelly and Wendy Smith for their comments and suggestions. Discussions with Nobue Suzuki motivated me to do the reading and (re)thinking which lead to the writing and revising of this chapter.
2  For men older than myself, I attach 'Mr' while to indicate men who were my age or younger I use only their family names without appellation.
3  With the continuing Heisei recession, many men outside of the working class have also had to face 'restructuring' and redundancy. For any individual man, whether working or middle-class, this can be a traumatic experience, but historically has *structurally* been more common among members of the working class.
4  Note that this appears to differ from what Mouer (1995) reports. However, there may be interesting gender-related dynamics at work in discouraging Mouer's informants from using their skills during their leisure hours, especially at home. Conversely, though still gender-relative, I consider it possible that Mouer's research method may not have encouraged the men to admit that they cook at home.

## References

Allison, A. (1993) 'Dominating men: male dominance on company expense in a Japanese hostess club', *Genders* 16: 1–16.
—— (1994) *Nightwork: Sexuality, Pleasure, and Corporate Masculinity in a Tokyo Hostess Club*, Chicago: University of Chicago Press.
Atsumi, R. (1979) '*Tsukiai*–obligatory personal relationships of Japanese white-collar company employees', *Human Organization* 38, 1: 63–70.
—— (1989) 'Friendship in cross-cultural perspective', in Y. Sugimoto and R. E. Mouer (eds) *Constructs for Understanding Japan*, New York: Kegan Paul.
Bird, S. R. (1996) 'Welcome to the men's club: homosociality and the maintenance of hegemonic masculinity', *Gender and Society* 10, 2: 120–32.
Bourdieu, P. (1984) *Distinction: A Social Critique of the Judgment of Taste*, Cambridge, MA: Harvard University Press.
Brinton, M. (1993) *Women and the Economic Miracle: Gender and Work in Postwar Japan*, Berkeley: University of California Press.
Chalmers, N. J. (1989) *Industrial Relations in Japan: The Peripheral Workforce*, London and New York: Routledge.
Cole, R. E. (1979) *Work, Mobility, and Participation: A Comparative Study of American and Japanese Industry*, Berkeley: University of California Press.
Connell, R. W. (1987) *Gender and Power: Society, the Person and Sexual Politics*, Stanford: Stanford University Press.
—— (1995) *Masculinities*, Berkeley: University of California Press.

— (1996) 'New directions in gender theory, masculinity research and gender politics', *Ethnos* 61, 3–4: 157–76.

di Leonardo, M. (1991) 'Introduction: gender, culture and political economy: feminist anthropology in historical perspective', in M. di Leonardo (ed.) *Gender at the Crossroads of Knowledge: Feminist Anthropology in the Postmodern Era*, Berkeley: University of California Press.

Donaldson, M. (1993) 'What is hegemonic masculinity?', *Theory and Society* 22: 643–57.

Dunk, T. (1991) *It's a Working Man's Town: Male Working-Class Culture*, Montreal and Kingston: McGill–Queen's University Press.

Fowler, E. (1996) *San'ya Blues: Laboring Life in Contemporary Tokyo*, Ithaca and London: Cornell University Press.

Gill, T. (2001) *Men of Uncertainty: The Social Organization of Day Laborers in Contemporary Japan*, Albany: SUNY Press.

Gilmore, D. (1990) *Manhood in the Making: Cultural Concepts of Masculinity*, New Haven and London: Yale University Press.

Gordon, A. (1985) *The Evolution of Labor Relations in Japan: Heavy Industry, 1853–1955*, Cambridge, MA: Harvard Council on East Asian Studies.

Hearn, J. and Morgan, D. (eds) (1990) *Men, Masculinities and Social Theory*, London: Unwin Hyman.

Imamura, A. E. (1987) *Urban Japanese Housewives: At Home and in the Community*, Honolulu: University of Hawaii Press.

Ishida, H. (1993) *Social Mobility in Contemporary Japan: Educational Credentials, Class and the Labour Market in a Cross-National Perspective*, London: Macmillan.

Kelly, W. W. (1986) 'Rationalization and nostalgia: cultural dynamics of new middle-class Japan', *American Ethnologist* 13, 4: 603–18.

— (1993) 'Finding a place in metropolitan Japan: ideologies, institutions, and everyday life', in A. Gordon (ed.) *Postwar Japan as History*, Berkeley: University of California Press.

Koike, K. (1983) 'The formation of worker skill in small Japanese firms', *Japanese Economic Studies*, Summer: 3–57.

Kondo, D. (1990) *Crafting Selves: Power, Gender and Discourses of Identity in a Japanese Workplace*, Chicago: University of Chicago Press.

Lie, J. (1996) 'Sociology of contemporary Japan', *Current Sociology* 44, 1.

Linhart, S. (1988) 'From industrial to postindustrial society: changes in Japanese leisure-related values and behavior', *Journal of Japanese Studies* 14, 2: 271–308.

— (1998) 'Introduction: the Japanese at play: a little-known dimension of Japan', in S. Linhart and S. Frühstück (eds) *The Culture of Japan as Seen Through Its Leisure*, Albany: SUNY Press.

MacLeod, J. (1995) *Ain't No Makin' It: Aspirations and Attainment in a Low-Income Neighborhood*, Boulder: Westview Press.

Mathews, G. (1996) *What Makes Life Worth Living? How Japanese and Americans Make Sense of Their Worlds*, Berkeley: University of California Press.

Moore, H. L. (1988) *Feminism and Anthropology*, Minneapolis: University of Minnesota Press.

Morgan, D. (1992) *Discovering Men*, London and New York: Routledge.

Mouer, R. (1995) 'Work – postmodernism or ultramodernism: the Japanese dilemma at work', in J. Arnason and Y. Sugimoto (eds) *Japanese Encounters with Postmodernity*, London and New York: Kegan Paul.

Nakane, C. (1970) *Japanese Society*, Berkeley: University of California Press.

Ogasawara, Y. (1998) *Office Ladies and Salaried Men: Power, Gender, and Work in Japanese Companies*, Berkeley: University of California Press.

Okano, K. (1993) *School to Work Transition in Japan: An Ethnographic Study*, Clevedon, UK: Multilingual Matters Ltd.

Ortner, S. (1996) *Making Gender: The Politics and Erotics of Culture*, Boston: Beacon Press.

Ortner, S. and Whitehead, H. (1981) 'Introduction: accounting for sexual meanings', in S. Ortner and H. Whitehead (eds) *Sexual Meanings: The Cultural Construction of Gender and Sexuality*, Cambridge: Cambridge University Press.

Plath, D. W. (ed.) (1983) *Work and Lifecourse in Japan*, Albany: SUNY Press.

Pyke, K. D. (1996) 'Class-based masculinities: the interdependence of gender, class and interpersonal power', *Gender and Society* 10, 5: 527–49.

Roberson, J. E. (1995a) 'Becoming *shakaijin*: working-class reproduction in Japan', *Ethnology* 34, 4: 293–313.

—— (1995b) 'After hours and private time: class, leisure and identity in Japan', *American Asian Review* 13, 2: 213–55.

—— (1998a) *Japanese Working Class Lives: An Ethnographic Study of Factory Workers*, London and New York: Routledge.

—— (1998b) 'People in small Japanese companies: diversity at work and play', in M. L. Shrestha (ed.) *Kigyō no Seichō to Gendai Shakai* (*Enterprise Growth and Modern Society*), Tokyo: Chikura Shobō.

—— (1998c) 'Manufacturing men: working-class masculinities in Japan', *Hitotsubashi University Journal of Social Sciences* 30, 1: 45–59.

Roberts, G. (1994) *Staying on the Line: Blue-Collar Women in Contemporary Japan*, Honolulu: University of Hawaii Press.

Rohlen, T. P. (1974) *For Harmony and Strength: Japanese White-Collar Organization in Anthropological Perspective*, Berkeley: University of California Press.

Sato, I. (1991) *Kamikaze Biker: Parody and Anomy in Affluent Japan*, Chicago: University of Chicago Press.

Seiyama, K. (1994) 'Labour market and career mobility', in K. Kosaka (ed.) *Social Stratification in Contemporary Japan*, London and New York: Kegan Paul.

Sugimoto, Y. (1997) *An Introduction to Japanese Society*, Cambridge: Cambridge University Press.

Vogel, E. F. (1971) *Japan's New Middle Class: The Salary Man and His Family in a Tokyo Suburb* (2nd edn), Berkeley: University of California Press.

White, M. (1987) *The Japanese Educational Challenge*, New York: Free Press.

Willis, P. (1977) *Learning to Labor: How Working-Class Kids Get Working-Class Jobs*, New York: Columbia University Press.

# 9 When pillars evaporate

## Structuring masculinity on the Japanese margins

*Tom Gill*

## Mobility – stasis – men

People desire to be dynamic, to travel, to be free, to be alone. People desire to settle down, to be loved, to have family and security and certainty in their lives. Men and women alike must negotiate these conflicting desires, but the unbalanced nature of gender relations has often excluded women from the issue. As Enloe (1989: 21) puts it: 'in many societies being feminine has been defined as sticking close to home. Masculinity, by contrast, has been the passport for travel'. Enloe's principal subject is international travel, but I would extend her observation to include more mundane forms of mobility, such as the simple journeying between home and workplace. To stay, or to go; to keep still or to move: these are issues for both genders, but the history of gender relations has perhaps made the issue of mobility/stasis more marked for men than for women.

In Japan masculine fantasies frequently stress the mobile: the sportsman, the traveler, the man of action, the magically endowed superhero. Traditional Japanese images of masculine mobility include wandering mendicant monks and pilgrims, roaming leaderless warriors and travelling actors. In contemporary Japan, the romanticized wandering vagabond lives on in the movies in the person of Tora-san, a lovable travelling pedlar who roams Japan, ageing through the decades but always unmarried.[1] More extreme media images of masculine mobility include the running, jumping, flying men seen in health-drink commercials (Roberson 1999) and the supersonic, jet-propelled heroes of children's TV dramas and animations targetted principally at boys (Gill 1998).

But alongside these images of men in motion, another set of cultural tropes, many of them very ancient, stresses the reverse theme, of immobility, expressed as solidity, endurance and strength. The Zen monk, achieving enlightenment by sitting still and emptying his mind; farmers staying on their ancestral lands across the generations; sumo wrestlers who should not be moved.

Perhaps the most telling traditional metaphor of static Japanese manhood is that of the *daikokubashira*, meaning the great central pillar that supports a house. In traditional farmhouses, there is a real *daikokubashira* holding up the roof, and the man of the house sits in front of that wooden pillar, in the place of honour around the *irori*, the square hearth set into the floor of the main living and dining room. In the image of the *daikokubashira*, man merges with pillar. It is an image of reliability, of strength, of stasis. The pillar that supports the household has honour, represented in its/his dominant central position, but also bears a heavy load – supporting the roof/supporting the family. The pillar is always there: male succession, ideally by the oldest son, is supposed to make the role of *daikokubashira* permanent even if the individual playing the role changes with the years.[2]

The modern, legalistic equivalent of the *daikokubashira* ideology is the *koseki* system under which the father of the house is designated as head of household in 98 per cent of Japanese families, and continues to be legally designated as such even after his death (Sugimoto 1997: 136–8). This system, along with the whole ideology of the male-centred family, is frequently and correctly denounced as deeply sexist and patriarchal (ibid.). Note, however, that as well as disempowering women, this ideology also puts a heavy stress on men, who carry the weight of traditional expectation and legal obligation to support both their parental and marital families.

## Two images of modern manhood

Modern fantasies of masculine mobility have a powerful appeal to 'salarymen' – men whose lifestyles are generally static and intellectual, who inhabit a world alienated from physicality, where the permanent is valued over the temporary, and brainwork over bodywork. Lifetime employment with a single employer and a steady home life with a wife and two kids are still the socially sanctioned ideals for Japanese men, even if the decade-long Heisei recession has made them increasingly difficult to attain. When men *do* move, it may well be involuntarily, in the form of forced *tanshin funin* transfers to distant branches of their company, which may separate them from their families.[3] For most men in Japan today, masculine mobility is an escapist fantasy; immobility, or involuntary mobility, is a dull, immovable reality.

The reader may object that this characterization of mainstream masculinity is (1) unrepresentative and (2) overly laden with negative value judgements. On the first issue, people are well aware these days that white-collar workers at large companies – the popular image of the salaryman – only account for a small minority of the working population, albeit one that has come to dominate the popular discourse on Japan 'as representations of a hegemonic masculinity in Japan' (Roberson 1998: 55). The salaryman has undoubtedly dominated images of Japan out of all proportion to his role in real-life society, but I think it is fair to say that imposed immobility and involuntary mobility are facts of life for most men in regular employment, whatever the colour of their collar.

As for the second issue, the meanings attached to the salaryman figure in Japanese culture are far from being unequivocally positive, as Matsunaga (2000) points out. There is also a large element of self-doubt, and a frustration and nostalgia for lost autonomy, in the salaryman discourse. Younger people often despise salarymen as lacking in independence and creativity. Salarymen are frequently derided in popular culture, and the discourse has darkened in recent years with the protracted recession in the Japanese economy and the dramatic rise in the male suicide rate.[4] Salarymen themselves may view their lives with a wry, self-deprecatory humour that acknowledges the limitations of personal agency in a corporate setting (Nakamaki 2000; see also Roberson 1999). More drastic are views such as that from the diary of salaryman Yagi Toshitsugu, who asks:

And can't it be said that today's armies of corporate workers are in fact slaves in almost every sense of the word? They are bought for money. Their worth is measured in working hours. They are powerless to defy their superiors.

(quoted in Smith 1997: 121)

It may well be argued, as Pyke (1996) does, that middle-class men are not under the same pressure as working-class men to assert their masculinity, and that when salary-men portray themselves as slaves of the company, they can afford to do so because their masculinity is not, in fact, under serious threat. However, perspectives that discount the complaints of salarymen as the ironic disclaimers of an unthreatened elite may risk naively equating an affluent middle-class lifestyle with contentment.

The men I shall discuss in this chapter constitute only a small minority of the Japanese male population, but they are of interest as instances of what happens when a man declines or breaks that contract of permanence and stasis that dominates the lives of so many of their brothers. Day labourers (*hiyatoi rōdōsha*) have a long, complex socio-economic history dating back at least to the sixteenth century, and at times have made up a substantial portion of the Japanese workforce (see Leupp 1992). Today, casual labour has become greatly diversified in Japan, and men living the traditional day-labouring lifestyle form a small and dwindling minority. These men look for casual work at early-morning street labour markets called *yoseba*, and tend to live in cheap lodging houses called *doya*, often concentrated in areas called *doya-gai*. In three famous cases (Kamagasaki, in Osaka; San'ya, in Tokyo, and Koto-buki, in Yokohama), the recruitment function of the *yoseba* coincides with the residential function of the *doya-gai*.[5] There is a massive Japanese-language literature on these places, and a fast-growing English-language literature too (e.g. Fowler 1996; Gill 1999, 2000, 2001; Marr 1997; Stevens 1997; Ventura 1992). Along with the street labour market, these districts also have public casual employment exchanges, reflecting the authorities' attempts over the years to regularize casual labour. Even so, the great majority of jobs are still negotiated on the street. Other major cities have *yoseba* without *doya-gai*, meaning that the men must find a room somewhere else and come to the *yoseba* by 5:00 or 6:00 am in the morning to try to get work.

Day labourers are of interest in the discourse on masculinities in Japan because, as stereotypes and to some extent in reality too, they are antithetical to salarymen (see Table 9.1).

*Table 9.1* Two models of manhood

| '*Salaryman*' | '*Day labourer*' |
| --- | --- |
| Lifetime employment | Employment by the day |
| Attached to large corporation | Unaffiliated |
| Substantial job security | No job security |
| Usually married by middle age | Usually single, separated or divorced |
| Intellectual labour | Manual labour |
| Generally seen as middle class | Working class or underclass |
| Many social constraints on freedom | No social constraints on freedom |

I have just discussed the lament for lost freedom that is part of the salaryman discourse. Day labourers, in contrast, sometimes celebrate their freedom and autonomy:

> SAKASHITA[6] did dangerous high-level construction work. He claimed that his lifestyle was designed to accommodate the possibility of sudden death:
>
> > I'm not afraid of death. I'm aware of the possibility. If you fall, that's it. It's all over in a flash. But I'm ready for death. I can go any time. I've designed my life that way: I've no wife, no kids and no regrets that I have no wife or kids. If I'd started a family, I'd have to take more care of my own life, I'd have to think of the others. I'm better off on my own. I can die any time and it won't bother anyone. That is real freedom. I'm that sort of guy and I can't change.

Narratives like this may fairly be read as a resistance strategy in response to marginalization (Day *et al.* 1999), or as an attempt to rationalize day labourers' essentially weak, low-status position in society. But when we attempt to move from the stereotype to the wide variety of human beings actually living in and around the *yoseba*, we find that libertarian themes form only one part of a complex day labourer discourse that in turn stands in complex relationship to the actual lives of day labourers.

## Double detachment

Most day labourers today are (a) aged between 45 and 65, (b) from rural rather than urban backgrounds and (c) of working-class origin, with a relatively low level of formal education.[7] However, the really definitive characteristic of day labourers is detachment: from the family and from the workplace.

First, detachment from the family. Only 6 of 76 day labourers in my study combined day labouring with married life. The few that do this tend to have better qualifications than most, and even then it is no easy matter for them:

> AOYAGI had just turned 60, but was still a tough and competent worker, with a sheaf of qualifications proving his ability to operate forklifts, large trucks, etc. These, and an encyclopaedic knowledge of the various kinds of benefit that could be extracted from the social services, made him one of the few day labourers capable of supporting a family. He had a house, a wife and two grown-up children. He had a bleak outlook on life, which he described as an endless struggle to sustain the household economy, and was especially bitter about the heavy costs he would have to bear when his daughter got married.

The overwhelming majority of day labourers are single men, perhaps roughly equally divided between lifelong bachelors and those who are separated or divorced from their wives. This has not always been so: prewar accounts of *doya-gai* life show that there were many day labourers who managed to sustain family life, often with whole families living in tiny *doya* rooms. As late as 1964, a large survey of several *doya-gai* found as many as 23 per cent of day labourers married (Caldarola 1968). Thus day labourers' detachment from family is not a culturally ordained constant, but the product of social and economic change. Marriage to a day labourer and life in a *doya* room is no longer an acceptable prospect to Japanese women. *Doya-gai* are increasingly becoming slum districts populated by single men, and comparisons with American skid rows are numerous (Aoki 1989; Caldarola 1968; Giamo 1994; Marr 1997; Tsuchida 1966; Yoshida 1995).

It is difficult to generalize about day labourers and marriage. There were cases where a man could not find a marriage partner because of the stigma or low economic status associated with being a day labourer, or had rejected marriage as part of his personal ethos. However, a common pattern is for men to arrive in the *yoseba* with one or more marriages or significant relationships behind them. Japan's divorce rate has doubled in the last three decades, but remains relatively low compared to other industrialized countries.[8] This may reflect the relatively strong disapproval with which divorce is viewed in Japan. To some men, the *yoseba* was a masculine refuge following the failure of these relationships:

SHIGERU was born in Iwate. He always wanted to become a bar tender in a smart hotel. He got married and had a son, but his bar-tending career got bogged down – he reckoned because he couldn't master the foreign languages needed in international hotels. His wife got fed up, mainly because of years of low income, and left him. He found he could make better money as a *tekkin-kō* – building the frameworks of steel rods used to reinforce concrete – and became a semi-skilled day labourer. He had not seen his wife or son for some ten years. He said he never sent them money: he spent what he earned, and looked for work again once he was cleaned out. He was based in San'ya but came to Kotobuki occasionally, usually when he had made some money to use on the services of the Yokohama prostitutes, who charged less than their Tokyo sisters.

Many day labourers are also detached from their parental family. Some feel ashamed to go home, having acquired a criminal record or failed in business. A marriage that ends in divorce or separation can lead to alienation from parents as well, so that links are severed with marital and parental families at the same time. Some younger men left home after getting into fights with their parents over their social behaviour, career plans, etc. Kuriyama, below, is an example. A more frequent motif of day-labourer narratives, however, was that of gradual alienation. Many day labourers have rural origins, and started their working careers as migrant labourers (*dekasegi rōdōsha*), supporting their impoverished parental family by sending money home (*shiokuri*). The cash remittances may gradually dry up, perhaps as a result of over-indulgence in drinking and gambling, leading to a slowly mounting embarrassment and a severing by degrees of relations with home.

There was a rather high proportion of eldest sons among my day-labourer informants: some 40 per cent, slightly higher than a random distribution would predict (Gill 2001: 115–22, 215). Given that these were men with largely rural backgrounds, born before, during or just after the war, this was a surprising result. In the households where they grew up, there would have been a strong expectation that they would inherit and maintain the household and its occupation under the principle of primogeniture[9] – to be the *daikokubashira*. By living away from their families and away from mainstream society in general, these first-born sons were flouting convention even more than the 60 per cent who were junior sons.

In some cases it is doubtless true that the man would not be welcome home; but in many other cases the family feels the loss of the son keenly. The *chōba-san* – concierges of *doya* – are frequently visited by mothers, fathers and siblings of missing men, carrying old photographs and asking if they ring a bell. In any case, the fact remains that in the *doya-gai*, as in skid row, the permanent and powerful ties of kinship give way to ties of friendship, usually less permanent and less powerful, and chosen by the individual on the basis of personal preference. Sometimes, however, men would attempt to model their friendships so as to resemble the kinship ties they had left behind:

KURIYAMA was still unmarried at the age of 40. He had been thrown out of his parental home after his irascible father, a career civil servant, lost patience with his heavy drinking. He had also lost his job as a short-order cook after getting into a fight. In the *yoseba* he recreated the seniority-based hierarchy of mainstream family and working life by taking up with two older men, whom he called his 'father-figure' (*oyabun*) and 'grandfather-figure' (*ō-oyabun*). These two men helped him to build his own shack, in a shrubbery next to the Nakamura River, which runs past Kotobuki. He tended to loneliness and adopted a stray cat. He was an only child, and once told me he had lost all interest in women after an intense love affair in his youth had ended badly.

Now for workplace detachment. Day labourers are the radical antithesis of the stereotypical salaryman. Lifetime employment? As the term suggests, these men often work on contracts that last just one day. Single-day contracts in fact account for roughly half of the work done by day labourers, the rest being done on contracts typically lasting between one week and one month. Work is negotiated formally at a public casual labour exchange or informally with a *yoseba* street-corner recruiter known as a *tehaishi*. The informal street market still dominates recruitment today, though overall job availability has fallen to disastrously low levels. There used to be a range of employing industries across the manufacturing, transportation and warehousing sectors. Now the construction industry is the only significant employer, although longshoring work at the Yokohama docks continues to provide a small but useful secondary category of employment in Kotobuki.

Workplace relationships are different when you work by the day or week rather than for decades. The powerful bonds of obligation between employer and worker, and between senior and junior workers, go out of the window. Day labourers can quit any time and frequently do. By the same token, they are the first to lose employment when recession reduces the demand for manpower – as they know from the bitter experiences of the Heisei recession. Just as some day labourers had come to the masculine community of the *yoseba* after previously trying married life, most of them appeared to have experienced more regular work arrangements before becoming day labourers. Often they would describe personal characteristics that made it difficult for them to fit in to the ordered hierarchy of working life at a company:

> OKADA was an elderly but well-built man who worked as a *tobi-shoku* – a construction worker specializing in high-level work. He was a self-styled individualist, and said that he had quit a steady job at Mitsubishi Electric because he couldn't stop getting into fights with the management – a frequent item in day-labourer narratives. In his cups, he would claim to be a descendant of Hannibal and Sitting Bull.

But if narratives of messy divorces were paralleled by tales of violent clashes with management, more positive narratives of life as a single man also had their parallel in accounts of day labouring as a positive, strategic choice. Day labourers can make slightly better money than men doing similar work as regular employees, provided they can get regular work and do without job security and non-wage benefits. A substantial number of building workers and carpenters left steady employment to work as casuals in Kōbe after the 1995 earthquake there, taking advantage of the higher rates of pay caused by the special post-disaster circumstances.[10] Some day labourers stress the merit of flexible working arrangements:

> KŌHEI was in his fifties, a diminutive but tough and resourceful man and a skilled worker – he was a ship's carpenter. He said he'd left a previous job working at a Nissan factory many years before when he realized that he could make better money as a day labourer in Kotobuki. He was well connected with the street-corner labour recruiters, and enjoyed the challenge of selling his labour to the highest bidder every morning. He cultivated many recruiters, to maximize his chances of getting work each day. He believed in developing bonds of reciprocity: he would help out recruiters when they were short-handed, in hopes that they would favour him when demand for casual labour declined.

## Physicality, immediacy, mobility

Detached from the family and the workplace, the two dominant institutions in the lives of many Japanese men, day labourers construct their identities in other ways. Three categories seem especially important: physicality, immediacy and mobility.

Looking first at physicality, day labourers like to stress that unlike the despised pen-pushing salaryman, to whom they like to conceptually oppose themselves, they work with their hands and bodies (cf. Connell 1987, 1995). As construction workers they make things, they leave their mark on the landscape. 'We built this city', they will tell you. That is a gross exaggeration, but not without a grain of truth. They sometimes express macho proletarian physicality visually, by wearing clothes clearly designed for physical labour – blue or grey boiler suits, and occasionally the more traditional baggy trousers (*shichibu-zubon*) and split-toe boots (*tabi*) – and by carrying leather bags of tools. Macho identity is linguistically expressed in the especially heavy use of marked masculine language such as the first-person pronoun *ore* and the sentence final particles '*zo*' and '*ze*' (Sturtz 1999). 'Talking straight' is valorized; some men told me that within the *doya-gai* there was no need for the complex shades of politeness used by many Japanese: everyone was in the same boat. To borrow Dorinne Kondo's term (Kondo 1990), there was no need to 'craft selves' – day labourers liked to present themselves as uncrafted nuggets of selfhood.

These postures may be read as a form of resistance to the mainstream, similar to that described by Pyke for working-class American men: '[M]en on the shop floor reconstruct their position as embodying true masculinity, an alternative to the hegemonic form associated with managers... whom they ridicule as conforming "yes-men" and "wimps" engaged in effeminate paper-pushing kinds of labour' (1996: 531; see also Collinson 1992).

An extension of straight talking was fighting, a common enough sight in the *doya-gai*. Sometimes physicality took the form of bullying – the raw expression of power over one's fellow man:

> RON-CHAN looked to be in his thirties. He said he was the youngest of five siblings, all brothers. The rest had gone to university and got good jobs, but he had joined a gang of *yakuza*. He left his gang after a few years but still had a magnificent dragon tattoo. He used to boast that it was easy to make money day labouring, and that he would soon save up enough money to set up his own little restaurant and leave the *yoseba*. In fact he very seldom worked, often slept rough and mostly acquired money and food by bullying it out of older, weaker men. He had an aggressive manner and was given to sudden violent outbursts. Several times I saw him beat and kick weaker men to the point where I feared for their lives.

A second theme is immediacy, an orientation to the present moment (Gill 1999). Postponement of reward – monthly salaries paid in arrears, and pay withheld for later transfer as bonuses and retirement payments – is an integral part of salaryman life, binding worker to employer. For day labourers, immediate payment implies both freedom and insecurity. A day's work is done; a day's pay is received. Very often it is spent that day as well. Shigeru, for instance, told me that he did not want a steady job because he couldn't afford to wait until the end of the month for his paycheque.

A third key theme is mobility. With no household or workplace to anchor their lives, day labourers are often on the move. They may move in search of work, or simply because they desire a change. Some travel cyclically from *yoseba* to *yoseba*; others spend periods working on rural construction sites; a few even travel internationally.[11] In any case the decision to move is made autonomously, not in response to an order from above as in the case of the *tanshin funin* salaryman. This positive view of mobility also has a long history – consider Andrew Gordon's account of deliberate job-switching by Japanese shipbuilding workers around the turn of the century (1985: esp. 33–6), or Okamoto (1993) for a similar case in the Meiji era textile industry.

KIRIMOTO was a perpetually cheerful man with a slight speech impediment who hailed from Nago, Okinawa. He was 42 when I met him in May 1994, and had just arrived in Kotobuki from Sasashima, the Nagoya *yoseba*. He was politically aware, supporting the day labourer unions and believing in the importance of comradeship. He had spent roughly three years based in Sasashima, two in San'ya and one in Kotobuki, but frequently travelled between the three. He would also return to Okinawa every couple of years to see his family and visit the family graves. I once asked a mutual acquaintance why Kirimoto was always on the move. 'He just has too many friends to visit', was the answer.

## Activism and passivism

I hope I have sketched the outline of an alternative narrative of Japanese masculinity, one very different to that focused on the *daikokubashira*, on which day labourers can call when constructing their own identity. These themes of physicality, immediacy and mobility are grounded in proletarian tradition, and they come together in two key words for day labourers: *genba* and *genkin*. Literally these words mean 'actual/ present place' and 'actual/present money'. They describe the construction worksite and the cash payment received by the worker. The idea is that real work is done, and real pay received – as opposed to the unreal, pen-pushing work that they associate with salarymen, rewarded by future bank transfers. The terms imply transience too: the workplace is temporary, lasting only until the building is finished, or the worker moves on, and the cash will soon be spent.

Now these three themes, of physicality, immediacy and mobility, carry in them the seeds of their own destruction. Physical power and mobility wane with age, and the ageing process is faster when hard manual labour is combined with a low standard of living, and sometimes with heavy drinking, heavy smoking and periods of living rough. As for immediacy, a culture based on living for the day will perish when tomorrow comes . . . and sooner or later, come it does. A *doya-gai* proverb puts it this way: '*Dokata korosu nya hamono wa iranu. Mikka no ame mo fureba ii*' (You don't need a knife to kill a day labourer. Three days of rain is all it takes). The idea is, of course, that you can't get work at a dock or building site on a rainy day; and that a stereotyped day labourer lacks the resources to last more than three days without income. Where salarymen can expect their income to gradually rise with age, day-labouring careers tend to follow the opposite pattern: earning power declines with age. Meanwhile the drinking and gambling pleasures of youth gradually become inescapable addictions, and the man eventually becomes unable to pay the rent on his *doya* room and takes to the street. The solitary lifestyle loses its intoxicating elements of freedom and autonomy and instead points the way to a lonely old age and unmourned death. Average age at death for day labourers is informally estimated at not much more than 60, some 15 years below the national male average. As employability falls, strategies based on playing off multiple labour recruiters in search of better terms may give way to clientelistic dependency on a single boss.

MASAYOSHI was 58 and had been in Kotobuki several decades. He started in construction, then switched over to dock work because it was better paid. He ran out of work there and moved back to construction, but now can't even find work there. He used to play the day-labouring game: working for various companies, through various *tehaishi*, going where the terms were best. In recent years he has found it more effective to stick with a single boss (*oyakata*). Nowadays the *oyakata* is unable to provide him with much work, but he does his best to take care of Masayoshi: for example, he will put employment stamps in his handbook and rubber-stamp them, even when no actual employment has occurred – enabling Masayoshi to claim the day-labourer dole.

What happens to day-labourer identity as decline sets in? For some men, the discourses of physicality, immediacy and mobility give way to a pervasive fatalism. Rather than accounting for their lives in terms of willed personal decisions, they present themselves as passive victims of inescapable tides that sweep them to their fate. These tides may be characterized in economic terms (bursting of the bubble economy, decline of the construction industry, etc.), in socio-biological terms (survival of the fittest, inevitable decline with old age, etc.) and not infrequently in metaphysical terms (some people are fated to hard lives and early deaths). For some, persistent long-term alcohol abuse appears to take on the character of slow suicide. Radical activists, alarmed at the quietism of many day labourers, struggle to goad them into action with slogans such as '*yararetara yarikaese*' (if they get you, get 'em back) and '*damatte notarejinu na*' (do not be silent and die in the gutter).[12]

The fact is that even today many day labourers *do* die in the gutter. Until quite recently, there was little alternative. With no pension rights, no money saved and no family support networks to fall back on, social welfare (*seikatsu hogo*, literally 'livelihood protection') is the only way to escape that fate for many day labourers – and this has not been easy to acquire. Many city authorities have refused to authorize welfare payments unless the applicant can prove his inability to work, through old age (at least 65) or physical incapacity (attested by a doctor's letter). These conditions are not stipulated by law – they are instances of *ad hoc*, ground-level regulation by local government officials who, motivated by the ideology of the *daiko-kubashira*, have often seen unemployment as shameful, rather than unfortunate.[13]

However, with sharply rising unemployment and vigorous campaigning by day-labourer unions, some city authorities have gradually eased their traditionally hard line. Yokohama has moved faster and further than most, so that 80 per cent of *doya* rooms in Kotobuki are now occupied by welfare recipients – a figure that has doubled in the last six years. Meanwhile it has become increasingly difficult for the traditional wandering day labourer to get a room in Kotobuki. In contrast, San'ya and Kamagasaki have more empty rooms and also far more homeless men around them.

So the ageing and weakening day labourer today is faced with a genuine but difficult choice. He can stubbornly maintain a self-image of tough, libertarian self-reliance to the bitter end, or he can find some way of justifying the decision to apply for welfare. Some choose the former, or attempt the latter but are turned away. Their home-made shacks can be seen on riverbanks, under railway bridges and in parks all over Japan. Some shacks are quite stoutly constructed: exemplars of the construction worker's craft *in extremis*. Again, masculinity is an important part of the cocktail of characteristics that contribute to homelessness: well over 90 per cent of all homeless people in Japan are male, reflecting in part the sexist attitude of welfare officials, to whom a homeless woman is a more disturbing prospect than a homeless man. Women are not expected to support themselves and so are more likely to be granted state support.

Day labourers who do apply for welfare justify the decision in a variety of ways. Some men see no contradiction in applying for welfare: unlike the salaryman, who predicates so much of his identity on his company, the man who works by the day is threatened only materially, not psychologically, by the loss of his job. Morgan correctly draws attention to the risk of making assumptions about the effects of unemployment on male psychology, particularly assumptions about the 'centrality of the male breadwinner role' (1992: 100). For other day labourers, welfare payments are just part of the natural abundance of the postmodern city, no different from the pay for a day's work: it is a survival game and one must take what one can get. More politically inclined men see success in obtaining welfare payments as a kind of revenge against the state, which has done them no favours in the past. Yet other men abstain from both employment and welfare:

LAZYBONES would not tell me his name. I met him in the street one winter morning in Nagoya. He said he had not been in the mood for working 'for twenty-five years'. He said he slept rough and lived off food past its sell-by date thrown out by supermarkets. He had enough futons to stay warm in winter, which was his favourite season because there were fewer people making a noise in the street. He claimed to be living entirely outside the cash economy.

He appeared to be in good health and good spirits. He said it was easy to live without cash in Japan, so long as one avoided alcohol. 'Once you start drinking, that's it – you're dead in a year or two.'

Activists and day-labourer unionists also show a variety of approaches to this issue. The Kotobuki Day Labourer Union (Junichirō) has campaigned long and hard for improved access to welfare for day labourers, whereas their counterparts elsewhere have tended to view welfare as demeaning to the workers' pride and accordingly have campaigned for jobs, not welfare. Junichirō has sought to resolve the psychological dichotomy of the self-reliant homeless man versus the weak and helpless welfare claimant by recasting the passive acceptance of government assistance as an active pursuit of one's legal rights. Union negotiations with the local authorities in Yokohama and Kawasaki, for example, were conducted with calculated, table-thumping aggression. These tactics have helped win a series of important welfare concessions, besides encouraging solidarity among the men and showing them that the struggle with the authorities is not necessarily a Kafkaesque battle against impossible odds.

Even so, getting welfare does inevitably affect one's personal identity. Solitary day labourers have already abandoned or rejected the image of the *daikokubashira* as a man supporting a household; once they apply for welfare, they effectively admit that they cannot even support themselves. Their lifestyles have to change as well. For example, the bid for financial security necessarily entails sacrificing a large degree of mobility. One must maintain a permanent address in order to continue claiming. Again, welfare claimants, more than day labourers, must mind their behaviour. A brush with the law can lead to suspension of payments, not just a night in the cells. Few day labourers would admit to being on welfare, but I gradually became aware of cases where men were lying about the matter, apparently out of shame. Thus themes of strength and weakness, independence and dependence, mobility and immobility, twine themselves around the day labourer's career and changing identity.

## Protean passivity at the margins

These ambiguities are expressed in some of the language associated with day labouring. They often describe themselves as having 'drifted' (*nagareru*) into the *doya-gai*, a term that elegantly combines the concepts of mobility and passivity. The imagery surrounding these drifting day labourers is often liquid and piscine. They are called 'angler-fish' (*ankō*) as they wait on the seabed of society for a job to come along. They may be caught in abusive labour camps called 'octopus traps' (*tako-beya*). When a man is mugged while sleeping in the street they call the incident a 'tuna' (*maguro*), likening the victim to a tuna helpless on a sushi chef's chopping board. Day labourers who fail to get a job say they have 'overflowed' from the market (*abureru*); if depressed they may 'drown themselves' (*oboreru*) in vice; and when troubles appear insurmountable, they may disappear overnight, or as they put it, 'evaporate' (*jōhatsu suru*).

The image of the evaporating day labourer is about as far as one can get from the solidity and permanence of the *daikokubashira*. I believe it is this polarization of lifestyles and their associated imagery that accounts for the mixture of romantic fascination and visceral hatred with which mainstream Japanese society views day labourers. The former is expressed in popular songs, novels and conversation,[14] the latter in violent attacks on homeless day labourers, which have been well documented for decades. When a day labourer is kicked to death by schoolboys, or thrown into the river by a drunken salaryman, the transformation from macho construction worker to helpless victim is complete.

Two other key *doya-gai* similes portrayed the *doya-gai* as an *ubasute-yama* ('mountain of abandonment') or as a *kakekomi-dera* ('temple of sanctuary'). Both connote detachment from mainstream society, the former in terms of expulsion, the latter in terms of escape. But it is interesting that both terms originally applied to institutions for women: in Japanese folklore, old women unable to work any more would be abandoned at the *ubasute-yama*, while in Tokugawa times, *kakekomi-dera* were nunneries to which a woman seeking a divorce could escape from her husband.

Thus, at some level, day labourers are perhaps associated with women, as people who are abandoned by, or who must or can escape from, mainstream masculinity. There may be evidence here to support Pyke's argument that class and gender hegemonies tend to 'enhance, legitimate and mystify the interpersonal power of privileged men relative to lower-status men and women in general' (1996: 527). It is very striking that the main *yoseba* district is adjacent to the city's most famous prostitution district in both Osaka (Kamagasaki adjoins Tobita) and Tokyo (San'ya adjoins Yoshiwara), and that districts with populations of *burakumin* and ethnic Koreans also rub shoulders or overlap with *yoseba* districts (Gill 2001: 172–5). Parallels between day labourers and prostitutes were acknowledged by several informants: the term *tachinbō* (literally 'one who stands') may be used of both day labourers and prostitutes since both stand in the street hoping to sell their labour. Day labourers use the term *nikutai rōdō* (physical labour, more literally 'bodily labour') about their own work, but occasionally also ironically about that of prostitutes.

## A masculine community

So far I have stressed the solitary, freelancing aspects of day-labouring life. However, there is also a kind of alternative masculine community in the *doya-gai*. While there are incidents of drunken brawling and occasional violent bullying, there is also genuine camaraderie. People can go and visit friends in their rooms to see if they have time for a conversation or a drink, whereas salarymen often live in different prefectures from their workmates. There are also general meeting spaces such as the bonfire in front of the Kotobuki Labour Centre – a kind of symbolic hearth that reminded me of the *irori* in front of the *daikokubashira* in the traditional Japanese farmhouse. It is this aspect of community, along with the strong identity with work and the day-labourer lifestyle, that most distinguishes my informants from the young unemployed Australian manual workers described by Connell (1995: 93–119), who come across as more solitary, rootless and apathetic than Japanese day labourers, seeking the human connection in sex or motorbike gangs, if anywhere, rather than with workmates.

In the last twenty-five years there has been a conscious effort by activists and politically aware workers to enhance this community aspect of the *doya-gai*. Summer festivals and winter survival campaigns (*Ettō* – see Gill 2001: 134–40; Stevens 1997) replicate the traditional activities of the mainstream midsummer and new year festivals of *Bon* and *Shōgatsu*, from which so many day labourers are excluded. But Kotobuki is not just presented as a substitute home village at festival time: a free all-day rock concert and ethnic events showcasing the district's Korean and Filipino minorities highlight the more modern, international aspects of what really is an alternative, and not just a substitute, community.

## Conclusion

Looked at a little more closely, the images of masculine mobility mentioned at the start of this chapter often turn out to gloss over the difficulties of living a free lifestyle as a Japanese man. The structure of a typical Tora-san movie, for example, entails our hero returning home to his parental family's household in the colourful Shitamachi district of Tokyo, getting involved in an adventure which takes him to some other part of Japan (virtually every prefecture has been featured), and falling in love with a much younger woman who likes him but ends up falling for a younger man, whereupon Tora-san returns home again before setting out on fresh travels in the final scene. To me, one reason for this movie series' enduring popularity lies in the way it gives the audience the best of both worlds: Tora-san can wander freely, but he can always come home to a cosy family situation. There is a poignancy in his inability to marry and settle down, but the parental family is always there for him.[15]

For non-fictional Japanese men, that balance is much harder to strike. Day labourers enjoy a degree of freedom of action that men in steady employment will admit to envying, but for most it comes at a high price. For many there is no welcoming parental family to go home to, and while some are lifelong bachelors like Tora-san, many others have abandoned marriage and family life. My enduring impression from a decade of studying day labourers is of the starkness of the choice confronting Japanese men. To truly fulfill the role of *daikokubashira* entails a heavy sacrifice of freedom. Despite gradual shifts in social and legal norms, custom and state institutions still tend to valorize the nuclear family centred on the male breadwinner; while in the workplace, the expectation of loyalty to the employing firm has arguably been strengthened by the decline of the union movement. Add to these socio-cultural factors the economic happenstance of inflated prices for housing and education and of increasing unemployment rates since the bubble economy burst at the start of the 1990s, and the web of family/work connections around the mainstream man start to appear as heavy shackles indeed. Men who reject that role, or who fail in it, may suffer social opprobrium and/or personal feelings of guilt.

Japanese men, it is true, continue to dominate Japanese society, industry and politics; but they are also more prone than women to alcoholism, homelessness, despair and suicide. To quote the title of the Tora-san movie series, 'It's hard to be a man' (*otoko wa tsurai yo*). The predicament of mainstream men perhaps helps to explain why the *yoseba*, despite their own high rates of alcoholism, crime and early death, may be read as therapeutic rather than pathological: as niches in Japanese society where some men at least, can find a degree of freedom without anomie. To the extent that researchers of Japanese society are themselves influenced by the salaryman paradigm, there is a danger of automatically pathologizing elements of the day-labourer lifestyle. Some paradigms may see them as unemployed because they have no formal employer, and as homeless because they live in accommodation normally thought of as temporary – see Somerville (1992) on the debate on 'roof-lessness' versus 'rootlessness'. Without minimizing the genuinely serious problems afflicting many day labourers, I think there is a risk of defining elements of their lifestyle as pathological when they may only be differing from middle-class norms.

It is an article of faith among *yoseba* activists that most *yoseba* men with dependencies on alcohol or gambling had developed those dependencies before they arrived: that the *yoseba*, far from being a socio-pathological environment, serves in part as a fracture clinic for the dysfunctions of mainstream masculinity. As for *yoseba* men themselves, they have many differing views of the place. Most, I think, would probably agree that life would be even worse if the place did not exist and men like themselves, outside regular employment and family life, had to improvise their lives and their identities without the company of fellow men struggling with similar challenges.

## Notes

1  Tora-san is the nickname affectionately bestowed upon Kuruma Torajirō, hero of a series of forty-eight films released by Shōchiku from 1969 to 1995 (see also Buruma 1984: 209–18; Shintani 1996). I discuss him briefly near the end of this chapter.

2  See Fukuzawa (2000: 40–1) for a moving description of a real *daikokubashira* by a homeless man who had himself abandoned the *daikokubashira* role. He recalls how his mother and grandmother would polish it assiduously every evening until it gleamed. Matsunaga (2000: 150–4) also has interesting material on the tensions inherent in the *daikokubashira* role and associated salaryman lifestyle.

3  The number of men practising *tanshin funin* passed 250,000 in 1992 (Shiina 1994; see also Wiltshire 1996). Hamada observes that 'it seems that the Japanese "cultural" norm of stressing children's education, female (maternal) nurturance and filial piety, all support the male's departure from the household' (1997: 6).

4  In 1998 the suicide rate for Japan shot up by 34.7 per cent, to 32,863 (National Police Agency 1999; see also Roberson and Suzuki, this volume, Introduction). At 26.0 per 100,000 people, the rate was second in the world behind Finland. Men accounted for 70 per cent of the total, with those in their forties and fifties registering especially high rates. In March 1998 came the first court ruling that a company had driven an employee to suicide by overworking him. Death by overwork (*karōshi*) ranks alongside *tanshin funin* as a recognized salaryman problem. Of course not all men who kill themselves are salarymen, but it is interesting that the domination of Japanese male stereotypes by salarymen extends to this grim area of society too.

5  Regularly or frequently working day labourers probably number no more than a few thousand in San'ya and Kamagasaki, and a couple of thousand in Kotobuki. In Japan as a whole some 40,000 men carry the white handbook needed to claim the Ministry of

Labour's unemployment payments for day labourers. Probably about the same number again work as day labourers without benefit of the handbook, while broader definitions of casual or insecure labour will generate much bigger head counts.

6 Some names of the men discussed here have been changed in the interests of privacy. Ages are as of the mid-1990s. Some of these men are introduced in greater detail in my book (Gill 2001).

7 In 1998 the average age of the 2,770 day labourers registered at the Kotobuki Labour Centre was 51.4, with 33 per cent aged 40–49 and 52 per cent aged 50–59. A 1992 survey by the Kotobuki Day Labourer Union (Junichirō) found that the major urban prefectures centred on Tokyo, Yokohama, Osaka, Nagoya and Fukuoka accounted for just 29 per cent of the men surveyed (sample size was unfortunately not available), although Koto-buki is located in the centre of Yokohama. Out of 56 men who told me their occupation before coming to Kotobuki, 45 mentioned working-class jobs and only 11 middle-class jobs – the last including vague terms such as 'engineer' and 'salaryman'. I lack statistical data on educational background, but most day labourers I knew had got as far as junior or senior high school.

8 Japan's divorce rate was 0.93 per 1,000 people in 1970, and had risen to 1.94 by 1998 (Ministry of Health and Welfare 1999). Figures from the late 1990s for other countries include: 4.3 for the United States, 2.9 for Britain and Australia and 1.9 for France.

9 See Dore (1978), esp. 133–42, for a highly readable discussion of the traditional house-hold system and the role of first-born sons within it.

10 Ministry of Labour interview, March 1995. The Kōbe earthquake caused a sudden 65 per cent increase in single-day contracts at the formal casual labour market in Kama-gasaki, the nearest *yoseba* to Kōbe (*Asahi Shinbun* 1995).

11 I met several day labourers in Kamagasaki who said that they were taking advantage of the strong yen to divide their lives between Japan and other Asian countries with lower costs of living. One man said he spent half of each year in the Philippines, where he had a house and a long-term girlfriend whom he was thinking of marrying. A man I met in Kotobuki was just back from several years working as a sushi chef and casual labourer in the United States.

12 Both these venerable slogans have become book titles: Funamoto 1985; Kama-kyōtō and San'ya Gentō'in 1974.

13 On January 20, 2001, the *Asahi Shinbun* reported that the Ministry of Health, Labour and Welfare was concerned about the tendency of regional welfare offices to refuse welfare payments to homeless peoples for the *ad hoc* reasons mentioned here, and was drafting a formal directive to this effect.

14 Popular songs about day labourers and their haunts include Mitsune Eiji's sentimental ballad of the 1950s, '*Kamagasaki Ninjō*' (Kamagasaki Kindness) and Okabayashi Nobu-yasu's celebrated 1980s pop ballad '*San'ya Burūsu*' (San'ya Blues). The film *Dokkoi Ikite iru* (*Living Tough*), directed by Imai Tadashi and released by Tōei in 1951, is among several that sympathetically portray the lives of day labourers within an atmosphere of grim realism.

15 On the basis of a few pages of Buruma's 1984 book, Gilmore (1990: 197) characterizes Tora-san as 'a classic father figure of the retiring, lovable sort', despite the fact that he is the most famous confirmed bachelor in Japanese popular culture. When Gilmore concludes that 'whether he chooses the battlefield or the office or wanders about the countryside doing good like Tora-San, the Japanese man is an engaged group player . . .' (ibid.: 198), one can only gasp at the sheer ignorance displayed in this, one of the most widely read general anthropological studies of masculinity.

# References

Aoki, H. (1989) *Yoseba Rōdōsha no Sei to Shi* (*The Life and Death of the* Yoseba *Worker*), Tokyo: Akashi Shoten.

*Asahi Shinbun* (1995) '*Osaka "Airin" niwaka ni kakki: shinsai fukkō ni muke kyūjin zattō*' (Osaka's Airin suddenly comes to life: a flood of personnel ads toward earthquake recovery), February 3, evening edn.

—— (2001) '*Hōmuresu seikatsu hogo: nenrei seigen wa dame*' (Homeless livelihood protection: age limits are no good), January 20.

Buruma, I. (1984) *Behind the Mask: On Sexual Demons, Sacred Mothers, Transvestites, Gangsters, Drifters and Other Japanese Cultural Heroes*, New York: Pantheon Books.

Caldarola, C. (1968) 'The *Doya-gai*: a Japanese version of skid row', *Pacific Affairs*, 41: 511–25.

Collinson, D. L. (1992) '"Engineering humor": masculinity, joking and conflict in shop-floor relations', in M. S. Kimmel and M. A. Messner (eds) *Men's Lives*, New York: Macmillan.

Connell, R.W. (1987) *Gender and Power: Society, the Person and Sexual Politics*, Stanford: Stanford University Press.

—— (1995) *Masculinities*, Berkeley: University of California Press.

Day, S., Papataxiarchis, E. and Stewart, M. (eds) (1999) *Lilies of the Field*, Oxford and Boulder: Westview Press.

Dore, R. (1978) *Shinohata: A Portrait of a Japanese Village*, London: Allen Lane.

Enloe, C. (1989) *Bananas, Beaches and Bases: Making Feminist Sense of International Politics*, London: Pandora.

Fowler, E. (1996) *San'ya Blues: Laboring Life in Contemporary Tokyo*, Ithaca and London: Cornell University Press.

Funamoto, S. (1985) *Damatte Notarejinu na* (*Do Not Be Silent and Die in the Gutter*), Tokyo: Renga Shobō Shinsha.

Fukuzawa, Y. (2000) *Hōmuresu Nikki 'Jinsei Suttonton'* (*Homeless Diary: Life in the Raw*), Tokyo: Shōgakkan.

Giamo, B. (1994) 'Order, disorder and the homeless in the United States and Japan', *Dōshisha Amerika Kenkyū* (Doshisha American Research) 13: 1–19.

Gill, T. (1998) 'Transformational magic: some Japanese superheroes and monsters', in D. P. Martinez (ed.) *The Worlds of Japanese Popular Culture: Gender, Shifting Boundaries and Global Cultures*, Cambridge: Cambridge University Press.

—— (1999) 'Wage hunting at the margins of urban Japan', in S. Day, E. Papataxiarchis and M. Stewart (eds) *Lilies of the Field*, Oxford and Boulder: Westview Press.

—— (2000) '*Yoseba* and *ninpudashi*: changing patterns of employment on the fringes of the Japanese economy', in J. S. Eades, T. Gill and H. Befu (eds) *Globalization and Social Change in Contemporary Japan*, Melbourne: Trans Pacific Press.

—— (2001) *Men of Uncertainty: The Social Organization of Day Laborers in Contemporary Japan*, Albany: SUNY Press.

Gilmore, D. D. (1990) *Manhood in the Making: Cultural Concepts of Masculinity*, New Haven and London: Yale University Press.

Gordon, A. (1985) *The Evolution of Labor Relations in Japan: Heavy Industry, 1853–1955*, Cambridge, MA: Harvard University Press.

Hamada, T. (1997) 'Absent fathers, feminized sons, selfish mothers and disobedient daughters: revisiting the Japanese *ie* household', Tokyo: Japan Policy Research Institute (JPRI Working Papers No. 33).

Kama-kyōtō and San'ya Gentō'in (1974) *Yararetara Yarikaese!* (*If They Get You, Get 'Em Back!*), Tokyo: Tabata Shoten.

Kondo, D. (1990) *Crafting Selves: Power, Gender and Discourses of Identity in a Japanese Workplace*, Chicago and London: Chicago University Press.

Leupp, G. (1992) *Servants, Shophands and Laborers in the Cities of Tokugawa Japan*, Princeton: Princeton University Press.

Marr, M. D. (1997) 'Maintaining autonomy: the plight of the American skid row and Japanese *yoseba*', *Journal of Social Distress and the Homeless* 6, 3: 229–50.

Matsunaga, L. (2000) *The Changing Face of Japanese Retail: Working in a Chain Store*, London and New York: Routledge.

Ministry of Health and Welfare (1999) *Jinkō Dōtai Tōkei (Vital Statistics)*, Tokyo: Ministry of Health and Welfare.

Morgan, D. H. J. (1992) *Discovering Men*, London and New York: Routledge.

Nakamaki, H. (2000) '*Senryū de miru gendai sararīman no jinseikan*' (The view of life of contemporary salarymen, as seen in their humorous verse), in N. Miyata and T. Shintani (eds) *Ōjōkō: Nihonjin no Sei, Rō, Shi (On Peaceful Passing: The Life, Old Age and Death of the Japanese)*, Tokyo: Shōgakkan.

National Police Agency (1999) *Keisatsu Hakusho (Police White Paper)*, Tokyo: NPA.

Okamoto, Y. (1993) *Chihō Bōseki Kigyō no Seiritsu to Tenkai (The Formation and Development of Local Cotton Spinning Firms)*, Fukuoka: Kyūshū University Press.

Pyke, K. D. (1996) 'Class-based masculinities: the interdependence of gender, class and interpersonal power', *Gender and Society* 10, 5: 527–49.

Roberson, J. E. (1998) 'Manufacturing men: working-class masculinities in Japan', *Hitotsubashi Journal of Social Studies* 30, 1: 45–59.

—— (1999) 'Fight! ippatsu!: "stamina" health drinks and the marketing of masculine ideology in Japan', paper presented at the 98th Annual Meeting of the American Anthropological Association, Chicago, November 17–21.

Shiina, M. (1994) 'Coping alone: when work separates families', *Japan Quarterly* 41: 26–35.

Shintani, T. (1996) *Tora-san no Minzokugaku: Sengo Sesōshi Danshō (Folklore Studies of Tora-san: Fragments of a Postwar History of Social Conditions)*, Tokyo: Kaimeisha.

Smith, P. (1997) *Japan: A Reinterpretation*, New York: Pantheon Books.

Somerville, P. (1992) 'Homelessness and the meaning of home: rooflessness or rootlessness?', *International Journal of Urban and Regional Research* 16: 529–39.

Stevens, C. (1997) *On the Margins of Japanese Society: Volunteers and the Welfare of the Urban Underclass*, London and New York: Routledge.

Sturtz, C. (1999) 'Sententializing masculinity: constructing male identity at the margins in Japanese', paper presented at the 98th Annual Meeting of the American Anthropological Association, Chicago, November 17–21.

Sugimoto, Y. (1997) *An Introduction to Japanese Society*, Cambridge: Cambridge University Press.

Tsuchida, H. (1966) '*Doya-gai no hikaku kenkyū*' (Comparative research on *doya-gai*), *Osaka Gakugei Daigaku Kiyō* 15: 203–15.

Ventura, R. (1992) *Underground in Japan*, London: Jonathan Cape.

Wiltshire, R. (1996) *Relocating the Japanese Worker: Geographical Perspectives on Personnel Transfers, Career Mobility and Economic Restructuring*, Folkestone, UK: Curzon Press.

Yoshida, R. (1995) '*Hobohemia to yoseba: yoseba no shakai hendō kenkyū e mukete*' (Hobohemia and *yoseba*: towards the social change study of *yoseba*), *Kyoto Shakaigaku Nenpō (Kyoto Journal of Sociology)* 3: 77–96.

# 10 Regendering batterers

## Domestic violence and men's movements*

*Tadashi Nakamura*

This chapter focuses on domestic violence (DV) and contemporary family relations in Japan from the viewpoint of clinical sociology. Centreing on violence used by husbands and fathers against wives and children, the chapter discusses the problems of adult male batterers and how we can eliminate violence between family members. I do this by placing DV in Japan in the contexts of marriage, the family and society as a whole. I also discuss an educational programme aimed at reorienting and regendering batterers. Programmes and policies supporting DV victims and survivors are obviously also important and I have discussed them elsewhere (Nakamura 2001: 62–93).[1] However, since gender is relational, and as various diversion programmes for batterers outside Japan have suggested, helping victims and survivors alone is insufficient to alleviate this complex problem. Because men in general are located at the centre of society, when they come to realize the constraints and antisocial behaviours as well as the power and privileges in their own gendered lives, their increased critical awareness and practices related to the construction of masculinity will, together with the efforts of women, engender the possibility for greater social change.

## Raising the issue of domestic violence

Although much concern about it has recently arisen, DV is not a new phenomenon. The home and intimate relations have in fact been dangerous sites in Japan for quite some time. For instance, while robbery, threat and theft tend to be committed by unrelated people, of the 1,222 cases of arrest for murder and injury in 1999, 42.6 per cent were committed by relatives and 44.3 per cent by acquaintances such as friends and colleagues (Ministry of Justice 1999).[2] In 2000, the Police Agency reported 1,096 DV-related criminal cases, double the 1999 total, including: murder 134; injury 838; and violence 124 (*Asahi Shinbun* 2001).[3] In addition, some 42 per cent of the 3,500 women housed at public women's consultation centres in 1999 had left home because of husbands' alcohol-influenced violence and aggression (ibid.). And, according to a Ministry of Health, Labour and Welfare survey, some 9,176 women visited prefectural counselling centres in 2000 seeking advice on domestic violence (see *Japan Times* 2001). These outnumbered women's consultations about divorce (8,585)[4] and poverty (6,206), and represent an increase of 1.8 times over the 1996 total of 5,000 consultations for domestic and alcohol-related violence by spouses or partners (ibid.).

Other local and national surveys also show the nature and prevalence of DV in Japan (see also Konishi 2001; Kusayanagi 1999; Nakamura 2001). The largest of these was conducted in 1999 by the Prime Minister's Office (2000). Among women respondents to this survey, 4.6 per cent reported having experienced at least one episode of spousal abuse where the women feared for their lives. Another 4.0 per cent of women similarly reported experiencing violence requiring medical attention and 14.1 per cent reported being the victims one or more times of physical abuse which they did not judge to need a doctor's attention. Being forced to have sex against their wishes on more than one occasion was reported by 17.7 per cent of women respondents. That DV may involve psychological as well as physical or sexual abuse is reflected in the fact 45.3 per cent of women reported being loudly yelled at by spouses or partners, among these 16.3 per cent on numerous occasions, 29 per cent at least once or twice. And, some 7.6 per cent of women respondents also reported having their social relations and telephone conversations subjected to close surveillance. Surveys in a number of urban areas (Tokyo, Nagoya, Kyoto) suggest that there are higher rates of (reporting) DV there than elsewhere (see Nakamura 2001: 21–4; *Asahi Shinbun* 1998).

DV thus reveals the fact that intimacy and violence coexist and potentially constitute two sides of the same coin. However, violence between spouses continues to be commonly overlooked as mere 'marital quarrels'. Commenting on the cases of forced sex, for example, Konishi notes that while these are essentially instances of marital rape, the idea that forced sex when married constitutes violence is still relatively new in Japan (2001: 88–9). Similarly, child abuse has often been dismissed as part of parental 'discipline' and 'punishment'. Abuse cases have been 'discovered' only after various surveys revealed the significance of their occurrence and social attention consequently began to be paid to them.

Behind these new findings is the rising awareness about human rights in the international community. In 1993, the United Nations defined three types of violence against women: violence inside the family, including physical, psychological, sexual and verbal assaults and economic deprivation; institutional violence such as sexual harassment, prostitution, violent media representations, battlefield rape and others; and state violence, including war and 'comfort women'. Before these UN definitions, DV in Japan tended to refer to violence in the home committed by adolescents. Subsequently, child abuse and violence between spouses have become recognized as social problems, shedding new light on pathologies inside the private space of the family. At the same time, definitions of DV have been broadened and contemporary use of DV refers to physical, psychological and sexual violence between people in intimate relations inside and outside the family unit. This understanding is important because DV thus becomes a social problem that can be linked to other types of violence caused by asymmetries in power and control.

The majority of DV assailants are men. To be clear, DV aggressors are not always men but men's generally higher positioning in the gender hierarchy, physical strength and economic power lead them to more frequently use violence against their wives and children.[5] Why do more men (and boys) employ violence against the people they (are supposed to) love? What relationships exist between violence against intimate others and masculinity and manliness? Batterers commit violence as individuals and as such there are discrete reasons for each case. Yet, beneath individual acts of violence also lie social–cultural notions of manliness and male roles. In order to untangle these links, I now turn to a consideration of the location of the family in contemporary social relations and institutional systems in Japan.

## Masculinity and the modern family system

On the one hand, DV can happen in anyone's home, but on the other hand it is not found in all families. DV perplexingly takes place in interrelations of protection, support and nurturing. It is often a cyclical problem, recurring after some interval of respite. Furthermore, the battered may unexpectedly be faithful to the batterer. How do we understand these paradoxes? First, we need to examine the structural attributes of the family that differ from those of other institutions.

As Michel Foucault (1980) has argued, modernity transformed the family into a site for the control of sexuality. According to Foucault, along with this rose the notions of sex as a personal and private matter and of sexual desires as appropriately satisfied only with designated partners. In order to confine sexuality, these partners and their relationships were legitimized through the institutions of marriage and the family. Provided with legality, the conjugal relation with its privileged access to pleasure came to form the primary space of biological and social reproduction as well as of the expression of love and emotions.

Thus, the family has historically been shaped by changing political–economic conditions and by the implicit and explicit controls of such social institutions in Japan as the family code, social security and welfare systems, education, employment fringe benefits and the tax system. These simultaneously work to shape our lives in order to produce 'proper' citizens. The family has embraced all this and has been designated by the Civil Code as the primary institution of biological and social reproduction and welfare (Ida 1995; Nakamura 1997; Ochiai 1994). The legal system requires support between family members up to the third degree of consanguinity. Livelihood Compensation is granted only when private resources are unavailable. The main earner (usually the husband) commonly receives a 'family wage' (*kazoku chingin*), which ideally provides for all family members for whom he is responsible. In order to receive the fringe benefits included in the main earner's 'family wage' package, this wage system limits the second earner's (usually the wife's) income to just over one million yen. The national pension system also advantages only certain wives. When primary earners are enrolled in welfare annuity plans for employees arranged by companies and institutions that pay both the basic (*kokumin nenkin*) and extra premiums (*kōsei* and *kyōsai nenkin*), spouses with limited or no incomes enjoy 'free-ride' coverage paid from the total annuity revenue pool. On the other hand, workers and their spouses who are not affiliated with such institutions must both pay their premiums individually without the 'free-ride' (Yamazaki and Ishikawa 1998: 52–5).

What these densely interwoven institutional arrangements suggest is the centrality in the modern marriage and family system of men's breadwinner role, not only for the everyday support of their families but also to provide for the future and for retirement. To funnel men into following this trajectory, a range of masculine images has been disseminated into the public sphere by networks of social institutions and the mass media. The most central of these masculine representations have been those of men as workers, taxpayers and family providers, which were especially dominant during the period of high economic growth beginning in the 1960s, but which have begun to diminish since the end of the bubble economy in 1991 (Okamoto and Sasano 2001).

At both school and workplace, men experience and are pressured by competition, the pursuit of possessions and interpersonal struggle (see also Itō 1996). Boys learn to (be expected to) excel in their endeavours, while in Japan's highly stratified education system, success later leads to better and more secure employment opportunities. Boys, who want their masculinity recognized by their peers, develop a collective consciousness, or perhaps an imagined community of masculinity, in which they monitor each other's behaviour. They may engage in other types of non-scholastic competition, making appeals for their sexual maturity and aggressiveness. Masculine peer pressure keeps essentially all young men inside the imagined community of masculinity and teaches them male 'pride' and the 'commonsense' of what 'men' 'ought to be'. While women's options in these social arrangements are usually the inverse of men's, expectations remain high for men to become 'correct citizen' workers, taxpayers and family breadwinners when they reach adulthood.

Despite the pervasiveness of such gendered constructions, Japanese men and manhood have started to waver, especially after the bursting of the bubble economy. There are many signs that changes in men's lifestyles are being caused by the collapse of the male-centred system, including the fact that even large companies have begun to breach the lifetime employment and seniority systems. Older and middle-aged men worry about restructuring and losing jobs, and they hope for 'soft landings' in retirement. Men in their forties increasingly wish to enjoy life apart from their work responsibilities and identities (Mathews, this volume, Chapter 7). Young people turn away from uniform-like business suits and instead project more androgynous images through trendy fashions and body aesthetics (Miller, this volume, Chapter 3). Young fathers commit themselves to doing housework and childrearing (Ishii-Kuntz, this volume, Chapter 12).

The emergence of these changes has been accompanied by other grim masculine trajectories. Even if one retains his job, already infamously long work hours are worsening. Unlike during the post-oil-shock recession from the mid-1970s through to the mid-1980s, during the current recession salarymen have been represented in the media as atomized and cut off from their families (Okamoto and Sasano 2001). Death by overwork (*karōshi*) and fatigue-induced suicide (*karō jisatsu*) are also on the rise. Suicide has become especially significant among middle-aged men. In 1999, some 22,402 men committed suicide, far exceeding the 9,189 deaths from traffic accidents (Ministry of Health, Labour and Welfare 2001). Life insurance companies have ironically even coined the term 'suicide during the thirteenth month', to refer to self-destruction committed during the thirteenth month of a policy, when companies begin paying premiums. Such suicide rates reflect the stress experienced by men under the now decade-long post-bubble recession. Yet many men who terminate their lives still do so in a 'manly' fashion, timing their deaths to ensure that their families are provided for.

On top of these trends, the national government now sends men the, in certain contexts harassing, message that 'A man who doesn't raise his children, we don't call a father'. This, however, does not mean that men's roles as workers, taxpayers and family providers have been lessened. Although they continue to be generally privileged *vis-à-vis* women, many men have become exhausted by these institutional demands and masculine constructions. If we understand Japan as a male-led society, these phenomena suggest its blockade, necessitating the transformation of male roles, institutions and the social system as a whole. DV and other tragic events and acts are intimately related to these historical and political–economic contexts.

### Labyrinth of love, power and control

Miller-Perrin and Miller (1999: 28–9) offer five characteristics of the family that create a clear boundary between it and the external world: family members spend a substantial length of time together; they live with dense emotions, dilemmas and tensions; there are physical and authoritative power inequalities; the family is walled within the idea of privacy, leading to the keeping of various secrets from the outside; and family members, especially parents and children, are linked by involuntary relations. Relations of power and control are thus interwoven into intimate relations among family members.

The effects of power and control in various kinds of criminal behaviour have been studied, especially in victimology. Psychiatrist Judith Hermann (1992: 118) has suggested that in providing psychological support for victims of wartime sexual aggression, natural disasters and rape, we need to consider the complex syndrome of prolonged, repeated trauma caused by conditions of physical and psychological confinement. Victims are often kept under the aggressors' surveillance. Similar situations inducing trauma among victims of violence can occur in the home as well. Women victims of DV find themselves surrounded by invisible walls, which are reinforced by the physical, economic, social, psychological and legal subordination of women to men (Hermann 1992). This condition is camouflaged by occasional 'rewards' granted by the aggressors in the form of gifts and words of affection, apologies and promises of change. The violence usually returns after some interval, and battered women come to have lowered self-esteem and to blame themselves because of inadequate gender-role performances, keeping them in the cycle of recurring violence (Walker 1980/1997).

In addition to the above five characteristics of the family and its traps, I want to emphasize that family members are related by the notions of love, care-giving and receiving and co-dependency. Co-dependency here refers to the need to be needed by someone in order to establish and reconfirm one's identity and usefulness. Casual observers of DV and other violence say that battered women suffer from masochistic personalities or that the victims are to blame for remaining in brutal situations that appear to have open exits available. However, these are simplistic responses to complicated problems and ignore battered women's structural disadvantages in society, as Hermann rightly points out. The subordination of women, especially those raising small children without their own incomes, is embedded in the gender and sexual politics of power and control. Thus the co-dependency relationship here is not that in which the two parties are equally responsible for violence.

It is essential to understand the relevant social mechanisms involved in DV since behind batterers' habitual violence lies a co-dependency addiction in the clinical sense that makes the vicious cycle of violence difficult to break. Intimate relationships, in which it is expected that one's basic desire to be recognized by another person will be satisfied, embrace this mechanism of co-dependency. One wishes that the relationship will (eventually) heal one's misery. Yet the couple thereby enters a labyrinth of love, power and control and begins to lose sight of the exit to the external world.

## Limits of the 'naturalness' of the family

Various forms of violence and abuse such as child abuse, DV, teenage–youth violence and elderly abuse are now recognized to exist inside the family. Public acknowledgement of these family pathologies has prompted the creation of new laws in Japan, including those intended to prevent child abuse and DV (see note 1). This indicates that actions within the formerly closed private and intimate family arena are being brought into the public domain. Before the institution of these new measures, the law was not actively enforced in dealing with what authorities defined as 'private affairs'. Similar to what feminism achieved with its claim that 'the personal is political', the institution of various laws concerning intimate relations has acted to transform the 'non-political' realm of the private into the political and public.

The exclusivity of marriage and the family, as Foucault discussed, has ironically been background to the tensions, dilemmas and explosions of emotions and violence and abuse between spouses and within the family. Though the family continues to be the primary institution fulfilling numerous domestic functions, it – or more specifically the wife – is increasingly relegating such tasks to commercial services. Women are also increasingly requesting that husbands share household chores, reproducing fewer children and working outside in paid employment both out of necessity and for personal fulfillment. On the other hand, men have become ever more unreliable earners under the prolonged recession. Because of these and various other changes in lifestyle, the 'naturalness' of the family in Japan is no longer so self-evident.

In addition, 'love' and 'marriage' may mean different things for women and men, further complicating gender relations (see Benjamin 1988). For example, upon marriage, the vast majority of Japanese men retain their family names[6] and keep working at the same place of employment. Women, on the other hand, take their husbands' name and are expected to resign from their jobs. Men's identities and lives may be punctuated by marriage but are not interrupted, as is the experience of their wives. This initial gap in entering marital life and forming a family may later seriously affect disjunctive relations.

## Gender gap and communication

Drawing on Judith Butler's notion of gender as performance, Deborah Cameron (1996) has suggested that gender is publicly displayed and reconfirmed through repetitive and ongoing performances. Gender is thus not a noun but a verb. Masculine styles of communication in Japan, characterized either by silence – commonly understood in terms of communication – or by aggressive speech do not simply serve as a mirror of masculinity but are instances of the constitution of men's masculine identities through everyday activities. The manner in which men tend (not) to speak is a gender issue.

While Japanese men learn to express themselves through competition, aggression and violence, for the most part they grow up not verbalizing their inner feelings. Indeed, one important social skill for 'masculine' men is control of emotions. Expectations of control are higher for men than for women, and for behaviour while in public more than in private places. Gender norms suggest to men not only that talkativeness cannot form or reconfirm their masculinity but that it may reveal 'unmanly' weaknesses, worries, pains and possibly tears. When men have to release these repressed feelings, they experience difficulty doing so in words, having (had) no appropriate model of verbal gender performance. Painfully pent-up emotions then become directed toward intimate others in the private arena of the home, men's only 'fort' for safely reconfirming their masculine identity and 'men's pride' (*otoko no koken*). Unfortunately, some men express 'unmanly' emotions in 'manly' fashion, using various (including verbal) forms of violence.

## Dealing with DV men

The theme of men, silence and violence has long been with us. For instance, Japanese soldiers who during the Second World War had sex with women forcibly taken to military 'comfort' facilities do not talk about their inner feelings but remain in hopeless silence. This contrasts sharply with the Asian women who have begun to speak out about their traumatic experiences. Those who initiate speaking have been the victims, the weak and the discriminated against who do not wish to remember their dreadful experiences but who nevertheless shoulder the burden of testimony. The same is true for the victims and survivors of rape and DV. Feminist counsellors and activists have supported these victims and survivors by assisting them in transforming their personal traumas into social narratives.

In this process of speaking, the men who have become assailants also need supporters. By saying this, I am fully aware that collectively men constitute the dominant group and I am not suggesting that the assailants' violence needs support. Violence must not be tolerated for any reason. Yet male aggressors too live in silence without the words with which to express themselves or describe their violent acts. It is not easy to release the encapsulated feelings of men who have harmed others. Men who have committed acts of violence often look nonchalant and their words sound emotionless. However, if their seemingly numbed emotions are also the effects of constructed manliness, then we are compelled to examine the technologies of gender at work in their silences.

Men as social beings are expected to assume roles and identities which will enhance upward mobility, but when they suffer setbacks in their roles as employees and family providers, such roles and identities tend to work adversely. When discouraged and under stress, men have tended to release their emotions in 'manly' fashion, such as through alcohol, gambling, violence, disappearance from the family (see Gill, this volume, Chapter 9) and suicide. The kinds of support male aggressors need, I suggest, are those through which we, and they, can view the connections between institutional(ized) systems and their constructed manliness and then disconnect this manliness from violence. In this way, the men will, it is hoped, reconnect themselves to family members and to society differently and non-violently.

### *Batterers*

One of the most active scholars of DV batterers is Donald Dutton (1995a, 1995b, 1998). He summarizes five major explanations for domestic violence. The first two are medical accounts which link domestic violence either to genetic causes or to some sort of brain damage. Such theses, however, do not explain why it is only wives, and only in private spaces, who are battered by such men. Next are feminist accounts which suggest that potentially any 'normal' man may batter his wife since the patriarchal system validates the use of violence in reconfirming male domination. Such feminist explanations shift our focus from the individual to the social and point to the important notions of power, control and privilege. Dutton (1995a) cautions, though, that one cannot dismiss the fact that there are also men in patriarchal societies who do not use violence.

Instead of homogenizing all men as (potential) batterers, he suggests in his fourth, social-psychological, type of explanation that we look into how batterers learn violence and are rewarded from it. Studies such as that by Kalmuss (1984) show that many men who become batterers were either childhood witnesses or victims of DV (see also below). Furthermore, men learn that they can 'win' quarrels with their wives and girlfriends by striking them. This kind of sociological account is important because it allows us to interpret the diversity of male behaviours and to connect DV to other types of violence in society. Finally, Dutton mentions discussions focusing on forms of PTSD (Post Traumatic Stress Disorder), suffered as a result of war experiences, childhood abuse and adult drug and alcohol abuse, which are connected with recurring violence as a means of coping with the psychological stresses suffered.

There are generally six attributes that batterers in many societies share. First, they shift their responsibilities for troubles at home on to the battered. Second, they tend to negate their partners' autonomy and to force the partners to fit what they want. Third, batterers do not see their partners as independent individuals but reduce them to symbols, particularly of mothers who will accept anything, even when the men use violence against them. Fourth, batterers want to keep their marriages and are not willing to negotiate about their strong expectations regarding wives' behaviours and roles. Fifth, the men believe that their partners love and need them, and that it is because of this that partners do not leave even if beaten. Sixth, batterers either develop relations with their wives which are unstable or they fail to establish truly intimate relationships at all. Under such circumstances, violence may be triggered by such things as wives' refusal to have sex; the men's dinner not being ready upon their return; children's misbehaviour when wives have asked the men to care for them; quarrels with wives; and frustrations over wives' directions about what to do.

In Japan, 30.9 per cent of the approximately 39,000 divorces submitted by wives in 1997 were filed on the basis of husbands' violence (Japanese Diet 1999). Although there is no definitive set of attributes, the batterers in these cases may be divided into four general categories. The first consists of men who rely heavily on their wives and demand unconditional spousal togetherness (*ittaikan*). They are often worrisome and jealous about their wives' activities. Even when wives refuse to do some trivial thing, the men feel that their wives are rejecting their entire persons. The men feel strongly they are the victims and use violence driven by emotions. The second consists of men who are not sociable with non-family members and use violence because they cannot express themselves well verbally. The third group consists of men who grew up experiencing violence at home and so became accustomed to violence in their lives. The fourth group comprises men who have developed pathological personalities under the influence of alcohol or drugs.

### Studies of masculinities and domestic violence

If women's studies is a discipline for empowering women, studies of masculinities should suggest ways of (re)engendering males and reconstructing positive masculine images and practices by squarely facing and overcoming the contradictions between the cultural objectification of masculinity as dominant and privileged and its dilemmas, pathologies and responsibilities. Thus, providing support to batterers requires having the men engage in such activities as pacifying their anger; stopping their violence; assuming social responsibilities by accepting their wives' petitions for divorce, alimony and child support; openly facing the stress from overwork, fatigue and fears of possible layoff; and untying the knots in their minds binding together male roles, pride, violence and aggression.

In grappling with these tangled problems, as our initial attempt to resocialize batterers, the Men's Center Japan[7] and the Study Group on Non-Violence for Men organized educational programmes for batterers in Osaka in 1998 and in Tokyo in 1999. We organized a 'diversion programme' based on my experiences at three programmes for DV batterers in the US[8] and on reference to key handbooks on DV (Sonkin 1995; Sonkin and Durphy 1989). A diversion programme is one which postpones legal action and handles certain types of criminals differently from others. If deemed appropriate, criminals are treated with measures that are less harsh and stigmatizing in order to enhance their reform. The programme we organized was called 'Men's Non-Violence Group Work' (hereafter workshop), and was initially run in Osaka from May to June 1999 for 2 hours on either of 2 days (Friday or Saturday) for 6 weeks.[9] There were four central tasks of the group work: first, the batterers performed activities through which they understood what violence is. Second, they worked to realize the imbalance in their emotions and learn to manage their anger. Third, they learned to express themselves verbally. Fourth, the men were taught to disconnect their anger from violence. All these activities were aimed at learning 'unmanly' communication skills in a broader sense. While I cannot describe all workshop activities in detail, below I introduce some of the main points (see Nakamura 2001 for more; see Kajiyama 1999 and Kusayanagi 1999 for brief descriptions of other programmes for batterers in Japan).

*Workshop*

The workshop was introduced in newspapers and on television, by flyers placed at consultation windows in women's centres, and through lawyers, counsellors, and psychiatrists. Participation was voluntary and some fifteen men joined each session. Participants were aged between their twenties and sixties. Occupations included salaryman, researcher, physician, welfare worker, unemployed and others. Before attending the workshop, some participants had been meeting counsellors and psychiatrists or were asked by their significant others to join. Others had been separated, and one was on probation for stabbing his girlfriend. Many participants had used violence against their spouses and lovers, a few men had done so against children and one man had used violence against aged patients whom he cared for at a home for the elderly. And approximately 80 per cent of the men were survivors of DV experienced either directly (having been beaten or neglected as children) or, more commonly, indirectly (witnessing violence between parents).

Each session had a theme:

1  Group Work Encounter: Meet Others and Know Yourself
2  Communicating Your Emotions 1: Learn about Your Own Emotions
3  Communicating Your Emotions 2: Expressing Your Feelings in Words
4  Communicating Your Emotions 3: Changing Your Perspectives
5  Changing Your Behaviour: Life Without Violence
6  New Self: Nurturing Rich Communication Skills

At the beginning of the workshop, participants were told that they were in a third space where they could feel safe and secure and that was different from homes in which there is violence or from workplaces with their superficial human relations. Emphasizing this context was ambivalent yet important because the men had 'come out of the closet' of the home and their participation alone speaks of the fact that they recognized that they are batterers. Placing them in a group of 'peers' was a way to have them learn from each other's experience (see also Kazama and Kawaguchi, this volume, Chapter 11) without criticizing the battered. Therefore, given the premises of the protection of privacy and of their own rights not to disclose personal experiences, participants were encouraged to share their reasons for attending the workshop and to listen to each other.

One of the main activities for workshop participants was to learn to express their inner feelings to an activity partner. They looked at drawings, adopted from the Manalive programme in San Francisco, of eight facial expressions – including those of being happy, satisfied, scared, angry, hurt, sad, excited by expectation and excited by enjoyment – and related their current feelings at the time of the workshop. Instead of speaking in abstract terms, activities revolved around the idea of 'here and now'.

In assertiveness training, inspired by the Manalive and Emerge programmes, participants were instructed to imagine a conversation between spouses and practise turning their negative feelings to positive ones. For instance, upon returning home and finding that supper is not ready, rather than yelling 'Hurry!', the men expressed themselves in more accepting terms like 'Well, she's trying', through which they could avoid using violence. Organizers asked participants how often they use words of praise and dispraise. They were then asked to work in pairs to exalt their partners for whatever they have or can offer. Becoming objects of heartening words, which they would probably have not themselves used with their wives, the men came to realize that being encouraged in this way feels good. Participants were also asked when the last time was that they said 'thank you' to someone close to them, not ritualistically but sincerely. To this question, many men had to think hard and could not recall when they had actually last uttered such words. Organizers told them, 'In your everyday life, there must be many things that you should be thankful for. This is especially so at home. As soon as you return home, start thinking of scenes in which you really should thank someone'. The workshop staff continued, telling the participants, 'Violence can occur for the smallest reason. Don't take for granted that chores and childrearing are solely your wives' jobs'.

During the workshop, participants were also encouraged to move around in order to relax through physical, bodily movement. In the activity of 'touching', for example, when the men heard the command, 'Touch blue!' they had to hurriedly touch blue objects in their surroundings. Other physical activities were designed to dislocate the men from the position of being the gazer to that of being, from various angles, the gazed at. In 'quiet movements', they all stood up and quietly decided upon two men whom they would stare at. While keeping equal distances from each other, the men moved around the room looking at the targetted individuals. In reflection, participants said that they were 'concerned about chasing the designated persons and forgot the fact that we were also the objects of observation'. This activity was intended to remind the men that their DV acts have witnesses such as children.

From another perspective, the participants became subjects of literally hierarchical relations as they looked at each other from two physically differentiated positions. One of the pair stood on a chair and looked down on his activity partner. They repeated this process, exchanging places and partners. After the activity, participants felt that: 'When I was above, I felt superior for no particular reason'; 'I felt overpowered when I was below'; 'Gazing from above is normal and I felt at ease'; 'I felt at loss when I was below because of my bald head'; and, 'I didn't realize that a hierarchical relation is so nasty'. The organizers explained that 'such physical hierarchy can also be seen in conceited positionings in speech and other behaviours. Verbally and behaviourally threatening from above makes the threatened person wither'. The participants then underwent image training in which, while closing their eyes, they imagined someone using violence against them. They found that they could only say, 'Stop it! It's my fault!', 'I'm sorry. Forgive me!' or 'I'll do what you want. So, please don't hit me!' The men learned that they feel frightened and apologize even when they have done nothing wrong or that they come to blame themselves for being threatened.

The MOVE Program (see note 8) has suggested the use of 'time out' periods in order to avoid direct confrontation with family members (see also Sonkin 1995). Our workshops in Japan have also instructed participants in employing these. When tension mounts, the angry man tells his wife, 'I'm angry and I need to take time out'. He goes outside and walks, runs or cycles, but does not drive, drink alcohol or take drugs. After one hour, he returns and asks his wife if she will talk with him. If she does not want to talk, he should respect her feelings. If they both agree to talk, the husband explains why he got upset. The next time he gets irritated, he takes time out again. In this way, he takes not just physical time out but psychological time out from frustrating situations. Workshop participants were reminded, 'Even if the cause of your anger is important to you, there is an even more important matter. That is to stop the violence. Otherwise, you will lose the people you love'.

To prevent DV from happening while participating in the programme, each man was given a 'symbolic ten yen coin' to help pacify rising frustrations at home by phoning workshop organizers. All of the men also received a key holder with the logo, 'Stop Men's Violence' to remind them of their participation in the programme. Some reported holding the key holder tight in their hands in order to keep their fists and frustrations from harming their families. Other participants continue to attend a self-help group, the Circle of Talking, which was established after the workshop ended. The reception and effectiveness of the workshop varied. Below, I introduce some of the participants' thoughts about the workshop.

*Reflections*

First is a 44-year-old man employed as a care provider for the disabled. His wife is 28 years old and works full time. They have been married for eight years and have two girls and one son. He described the process of his change as follows:

> In my case, I just beat our son endlessly. Our friends even said, 'Hey, that's too much!' Because of my violence, my wife and I were separated for a while. Then, I learned about the workshop. Recently, we've started to live together again.
>
> I grew up in a difficult family. After graduating from junior high school, I left home. I just didn't want to live with my parents. It was my stepfather. I have never met him since leaving home. While in junior high, he hit me for no reason. It was unbearable. Even when I think about that time, I know I didn't do anything wrong. It just didn't make sense to me.

Then, I beat my own son because he was naughty. It was good that I participated in the workshop. 'Time out' does work. The kids tell me, 'When you feel like raising your fist, say "time out!"' At least, I don't use violence lately. Now, my wife shows some signs of concern for me. So, we can avoid a divorce.

Next is a 28-year-old physician of internal medicine who works at a hospital. He has been married for three years and his wife is a full-time housewife. She had a job but left it on marriage because her mother-in-law told her to do so. He learned about this only afterwards. This was stressful for his wife because she was left alone at home and he does not talk to her much. For him, life was normal, but his wife wanted him to sense the problems she was experiencing. She talked to him a lot but his senses were turned off as soon as he was released from his daily medical practice, which requires intense concentration. He believed that family life runs with the same pace and style he was accustomed to when growing up. However, his father banged objects when angry, which the physician disliked. He also witnessed his father uni-laterally scolding his mother. Nevertheless, the physician ironically transposed the same communication styles to his own conjugal relation. His case started this way:

I often hit my wife and she said that my words were harsh. I never thought about things that way. Usually, I just slapped her lightly. Now, when I feel like we're going to have an argument, I keep my distance from her. I'm getting better than before. But my wife still says, 'You haven't really changed. You're no good'. I don't like that. I remember that I used violence before we were married. I didn't see any problem with that because I'm a man. One year after marriage, I butted her with my head and cracked her cheekbone. We were fighting and she had pushed me against the chest of drawers. With excessive strength, it just happened. While arguing, I lose words with which to rebut her. I hit her and bang the things around me. I thought that was common. When I start to calm down, I feel I should apologize to her. But I can't.

I started to visit a counsellor twice a month. Then, my wife learned about this workshop and insisted that I attend. My counsellor also recommended it. Now, when I attend this 'Circle of Talking', I feel at ease. Someone listens to me. I like the atmosphere, where no one blames me. I know what's wrong with me. I can't talk about my problems to people at work. Relationships there exist only within the context of our work routines. Reading books about DV doesn't help because they only say that men are at fault. I want to know what I can do. Recently, I have started to skip some work and try to think more about home.

In addition to these two men, other workshop participants' previously untold problems and backgrounds began to be disclosed in the Circle of Talking. These include:

- A man who was depressed after losing his job and whose family criticized him for 'having no capability' (*nō nashi*).
- A divorcee heading a single-father family who feels overburdened by the two roles of work and of caring for his children.

- A 65-year-old man who must attend to his 84-year-old parent's needs. He feels depressed when he verbally and uncaringly treats his parent badly.
- A father who suffers from his inability to stop his teenage children's violence and contempt.
- A man who is criticized by his full-time homemaker wife, who wants him to share chores and childrearing.
- A man undergoing divorce arbitration.
- A man trying to restart marital life with his current wife on the condition of participating in the workshop.

These examples demonstrate the complex ways in which, on the one hand, men are still expected to provide for the family or to concentrate on their work, relegating household chores to wives who, on the other hand, live in isolated homes and have little communication with their husbands. As in the case of the physician, such gender-role assignments may even be encouraged by older female family members such as mothers(-in-law). For the doctor, being such a man was further legitimated by having seen his father overpowering his mother, thus granting him the 'natural' male authority to hit his wife. This marital–family situation was further compounded by the nature of the hospital as workplace, with its psychological demands and unsociable relationships. His home thus became a masculine haven where he thought that even his emotional, verbal and physical abuse would be accepted because of his gender, and because of his wife's.

Participants' childhood experiences or their own teenage children's (usually boys') violence have also become interwoven into family relations, triggering acts of physical and verbal violence not just against women but also against the weak and/or suffering in the family, whether female or male. The family as the locus of care-giving, care-receiving and co-dependency has in many cases absorbed such tensions, but in some families these forces have not been so easily controlled. This situation, in which the family as a self-contained unit remains dominant in the social imagination yet in fact is increasingly unable to contain its tensions, is exacerbated by social mechanisms driven by gender-based role divisions. In some cases, this family–society nexus has provided inadequate social support not only for battered women but also for elderly family members and for men. At the same time, some women have come to expect that their partners will share housework and childcare. These and other women may also insist that their partners work to transform their male roles and masculine pride and behaviour. If the men do not respond positively, the women declare that they will not continue to tolerate their present situations, which for many include violence, and demand divorces. Yet, for men, marriage and the family continue to be important because these institutions legitimize their role as provider, which gives them power and authority, and as pointed out earlier is connected with their 'correct citizenship'. Caught between these tangled institutional and personal politics and relations, some men's emotional equilibrium has been stretched to the point that they blame and abuse the weak as a method of alleviating their own distress.

Some men have come to realize that what they have been doing is not just engaging in spousal quarrels but committing DV. They try to suppress and control their negative emotions, as seen in the welfare worker's case. This means that they have begun to overcome the batterer's tendencies to deny their own responsibility, the damage they have caused and the presence of victims. On the other hand, as in the case of the physician, other men continue desperately to defend their male privileges and reject criticisms, especially those coming from women. Both the doctor and the welfare worker also express desire for their wives' attention and concern for them.

The organizers of the workshop realize that participating in a six-week programme alone will not suddenly transform DV batterers into non-violent and socially communicative men. Whether or not a diversion programme for DV batterers is truly effective also depends on the degree to which the infrastructures of community treatment have been developed to change the relations of power, control and violence and to offer alternative masculine roles and identities. What the workshop has done, we believe, is to begin to change the men's perspectives on their lives and loved ones. The participants joined the programme without knowing exactly what would happen during and after the workshop, but, without skipping any sessions, they thought about domestic violence for six weeks. They have become more aware of what the social construction of masculinity may do to the less powerful and privileged (female and male) and to themselves. Even should their violence recur, the men have learned that DV is largely a problem of masculinity-making and is therefore a social as well as a personal problem. Having realized their gendered being and having gradually come to express themselves in words, the men have learned to face their own individual selves, gender and problems.

The workshop has come under criticism for using the dynamics of same-sex group work. Yet making the technology of gender and masculinity visible to the DV batterers and making them aware of their own acts as those of masculine violence generated by their power and control over the battered, the programme has planted a seed in the participants' minds potentially blossoming into personal and social transformation. Without simply shifting the responsibility for their individual aggression on to society, the men may begin to regender themselves and to reconnect themselves differently to society through everyday acts as, or at least remembering that they can be, non-violent and self-reflective men in intimate relationships with others.

## Men's movements and DV: what are we supporting?

While providing support for DV batterers, I personally have been faced with many difficulties not only as one of the organizers of the programme but as a husband, father and man. I too embody the same gender technologies and my clients demonstrate problems that I myself must constantly reflect on as a member of this sex and gender. As I similarly share socially constructed consciousness and roles, I too have had to think deeply about the links between violence and intimacy, masculinity and society.

R. W. Connell (1987, 1995) has emphasized analyses of the processes through which males are engendered and masculine consciousness and values are embedded in modern social institutions. He has also contended that because of this embeddedness of gender, the possibility for social change emerges when men begin to question their power and privilege. This requires that we break the singularity of masculinity and of masculine experiences as being dominant *vis-à-vis* women and recognize the plurality among men and the actual diversity of masculine position-alities and functions. The importance of social movements is, then, that they attempt to allow us to go beyond the universality of male domination and shed light on men's divergent lives. Although the main function of the provider role has not been ideologically abandoned (as seen in the chapters by Roberson, Gill and Ishii-Kuntz, in this volume, Chapters 8, 9 and 12, respectively), there are many practices that demand popular and state acknowledgment of alternative lifestyles among men in Japan. Connell maintains that this will begin to shake the foundation of male-led society.

Questioning the construction of masculinity, then, begins to render social meanings. It serves as a critical thrust into the core of Japanese society, which is built on male power and privilege as well as gender-specific constraints and trajectories. It also makes visible the effects of gender technologies and gender performances on the lives of both men and women. Thus, even if at present support activities intended to resocialize DV batterers largely remain acts of consciousness-raising, projecting alternatives to existing gender models is a way to make the restructuring and transformation of men and masculinity possible. To be sure, I am not suggesting that women and men swap roles, since the simple act of trading roles will not change the gendered social structure and institutions. Rather, with Connell, I suggest that the emergence of new models, consciousness and lifestyles will gradually project into and circulate within the public sphere gender relations that are more desirable than those at present. In the meantime, what men's movements such as the DV batterers' support workshop can do is to continue to destabilize the pervasive 'naturalness' of the gender hierarchy and roles, help establish alternative infrastructures of affective relationships and tap into men's rising awareness of masculinity that has begun to waver in Japan at the turn of the century.

## Notes

* Translated by Nobue Suzuki and James E. Roberson.
1 The 'Law for the Prevention of Spousal Violence and the Protection of Victims' (*Haigūsha kara no Bōryoku Oyobi Higaisha no Hogo ni Kansuru Hōritsu*) was passed by the Diet on April 6 and put into effect in October 2001 (Japanese and English versions may be found at <http://www8.cao.go.jp/danjyo/dv/dvhou.html>). Domestic violence against women in Japan is also discussed by Kajiyama (1999); Konishi (2001); Kusayanagi (1999); Nihon Bengoshi Rengōkai (2000); Nihon DV Bōshi Jōhō Sentā (1999); and Otto (Koibito) kara no Bōryoku Kenkyūkai (1998).
2 Victims included parents 10 per cent; spouses 13 per cent; children 7 per cent; siblings 3 per cent; and others (Ministry of Justice 1999).
3 While such figures might appear to be relatively small, one must remember that many victims do not report their cases to the police and that the police may even then not include such reports in their case numbers (see Konishi 2001: 81).

4  Konishi (2001) points out that in cases filed with the Family Court in 1998, the second most common reason for divorce after incompatibility of characters was husband's violence (30.7 per cent of cases), followed by psychological abuse (20.7 per cent of cases). Divorce and domestic violence are thus in fact closely linked, as will be discussed again below.
5  Although women do become batterers, in many cases their violence is used as a(n excessive) form of self-defence or in reaction to violence first used against them.
6  Nearly all (97 per cent) couples in Japan assume the husbands' surname (Takeda 1999).
7  The non-profit Men's Center Japan was opened in Osaka in 1995. It publishes a bimonthly newsletter called *Men's Network*. In addition to the workshops on domestic violence discussed here, activities include: organizing classes to enhance communications skills for men; offering counselling sessions for workaholic men and other problems, and pursuing men's studies (for brief discussions see Men's Center 1996, 1997). Men's Center Japan also sends lecturers to various other seminars to help men become more aware of and better understand gender problems. We work to develop an environment for men's liberation from masculine stereotypes and to advance and realize gender equality in Japanese society.
8  These are Manalive in San Francisco; Men Overcoming Violence (MOVE) in Amherst, Massachusetts (<http://www.mrc-wma.com/move.html>), and Emerge in Cambridge, Massachusetts (<http://www.emergedv.com>).
9  Many programmes in the US are much longer. Emerge, for example, runs a weekly two-hour session for two months and a 'second stage' that lasts between 11 and 24 months.

## References

*Asashi Shinbun* (1998) '*Otto naze tsuma o naguru no ka?*' (Why do husbands strike their wives?), September 10.
—— (2001) '*Fūfu no bōryoku bōshi e ippo*' (One step toward the prevention of spousal violence), April 7.
Benjamin, J. (1988/1992) *The Bonds of Love: Psychoanalysis, Feminism and the Problem of Domination*, trans. M. Terasawa, Tokyo: Seidosha.
Cameron, D. (1996) 'Performing gender identity: young men's talk and the construction of heterosexual masculinity', in S. Johnson and U. H. Meinoff (eds) *Language and Masculinity*, Oxford: Blackwell.
Connell, R. W. (1987) *Gender and Power*, Stanford: Stanford University Press.
—— (1995) *Masculinities*, Berkeley: University of California Press.
Dutton, D. G. (1995a) *The Batterer: A Psychological Profile*, New York: Basic Books.
—— (1995b) *The Domestic Assault of Women*, Vancouver: The University of British Columbia Press.
—— (1998) *The Abusive Personality: Violence and Control in Intimate Relationships*, New York: The Guilford Press.
Foucault, M. (1980/1988) *The History of Sexuality Volume I*, trans. M. Watanabe, Tokyo: Shinchōsha.
Hermann, J. L. (1992) *Trauma and Recovery*, New York: Basic Books.
Ida, H. (1995) *Sei Sabetsu to Shihonsei* (*Sexism and Capitalism*), Kyoto: Keibunsha.
Itō, K. (1996) *Danseigaku Nyūmon* (*Introduction to Men's Studies*), Tokyo: Sakuhinsha.
*Japan Times* (2001) 'More women seeking help over domestic violence', September 6.
Japanese Diet (1999) 145th House of Councillors Parliamentary Meeting, Minutes of the Research Committee on Society of Co-operative Way of Life, February 10.
Kajiyama, T. (1999) *Onna o Naguru Otokotachi: DV wa Hanzai de Aru* (*Men Who Beat Women: DV is Crime*), Tokyo: Bungei Shunjū.

Kalmuss, D. (1984) 'The intergenerational transmission of marital aggression', *Journal of Marriage and the Family*, 46, 1: 11–19.

Konishi, T. (2001) *Domesutikku Baiorensu (Domestic Violence)*, Tokyo: Hakusuisha.

Kusayanagi, K. (1999) *Domesutikku Baiorensu: Dansei Kagaisha no Bōryoku Kokufuku no Kokoromi (Domestic Violence: Attempting to Conquer Male Assailants' Violence)*, Tokyo: Iwanami Shoten.

Men's Center Japan (eds) (1996) *'Otoko Rashisa' kara 'Jibun Rashisa' e (From 'Manliness' to 'Being Myself')*, Kyoto: Kamogawa Shuppan.

—— (1997) *Otokotachi no 'Watashi' Sagashi (Men's Search for Themselves)*, Kyoto: Kamogawa Shuppan.

Miller-Perrin, C. L. and Miller, R. D. (1999) *Child Maltreatment*, Thousand Oaks: Sage.

Ministry of Health, Labour and Welfare (2001) 'Vital statistics', <http://www1.mhlw.go.jp/toukei-i/toukeihp/11nenpo_8/deth11.html> (August 25).

Ministry of Justice (1999) *White Paper on Crime*, Tokyo: Ōkurashō.

Nakamura, T. (1997) *Kazoku no Yukue (Whereabouts of the Family)*, Kyoto: Jinbun Shoin.

—— (2001) *Domesutikku Baiorensu: Kazoku no Byōri (Domestic Violence: Pathology of the Family)*, Tokyo: Sakuhinsha.

Nihon Bengoshi Rengōkai (2000) *Domesutikku Baiorensu Bōshi Hōritsu Handobukku (Legal Handbook for the Prevention of Domestic Violence)*, Tokyo: Akashi Shoten.

Nihon DV Bōshi Jōhō Sentā (1999) *Domesutikku Baiorensu e no Shiten: Otto, Koibito kara no Bōryoku Konzetsu no Tame ni (Views of Domestic Violence: Terminating Violence by Husbands and Boyfriends)*, Osaka: Toki Shobō.

Ochiai, E. (1994) *21 Seiki no Kazoku e (For the Family of the 21st Century)*, Tokyo: Yūhikaku.

Okamoto, T. and Sasano, E. (2001) *'Sengo Nippon no "sararīman" hyōshō no henka: Asahi Shinbun o jirei ni'* (Changes in representations of 'salaried men' in postwar Japanese newspapers: a reexamination of *Asahi Shinbun*, 1945–1999), *Shakaigaku Hyōron (Japanese Sociological Review)* 52, 1: 16–32.

Otto (Koibito) kara no Bōryoku Kenkyūkai (1998) *Domesutikku Baiorensu (Domestic Violence)*, Tokyo: Yūhikaku.

Prime Minister's Office (Sōrifu Danjokyōdō Sankakushitsu) (2000) 'Danjokan ni okeru bōryoku ni kansuru chōsa' (Survery on violence occurring between men and women) <http://www8.cao.go.jp/danjyo/yoron/bouryoku/bouryoku.html> (September 10, 2001).

Sonkin, D. J. (1995) *The Counselor's Guide to Learning to Live without Violence*, Volcano, CA: Volcano Press.

Sonkin, D. J. and Durphy, M. (1989) *Learning to Live without Violence: A Handbook for Men*, Volcano, CA: Volcano Press.

Takeda, M. (1999) 'Fūfu bessei to koseki' (Separate husband–wife names and the family register), in T. Inoue and Y. Ehara (eds) *Josei no Dētabukku (Women's Data Book)*, Tokyo: Yūhikaku.

Walker, L. E. (1980/1997) *The Battered Woman*, trans. M. Saitō *et al.*, Tokyo: Kongō Shuppan.

Yamazaki, H. and Ishikawa, A. (1998) *Shōshika Kōreika Jidai no Zeikin, Nenkin Nyūmon (Introduction to Tax and Annuity in the Age of Fewer Children and Ageing)*, Tokyo: Iwanami Shoten.

# 11 HIV risk and the (im)permeability of the male body

## Representations and realities of gay men in Japan*

*Takashi Kazama and Kazuya Kawaguchi*

In the United States, especially following the Stonewall Riot in 1969,[1] lesbians and gays have gained some power of social expression and other rights. Lesbian and gay activism has also succeeded in achieving the de-pathologization of homosexuality.[2] However, the disease later named AIDS was discovered in 1981 and was initially identified as a disease peculiar to (male) homosexuality. This contributed to the remedicalization of homosexuality (Blasius 1994: 153–4), and as such the regulatory discourse on AIDS in the US may be seen as a reaction against the rights won by lesbian and gay movements. On the other hand, when 'the first AIDS patient' was discovered in Japan in 1985, there was essentially no similar power of social expression or political activism among lesbians and gays. Japanese homosexuals were thus thrown into the midst of the age of AIDS and their struggles with pathologization continued until 1995, when the Japanese Society of Psychiatry and Neurology (finally) declared the de-medicalization of homosexuality.

This chapter elucidates how gay men and gay and lesbian activist groups in Japan have experienced and engaged with the social phenomena surrounding AIDS in contexts different from those in the US. In Japan, HIV infection risks have been chiefly attributed to male homosexuality and foreign sex workers. Here, we pay particular attention to the shift in public health concepts from 'risk group' to 'risk behaviours' which have been used both in Japan and in the West. These concepts have depicted both homosexual identity and male same-sex sexual acts as two major risks in contracting HIV. We contend that behind this conceptualization of gay men – as well as foreign sex workers – lies a desire to protect the representational – and illusionary – boundary of the Japanese nation-state and of the (heterosexual) male body as (im)permeable and (in)penetrable.

Responding to these, we provide an alternative view of 'intersubjective risk' that differentiates gay men from those constituting a 'risk group' or engaging in 'risk activities'. Through an analysis of events promoting HIV prevention organized by a Tokyo-based lesbian/gay group, OCCUR (Ugoku Gei to Rezubian no Kai [Japan Association for the Lesbian and Gay Movement]), we suggest that intersubjective risk may serve as a mechanism of resistance to the homophobia exemplified in the heterosexist/nationalist representations of permeable and impermeable bodies.

# The construction of risk in public health discourse

## Male homosexuality as identity

Four years after the discovery of AIDS in the US, 'the first person with AIDS (PWA)' in Japan was identified in March 1985. This person was a gay Japanese artist living in the US who was diagnosed as HIV-positive after undergoing an antibody testing during a return visit to Japan. However, as the Ministry of Health and Welfare (MHW) later acknowledged, there were a number of people who had contracted the HIV virus through infected blood products before this (Hirokawa 1993). This was a result of the Ministry's failure not to advise the use of heat-treated blood products. Identifying the gay artist as 'the first PWA' displaced the risk of contagion on to gay men and things foreign (or, foreigners; see Buckley 1997), and allowed the MHW and pharmaceutical companies to conceal their fatal mistake that had caused numerous other cases of HIV infection (Kazama 1997). A discursive map was thus constructed which engendered an exclusionist consciousness against foreigners and has generated a cognitive framework involving the gaying of AIDS, in which risks of contracting HIV are linked to gay identity (Buckley 1997; Treat 1994).

An illuminating example of the gaying of AIDS is found in the classification of infection routes used by the MHW's AIDS Surveillance Committee between 1985 and 1993 (Japan Public Health Association 1990: 106):

1   Opposite-sex sexual contact
2   Male homosexuality
3   Drug abuse
4   Foetal transmission
5   (Use of) infected blood products[3]

In this scheme 'male homosexuality' stands out in comparison with the other categories since without 'contact' appended – as is done in the case of heterosexual sexual contacts – it refers to an *identity* called 'male homosexuality' based on sexual orientation while the other four items suggest some kind of 'behaviour' (Vincent *et al.* 1997: 124–7).

We underscore the problem of jumbling the two different criteria of 'identity' and 'behaviour' because the choice of sexual partners based on sexual identity and the actual sex partner may not always be identical. For instance, there is no guarantee that a person with a homosexual identity will have sex only with a same-sex partner nor does a person with a heterosexual identity necessarily always have sex with an opposite-sex person.[4] For example, it is unclear which category, 'sexual contacts between heterosexuals' or 'homosexuality', would be used in the case of a man with homosexual identity who has sex with a woman and thereby contracts HIV. Thus any attempt to understand reality based on this confused categorization of causality in the spread of infection may actually invalidate the functions of AIDS prevention surveillance. That this kind of confusion has been accepted not only by the MHW but also by 'AIDS experts' in Japan indicates that homosexual identity itself is considered a cause of AIDS.

It is also important to keep in mind that the classification scheme used in AIDS surveillance in Japan lacks an item for female same-sex contraction. While to this time there has been no reported case of sexual contact between females leading to HIV infection, the absence of a relevant category speaks beyond the actual presence of such cases and empowers the de-sexualization of female sexuality. When, together with this, male homosexual *identity* is constructed as a risk factor in HIV infection, the AIDS phenomena work to stigmatize *male* homosexuality. This simultaneously strengthens the negative visibility of gay men while rendering lesbians invisible. Moreover, this has contributed to the representation of (gay) men as essentialized sexual subjects (Takemura 1997: 78).

In addition to the above classification of infection routes, Japanese AIDS surveillance has also employed a categorization by nationality. In the case of domestic transmission, for example, there is no category showing the nationality of the infected partner and yet foreign sex workers have been blamed as risk carriers (Buckley 1997).

### Emergence of the concept of risk groups

The consciousness that links risk of HIV infection with homosexual identity and the foreign is also found in epidemiological research. In this section, we examine how the idea of 'high-risk group' has been used in epidemiological discourse in Japan. This concept was first employed in AIDS epidemiology in 1988, when the MHW's AIDS Research Team was instituted (Shigematsu 1988). A nationally circulated newspaper translated 'high-risk group' as 'AIDS danger stratum (*eizu kiken sō*)' and identified male homosexuals, drug abusers and women sex workers as belonging to this stratum (*Asahi Shinbun* 1988). Consequently, these people came to be considered 'HIV infection high-risk groups'.

The categorization of (foreign) women sex workers as members of a 'high-risk group' in Japanese AIDS surveillance research seems to reflect cases such as the 1986 'Matsumoto Incident' in which a Filipina working in the sex industry in Matsumoto, Nagano Prefecture, was reported to have contracted HIV. In a report on 'women sex workers', Shiokawa Yūichi wrote that 'foreign women are an important source of AIDS infection in our country' (Shiokawa 1997: 9).[5]

Other incidents indicate how gay men were consistently categorized as a risk group in Japan's AIDS policy and in epidemiological studies in the 1980s. One example is the 'Kōbe Incident'[6] in 1987 in which the first Japanese heterosexual woman, an alleged prostitute, was diagnosed as carrying HIV. Shiokawa, chair of the Council of AIDS Policy Experts, proclaimed 1987 to be 'AIDS Year One' and commented:

> The emergence of AIDS through heterosexual sexual intercourse means that we must develop renewed AIDS strategies in our country. This is because the disease is not limited to a small number of homosexuals but now shows a

dangerous sign of spreading to people who are leading ordinary lives. We take this 'AIDS Year One' seriously.

(Asahi Shinbun 1987)

Despite the previous recognition of male homosexuals and foreign sex workers as forming 'high-risk groups', HIV infection among both was apparently not deemed worth acknowledging as 'AIDS Year One', nor were actual preventive measures put into action. For the Japanese state, then, male homosexuals and foreigners were not 'people leading ordinary lives', and so were not considered in need of infection prevention but were located outside the scope of such measures. The notion of 'high-risk group' has been used as a way of identifying AIDS as a disease associated with people belonging to that group, simultaneously engendering the notion of 'normal' people as those originally 'unrelated' to AIDS and in need of protection.

Contrary to this sort of conceptualization, in epidemiology elsewhere, risk groups are understood differently. According to Simon Watney,

> Epidemiologists use the term risk groups to refer to defined groups at demonstrably increased risk from particular medical conditions, compared to the rest of the population . . . Further, those at highest statistical risk are sometimes referred to as high risk groups.

(1996: 431–2)

Here, risk refers to 'victims to be protected' and

> [t]he aim of defining such risk groups is to contribute to prevention, including to marshal adequate and appropriate resources for those in greatest need. In an epidemic, such resources will include preventive measures, care and service provision, which need to be targetted to those at greatest predictable risk.

(ibid.)

Obviously, epidemiological research in Japan did not evolve in this fashion. The ways in which resources for preventive measures are allocated to groups identified as at high risk serve as a good indicator of how the Japanese state has dealt with this issue. For instance, it was only in 2001 that, for the first time, the national budget included monies in its AIDS policy funds for prevention promotion campaigns aimed at homosexuals. That is, if one takes the availability of state budgeting for AIDS-related policies for homosexuals as an indication, homosexuals have until very recently not been considered 'victims to be protected' but rather dangerous objects to be excluded from social support.

The Matsumoto and Kōbe incidents, both involving heterosexual contacts, caused a 'panic' in Japanese society, where AIDS had previously been 'safely' associated with homosexuals.[7] The Japanese government attempted to appease the rising worries among citizens by instituting an AIDS Prevention Law (Japan Public Health Association 1990: 98–101). The bill that was passed in 1987 and which took effect in 1988 included the following provisions:

1    When doctors believe that persons with HIV are not following their instructions and are deemed likely to spread the disease, the physicians are obligated to report the patients' names, addresses and other information to the prefectural governor.
2    When the governor deems that individuals justifiably suspected to be HIV carriers may spread the disease to an unlimited number of other people, or when s/he otherwise decides it necessary, s/he may require those persons to undergo physical examinations. If diagnosed to have contracted HIV, the governor may issue further prevention-oriented directives.
3    Foreigners with HIV or PWAs who are suspected as likely to spread the disease may not enter Japan.

This bill essentially treats all people suspected of possible HIV infection – essentially, homosexuals and foreigners – as potential assailants and legitimates the strengthening of state surveillance and control over these people. Conversely, the construction of 'risk groups' has also worked to locate Japanese heterosexual men in the position of 'ordinary people' who must be protected from harm.

### From risk group to risk behaviours

OCCUR has criticized the notion of high-risk groups used in the above epidemiological research and has demanded that the surveillance report alter the category of homosexuals' *identity* in the list of causes of HIV infection (Kazama 1997, 1998). Subsequently, in 1993 the surveillance research team changed this item from 'male homosexuality' to 'same-sex sexual contacts'. Although this change is important as one of the fruits of lesbian/gay activism in Japan, we should not ignore two important background factors that were concurrently emerging in public health research.

Behind this terminological alteration lies a conceptual transformation from 'risk group' to 'risk behaviours' in public health discourse in Western countries in the 1990s that by 1993 had also begun entering Japan. Watney notes that '[b]y 1988 it had become an axiom that risk for HIV comes not from who you are, but from what you do' (1996: 431–2). In other words, contracting HIV is not the problem of certain groups but of individuals who engage in behaviours that potentially lead to infection. This newly emerging discourse required the revision of the existing conceptual framework of risk groups in dealing with AIDS and HIV infection.

A significant factor contributing to this conceptual change was that Japanese statistics on HIV-infected persons and PWAs began to show remarkably different patterns after 1992. Persons with HIV and PWAs through same-sex sexual contacts numbered 43 in 1991 and 58 in 1992. In contrast, the numbers of people who contracted HIV and AIDS heterosexually soared from 123 in 1991 to 253 in 1992 (National AIDS Surveillance Committee 2000 [1999]). The transformation of concepts of risk in public health administration is thus also a result of the realization that then current terminology did not reflect the fact that the previously dominant route of HIV infection through male same-sex sexual contact had been surpassed by the rising cases of infection through heterosexual sexual contact (*Tokyo Shinbun* 1993). The view of AIDS as a 'gay disease' disregarded transmission from (Southeast

Asian) sex workers (in Japan) to heterosexual Japanese men while existing preventive measures thereby became inappropriate in attempting to protect even these men.

The state's concern with the protection of heterosexual men is exemplified by a poster for the promotion of AIDS prevention created in 1991 by the Japan Foundation for AIDS Prevention, which featured a Japanese man wearing a business suit and shielding his face with a Japanese passport. The caption read: 'Bon voyage. Watch out for AIDS'. This poster was made during the time when Japanese men's sex tourism to Southeast Asia was widespread,[8] and whatever the intentions of its creator, when viewed in this context speaks clearly about whom the government wanted to protect and about whom it saw as the source of risk. Having the man in the poster hide his face with his passport is, further, a way to remove his individuality. The object of the phrase 'Watch out for AIDS', the person to be protected, may thus be understood to refer to the Japanese heterosexual male population as a whole (Ōishi and Kawaguchi 1998: 171–2).

Recently, a pamphlet created by Osaka Prefecture (1997) promoting human-rights protection wrote:

> Why is there prejudice against [AIDS] patients and [HIV]-infected people? This is because of the spread of the mistaken image that 'AIDS is a terrifying disease' and that 'it is a particular disease spread among people like homosexuals'.

The meaning of the latter phrase, 'disease of particular people like homosexuals', is particularly rich in suggestion when we consider the effects on gay men of the de-gaying of AIDS resulting from the shift of focus to risk behaviours. It might appear that the change in focus of risk factors reflects a correction to the gaying of AIDS. Yet quite the contrary is true. Commenting on the question – 'Is AIDS a disease of homosexuals?' – and answer – 'Of course, it's wrong. Anyone can contract AIDS' – which appeared in a widely circulated pamphlet, Buckley has argued that:

> The question and answer reinforce the fact that in this brochure AIDS is treated as a heterosexual issue. In clarifying that AIDS is not a homosexual disease, the statement also appears to reinforce a negative and deviant marking of male gay identity by uncritically linking discrimination toward PWAs with gay identity.
>
> (1997: 278–9)

An issue of the newsletter *Confronting HIV* published in October 1998 included the equation '489 + 1,281 = 1,770' on its cover (*Confronting HIV* 1998). The explanation printed on the inside of the cover reads:

> As of April 1998, the number of HIV-positive persons and PWAs infected through heterosexual intercourse in Japan numbered 489 and 1,281. While the numbers of new HIV cases are beginning to decrease in several western countries, they continue to increase in Japan.
>
> (ibid.)

The cover page sends a message warning about the spread of HIV infection and calling for the need to reduce the number of new patients. What is important here is that homosexuals are not included in these concerns. Thus, as focus was turned to heterosexual contacts, the problem of same-sex sexual contacts became invisible with the de-gaying of AIDS.

While the gaying of AIDS in Japan might be seen to have contributed to the concealing of HIV infection cases resulting from medication with non-heat-treated blood products, the de-gaying of AIDS in Japan may also be seen to have been speeded up by the rise of support for and the protest movement surrounding 'Medical AIDS' cases. After 1995, mass media coverage changed completely, with a great decrease in reports regarding sexually transmitted infection and a huge increase in reports about 'Medical AIDS' cases. Coupled with this, the fact that only the secondary infection of heterosexual partners was focused on advanced the de-gaying of AIDS to another level.

### Emphasis on sex acts in MSM research

The de-gaying of AIDS has not only rendered HIV infection among homosexuals invisible but has simultaneously maintained a particularizing view of sex between men. For example, the change in views of risk influenced the blood donation policy that the Japan Red Cross (JRC) had employed since the discovery of the 'first AIDS patient' to 'refuse blood donations from homosexuals, bisexuals and those who had sexual contacts with these people'. The JRC now refuses donations from 'those who have had sexual contacts with an unknown number of people and those who have had sexual contacts with people of the same sex' (Kazama 1998: 248). This revision indicates that blood donations from homosexuals are no longer rejected on the basis of their sexual identity. However, regardless of whether they are practising safer sex or not, sexual intercourse with same-sex individuals itself has come to be considered a risk. The basis of the judgement here is not homosexual identity but sexual activity.

The same dynamic has also been observed in epidemiology, which while moving from a focus on 'homosexuality' to MSM or 'Men who have Sex with Men' has none the less retained a particularistic view of same-sex sexual activities. The category 'same-sex sexual contact' was first used in Japanese epidemiology research by the Epidemiology Research Team's Subgroup on High Risk in its 'Epidemiological Report on Groups of Men who have Sex with Men (MSM) in the Kantō Region' (Ichikawa *et al.* 1995: 155–9).

In research conducted in 1995, Public Health Office employees collected trash from individual and shared rooms at two gay bathhouses in Tokyo over a three-day period from Friday to Sunday. The objectives of this research were to calculate 'rates of anal sex', 'rates of condom use', 'syphilis infection rates' and 'HIV infection rates' from the semen and faecal matter extracted from the used tissue papers and condoms collected from each room. Researchers distributed condoms to further check condom use rates and to measure the effectiveness of measures promoting infection prevention. The trash collected from each room was separated by item and placed in plastic bags. Researchers then examined:

1   the presence or absence and the number of condoms
2   the presence or absence of traces or the odour of semen
3   the presence or absence of traces of faecal matter

4   the presence or absence of drugs
5   the weight of the bags.

The presence of semen was understood as evidence of sexual contact and traces of faecal matter as that of anal sex. The trash was further chemically treated to extract semen or faeces from used tissue papers in order to measure the rates of sexually transmitted diseases such as HIV, syphilis, chlamydia and hepatitis B virus.

Criticism of ethical and methodological problems led several gay/lesbian organizations brought together by OCCUR to demand the termination of this project for the following reasons: (1) researchers had not obtained the consent of research subjects; (2) the probable rates of disease infection calculated are those of the rooms and not of each man; and (3) research results could, however, be interpreted as indicating the HIV infection rates of individual (gay) men. The MHW research group refused to take this request into consideration, drawing on the epidemiological concept of the 'unlinked anonymous' approved by ethics committees at American universities, which suggests that as long as anonymity is preserved, unlinked to particular individuals, that is sufficient.

As is reflected in the term MSM, this research was concerned only with the subject of men's sexual practices. It might appear that it had taken into consideration demands to change the orientation of AIDS surveillance from a focus on homosexual 'identity' to a concentration on 'behaviours'. Yet OCCUR had no choice but to protest against this research since it failed to obtain the informed consent of its subjects. Behind this situation also lay the fact that the shift of research focus from homosexual identity to practice had not changed the continuing particularized gaze at male same-sex sexual intercourse and the related fact that the researchers were attempting to concentrate on the education of heterosexual men. Thus this MSM research appears to have been an attempt to observe the sex acts of the users of gay bathhouses as a peculiar and dangerous form of behaviour. Furthermore, by disregarding the necessity to obtain the informed consent of its subjects, this research's focus on activities may be seen as closely related to a disparaging view of (male) homosexual identities and subjectivities.

### Dangerous anal sex

Both views of risk focusing on homosexual identity and on behaviours have disadvantaged homosexuals. We now discuss this through a consideration of representations of risk and the (im)permeability of the male – and national – body. In doing this, we analyse epidemiological research projects directed by Isomura Shin. This research was initially conducted between 1986 and 1996 under the title 'Serum Epidemiological and Behavioural Research on HIV Infection among *Male Homosexual* Groups in the Tōkai Region' (Isomura 1997: 165–7; emphasis added). From 1997, the research was renamed 'Serum Epidemiological and Behavioural Research on HIV Contract among *MSM* Groups in the Tōkai Region' (ibid.). What is curious about these research projects is that while the focus on risk shifted from the identity of 'homosexual groups' in the former to the behaviours of MSM in the latter, no consequent change in research content may be found.

This research examined shifts in the estimated rates of HIV-positive persons based on free and anonymous blood tests conducted, with consent, among the patrons of gay bathhouses in the Tōkai region. Upon reporting test results over the phone, research subjects were asked questions about six further sets of items:

A   Homosexual, heterosexual and marriage histories
B   Current age; the age at which one became homosexual; and the number of years of homosexual experience
C   Number of sex partners during the past year
D   (Non-)practice of anal sex; roles during sex acts; (non-)use of condoms during the past year
E   History of STD contraction and serum syphilis reaction
F   (Non-)engagement in sex with foreigners; drug use.

Again, these questions make foreigners and gay men 'risks', and through this Japanese heterosexual identity is 'naturalized' and Japanese heterosexuals are given the status of 'victim'. Item F, for example, reveals that HIV/AIDS-related research in Japan continues to view foreigners as a 'risk factor', and that representations of 'the foreign' are connected not just to female sex workers but also to gay men. This stubbornly repeats the dynamics of the discovery of the 'first AIDS patient', discussed earlier. Item A, which asked not only about sexual orientation but also about marriage history, implies that homosexuals are a 'source of infection' potentially spreading HIV to heterosexuals through marriage. Furthermore, Item B assumes the 'natural' state of heterosexuality before the 'start' of homosexuality, which for some unknown reason 'begins'.

The representation of anal sex in Item D works together with that of the (im)permeability of the male body to form a discursive structure linking gay men and contraction risks. Isomura's team asked not only about the presence or absence of anal sex but also about the 'roles' in sex acts. The report identifies three roles: 'male', 'female' and 'both' (Isomura 1997: 173). Although no further description of the behaviours assumed to be associated with each of the 'roles' is provided, it is easy to imagine that Isomura based these on the dichotomy of manliness/womanliness (Takemura 1997: 76). This dichotomy not only suggests that gendered relations are asymmetrical but that sexual positionalities are as well. In both, men are assumed to perform active and women passive roles. Isomura's use of 'male' thus suggests an 'active' penetrating role while 'female' implies a 'passive' penetrated role (ibid.).

Epidemiologists are concerned about the roles performed in anal sex because they consider the anus to be the most dangerous body part in terms of HIV infection. This discourse views the anus as a site of ready viral absorption and treats anal sex without the use of condoms as one of the riskiest of sexual acts. It further views the men playing the 'female role', inside of whom semen is ejaculated, as at particular danger. For example, Abe Takeshi[9] wrote that:

> the anus and the connected rectum have delicate yet flexible internal skin, surrounding muscles and ligaments so that they can adjust to faeces of any

shape and hardness. Furthermore, they efficiently maintain the pressure in the abdomen in order to control the flow and amount of blood. However, when a hardened penis is inserted with great force, these organs are easily injured. Bleeding may also occur. Therefore, anal sex has been seen as the sexual act at highest risk in contracting HIV.

(1986: 43)

Treichler (1987/1993: 238) has argued that a discourse that emphasizes the risks involved in anal sex in comparison with other forms of sexual practice is grounded in homophobia. Judith Butler, meanwhile, has analysed the reason why male same-sex acts are considered menacing as follows:

Since anal and oral sex among men clearly establishes certain kinds of bodily permeabilities unsanctioned by the hegemonic order, male homosexuality would, within such a hegemonic point of view, constitute a site of danger and pollution, prior to and regardless of the cultural presence of AIDS.

(Butler 1990: 132/1999: 234)

One of Butler's points here is that sex between men is accompanied by the representation of permeability, which is not accepted in the 'hegemonic order of the body'. Such permeability constitutes the male homosexual body as a site of danger and pollution. The 'hegemonic order of the body' refers not only to the physical boundary in which 'men' are active and 'penetrate' and 'women' are passive and 'penetrated'. Instead, this sex/gender distinction is a reflection of one of the dominant norms constituting modern society (Takemura 1997: 75–7). Since the rise of industrial capitalism, there has been a division of male and female spheres of labour. For example, in the arenas of paid labour and politics, men have largely monopolized public, active functions, while women have been pushed into private, passive domestic roles. From this perspective, anal and oral sex between men, accompanied by acts of active and passive penile penetration, is an abrogation of the assumed 'male' physical role and a danger to the hetero/sexist modern social order – of (male) impermeability – and must therefore be abolished.

Although men performing this impermeable, penetrating 'male role' might appear to be qualitatively similar to heterosexual men, the fact that they penetrate into other men makes them a threat to heterosexual men, endangering the supposedly impermeable male body (politic). With the link between the permeated/penetrated and 'women', anal sex becomes a juncture where men feminize other men. The social imagination of heretofore 'hegemonic' men becoming 'feminized' through penetration breaks the presumed coherence among men as a unified group located above women in the existing gender hierarchy, which then itself becomes at risk of being subverted.

However, it must not be forgotten that sex between men is not just 'dangerous' and 'a site of pollution' but may in some ways also be seen to be necessary for the (compulsory) heterosexist system (see also Rich 1980; Takemura 1997). The view of 'male' and 'female' roles in male same-sex sexual intercourse suggests that even when performed by same-sex individuals the actors' roles in sex may thus be conceptualized as essentially heterosexual(-like) and as such do not deviate from the hegemonic gender code but rather become copies of the normative dominant/dominated male–female relationship (Butler 1990/1999). As Butler (1993: 313/1996: 125) has argued, this original–copy relationship is a part of the necessary process in which heterosexuality is asserted to be the original of all other sexual identities and relations.

Thus, on the one hand, anal sex as the representation of sex acts among homosexuals endangers male identity since it deviates from normative gender roles and divides the collective male hegemony. It is also viewed as a destructive form of sex, leading to death by AIDS. On the other hand, through heterosexually marking roles as active 'male' and passive 'female', homosexuals are recognized as copies that imitate and legitimate the gender roles in heterosexual sex and society (Bersani 1988). While for the system of compulsory heterosexism based on such a male–female dichotomy sex between men is dangerous and sex between women is made invisible and de-sexualized, heterosexuality is taken as the original. Furthermore, homophobia, denying the legitimacy of homosexuality, is at the same time also necessary in order for the heterosexist system to keep its dependency on homosexuality concealed (Takemura 1997).

## *Deai* Events[10] as political space

We have thus far discussed the ways in which concepts of AIDS/HIV risk in Japan have been constructed and how heterosexism and homophobia have worked together in this process. In the following, we examine '*Deai* Events' organized for the past few years by OCCUR as an example of a concrete HIV-preventive intervention initiated by gay men themselves which also acts to resist homophobic risk concepts.

### Isolated homosexuals

It will first be useful to examine briefly the situation of lesbians and gays in contemporary Japan. Since the 1990s, the amount of information available in Japan regarding homosexuality has been on the rise. Yet this has largely been composed of images of homosexuality or of homosexuals as constructed by heterosexist society. Lesbians' and gays' own voices and lived experiences have for the most part remained unheard within the dominant discourse, hidden behind the socially constructed images of homosexuality. For many gays and lesbians, those images simultaneously participate in the construction of a harsh reality of discrimination.

There are no laws in Japan similar to those prohibiting sodomy in the West, nor are there clear religious bans on homosexuality. However, this does not mean that Japanese society tolerates homosexuality without any discrimination. Rather, the problem lies in the fact that there is no clear or obvious homosexual 'object' of prohibition. If, as Foucault (1987) has said, 'prohibition' or the 'prohibition of desire' generates its objects and if bans invite resistance, then Japanese society offers no locus for homosexuals' resistance. Under these circumstances, individual homosexuals have been isolated and placed in contexts where it is difficult for them to organize or form groups.

In response to this situation, since 1987 OCCUR has been offering telephone peer counselling to lesbian and gay callers so that people suffering from or worried about their sexual orientation can feel at ease in talking with someone with the same sexual orientation. Some one thousand calls per year are received from gay clients alone. Many callers experience finding for the first time in their lives that there are other men or women who love men or women, respectively. Callers feel relieved to hear reassuring comments such as 'I'm the same as you' from the peer counsellors. This telephone peer counselling is also a site where homosexuals can in their own words begin to talk about the various forms of oppression they experience in their daily lives.

Callers' comments reveal that their greatest concern is isolation. The majority worry or hold negative feelings when they realize that they are attracted to members of the same sex, reflecting (stereotypical) negative images about homosexuality in Japanese society. Whether or not they hold a conscious homosexual identity, many callers feel that they cannot reveal their attraction to people of the same sex but must keep their feelings secret. Many people look up 'homosexuality' in dictionaries and encyclopaedias when worried about their sexuality only to find descriptions like 'perversion' and 'abnormality'. Their worries are thereby exacerbated rather than relieved.

Under such conditions – of the circulation of misinformation or of the lack of information altogether – it is especially difficult for gay men to win parents' and families' understandings. Many families put pressure on children to marry even after learning about their homosexuality, not to mention prior to this. Due to the Japanese notion of *seken* (the public eye) some families feel ashamed of homosexual members and, just like the isolation felt by homosexuals themselves, parents and families also tend to become isolated when family members come out as homosexuals. By creating this situation, whether consciously or not, the ubiquitous homophobia in Japanese society has made (or tries to make) the existence of homosexuals publicly invisible.

The Japanese media, further, often make teasing and disparaging comments about homosexuals. While for heterosexuals such representations may appear to be 'just for fun' within the context of Japanese 'culture', for homosexuals these may be deeply humiliating. However trivial they may appear on the surface, such comments are factors in the self-negation felt by many homosexuals. Under these conditions, gay men (and lesbians) tend to be isolated and it is difficult for them to meet each other (Kawaguchi 2000: 70–3).

While it is true that since the 1990s gay subcultures in Japan have gained in popularity as seen in the cultural phenomenon of the 'gay boom', these tend to exist only in certain sections of urban centres and to have a commercial(ized) character. That people from throughout Japan who contact OCCUR for telephone peer counselling are willing to pay high long-distance phone rates suggests the need felt for such consultation and demonstrates that venues for homosexual men and women to meet each other are still limited.[11] Even when they do not have any clear reason or serious problem to discuss, there has always been a number of callers who just want to talk with other homosexuals. For these isolated homosexual individuals, telephone counselling has served as a vital lifeline in locating and communicating with peers.

## Epidemiological risks and intersubjective risks

As mentioned above, contemporary Japanese epidemiology has focused on those who are engaged in risky activities or on one particular group as a risk entity. This implies that a person's identity or individual acts are the reasons s/he is faced with the risk of contracting AIDS. Individuals are thus held liable for taking risks. In fact, Japanese scientists, medical experts and bureaucrats have commonly adopted this perspective when designing HIV/AIDS prevention measures and when disseminating information regarding safer sex practices. They have assumed that a 'rational' individual receiving information will not be influenced by external factors but will instead passively receive information and act as instructed. There is no active individual here who takes initiative in his or her own behaviour. And, while the availability of preventive knowledge about AIDS is of course important, the diffusion of accurate information about AIDS and of preventive knowledge does not guarantee that people will necessarily practice safer sex (see Davis 1994; Kendall 1995).

Sexual acts are not just individual practices but are social practices performed as part of a relationship between two (or more) individuals. Discussions of homosexual sexual behaviours must also take homophobic and heterosexist social contexts into consideration. Yet the influence of 'external conditions' such as the isolation, homophobia and other social constraints experienced by homosexuals has seldom been taken into account when the problems of epidemiological risk and of preventive or care-giving measures have been discussed in Japan. Until recently the involvement of social scientists in Japanese AIDS research was insignificant and AIDS policies consequently failed to build links with community-based non-government organizations (NGOs), thereby limiting the acquisition of information regarding the situations and needs of people influenced by AIDS. In preventive education, moreover, policies have been unable to connect research results with effective preventive practices.

Consideration of such social dimensions demands that 'risk' be reconceptualized. Risks, we discuss here, are not fixed or predetermined. Rather, they are generated or constructed between a multiple number of individuals or subjects as they form social relationships. This new conceptualization of risk may be called that of 'intersubjective' or 'sociological' risk in order to differentiate it from epidemiological risk.

Given the social isolation of homosexuals in Japan, their opportunities and means for communication have been very limited. This is quite different from the situation in metropolitan areas in advanced countries in the West, where homosexuals have formed their own distinctive 'communities'. In Japan, the presence of homosexuals, with the exceptions of certain celebrities, has become visible primarily only because of the problem of AIDS. In these circumstances, homosexuals in Japan have themselves been compelled to deal with the threat of AIDS and to intervene in its spread. In the following, we introduce OCCUR's '*Deai* Events' as an example of a concrete preventive practice utilizing an intersubjective concept of risk that intervenes against AIDS and the de-gaying of the AIDS discourse.

## Outline of 'Deai Events'

Starting from its establishment the mid-1980s, OCCUR has organized various educational activities for AIDS prevention. In the beginning, we distributed information about AIDS at bars in urban entertainment districts where homosexuals gather. Subsequently, we simultaneously distributed AIDS prevention goods such as condoms. These actions were taken amid the 'AIDS Panic' when institutionally organized prevention measures generally only stirred a sense of fear. Our efforts did provide accurate information about AIDS, but like other prevention education groups we soon realized that information and knowledge alone do not necessarily lead to safer sex.

As a result, from 1997 OCCUR began implementing a new programme which took a completely different form. Based on what we had learned about the situations of gays in Japan, OCCUR established a space in which homosexuals can gather and communicate among themselves. We call this programme '*Deai* Events'. The goal is to enhance the number of occasions for gays to meet and gain knowledge about AIDS and safer sex through rounds of communication exchange. Actual activities include 'circulating talk' in which participants rotate, introducing themselves to each other, and quiz games played in groups where participants try to answer questions about AIDS and homosexuality. These activities are designed to enhance cooperation and communication skills with peers, especially listening. As the name suggests, this space also allows participants to meet others and potentially to find friends and lovers. Blank cards are circulated on which participants can express their feelings and which they can give to the relevant person during the course of the *Deai* Event. Throughout, OCCUR staff provide support to ensure smooth communication. The masters of ceremony include someone who is gay and/or HIV-positive, who talks with participants about his own experiences.

## Meanings of Deai Events

As noted above, efforts to prevent AIDS in Japan have thus far relied chiefly on the dissemination of information to both homosexuals and heterosexuals. While still useful, the generation of information for these two sexually different groups has not been symmetrical. Administratively proffered information about AIDS has for the most part focused on sexual behaviour between members of the opposite sex. Information dissemination targetted at homosexual sex has been relegated to NGOs. One positive result of this has been that, because these are NGOs formed by gays themselves, the information circulated for homosexuals reflects their (particular) needs. Methodologically, the governmentally administered schemes potentially disregard individuals as active agents. *Deai* Events fill the gap between the institutional measures and local needs by emphasizing the importance of enhancing communication between sexual partners.

This difference in methodology coincides with a shift in views from epidemiological to intersubjective risk defined not by individual identity but constructed in practice between sexual subjects. The goal of the *Deai* Events is to intervene into the epidemiological view of risk that sees homosexual identity and the related actions of

194 Takashi Kazama and Kazuya Kawaguchi

individuals as the source of problems such as AIDS, viewed as the 'gay disease'. Thus the events politically symbolize acts of resistance against homophobia. These acts of resistance are not limited to attempts to have society accept homosexual sex acts. We are also working to disrupt the reductionistic link between homosexuality and (anal) sex and to make visible, as in Foucault's (1987) argument, other 'gay lifestyles'. In the context of Japanese society, same-sex sexual acts – not just as 'sex acts' but as 'love' and 'lives' based on sexual unions – are seen as a disturbance and threat to heterosexist social institutions.

Conversely, gatherings of homosexuals create a space in which they can disregard sexual orientation as a significant mark of difference. In this regard, they may themselves enjoy opportunities to transform socially constructed images of homosexuals as simply (and dangerously) sexualized beings. As in the dominant space for heterosexuals, a space in which homosexuals can remain 'unconscious' about their sexual orientation helps individual wholeness and differences come into view. These differences include those of age, sexual leader–follower, economic power, nationality and the like. When they begin to see each other as different individuals, *Deai* Event participants are compelled to communicate with each other in order to understand and overcome personal differences in points of view, experience and power.

Though many initially feel unable to express themselves well, participants begin to acquire better communication skills. This is possible only in contexts where being homosexual is taken for granted, and these skills can subsequently be pragmatically utilized to ensure safer sex practices. Mutual communication makes one aware that one's self is not inherently complete but rather is socially and intersubjectively defined and constructed. Likewise, the line between 'safe' and 'dangerous' practices is not absolute, and as such safer sex acts are learned and practiced in inter-relationships between homosexual individuals placed within shifting power relations. Hence, the divided categories of 'identity' and 'behaviour' based on risks involved in HIV infection become meaningless. By uniting these two politically divided categories, *Deai* Events organized by OCCUR have served as an alternative programme to help reduce HIV/AIDS infection by redefining (homosexual) selves and practices within social relationships based on intersubjective communication.

## Conclusion

In this chapter, we have delineated ways in which gay men in Japan have come to face and experience various problems associated with AIDS. A discourse using the notions of 'risk group (identity)' and 'risk behaviour' linked homosexuals with AIDS and generated both the gaying and de-gaying of AIDS. Drawing on an analogy between the (im)permeability of the (heterosexual) masculine body and of the nation-state and its protective boundaries, this discourse has attempted to exclude or expel HIV/AIDS and its supposed carriers from the Japanese body (politic). This was evidenced in the Matsumoto and Kōbe incidents, where 'foreign' and 'non-domestic' Japanese women, respectively, were deployed to confirm the argument that such external agents are to blame for infecting the Japanese male/national body. Those deserving protection in this discourse are (heterosexual) Japanese men in their prime working ages living in Japan. In this view, heterosexual males (as individuals and as nation) possess bodies that not only must not be infected but, furthermore, must not be penetrated (violated) and thereby feminized.

We have also discussed the impact of the AIDS discourse upon lesbian/gay movements and the ways in which certain gay men have worked to resist the regulatory discourse. The division of identity and practice among homosexuals in the AIDS discourse, we argue, needs to be politically contextualized. When the discourse of 'gay = AIDS' spread, it worked to exclude homosexuals from ('healthy') society, from social–sexual citizenship. Moreover, the category of 'practice' has consistently reduced homosexual sexual behaviour to the act of anal sex. Homosexual relations or MSM have been viewed as a category of 'practice' separate from 'identity'. By focusing exclusively on the practice of anal sex, the AIDS discourse has obscured other dimensions of the lifestyles of and problems among homosexuals.

Through its critique of problematic research, telephone peer counselling and *Deai* Events, OCCUR has attempted to construct a locus linking intersubjective identities and practices in responding to constructions of HIV risks and the (im)permeable body (politic) in the representations and realities of gay men in contemporary Japan. As Foucault (1987: 71) noted, making gay lifestyles, not just homosexual sex acts, publicly visible is one way to organize political resistance against homophobia.

## Notes

\* Translated by Nobue Suzuki and James E. Roberson.
1 The Stonewall Riot refers to protests by gays and drag queens in New York City against the suppression of gay businesses by police, who in this case used ostensible liquor violations in an attempt to shut down the Stonewall Inn. This incident is taken to mark the beginning of gay/lesbian liberation movements.
2 The American Psychiatric Association removed homosexuality from *DSMII* (*Diagnostic Statistical Manual of Psychiatric Disorders II*) in 1973 (Conrad and Schneider 1992: 204–9). In this chapter, 'homosexuality' refers to male homosexuality and 'homosexuals' to gay men unless otherwise noted.
3 This item was removed after the AIDS Prevention Law was instituted in 1989. Doing this worked to conceal the responsibility of the MHW, pharmaceutical companies and medical practitioners who had caused HIV infection among haemophiliac patients. Similar to the case of the discovery of the 'first AIDS patient', its effect was to transform AIDS from a problem caused by medical mismanagement to one caused by sexual acts.
4 In fact, there are many homosexuals who are forced into heterosexual marriages because of social pressure, including that which comes from families and companies (see also below).
5 The MHW's statistics on HIV-infected persons and PWAs provides numbers by region only. Those by country are not made available. In either case, the 'external' cause for the rise in the disease is evident here.
6 The media represented this incident as '"The complete disembarkation of AIDS" from across the seas' (*Friday* 1987: 4).
7 This report resulted in a panic in Hyōgo Prefecture, where Kōbe is located. One magazine reported that 'There were numerous inquiries at public health offices in Kōbe City as well as at other municipalities in the prefecture, more than 2,000 over only three days in Kōbe alone. There were 751 people who underwent blood testing' (*Friday* 1987: 4).
8 The producer of this poster seems to have intended to protect heterosexual men from

HIV infection from female prostitutes although, while much less frequently, Japanese men's sex tours also include those involving male and child prostitution.

9  Abe Takeshi, former Vice President of Teikyō University and former Chair of the Epidemiology Research Team's Subgroup on High Risk is currently being sued for having caused HIV infection, leading to death, among haemophiliac patients, for whom it is claimed that he recommended the use of non-heat-treated blood products (*Asahi Shinbun* 1996).

10  '*Deai*' is a Japanese word meaning 'encounter' or 'meet'.

11  As is well known, there are several hundred gay bars in the 2-Chōme district of Shinjuku in Tokyo. However, a distinction must be drawn between the presence of such commercial establishments as sites for meeting friends and possibly lovers and the remaining necessity for venues such as that offered by OCCUR for critical, educational and alternative activities, conversations and relations.

# References

Abe, T. (1986) *AIDS to wa Nani ka: Nazo no Shōtai ni Semaru* (*What is AIDS? Approaching the True Character of a Mystery*), Tokyo: Nihon Hōsō Kyōkai.

*Asahi Shinbun* (1987) '*AIDS, hatsu no josei kanja*' (AIDS: the first female patient), January 18.

—— (1988) '*AIDS, zenkoku chōsa*' (AIDS, nationwide survey), Osaka Edition, May 8.

—— (1996) '*Abe zen fukugakuchō o taiho*' (Former Vice President Abe arrested), Osaka edition, May 8.

Bersani, L. (1988) 'Is the rectum a grave?', in D. Crimp (ed.) *AIDS: Cultural Analysis/Cultural Activism*, Cambridge, MA: MIT Press.

Blasius, M. (1994) *Gay and Lesbian Politics: Sexuality and the Emergence of a New Ethic*, Philadelphia: Temple University Press.

Buckley, S. (1997) 'The foreign devil returns: packaging sexual practice and risk in contemporary Japan', in L. Manderson and M. Jolly (eds) *Sites of Desire, Economies of Pleasure*, Chicago: University of Chicago Press.

Butler, J. (1990/1999) *Gender Trouble: Feminism and the Subversion of Identity*, trans. K. Takemura, London and New York: Routledge; Tokyo: Seidosha.

—— (1993) 'Imitation and gender insubversion', in H. Abelove, M. A. Barale and D. Halperin (eds) *Lesbian and Gay Studies Reader*, London and New York: Routledge; trans. E. Sugiura, 1996, '*Mohō to Jendā e no Teikō*', *Imāgo* 7, 6: 116–35.

*Confronting HIV* (ed.) (1998) *Confronting HIV*, No. 8, Tokyo: Standard Macintyre, Inc.

Conrad, P. and Schneider, J. W. (1992) *Deviance and Medicalization: From Badness to Sickness*, Philadelphia: Temple University Press.

Davis, P. (1994) 'Acts, sessions and individuals: a model for analyzing sexual behaviour', in M. Boulton (ed.) *Challenge and Innovation: Methodological Advances in Social Research on HIV/AIDS*, London: Taylor & Francis.

Foucault, M. (1987) *Homosexuality and the Aesthetics of Life* (*Dōseiai to Seizon no Bigaku*), trans. K. Masuda, Tokyo: Tetsugaku Shobō.

*Friday* (1987) '*Umi no mukō kara "AIDS" kanzen jōriku*' (Complete landing of AIDS from the other side of the sea), February 6: 4–5.

Hirokawa, R. (1993) *Nihon no AIDS: Yakugai no Giseishatachi* (*AIDS in Japan: Victims of Contaminated Blood Products*), Tokyo: Tokuma Shoten.

Ichikawa, S. *et al.* (1995) '*Kantō chiku ni okeru dansei-dōsei kan seiteki sesshokusha (MSM) dantai ni okeru seikōdō ekigaku chōsa*' (An epidemiological survey of sexual practices among men having sex with men in the Kantō Region), in *HIV no Ekigaku to Taisaku ni Kansuru Kenkyū* (*Research Report on HIV-Related Epidemiology and Policy*), Tokyo: MHW.

Isomura, S. (1997) '*Tōkai chiku kyojū dansei dōseiaisha shūdan ni okeru HIV kansen ni kansuru kessei narabi ni kōdō chōsa*' (Research on serum and behaviours relating to HIV infection among male homosexual collectives in the Tōkai Region), S. Yamazaki (primary investigator) *HIV no Ekigaku to Taisaku ni Kansuru Kenkyū: Heisei 9 Nendo Kenkyū Hōkokusho* (*1997 Research Report on HIV-Related Epidemiology and Policy*), Tokyo: MHW.

Japan Public Health Association (1990) *HIV to Kaunseringu* (*HIV and Counselling*), Tokyo: Nihon Kōshūeisei Kyōkai.

Kawaguchi, K. (2000) '*Dōseiaisha to pia kaunseringu: akā no denwa sōdan no keiken kara*' (Homosexuals and peer counselling: from the experience of telephone advice at OCCUR), *Rinshō Shinrigaku Kenkyū* (*Clinical Psychology*) 37, 4: 70–3.

Kazama, T. (1997) '*AIDS no gei-ka to dōseiaishatachi no seijika*' (The gaying of AIDS and the politicization of homosexuals), *Gendai Shisō* 25, 6: 405–21.

—— (1998) '*Hyōshō/aidentiti/teikō: ekigaku kenkyū ni okeru AIDS to gei dansei*' (Representation/identity/resistance: AIDS and gay men in epidemiological research), in Ugoku Gei to Rezubian no Kai (ed.) *Jissen Suru Sekushuariti* (*Practising Sexuality*), Tokyo: Ugoku Gei to Rezubian no Kai.

Kendall, C. (1995) 'The construction of risk in AIDS control programmes', in R. G. Parker and J. H. Gagnon (eds) *Conceiving Sexuality: Approach to Sex Research in a Postmodern World*, London and New York: Routledge.

National AIDS Surveillance Committee 2000 (1999) *Heisei 11 Nendo AIDS Hassei Dōkō Nenpō* (*1999 Annual Report on New AIDS Cases*), Tokyo: MHW.

Ōishi, T. and Kawaguchi, K. (1998) '*AIDS o meguru gensetsu, kisei, kanja/kansensha: soshite kyōsei e*' (Patients/infected persons, restrictions, discourses surrounding AIDS: towards symbiosis), in K. Ōba, H. Kanegae, M. Hasegawa, K. Yamazaki and T. Yamazaki (eds) *Shirīzu: Sei o Tou; 5 Yuragi* (*Series: Questioning Sex; 5 Shifts*), Tokyo: Senshū Daigaku Shuppankyoku.

Osaka Prefecture (1997) *Hitori-Hitori ga Kagayaku Tame ni* (*So That Everyone May Glow*), Osaka: Osaka Prefecture.

Rich, A. (1980) 'Compulsory heterosexuality and lesbian existence', *Signs* 5, 4: 631–60.

Shigematsu, I. (1988) *HIV Ekigaku Kenkyūhan: Shōwa 63 Nendo Hōkokusho* (*HIV Epidemiology Research Team: 1988 Research Report*), Tokyo: MHW.

Shiokawa, Y. (1997) '*Fūzoku sangyō josei no HIV kōtai hoyū oyobi seikansenshō no jittai ni kansuru kenkyū*' (Research on the situation of HIV immunity and sexually transmitted diseases among women sex workers), in *Heisei 5 Nendo Tokyoto AIDS Kenkyūhan Hōkokusho* (*1993 Tokyo Metropolitan AIDS Research Team Report*), Tokyo: TMG.

Takemura, K. (1997) '*Shihoshugi to sekushuariti*' (Capitalism and sexuality), *Shisō* 97, 9: 71–104.

*Tokyo Shinbun* (1993) '*Nisseki "sakujo shi aratamemasu"*' (Japan Red Cross, 'remove and change'), February 18.

Treat, J. W. (1994) 'AIDS panic in Japan, or how to have a sabbatical in an epidemic', *positions* 2, 3: 629–79.

Treichler, P. A. (1987) 'AIDS, homophobia and biomedical discourse', in D. Crimp (ed.) *AIDS: Cultural Analysis/Cultural Activism*, trans. J. Kikuchi (1993) '*Imi no densenbyō*' (Epidemic of meaning), in H. Tazaki (ed.) *AIDS Nante Kowakunai*, Cambridge, MA: MIT Press/Tokyo: Kawade Shobō Shinsha.

Vincent, K., Kazama, T. and Kawaguchi, K. (1997) *Gei Sutadīzu* (*Gay Studies*), Tokyo: Seidosha.

Watney, S. (1996) 'Risk groups or risk behaviours', in J. Mann and D. Tarantola (eds) *AIDS in the World II*, Oxford: Oxford University Press.

# 12 Balancing fatherhood and work

## Emergence of diverse masculinities in contemporary Japan

*Masako Ishii-Kuntz*

### Introduction: emergence of diverse masculinities

In this chapter, I discuss the emergence of diverse masculinities in contemporary Japan by examining how 'childcaring' fathers construct and maintain their masculinities. I first describe the interrelated theoretical concepts of hegemonic and marginalized masculinities and then trace the political–social–economic context in Japan in which alternative masculine identities and practices focusing on family and fatherhood have begun to appear. Second, I discuss data from interviews and observations of fathers who are actively involved in parenting and housework. Most of these men belong to Otoko mo Onna mo Ikuji Jikan o Renrakukai (Childcare Hours for Men and Women Network, also known as Ikujiren), a Japanese advocacy group for fathers' active involvement in childcare. I illustrate how these active family men utilize their childcaring experiences to construct and redefine their masculinities.

It has been argued that hegemonic masculinity is learned in childhood (Bem 1993) and maintained and reinforced through adulthood by gendered experiences in college (Eisenhart and Holland 1992), the workplace (Reskin 1993) and the family (Ishii-Kuntz 1996). Boys are encouraged to be strong, self-reliant, competitive, aggressive and successful (Itō 1993). These gendered characteristics are also constructed within contexts of social interaction, in which a man needs constantly to construct a masculine image that will be accepted by others (West and Zimmerman 1987).

In every culture, the definition of what it means to be a man or a woman differs in many respects. However, in most societies 'masculinity' exists in contrast to 'femininity' (Connell 1995), and this contrast makes reconstructing 'gender' possible. In most instances, a violation of gender norms is unacceptable for either gender, but 'crossing the gender boundary has a more negative cultural meaning for men than it has for women' (Bem 1993: 149–50). To avoid being stigmatized, men must learn to avoid behaviours that are considered 'feminine' (Harris 1995). Men continue to perform gender to others (Butler 1990) out of need for acceptance and out of fear of appearing feminized, or emasculated (Kimmel 1996).

Connell (1995) argues, however, that one needs to speak of masculinities in the plural. The central concept of hegemonic masculinity reflects the ideal of those in power and all other masculinities are measured against it. Kimmel (1996) traces the story of dominant males and the ever-changing manner through which masculinity is defined in the West. In this, he shows how the dominant group has used the presence of lower-class men, gay men, men of colour and immigrants – as well as women – in the construction of hegemonic masculinity. It is the formation of other or marginalized masculinities that in Western societies assists a white, middle-class and heterosexual native-born male in defining his own masculinity, by presenting these marginalized masculinities as either hypermasculine or effeminate.

In Japan, ideal hegemonic masculinity has been constructed and maintained through 'salarymen's' roles as breadwinners for their families. The male economic provider role has required men's strong psychological and physical commitment to work (Reischauer 1981). The corporate environment in Japan is, further, dominated by competition, with those who rise above others perceived as the most prestigious. Being 'truly' masculine is thus equated with competence and control over self and others, including women and children.

Men's long work hours have contributed to their family's financial resources and, in a larger context, to Japan's postwar 'economic miracle' (Vogel 1979). At the same time, however, this has resulted in men's limited involvement with their families, including caring for their children (Ishii-Kuntz 1992, 1993). Comparative studies report that Japanese fathers spend much less time with their children than do their counterparts in other countries (Ishii-Kuntz 1994, 1998, 1999; Makino 1995). According to a 1994 survey, Japanese fathers spent, on average, 3.8 hours per day with their children aged three or younger. This was significantly less than in the United States (5.35 hours), the UK (6.45 hours), Korea (4.12 hours) and Thailand (7.17 hours). Furthermore, the most frequent father–child interaction in Japan was 'playing' rather than routine physical care of children as reported for fathers in other countries (Japan Association for Women's Education 1994).

Due to this shallow and non-routine involvement of fathers at home, Japanese families have been frequently characterized as 'fatherless', and fathers' existence seems to be appreciated when they are 'healthy and out of the house' (Ishii-Kuntz 1992). Some Japanese fathers, further, seem to consider their absence from home due to work demands an important factor contributing to their masculinities (Ishii-Kuntz 1993), enabling them to maintain an authoritarian image at home (Wagatsuma 1977). This construction of masculinity also coincides with children's preferences for their fathers to be strongly work-oriented (Office of the Prime Minister 1981). Miwa (1995) reported that some 90.5 per cent of fifth-graders surveyed thought that their fathers' primary responsibility is to work outside while 80.1 per cent thought that their mothers are suited to be the primary caretaker at home. Japanese fathers' hegemonic masculine identity has thus not only been maintained by their own commitment to work and the subsequent distancing from their families but also by the manly provider images held by their wives and children.

Although there is a dominant ideology concerning masculinity in contemporary Japan, it is also important to recognize that a multiplicity of masculinities is becoming more evident. There are several reasons why the dominant ideology concerning men's breadwinning role is undergoing a transition. First, with the current economic recession, an increasing number of Japanese men are becoming discontented with their jobs and the workplace (Ishii-Kuntz 1996). According to a nationwide survey, 24 per cent of Japanese men in 1978 considered paid work the most important aspect of their lives (Management and Coordination Agency 1990). However, this figure declined to 8 per cent in 1989.

Second, while from 1986 to 1997 the labour force participation of Japanese men remained relatively unchanged, women's labour force participation increased from 48.6 to 50.4 per cent (Ministry of Health, Labour and Welfare 2000a). This increase is particularly evident among women of childbearing years. For example, the labour force participation rate among women between 25 and 29 years of age increased from 56.9 per cent in 1986 to 68.2 per cent in 1997, while for women in their early thirties it went from 50.5 per cent to 56.2 per cent. Conversely, the number of Japanese women interested in pursuing a homemaker role upon the birth of their first child declined from 33.6 per cent in 1987 to 20.6 per cent in 1997 (ibid.). The number of double-earner families has consequently increased, suggesting that the traditional division of household labour where a man is the sole financial provider for the family may no longer be the dominant pattern in many families. It should be noted, however, that many women, working-class in particular, work to supplement family income – even in the early 1970s when the majority of married women stayed at home (see also Roberts 1994). Therefore, this decline of traditional gender roles may be more prevalent in middle-class Japanese families.

Third, there has been a sharp decline in the birthrate in Japan over the last decade. This has been partly attributed to women's reluctance to have babies due to their husbands' lack of participation in childrearing (Jolivet 1997; Kansai Economic Union Association 1998). The declining birthrate has also been a serious concern among Japanese government officials (Ministry of Health, Labour and Welfare 2000b), generating a 1999 campaign appealing for greater paternal involvement among men. The Ministry of Health, Labour and Welfare even produced a series of TV commercials and posters with the controversial slogan, 'A man who doesn't raise his children can't be called a father'. This can be seen as an attempt to reconfigure ideal hegemonic masculinity by emphasizing that men's familial involvement is an important part of responsible masculine behaviour.

These governmental efforts can be seen as a significant transition in terms of the state's attitude toward the family. The Japanese state was committed to relegating welfare responsibilities to the *ie* during the prewar period (Garon 1997), and then shifted to the 'family' and 'married couples' during the postwar period. However, the 'family' and 'married couples' imply and rely on the traditional gender-role division of labour (Ochiai 1998). In contrast, current emphasis is on the individual responsibilities of family members, as is reflected in the phrase '*kateinai no kojin no dokuritsu*' (individual independence within the family; Ministry of Health, Labour and Welfare 2000b).

The state has proposed policy changes which would pragmatically encourage or allow for shared caretaking between spouses. These proposals include (1) providing societal support for childcare; (2) reducing the economic burden placed on parents with younger children by providing childcare allowances and/or reducing taxes; and (3) creating policies to enable parents to balance work and childcare (ibid.).

However, the government has yet to implement any of these proposals. The Ministry of Health, Labour and Welfare has also recently proposed providing financial support for mid- to large-size companies that allow employees on childcare leave to return to the same pre-leave position. Companies will be financially compensated for the cost of hiring temporary replacements: 3,350,000 yen and 2,300,000 yen per substitute employee (and up to twenty such employees at a time) in mid- and large-size companies, respectively.

Thus, while the status of 'salarymen' empowers Japanese men since it is the source of dominant masculine identity, various economic, demographic and attitudinal changes suggest that the hegemonic model of masculinity is being transformed not only by younger generations of Japanese men and women but also by the state. For many younger Japanese men, commitment to work and the breadwinning role may no longer be the primary sources of their masculine identity. Toyoda (1997), for instance, describes how men who are 'corporate dropouts' seek alternative masculine identities in support groups such as their family and/or by pursuing other work that is not competitive in nature (see also Miller and Mathews, this volume, Chapters 3 and 7, respectively).

In contrast to the idealized salaryman, a 'family man' who actively participates in childcare and housework – both unpaid 'feminine' work – may be identified by those in power as manifesting a marginalized masculinity. While the creation of a framework of masculinities centred on what is 'dominant' simultaneously constitutes marginalized or feminized 'others', this does not presuppose that these marginalized groups are unable to define themselves as masculine. The emergence of diverse forms of masculinity in contemporary Japan is evident among a small but ever-increasing group of younger men who actively engage in childcare and housework. This emerging phenomenon among younger fathers enables us to examine the diversity of masculinities in contemporary Japan.

## Fathering masculinities: Ikujiren men

In order to assess how Japanese childcaring men evaluate and define their masculinity, interviews were conducted in 1999 with 17 men, most of whom (14) belong to Ikujiren. This Tokyo-based association aims to increase paternal involvement in childcare as well as to reduce parents' work hours in order to accomplish that goal. It holds monthly meetings, publishes a bimonthly newsletter with a circulation of more than 500, maintains an Internet discussion list and home page, holds symposia and its members give lectures to many community groups (Ikujiren 2000a). Recent activities also include: (1) creating a poster in response to the government's 1999 campaign, with the phrase 'A man who doesn't raise his children can't be called a father. Then let us care for our children without any hesitation' (Ikujiren 2000b); (2) delivering a letter in the spring of 2000 to British Prime Minister, Tony Blair, requesting that he take parental leave upon the birth of his baby (Ikujiren 2000c); and (3) conducting an opinion poll on childcare issues among political candidates running for Japanese parliamentary election in June 2000 (Ikujiren 2000d).

In addition to Ikujiren members, three more fathers actively engaged in childcare were located using snowball sampling. Whenever possible, wives were also interviewed. The interview format was mostly open-ended with a few structured questions. Questions addressed the motivation behind shared childcaring, the extent of sharing, and several questions concerning gender identities. Interviews were conducted at men's offices, nearby coffee shops, or their homes, and lasted between one and three hours. Children were present during several interviews, and fathers' interactions with their children were also observed.

Table 12.1 presents the major characteristics of the men in the sample. The ages of the men ranged from 29 to 49, while the majority are in their thirties. Seven men

*Table 12.1* Sample characteristics

| Name | Age | Occupation | Daily work hours | Education | Sex and age of child | Parental leave | Wife's employment |
|---|---|---|---|---|---|---|---|
| Doba | 34 | Professor | 7.0 | College | M(1) | No | Part-time (Research assistant) |
| Enami | 36 | Teacher | 8.5 | College | M(5) M(3) | Yes | Full-time (Teacher) |
| Hosoya | 30 | Engineer | 9.0 | College | F(2) | No | Full-time (Teacher) |
| Inaba | 36 | Professor | 9.8 | College | M(5) | No | Full-time (Reporter) |
| Kagaya | 31 | Engineer | 11.0 | College | F(4) M(2) | Yes | Full-time (Teacher) |
| Kaji | 42 | Clerical | 9.0 | Vocational School | M(6) | No | Full-time (Clerical) |
| Katayama | 37 | Banker | 11.0 | College | F(4) F(1) | No | Full-time (Manager) |
| Matsuda | 36 | None | 0 | College | M(6) | No | Full-time (Pharmacist) |
| Oguro | 35 | Engineer | 9.0 | College | M(5) M(2) | Yes | Full-time (Clerical) |
| Ōta | 41 | Manager | 11.0 | College | F(7) M(4) | Yes | Full-time (Manager) |
| Ōkoshi | 42 | Engineer | 9.5 | College | F(14) F(11) | No | Full-time (Nurse) |
| Tajiri | 49 | Engineer | 8.2 | College | F(13) F(9) | No | Full-time (Clerical) |
| Takenaka | 42 | Civil worker | 10.0 | College | M(8) M(4) | No | Part-time (Manager) |
| Tanaka | 32 | Engineer | 8.5 | College | M(2) | Yes | Full-time (Teacher) |
| Tominaga | 47 | Civil worker | 9.0 | Junior College | F(10) M(8) | Yes | Full-time (Teacher) |
| Wakita | 32 | Engineer | 8.0 | College | M(5) M(2) | Yes | Full-time (Clerical) |
| Yamamoto | 29 | Physiotherapist | 11.0 | College | F(2) | Yes | Full-time (Therapist) |

have one child, and ten have two children. The average age of children is 5.4 years. Overall, these men are 'salarymen' who are college graduates and work for middle- to large-size companies or as civil servants. On average, these fathers worked 8.79 hours per day and had two days off per week. These men and their wives are also dual-worker couples. The majority of wives are also professionals employed full-time. Of the seventeen men, eight have taken parental leave from work to care for their infants. Another six men have taken childcare hours from work in the form of flexitime. One man went on a union-backed 'childcare strike' by taking one hour off every morning in order to take his children to a daycare centre. Since only 0.16 per cent of male civil servants and 0.02 per cent of private sector employees take advantage of parental leave from work annually (Hisatake *et al.* 1998; Ōta 1999), the sample over-represents those fathers who take extensive leave from work to care for their children. However, the purpose of my study is to explore how these men's experiences as childcaring men influence their masculinities rather than to generalize my findings against a larger population of fathers.

Some Ikujiren men's experiences may have indirectly contributed to the creation of the 1992 Parental Leave Law allowing men, for the first time, to take leave from work or to use flexitime schedules to care for their children (Ikujiren 1995). In two men's cases, their unions took serious interest in their cause and included childcare issues in their demands to their companies. Extensive media coverage of these childcaring men in the late 1980s and early 1990s caught the attention of the government as well as of the Japanese public.

Before 1992, only women were allowed to take leave from work to care for their infants. However, due to governmental concern over the declining birthrate and the subsequent campaign to encourage women to bear more children, the Parental Leave Law, rejected in previous years, was hastily established in 1991. Except for companies with fewer than thirty employees that were granted a three-year extension, the law was enacted in April 1992. Under this law, both male and female employees with a child younger than twelve months can apply for parental leave, and employers cannot deny the request. Additionally, employers are prohibited from firing or demoting employees solely on the basis of their taking parental leave. Employees are also allowed to shorten work hours for childcare instead of taking leave.

In 1995, the Parental Leave Law was expanded to include leave for family caregiving including eldercare. The low rate of Japanese men taking childcare leave as previously described is perhaps due to the low level of compensation during the leave (since 1995 only 25 per cent of salary is guaranteed by Employment Insurance), problems associated with post-leave positions and poor quality or lack of substitute employees.

Despite these problems, many Ikujiren men have taken leaves and/or childcare hours from work and their experiences have been reported in several newspaper articles and books (*Asahi Shinbun* 1997–8; Ikujiren 1989, 1995; Ōta 1992, 1999; Tajiri 1990). For example, a nationally circulated newspaper, the *Asahi Shinbun* (ibid.), featured a year-long series with four fathers writing about their experiences as childcaring men. Three of these fathers are members of Ikujiren.

## Paternal involvement and masculinities

There are diverse reasons why these men are motivated to take an active part in childcare. Here I examine how some of these reasons are related to their constructions of masculinity. These motivations can be largely divided into (1) parental responsibilities; (2) providing better and diverse familial environments for their children; (3) fathers' own childhood socialization; and (4) spouses' attitudes towards active paternal involvement.

### *Parental responsibility*

An important part of being masculine for these men is showing responsibility for their own actions. Although many Japanese men consider their breadwinning role to be their major familial responsibility, sample fathers consider childcaring to be primary. This does not mean, however, that these men will leave their largely high-paying jobs for childcaring as numerous women have done. Rather, they tend to give more weight to their childcaring role than that of being a financial provider. In this respect, being masculine to these fathers means being a responsible parent by taking an active part in childcare. Unlike fathers involved in 'intrinsically fun' activities with their children such as sports, these men are frequently in charge of routine and 'unpleasant' childcare activities such as changing, feeding, cleaning up, bathing and caring for sick children (see Hochschild 1989). Mr Kaji,[1] a 42-year-old father of a 6-year-old son, talked about his responsibility this way:

> For me, taking physical care of our son is a part of my responsibility as a father and a man. Unless you are a responsible parent by being involved in your child's life from early on, you are not a real man. It really doesn't matter how successful you are at work. What is important in your life is to be responsible as a father for your children.

A 49-year-old father of two daughters, Mr Tajiri, is one of the founding members of Ikujiren. When asked about his commitment to the breadwinning role, he confessed that he was never fully committed to his work. He lives with what he calls a '*Ganbaranai*' (Not doing my best) philosophy which is opposite from the competitive component of hegemonic masculinity (Tajiri 1995: 210). He gains a sense of responsibility from his experiences as an involved father and in this respect can be seen as constructing an 'other' kind of masculinity by being involved in 'women's' activities.

A similar sentiment was echoed by Mr Tominaga, one of the first civil servants in Japan to take childcare leave hours and a one-month parental leave from work:

> When I was 20 years old, I went to a meeting where feminism was discussed. I heard many women saying that they have been eating 'cold rice' (being disadvantaged) due to societal expectations for them to be the primary childcare provider at home. When they confronted me with the issue of why only men

can get away from parental responsibilities, I was unable to respond to them. This experience taught me the lesson that men, too, should be more responsible for childcare. Unless men can become involved parents and good providers, we cannot justify our masculinity.

Mr Tominaga also does a major part of the housework, including cooking family meals with a variety of dishes which combine 'at least sixteen different food items'. To him, being an involved father and sharing housework are important pre-requisites of being a manly man.

### Providing a diverse environment

Another source of masculinity is derived from fathers' determination to provide their children with a diverse environment where they are exposed to more than one adult (i.e. mothers) when growing up. The implicit assumption is that although fathers are engaged in similar childcare activities as are mothers, what men can provide is unique and different, and thus children with an involved father are more likely to be exposed to various stimuli and options than are children with a non-involved father. Mr Matsuda, a 36-year-old father – who recently resigned from the job he had held for ten years in order to pursue his 'dream of visiting Scandinavian countries to study fathers who are actively involved in childcare' – emphasized the uniqueness of fatherhood, saying: 'Because my wife and I are very different, I think it is important to share childcare so that our son will be exposed to diverse personalities and environments'.

Although Mr Matsuda is currently not employed full-time, his wife is a licensed pharmacist who earned more money even during his job tenure. Studies in the US have found that men with less income than their wives tend to do fewer chores and the 'second shift' at home than their wives (Hochschild 1989; Pyke 1996). However, in Mr Matsuda's case, lower income is associated with greater childcare participation, although he did not directly state this income discrepancy as a reason for his motivation for more involvement in childcare activities. His sense of masculinity is now derived from his role as a father who can provide a different kind of environment for their son. Mr Matsuda, however, admits that since he pays income tax based on his part-time jobs and the honoraria he receives from public lectures, he is not 'completely unemployed'. This suggests that while a major part of Mr Matsuda's masculinity is derived from his paternal role, having a part in earning money for the family is also important.

Mr Ōta, father of a daughter and a son, is in a management position in a large corporation and was the first father to take a parental leave from work in the private sector. He also talked about the different perspective from that of his wife's that he provides his children:

> I try not to expect too much from my children. Children who are expected to be high achievers frequently end up misbehaving. So what I want our kids to learn is to have the strength to live and to acquire skills to survive no matter what the

future holds for them. My partner[2] does not want to force our children to go to a prestigious college, but since she is a graduate of a very prestigious school she tends to expect more from our children. In this sense, I believe what I can provide our children is different from that of my partner.

Apparently, his wish for his children to 'acquire skills to survive' reflects his view of the current economic stagnation and of less hopeful future prospects.

In summary, these quotes illustrate that a part of masculine identities may be formed not only in being responsible for taking care of children but also in providing different environments for them. This perception is also shared by some of their wives and children. Ms Nitta,[3] partner of Mr Tajiri, was once told by a close friend that she was much more 'manly' than her husband. However, Ms Nitta believes that this difference is merely a reflection of their different personalities. Moreover, she was pleased to hear her 10-year-old daughter's comments about liking her father because he is different from other fathers.

### Men's childhood socialization

Fathers' own childhood socialization also plays a key role in how active paternal involvement can be a source of masculine identity. The majority of sample fathers grew up in traditional home environments. However, these men did not necessarily admire their fathers' masculine breadwinning role, as is expressed by Mr Ōkoshi, a 41-year-old father of two daughters:

> Because my parents were extremely traditional with my father as the authority figure, I often felt that he was controlled to be that way by society. To escape from that pressure, my father ended up drinking alcohol heavily and that was the only image I had of him. I don't have any recollection that my father played with me. He was rather a mean figure. Looking back on my childhood, I think I just obeyed my father even though I did not particularly like it. I don't want to be like my father, and I'd rather be free from that kind of pressure. By being an active childcaring father, I feel that I have accomplished that.

In a popular 1996 book, Hayashi argues that Japanese fathers are becoming less authoritarian at home and that 'strong' fathers should be reinstituted in order to re-establish 'healthy' families. In contrast, the sample fathers frequently expressed resentment toward their own fathers' authoritarian image. As a result, they were not engaged in activities that are closely associated with the hegemonic masculine image.

Sport, for example, is one of the primary arenas through which hegemonic masculinity is learned and perpetuated. In fact, some argue that it is one of the last male havens (Connell 1995; Messner 1992). Except for two men, most of the sample men were not interested in sport during their childhoods, although in some cases they were encouraged or forced to participate in these 'masculine' activities by their fathers. Instead, many men preferred reading and other hobbies. When asked about his childhood activities, Mr Ōta, for example, stated:

I used to cry easily and was bullied. Other kids probably thought I was strange. I didn't like rough and tumble play with other boys. I was not engaged in any sports. I rather wanted to read alone or ride a bike by myself. Those are the kinds of things I used to do as a child.

Mr Ōta obviously did not mind being a 'loner' and felt quite comfortable pursuing activities that were not in line with dominant masculine values. A few men in the sample not only lacked interest in 'manly' activities such as sports but also felt inferior about their own bodies. Gerson (1993) shows that men with troubled masculine identities increased paternal involvement as a form of compensation to their 'lack' of masculine power. Mr Enami, an elementary school teacher, fits this pattern. He talked about his short height as a source of inferiority but at the same time a source of motivation to do 'other' activities not traditionally considered 'masculine'. Ms Takasu, Mr Enami's wife, added:

When we started dating, my husband used to tell me repeatedly that he could not play baseball . . . When a man sees sports as a source of confidence, he cannot think that there are other important activities that they can gain confidence from. In my husband's case, being an involved father was perhaps one of the ways to overcome his inferiority from being short.

In summary, many sample fathers' own childhood socialization, having an authoritarian father and lacking interests in 'manly' activities such as sports, appear to have contributed to their redefinition of their masculinities. Instead, they have chosen to become involved fathers in order to seek other sources of masculine confidence and identity.

### Spousal attitudes

Another important factor affecting sample men's sense of masculinity through their involvement in parenting is the attitudes frequently displayed by their wives. Overall, these wives are successful in their jobs and have liberal attitudes towards men's involved parenting. Instead of relying on their husbands for the breadwinning role, these women tend to earn comparable incomes and demand equal participation in childcare and housework. The majority of sample men became active fathers because of 'forceful' encouragement from their wives.

Mr Ōkoshi, for example, commented on his wife's role in motivating him to take on childcare activities:

When I got married, I didn't think about who would be responsible for childcare when we became parents. I thought that my partner would continue working since she took pride in her job (nurse). So when she had the baby, she told me that since both of us are professionals with equal amounts of commitment to work, we should share the childcare . . . As a result of my wife's strong persuasion and after many arguments, I decided to be more involved in childcare. After a while, I found childcare to be more rewarding than my work.

Mr Wakita, an engineer who took parental leave to care for his second son, also talked about his wife's stressful experience with their first baby, and said: 'So when she was pregnant with our second baby, I decided to take parental leave. I am happy I did because now I understand what my partner had to go through with our first baby'. Mrs Wakita, a corporate woman, reflected on her own changes in attitude towards shared childcaring after her experience with her first son:

> When we got married, I had a somewhat romanticized notion of motherhood. I didn't mind quitting my job to become a full-time homemaker . . . Although being a parent is overall a rewarding experience, the daily routine of childcare became very stressful. At the same time, I started thinking it was unfair that I take the sole responsibility for caring for our son. So before our second son was born, I demanded that my husband have his turn to take care of the baby. I think he would have taken childcare leave without my asking, because he knew how tired and stressed out I was during my childcare leave.

These comments suggest that the support, encouragement, understanding and demands of their spouses are important for the sample fathers in associating their negotiated masculine identities with what they do as involved fathers. Although some wives are still hopeful that their husbands will do more of the housework, both the sample fathers and their spouses seem to consider that they are much better than 'ordinary' Japanese husbands who do very little childcare.

## Work environment and masculinities

The work environment is equally important as familial factors in the construction of sample men's masculinities through their childcare activities. Institutional contexts can constrain men's childcare involvement but can also facilitate greater commitment to the family. This also applies to parental leave and to the practice of flexitime that many sample fathers have made use of. The 1987 revision of the Labour Standard Law allows flexible work schedules except for the 'core' hours between 10:00 am and 3:00 pm. Employees are required to work during this five-hour period but the additional three hours of work time can be arranged either before 10:00 am or after 3:00 pm. Mr Hosoya, for example, took advantage of this policy by reporting for work at 10:00 am after getting his children ready for the day and taking them to their daycare centre.

Although these are policies backed by the law, whether or not men actually use them still depends on the 'family-friendly' atmosphere of their workplace. In a negative case, these men can be bullied by their bosses and/or colleagues with threats of single transfer (*tanshin funin*) to remote areas. In fact, one Ikujiren member who took parental leave was transferred to China almost immediately upon his return to work. When there are constraints, criticisms and threats within their workplace, many of the sample men have decided to excel at other work-related abilities rather than working longer hours. Mr Takenaka, a civil servant with two sons, talked about how he managed to survive the harsh criticism expressed by his colleagues about his heavy involvement in childcare:

> Prior to my association with Ikujiren, I had no place where I could talk about parenting. When I talked about my childcare experiences at work, my colleagues teased me by saying that 'Real fathers don't do such a thing' or 'You don't need a wife, do you?' Since I was rather quiet, I was called a 'men's embarrassment' (*otoko no haji*) or 'men's enemy' (*otoko no teki*) . . . I used to finish my work at the same time as my female colleagues so my boss used to say that I could not have finished because of my early departure. In order to excel, I studied during my childcare hours to get a certificate in computer communications . . . Once I established their respect by passing a rather difficult exam and obtaining the certificate, nobody complained about my leaving earlier than other men as long as I finished my work.

Excelling over his colleagues in ways other than working longer hours helped Mr Takenaka feel and be perceived as masculine at his workplace. Other men also had to overcome hostility from colleagues. Mr Tominaga talked about his own negative experiences:

> When I decided to take a parental leave from work, I was asked questions like 'what will you do during the daytime when you take childcare leave?' I was speechless especially because these questions were asked by some leaders of my labour union. Of course, I would take care of my child during my leave rather than playing *pachinko* (pinball) or mahjong. During my parental leave, I was featured in the *Asahi Shinbun*. When I was quoted as saying that 'this is a wonderful experience despite some criticisms toward me at work', two guys in my office posted a copy of that newspaper article on the office wall with some negative comments.

Despite this hostility at work, Mr Tominaga tried to understand the reaction of his colleagues in terms of how Japanese society expects everyone to act in a similar way. If one acts differently, there is a negative sanction. His decision to take childcare leave deviated from masculine 'norms'. Mr Tominaga had thus willingly marginalized himself socially. However, his personal sense of masculinity cannot be easily characterized as 'marginal', but instead derives more from his active paternal involvement and much less from his role at work.

Other men in the sample attempted to pursue alternative ways to escape pressure at work. Mr Inaba, a college professor, spoke of his one-time desire to become a full-time homemaker in order to escape the isolation and pressure to succeed at work that he felt because of his involvement in childcare at home. Mr Inaba may have romanticized the 'easy' and 'less pressured' homemaker role, but he decided to stay with his profession while taking a major responsibility in caring for his son. Mr Ōta also described initial feelings of total isolation (*Asahi Shinbun* 1998).

Another way of surviving the hostility at work is to redefine one's commitment to work and the family, as Mr Ōkoshi states:

> I told myself that I had not 'sold my soul to my company', meaning that my company cannot control my own life. Thinking that way made it easier for me to leave from work earlier than my colleagues. I knew that my family and childcare activities, in particular, were much more important sources of my own gratification than my work.

While some sample men experienced negative reactions at work, other men experienced almost no negative consequences as a result of their active paternal involvement. Mr Yamamoto, a 29-year-old father, experienced 'little difficulty at work' when he decided to take parental leave from the hospital where he worked as a physical therapist. This is perhaps due to the more 'humanistic' work environment he was in and may also be due to the greater ratio of female workers such as nurses who showed more sympathetic attitudes toward Mr Yamamoto's childcare leave.

Others, with careful planning, also experienced little hostility at their workplace. When his wife found out she was pregnant with their second child, Mr Wakita immediately asked his boss if he could take parental leave. He also planned his work accordingly. Thus, by the time his leave started, he experienced few problems both in terms of his work and the reactions of his colleagues. Other men such as Mr Oguro and Mr Tanaka also found their workplace environments more understanding and tolerant for fathers' childcare leave since there was a precedent in those companies and communities.

Finally, in Mr Tajiri's case, some colleagues were quite understanding toward his taking childcare leave and even told him to 'be proud of what he was doing as Mr Tajiri had already made great contributions to the company' (Tajiri 1995). Although at the beginning even union members were sceptical about the importance of men's involvement in childcare, Mr Tajiri eventually received strong support for his 'childcare strike'. While unions can be strong allies to childcaring men, this is not always the case. Mr Tominaga devoted most of his adult life to his labour union and was thus shocked by negative comments about his parental leave from certain union leaders.

These Ikujiren members' experiences of taking parental leave and/or childcare hours remain unique as few other co-workers have done so. Even the companies that granted parental leave were not always supportive. The Heisei economic recession has also made it more difficult for men to take childcare leave today. In most cases, parental leave was granted because the men's individual initiative and strategic planning helped prevent problems at work. This suggests that with their pre-childcare leave efforts, some sample fathers' masculinities were not threatened as much as other men who had more negative experiences at their workplace.

In addition to work environments, institutional constraints such as gender-based salaries and hiring practices also affect the relationship between childcaring and the masculine identities of these fathers. Although women's incomes have recently increased, there is still a significant gender-based income gap in Japan. Women with full-time jobs on average earn only 60 per cent of what their husbands make (Ministry of Health, Labour and Welfare 2000a). Gender discrimination in salaries is prohibited by law but since women's occupations are concentrated in female-dominated areas, their salaries are more likely to be lower than those of men. As previously described, an employee on parental leave receives just 25 per cent of his or her salary as a form of Unemployment Compensation Insurance. Since wives' earnings are most likely to be lower than their husbands', it is usually more reasonable for the wives to take parental leave. Sample fathers who have taken childcare leave are those whose wives earn as much or nearly as much as they do. A smaller gender gap in earning between husbands and wives makes it easier for many childcaring husbands to take parental leave or childcare hours. As long as there are such state-level barriers against men's taking childcare leave, contradicting its other policies (see above), the government's campaign to encourage men to become more active as fathers will remain rather empty. Instead, effort needs to be focused on more progressive legislation increasing compensation during parental leave and on tax benefits for those who take childcare leave.

It should also be noted that although job security is not nearly as assured as it once was, company loyalty still stands as an admired tradition. Mr Ōta talked about how he was considered to be 'very brave' for taking childcare leave at the risk of appearing disloyal to his company. Despite this, Mr Ōta has been promoted to a managerial position. While childcaring roles may not be compatible with what companies expect from employees, by working harder than others, men like Mr Ōta demonstrate that they are capable of working and childcaring at the same time. As in Mr Takenaka's case, this added effort is perhaps a way masculine values can be maintained despite the 'feminine' childcaring experience.

In addition, these men face '*tsukiai*' (socializing) pressures from their bosses and co-workers when they are asked to join after-work entertainment. Allison (1994) places great emphasis on this 'male-bonding' ritual in the reproduction of a 'corporate masculinity'. Atsumi (1979) also describes the obligation to engage in frequent after-hours socializing in corporate workplaces. Some sample fathers described such pressures, but many eventually succeeded in escaping from or resisting them by establishing reputations as childcaring fathers. Interestingly, identification with female colleagues with childcaring responsibilities also made it easier for many of the sample fathers to resist such social pressure.

Institutional factors such as the father-friendliness of the work environment, the gender gap in earnings, the loyalty demanded by companies and the socializing pressed by colleagues can thus either constrain or facilitate men's childcaring experiences. Although the fathers in my sample are varied in terms of how they handle work-related concerns, most of these men have managed to maintain their own masculinities at their workplace.

However, what the sample fathers, most of whom work for large corporations, experience cannot necessarily be generalized to Japanese working-class men. Neither these latter men nor their companies can as easily afford to demand or allow men's childcare leave. It is extremely rare for working-class men to take parental leave and if they do, it may be because they have no other choice but to take care of their children. In this sense, working-class men do not enjoy the same 'luxury' as middle-class salaryman fathers. This was frequently the focus of debate between Ikujiren and Otoko no Kosodate o Kangaeru Kai (The Men's Group for Rethinking Childcare), a group established in 1978 by men of predominantly working-class backgrounds. Moreover, their high incomes give the middle-class wives of the Ikujiren men a stronger voice in demanding their husbands do more childcare.

## Emergence of alternative gender practices and identities

Just as it is a challenge for many Japanese women to balance work and the family (Kuroda 1994; Sodei 1996), so fathers who are involved in childcare and housework also face many obstacles (Ishii-Kuntz 1996; Katō *et al.* 1998). Other than the 1999 campaign, the state has yet to endorse and implement the scheme promoting equality in childcaring. The state continues to relegate caretaking work to the family with little actual support. By practising the newly state-sanctioned childcare, the fathers discussed here, however ironically and unintentionally, may be supporting the state's twin goals of population maintenance and of non-commitment in providing much-needed welfare for its citizens.

Childcaring 'salarymen' are simultaneously engaged in activities considered 'masculine' and 'feminine'. The salaryman model and the traditional definition of hegemonic masculinity in Japan fail to describe the activities that these men are engaged in. However, this does not mean that these men are unable to construct and present masculine identities. Rather, they must rely on alternative methods and symbols to represent their masculinities, such as their parental responsibilities and the provision of diverse familial environments for their children. These men refuse to fit in with the ideal expectation of hegemonic masculinity and take advantage of their 'other' or 'different' experiences to construct alternative forms and practices of masculinity.

If 'marginalized' masculinity refers only to those of lower status in the social hierarchy, then my informants are not 'marginal' since many are employed in large corporations and, except for their childcare activities, may be considered 'elite salarymen'. In his study of Japanese working-class men, Roberson (1998, this volume, Chapter 8) suggests that socio-economically marginalized men hold different class-related notions of masculinity. Although the white-collar fathers in my study are not marginalized in the social hierarchy, their childcaring experiences none the less dissociate them from hegemonic masculine roles. Thus, if the meaning of 'marginalized' masculinities is expanded to include those men who do not hold hegemonic masculinity, then these fathers may indeed be considered marginalized.

It is also interesting to note that the term 'masculinity' was hardly mentioned in interviews. These men consider what they do as providers and caretakers part of their *ningen rashisa* (humanity) rather than of their 'masculinity' or 'femininity'. This is perhaps similar to the slogan of women's and men's movements to live free from gender expectations (e.g. Toyoda 1997). By being responsible parents who can provide a better environment for their children, who are not like their authoritarian fathers, and who receive spousal support for their childcare involvement, these men affirm and define their identity as a 'person'. Their efforts and strategies at the workplace to maximize their paternal involvement can also be seen as a process of constructing their humanity.

While the salaryman model remains a dominant representation of masculinity in Japan, the examples of the fathers cited in this chapter raises the need to examine diverse forms of gender identities, including masculinities, in contemporary Japan. The experiences and the actions of groups like Ikujiren also call for changes in state and company policies and practices concerning men's childcaring roles. The traditional salaryman model of masculinity fails to describe emerging gender identities among younger and upper-middle-class Japanese fathers.

Furthermore, my study suggests that the presentation of masculinity and femininity may not be sex-specific since what these fathers experience as economic providers and caretakers may be quite similar to what employed Japanese mothers experience in everyday life. That is, an individual's assumed identity of either masculinity or femininity may or may not be in congruence with an individual's sex category (Wiley 1995; see also Lunsing, this volume, Chapter 2). At the same time, however, childcaring fathers in my sample frequently found it difficult to associate with full-time homemaker mothers even during childcare leave when they were full-time househusbands.

Finally, it is necessary to examine carefully the experiences of and the enabling and constraining contexts related to the emergence of diverse masculinities. Fathers in my sample construct and define their own masculinities within the everyday practices of childcare and work. Perhaps, as the gender literature has shown, a more constructive approach to understanding masculinities in contemporary Japan would be to define gender as the product both of social interaction and everyday practice and of governmental schemes, ideologies and institutions. The role of the state is crucial here, in constructing the legal, institutional and ideological contexts that influence fathers' participation in childcare. The majority of Japanese men still feel that their main familial role is that of economic provider (Ishii-Kuntz 1994) and their participation in childcare is thus considerably less than that of their wives. Recent governmental efforts are targetted at changing these men's attitudes about child-caring roles. Without concerted efforts to change the legal and institutional contexts, however, many Japanese men may find it difficult to take a major part in childcaring activities (see Mathews, this volume, Chapter 7).

In this respect, some Ikujiren fathers are active in organizing themselves as part of a movement to promote active paternal involvement. However, not all these men consider it necessary for the association to become more politically active. Indeed, some members are attracted to Ikujiren simply because of the psychological support it provides for childcaring fathers. Still, all the male Ikujiren members share the common and unique experience of being childcaring men in a society dominated by non-involved fathers. Therefore, many of the public as well as individual activities in which Ikujiren members are involved can be seen as further efforts to promote examples of how Japanese men can be a part of the movement to create the social–ideological space needed for alternative gender practices and identities to emerge.

## Notes

1 Based on their stated preferences, the names used in this chapter are informants' real names.
2 Many Ikujiren men used the term '*pātonā*' (partner) rather than '*kanai*' (wife) to refer to their spouses. The former term is also frequently used by Japanese men who are involved in Men's Lib Movement (Toyoda 1997). This suggests that, to these men, 'partner' implies more equal status than the conventional term '*kanai*', which literally means 'a person inside the house'.
3 Japanese civil law does not currently allow married couples to carry separate last names. Because of this discriminatory law, one spouse is forced to 'abandon' his/her surname upon marriage. Although couples are free to choose either the husband's or the wife's name, in reality 98 per cent adopt the husband's last name (Hisatake *et al.* 1998). Those couples who wish to use separate last names must choose either '*jijitsukon*' (common-law marriage) or separate common (not legal) names upon marriage. In the case of Mr Enami and Ms Takasu, they decided not to marry legally in order to keep their separate surnames. This is quite common among Ikujiren couples, and can be seen as another example of sample men and women practising gender equality.

## References

Allison, A. (1994) *Nightwork: Sexuality, Pleasure and Corporate Masculinity in a Tokyo Hostess Club*, Chicago: University of Chicago Press.
*Asahi Shinbun* (1997–8) '*Ikukyū Tōsan no Seichō Nisshi*' (Diary of a Father Who Took Parental Leave from Work), October 1997–August 1998.
Atsumi, R. (1979) '*Tsukiai* – obligatory personal relationships of Japanese white-collar company employees', *Human Organization* 38, 1: 63–70.
Bem, S. L. (1993) *The Lenses of Gender*, New Haven: Yale University Press.
Butler, J. (1990) *Gender Trouble*, New York: Routledge.
Connell, R. W. (1995) *Masculinities*, Berkeley: University of California Press.
Eisenhart, M. A. and Holland, D. C. (1992) 'Gender constructs and career commitment: the influence of peer culture on women in college', in T. L. Whitehead and B. V. Reid (eds) *Gender Constructs and Social Issues*, Urbana: University of Illinois Press.
Garon, S. (1997) *Molding Japanese Minds*, Princeton: Princeton University Press.
Gerson, K. (1993) *No Man's Land: Men's Changing Commitments to Family and Work*, New York: Basic Books.
Harris, I. M. (1995) *Messages Men Hear: Constructing Masculinities*, Bristol: Taylor & Francis.
Hayashi, M. (1996) *Fusei no Fukken* (*Restitution of Paternity*), Tokyo: Chūō Kōron Shinsho.
Hisatake, A., Kainō, T., Wakao, N. and Yoshida, A. (1998) *Kazoku Dēta Bukku* (*Family Data Book*), Tokyo: Yūhikaku.
Hochschild, A. (1989) *The Second Shift*, New York: Avon.
Ikujiren (1989) *Otoko to Onna de Hanbunko-ism* (*Half-ism by Men and Women*), Tokyo: Gakuyō Shobō.
—— (1995) '*Ikuji de kaisha o yasumu yōna otokotachi*' (*Men who take leave from work due to childcare*), Tokyo: Yukkusha.
—— (2000a) '*Ikujiren homepage*', <http://eqg.org/index.html> (June 30).
—— (2000b) '*Ikujiren poster*', <http://eqg.org/project/poster99.html> (June 30).
—— (2000c) '*A letter to Prime Minister, Tony Blair*', <http://eqg.org/project/letter/index.html> (June 30).
—— (2000d) '*Senkyo ankēto*' (*Election survey*), <http://www.eqg.org/project/2000senkyo/index.shtml> (June 30).

Ishii-Kuntz, M. (1992) 'Are Japanese families "fatherless"?', *Sociology and Social Research* 76, 3: 105–10.

—— (1993) 'Japanese fathers: work demands and family roles', in J. Hood (ed.) *Men, Work and Family*, Newbury Park: Sage.

—— (1994) 'Paternal involvement and perception toward fathers' roles: a comparison between Japan and the United States', *Journal of Family Issues* 15, 1: 30–48.

—— (1996) 'A perspective on changes in men's work and fatherhood in Japan', *Asian Cultural Studies* 22, 1: 91–107.

—— (1998) 'Fathers' involvement and children's social network: a comparison between Japan and the United States', *Journal of Family Education Research Centre* 20, 1: 5–16.

—— (1999) 'Children's affection toward fathers: a comparison between Japan and the United States', *International Journal of Japanese Sociology* 8: 35–50.

Itō, K. (1993) *Otoko Rashisa no Yukue: Dansei Bunka no Bunka Shakaigaku* (*Direction of Manliness: Cultural Sociology of Male Culture*), Tokyo: Shin'yōsha.

Japan Association for Women's Education (1994) *International Comparative Research on 'Home Education': Survey on Children and the Family Life*, Tokyo: Japan Association for Women's Education.

Jolivet, M. (1997) *Japan: A Childless Society?*, London and New York: Routledge.

Kansai Economic Union Association (1998) *Shōshika Mondai ni Kansuru Jisedai no Ishiki Chōsa Hōkokusho* (*Report on a Survey of Attitudes Among the Next Generation Concerning Declining Birthrates*), Osaka: Shōshi Kōrei Taisaku Iinkai (Committee on Declining Birth and Ageing).

Katō, K., Ishii-Kuntz, M., Makino, K. and Tsuchiya, M. (1998) '*Chichioya no ikuji sanka o kiteisuru yōin: dono yōna jōken ga chichioya no ikuji sanka o susumeru no ka*' (Factors affecting fathers' childcare participation), *Journal of Family Education Research Center* 20, 1: 38–47.

Kimmel, M. (1996) *Manhood in America*, New York: The Free Press.

Kuroda, A. (1994) *Mama de Nakya Dame: Wākingu Ūman no Kosodate Sensō* (*I Only Want Mommy: Childcare Battle Among Working Women*), Tokyo: Magazine House.

Makino, K. (1995) '*Chichioya to kodomo to katei*' (Fathers, children and the family), *Shakai Anzen* 18: 22–9.

Management and Coordination Agency (1990) *Nihon no Chichioya to Kodomo* (*Report on Japanese Fathers and Children*), Tokyo: Ministry of Finance Printing Office.

Messner, M. A. (1992) *Power at Play: Sports and the Problem of Masculinity*, Boston: Beacon Press.

Ministry of Health, Labour and Welfare (2000a) 'White Paper on women's labour force participation', <http://www.mhlw.go.jp/wp/hakusyo/josei/00/gaiyo1.html> (October 21, 2001).

—— (2000b) 'White Paper on declining birth rate', <http://www1.mhlw.go.jp/wp/ 98index.html > (October 21, 2001).

Miwa, S. (1995) '*Kodomo kara mita oyako kankei*' (Parent–child relationships from children's point of view), in Nagoyakai (ed.) *Gendai no Kosodate to Oyako Kankei* (*Contemporary Child-rearing and Parent–Child Relationships*), Nagoya: Nagoyakai.

Ochiai, E. (1998) *21 Seiki Kazoku e* (*For Families in the 21st Century*), Tokyo: Yūhikaku.

Office of the Prime Minister (1981) *Gendai no Wakamono: Jūnen Mae to no Hikaku* (*Today's Youth: A Comparison with Those Ten Years Ago*), Tokyo: Office of the Prime Minister.

Ōta, M. (1992) *Otoko mo Suru Nari Ikuji Kyūshoku* (*I Would Take Parental Leave for Childcare as a Man*), Tokyo: Shin Hyōron.

—— (1999) 'Dad takes childcare leave', *Japan Quarterly* 146: 83–9.

Pyke, K. D. (1996) 'Class-based masculinities: the interdependence of gender, class and interpersonal power', *Gender and Society* 10, 5: 527–49.

Reischauer, E. O. (1981) *The Japanese*, Cambridge, MA: Harvard University Press.

Reskin, B. (1993) 'Sex segregation in the workplace', *Annual Review of Sociology* 9: 241–71.

Roberson, J. E. (1998) 'Manufacturing men: working-class masculinities in Japan', *Hitotsubashi Journal of Social Studies* 30, 1: 45–59.

Roberts, G. (1994) *Staying on the Line: Blue-Collar Women in Contemporary Japan*, Honolulu: University of Hawaii Press.

Sodei, T. (1996) '*Shigoto to katei o dō ryōritsu saseru ka*' (How to balance the family and work), in N. Toshitani, Y. Yuzawa, T. Sodei and E. Shinotsuka (eds) *Kōgakureki Jidai no Josei* (*Women in a Highly Educated Era*), Tokyo: Yūhikaku.

Tajiri, K. (1990) *Tōsan wa Jitensha ni Notte: Otoko no Ikuji Jikan Suto Tenmatsuki* (*Dad on a Bike: Story of a Man's Childcare Hour Strike*), Tokyo: Yukkusha.

— (1995) '*Ganbaranai tetsugaku*' (Not doing my best philosophy), in T. Inoue, C. Ueno and Y. Ehara (eds) *Danseigaku* (*Men's Studies*), Tokyo: Iwanami Shoten.

Toyoda, M. (1997) *Otoko ga 'Otoko Rashisa' o Suteru Toki* (*When Men Abandon Their Masculinity*), Tokyo: Asuka Shinsha.

Vogel, E. F. (1979) *Japan as Number One: Lessons for America*, Cambridge, MA: Harvard University Press.

Wagatsuma, H. (1977) 'Some aspects of the contemporary Japanese family: once Confucian, now fatherless?', *Daedalus* 106: 181–210.

West, C. and Zimmerman, D. H. (1987) 'Doing gender', *Gender and Society* 1, 2: 125–51.

Wiley, M. G. (1995) 'Sex category and gender in Social Psychology', in K. Cook, G. A. Gine and J. House (eds) *Sociological Perspectives on Social Psychology*, Boston: Allyn and Bacon.

# Index

Note: 'n' following a page number indicates that the entry can be found in a note, e.g. 14n refers to a note on page 14.

CPSIA information can be obtained
at www.ICGtesting.com
Printed in the USA
BVHW082033060819
555251BV00004B/45/P